Alan Rogers

CW01640485

Alan Rogers

Spain
& Portugal

Quality camping & caravanning sites

INSPECTED CAMPSITES & SELECTED

Compiled by: Alan Rogers Guides Ltd

Designed: Paul Effenberg, Vine Design Ltd

Maps created by Customised Mapping (01769 560101)
contain background data provided by GisDATA Ltd
Maps are © Alan Rogers Guides and Gis DATA Ltd 2004

© Alan Rogers Guides Ltd 2005

Published by: Alan Rogers Guides Ltd,
Spelmonden Old Oast, Goudhurst, Kent TN17 1HE
www.alanrogers.com Tel: 01580 214000

British Library Cataloguing-in-Publication Data:
A catalogue record for this book is available from the British Library.

ISBN: 0-9545271-4-3

Printed in Great Britain by J H Haynes & Co Ltd

Cover photography

We would like to thank Campings Cambrils Park and Sanguli (pages 54 and 56 of this guide) for the use of our main cover image.

While every effort is taken to ensure the accuracy of the information given in this book, no liability can be accepted by the authors or publishers for any loss, damage or injury caused by errors in, or omissions from, the information given.

All rights reserved. No part of this publication may be reproduced, stored in a retrieval system or transmitted, in any form or by any means, electronic, mechanical, photocopying, recording or otherwise, without prior permission in writing from the publishers.

CONTENTS

the Alan Rogers approach

IT IS NEARLY 40 YEARS SINCE ALAN ROGERS PUBLISHED THE FIRST CAMPSITE GUIDE THAT BORE HIS NAME. SINCE THEN THE RANGE HAS EXPANDED TO SIX TITLES WITH GUIDES TO ITALY AND SPAIN & PORTUGAL ADDED IN 2004, AND A NEW GUIDE TO CENTRAL EUROPE AND CROATIA FOR THIS YEAR. WHAT'S MORE, ALAN ROGERS GUIDES HAVE BECOME ESTABLISHED IN HOLLAND TOO: ALL SIX TITLES ARE ALSO AVAILABLE IN THE NETHERLANDS, STOCKED BY WELL OVER 90% OF ALL DUTCH BOOKSHOPS.

There are many thousands of campsites in Spain and Portugal of varying quality: this guide contains impartially written reports on over 220 of the very finest, each being individually inspected and selected. Plus it incorporates a new section on our popular Travel Service (page 8), as well as all the usual maps and indexes, designed to help you find the choice of campsite that's right for you. We hope you enjoy some happy and safe travels – and some pleasurable 'armchair touring' in the meantime!

INDEPENDENT AND HONEST

Whilst the content and scope of the Alan Rogers guides have expanded considerably since the early editions, our selection of campsites still employs exactly the same philosophy and criteria as defined by Alan Rogers in 1968.

'warts and all'

Firstly, and most importantly, our selection is based entirely on our own rigorous and independent inspection and selection process. Campsites cannot buy their way into our guides – indeed the extensive Site Report which is written by us, not by the site owner, is provided free of charge so we are free to say what we think and to provide an honest, 'warts and all' description. This is written in plain English and without the use of confusing icons or symbols.

"...the campsites included in this book have been chosen entirely on merit, and no payment of any sort is made by them for their inclusion."

Alan Rogers, 1968

INSPECTED & SELECTED SINCE 1968

A question of quality

The criteria we use when inspecting and selecting sites are numerous, but the most important by far is the question of good quality. People want different things from their choice of campsite so we try to include a range of campsite 'styles' to cater for a wide variety of preferences: from those seeking a small peaceful campsite in the heart of the countryside, to visitors looking for an 'all singing, all dancing' site in a popular seaside resort. Those with more specific interests, such as sporting facilities, cultural events or historical attractions, are also catered for.

The size of the site, whether it's part of a campsite chain or privately owned, makes no difference in terms of it being required to meet our exacting standards in respect of its quality and it being 'fit for purpose'. In other words, irrespective of the size of the park, or the number of facilities it offers, the essentials (the welcome, the pitches, the sanitary facilities, the cleanliness and the general maintenance) must all be of a high standard.

Expert opinions

We rely on our dedicated team of Site Assessors, all of whom are experienced campers, caravanners or motorcaravanners, to visit and recommend sites. Each year they travel some 100,000 miles around Europe inspecting new campsites and re-inspecting the older ones. Our thanks are due to them for their enthusiastic efforts, their diligence and integrity and their commitment to the philosophy of the Alan Rogers Guides.

We also appreciate the feedback we receive from many of our readers and we always make a point of following up complaints, suggestions or recommendations for possible new sites. Of course we get a few grumbles too – but it really is a few, and those we do receive usually arrive at the end of the high season and relate mainly to overcrowding or to poor maintenance during the peak school holiday period.

Please bear in mind that although we are interested to hear about any complaints we have no contractual relationship with the campsites featured in our guides and are therefore not in a position to intervene in any dispute between a reader and a campsite. If you have a complaint about a campsite featured in our guides the first step should be to take the matter up with the site owner or manager whilst on the campsite.

Widely regarded as the 'Bible' by site owners and readers alike, there is no better guide when it comes to forming an independent view of a campsite's quality. When you need to be confident in your choice of campsite, you need the Alan Rogers Guide.

- ✓ Sites only included on merit
- ✓ Sites cannot pay to be included
- ✓ Independently inspected, rigorously assessed
- ✓ Impartial reviews
- ✓ 36 years of expertise

INSPECTED & SELECTED CAMPSITES

Written in plain English, our guides are exceptionally easy to use, but a few words of explanation regarding the layout and content may be helpful. In Spain we have used the 15 official administrative regions, whilst in Portugal we use the five regions defined by the Portuguese Tourist Board. We provide a full page introduction to each region highlighting its main areas of interest and places to visit with details of the local cuisine.

Indexes

Our three indexes allow you to find sites by site number and name, by region and site name or by the town or village where the site is situated.

Campsite Maps

The maps will help you to identify the approximate position of each campsite within its region.

Region

The Site Reports – *Example of an entry*

Site no **Site name**

Postal Address (including county)

A description of the site in which we try to give an idea of its general features – its size, its situation, its strengths and its weaknesses. This column should provide a picture of the site itself with reference to the facilities that are provided and if they impact on its appearance or character. We include details on pitch numbers, electricity (with amperage), hardstandings etc. in this section as pitch design, planning and terracing affects the site's overall appearance. Similarly we include reference to pitches used for caravan holiday homes, chalets, and the like. Importantly at the end of this column we indicate if there are any restrictions, e.g. no tents, naturist sites.

Facilities

Lists more specific information on the park's facilities, as well as certain off site atractions and activities.

At a glance

Welcome & Ambience	✓✓✓✓	Location	✓✓✓✓✓
Quality of Pitches	✓✓✓✓✓	Range of Facilities	✓✓✓✓

Our inspectors grade each site out of five, giving a unique indication of certain key criteria that may be important when making your decision.

Directions

Separated from the main text in order that they may be read and assimilated more easily by a navigator en-route. Bear in mind that road improvement schemes can result in some road numbers being altered. Websites like **www.mappy.com** and others give detailed route plans.

Charges 2005

Reservations

including contact details

Open

Site opening dates.

Facilities

Toilet blocks: We assume that toilet blocks will be equipped with at least some British style WCs, washbasins with hot and cold water and hot showers with dividers or curtains, and will have all necessary shelves, hooks, plugs and mirrors. We also assume that there will be an identified chemical toilet disposal point, and that the campsite will provide water and waste water points and bin areas. If not the case, we comment. We mention certain features that some readers find important: washbasins in cubicles, facilities for babies, facilities for those with disabilities and motorcaravan service points. Readers with disabilities are advised to contact the site of their choice to ensure that facilities are appropriate to their needs.

Shop: Basic or fully supplied, and opening dates.

Bars, restaurants, takeaway facilities and entertainment: We try hard to supply opening and closing dates (if other than the campsite opening dates) and to identify if there are discos or other noisy entertainment.

Children's play areas: Fenced and with safety surface (e.g. sand, bark or pea-gravel).

Swimming pools: If particularly special, we cover in detail in the first column but reference is always included in the second column. Opening dates, charges and levels of supervision are provided where we have been notified.

Leisure facilities: E.g: playing fields, bicycle hire, organised activities and entertainment.

Dogs: If dogs are not accepted or restrictions apply, we state it here. Check the quick reference list at the back of the guide.

Off site: This briefly covers leisure facilities, tourist attractions, restaurants etc nearby. Geographical tourist information is more likely to be in the first column.

At a glance: All Alan Rogers sites have been inspected and selected – they must meet stringent quality criteria. A campsite may have all the boxes ticked when it comes to listing facilities but if it's not inherently a 'good site' then it will not be in the guide.

These 'at a glance' ratings are a unique indication of certain key criteria that may be important when making your decision. Quite deliberately they are subjective and, modesty aside, are based on our inspectors' own expert opinions at the time of their inspection.

Charges: These are the latest provided by the parks. In those few cases where 2004 or 2005 prices are not given, we try to give a general guide.

Telephone numbers: All numbers assume that you are phoning from within Spain or Portugal. To phone Spain from outside that country, prefix the number shown with the International Code '00 34' and then the number indicated. To phone Portugal pefix the number shown with the International Code '00 351'.

Opening dates: Are those advised to us during the early autumn of the previous year – parks can, and sometimes do, alter these dates before the start of the following season, often for good reasons. If you intend to visit shortly after a published opening date, or shortly before the closing date, it is wise to check that it will actually be open at the time required. Similarly some sites operate a restricted service during the low season, only opening some of their facilities (e.g. swimming pools) during the main season; where we know about this, and have the relevant dates, we indicate it – again if you are at all doubtful it is wise to check.

Reservations: Necessary for high season (roughly mid-July to mid-August) in popular holiday areas (ie beach areas). You can reserve via our own Alan Rogers Travel Service or through tour operators. Or be wholly independent and contact the campsite(s) of your choice direct, using the phone or e-mail numbers shown in the site reports, but please bear in mind that many sites are closed all winter.

Our Accommodation Section

Over recent years, more and more campsites have added high quality mobile home and chalet accommodation. In response to feedback from many of our readers, and to reflect this evolution in campsites, we have now decided to include a separate section on mobile homes and chalets.

We have chosen a number of sites offering some of the best accommodation available and have included full details of one or two accommodation types at these sites. Please note however that many other campsites listed in this guide may also have a selection of accommodation for rent.

Points to bear in mind

Some site owners are very laid back when it comes to opening and closing dates. They may not be fully ready by their opening date – grass and hedges may not all be cut or perhaps only limited sanitary facilities open. At the end of the season they also tend to close down some facilities and generally wind down prior to the closing date. Bear this in mind if you are travelling early or late in the season – it is worth phoning ahead.

The Camping Cheque low season touring system goes some way to addressing this in that participating campsites are encouraged to have all facilities open and running by the opening date and to remain fully operational until the closing date.

Whether you're an 'old hand' in terms of camping and caravanning or are contemplating your first trip, a regular reader of our Guides or a new 'convert', we wish you well in your travels and hope we have been able to help in some way. We are, of course, also out and about ourselves, visiting sites, talking to owners and readers, and generally checking on standards and new developments.

The Alan Rogers Team

Alan Rogers

VALUE, VALUE, VALUE

service and value

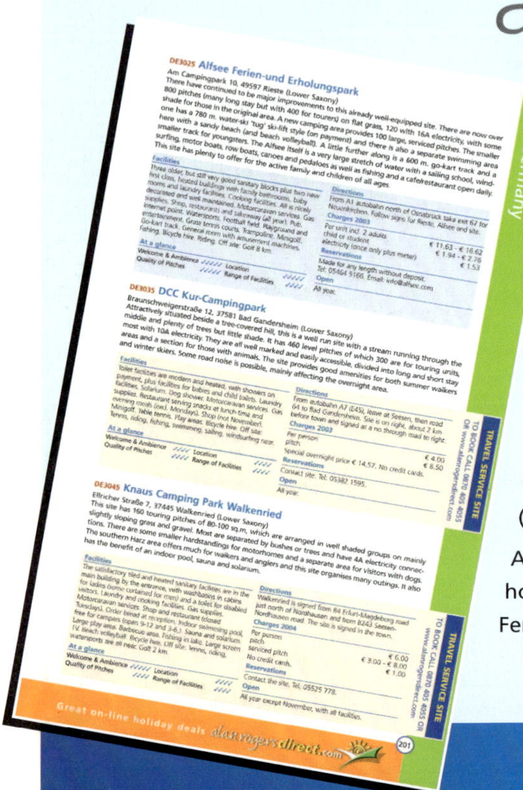

DE3025 **Alfsee Ferien-und Erholungspark**

Am Campingpark 10, 49597 Rieste (Lower Saxony)

There have continued to be major improvements to this already well-equipped site. There are now over 800 pitches (many long stay but with 400 for tourers) on flat grass, 120 with 16A electricity, with some shade for those in the original area. A new camping area provides 100 large, serviced pitches. The smaller one has a 780 m. water-ski 'tug' ski-lift style (on payment) and there is also a separate swimming area here with a sandy beach (and beach volleyball). A little further along is a 600 m. go-kart track and a smaller track for youngsters. The Alfsee itself is a very large stretch of water with a sailing school, windsurfing, motor boats, row boats, canoes and pedaloes as well as fishing and a cafe/restaurant open daily. This site has plenty to offer for the active family and children of all ages.

Facilities

Three older, but still very good sanitary blocks plus two new first class, heated buildings with family bathrooms, baby rooms and laundry facilities. Cooking facilities. All is nicely decorated and well maintained. Motorcaravan services. Gas supplies. Shop, restaurants and takeaway (all year). Pub. Internet point. Watersports. Football field. Playground and entertainment. Grass tennis courts. Trampoline. Minigolf. Go-kart track. General room with amusement machines. Fishing. Bicycle hire. Riding. Off site: Golf 8 km.

At a glance

Welcome & Ambience ✓✓✓✓✓ Location ✓✓✓✓✓
Quality of Pitches ✓✓✓✓✓ Range of Facilities ✓✓✓✓

Directions

From A1 autobahn north of Osnabrück take exit 67 for Neuenkirchen. Follow signs for Rieste, Alfsee and site.

Charges 2003

Per unit incl. 2 adults € 11.63 - € 16.62
child or student € 1.94 - € 2.76
electricity (once only plus meter) € 1.53

Reservations

Made for any length without deposit. Tel: 05464 5166. Email: info@alfsee.com

Open

All year.

DE3035 **DCC Kur-Campingpark**

Braunschweigerstraße 12, 37581 Bad Gandersheim (Lower Saxony)

Attractively situated beside a tree-covered hill, this is a well run site with a stream running through the middle and plenty of trees but little shade. It has 460 level pitches of which 300 are for touring units, most with 10A electricity. They are all well marked and easily accessible, divided into long and short stay areas and a section for those with animals. The site provides good amenities for both summer walkers and winter skiers. Some road noise is possible, mainly affecting the overnight area.

Facilities

Toilet facilities are modern and heated, with showers on payment, plus facilities for babies and child toilets. Laundry facilities. Solarium. Dog shower. Motorcaravan services. Gas supplies. Restaurant serving snacks at lunch-time and evening meals (excl. Mondays). Shop (not November). Minigolf. Table tennis. Play areas. Bicycle hire. Off site: Tennis, riding, fishing, swimming, sailing, windsurfing near.

At a glance

Welcome & Ambience ✓✓✓✓ Location ✓✓✓✓
Quality of Pitches ✓✓✓✓ Range of Facilities ✓✓✓✓

Directions

From autobahn A7 (E45), leave at Seesen, then road 64 to Bad Gandersheim. Site is on right, about 2 km before town and signed as a no through road to right.

Charges 2003

Per person € 4.00
pitch € 8.50
Special overnight price € 14,57. No credit cards.

Reservations

Contact site. Tel: 05382 1595.

Open

All year.

DE3045 **Knaus Camping Park Walkenried**

Ellricher Straße 7, 37445 Walkenried (Lower Saxony)

This site has 160 touring pitches of 80-100 sq.m, which are arranged in well shaded groups on mainly slightly sloping grass and gravel. Most are separated by bushes or trees and have 4A electricity connections. There are some smaller hardstandings for motorhomes and a separate area for visitors with dogs. The southern Harz area offers much for walkers and anglers and this site organises many outings. It also has the benefit of an indoor pool, sauna and solarium.

Facilities

The satisfactory tiled and heated sanitary facilities are in the main building by the entrance, with washbasins in cabins for ladies (some curtained for men) and a toilet for disabled visitors. Laundry and cooking facilities. Gas supplies. Motorcaravan services. Shop and restaurant (closed Tuesdays). Order bread at reception. Indoor swimming pool, free for campers (open 9-12 and 3-6.). Sauna and solarium. Large play area. Barbecue area. Fishing in lake. Large screen TV. Beach volleyball. Bicycle hire. Off site: Tennis, riding, watersports are all near. Golf 2 km.

At a glance

Welcome & Ambience ✓✓✓✓✓ Location ✓✓✓✓
Quality of Pitches ✓✓✓✓ Range of Facilities ✓✓✓✓

Directions

Walkenried is signed from B4 Erfurt-Magdeburg road just north of Nordhausen and from B243 Seesen-Nordhausen road. The site is signed in the town.

Charges 2004

Per person € 6.00
pitch € 3.00 - € 8.00
serviced pitch € 1.00
No credit cards.

Reservations

Contact the site. Tel: 05525 778.

Open

All year except November, with all facilities.

The Alan Rogers Travel Service was set up to provide a low cost booking service for readers. We can tailor-make a holiday to suit your requirements, giving you maximum choice and flexibility: exactly what we have been offering for some 5 years now.

Alternatively you can opt for one of our new Value+ holidays, pocketing a 20% saving off base price in return for accepting various restrictions (see opposite).

And because we organise so many holidays we can offer outstanding Ferry Deals too!

Unbeatable Ferry Deals

WE ARE ALWAYS NEGOTIATING NEW OFFERS ON CHANNEL CROSSINGS. MAKE SURE YOU ASK US ABOUT OUR FAMOUS DEALS!

- ✓ **CARAVANS GO FREE**
- ✓ **TRAILERS GO FREE**
- ✓ **MOTORHOMES PRICED AS CARS**

SEE PAGES 15-16

At the Alan Rogers Travel Service we're always keen to find the best deals and keenest prices. There are always great savings on offer, and we're constantly negotiating new ferry rates and money-saving offers, so just call us on

0870 405 4055

and ask about the latest deals.

or visit

www.alanrogersdirect.com

THE AIMS OF THE TRAVEL SERVICE ARE SIMPLE.

- To provide convenience - when booking a campsite yourself can be anything but convenient.
- To provide peace of mind - when you need it most.
- To provide a friendly, knowledgeable, efficient service - when this can be hard to find.
- To provide a low cost means of organising your holiday – when prices can be so complicated.

HOW IT WORKS

1 Choose your campsite(s)

2 Choose your dates

3 Choose your ferry crossing

Then just call us for an instant quote

0870 405 4055

or visit

www.alanrogersdirect.com

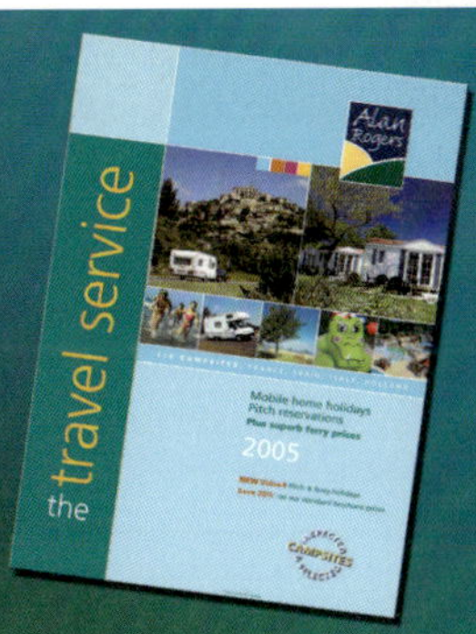

LET US BOOK YOUR PITCH AND FERRY FOR YOU

For full details see our FREE 2005 brochure

0870 405 4055

Ask about our incredible Ferry Deals:

- ✓ Caravans GO **FREE**
- ✓ Motorhomes Priced as Cars

NEW Value+ Holidays SAVE 20%

We can book many campsites for you, with complete flexibility: any dates, any duration, any arrival/departure day, any ferry and so on.

But some readers do not necessarily need such choice and would prefer 'off the shelf' convenience and even lower prices. So for 2005 we are introducing our new **Value+** holidays where, in return for meeting certain conditions, we can reduce your base price by a massive 20%.

We can offer **Value+** holidays at over 50 campsites within our 2005 programme. To qualify for huge savings please understand that your holiday must be...

- + Ferry-inclusive
- + Single site only – no overnight campsite stops
- + Minimum of 7 nights
- + Either 7, 14 or 21 nights duration
- + Booked at least 30 days in advance of travel
- + Subject to availability on each site

See our new 2005 brochure for details
or call us today for a no-obligation quote.

0870 405 4055

PRICING YOUR HOLIDAY

WE ACT AS AGENTS FOR ALL THE CAMPSITES AND FERRY OPERATORS FEATURED IN THE TRAVEL SERVICE. AS SUCH, WE CAN BOOK ALL YOUR TRAVEL ARRANGEMENTS WITH THE MINIMUM OF FUSS AND AT THE BEST POSSIBLE PRICES. THE BASE PRICES BELOW INCLUDE 14 NIGHTS PITCH FEES AND RETURN FERRY CROSSING.

	Base Price 2 adults + car 14 nights		Extra adult		Child	Extra/fewer nights	
First night on site	Tailormade	**Value+**	Tailormade	**Value+**	(0-13)	Tailormade	**Value+**
Before 17 May	£318	£254.40	£25	£20	FREE	£12	£9.60
17/5 - 17/6	£338	£270.40	£25	£20	FREE	£12	£9.60
18/6 - 1/7	£369	£295.20	£25	£20	FREE	£12	£9.60
2/7 - 12/8	£439	£351.20	£25	£20	FREE	£12	£9.60
13/8 - 22/8	£399	£319.20	£25	£20	FREE	£12	£9.60
From 23/8	£338	£270.40	£25	£20	FREE	£12	£9.60

The base price of your holiday includes 14 nights pitch fees and a mid-week return ferry crossing from Dover to Calais with P&O Ferries for a car and 5 passengers (outward sailing times must be between 14:01 and 06:59. Inward sailing times must be between 20:01 and 14:59). Additional supplements are payable for caravans, trailers and motorhomes at many times and for cars at weekends and times outside those given above. There will also usually be a campsite supplement payable (see opposite). Call us on **0870 405 4055** for details and a quote.

If your holiday is longer or shorter than 14 nights, simply add or subtract the extra/fewer night rate. Tailor-made holidays must be for a minimum of 3 nights, with ferry (many sites have a minimum stay requirement). For holidays longer than 21 nights please call for a quotation. You may stay on as many sites as you wish, subject to individual site requirements, with a one-off £10 multi-site fee. Value+ holidays are subject to various restrictions. Please see page 9 for details.

LOW £100 DEPOSIT

A special low deposit of just £100 secures your holiday

(full payment is required at the time of booking for travel within 10 weeks)

14 nights pitch fees + ferry for car and passengers	from **£324** DOVER - CALAIS
14 nights pitch fees + ferry for motorhome and passengers	from **£346** PORTSMOUTH - LE HAVRE
14 nights pitch fees + ferry for car and caravan and passengers	from **£324** DOVER - CALAIS

Sample Value+ holiday at Camping Jarny Ocean, Vendée in May.

Motorhomes
Priced
as Cars

Caravans
and Trailers
GO FREE

Site Supplements

All sites operate their own independent pricing structure, and in order to reflect the differences in cost from one site to another, a nightly 'site supplement' needs to be added to the Base Prices indicated above.

All supplements are given in our 2005 brochure. Additional supplements can often apply for electricity, water and drainage or special pitches.

The simplest next step is to request a brochure or just call us for an immediate price quotation for your chosen site and all the available options, as well as any other important information, such as any minimum stay requirements.

CALL US NOW 0870 405 4055 FOR AN INSTANT QUOTE
OR VISIT www.alanrogersdirect.com

Leave The Hassle To Us

- **All site fees paid in advance – you won't need to take extra currency with you.**
- **Your pitch is reserved for you – travel with peace of mind.**
- **No endless overseas phone calls or correspondence with foreign site owners.**
- **No need to pay foreign currency deposits and booking fees.**
- **Take advantage of our expert advice and experience of camping in Europe.**

Already Booked Your Ferry?

We're confident that our ferry inclusive booking service offers unbeatable value. However, if you have already booked your ferry then we can still make a pitch-only reservation for you. Your booking must be for a minimum of 10 nights, and since our prices are based on our ferry inclusive service, you need to be aware that a non-ferry booking will always result in somewhat higher prices than if you were to book direct with the site.

You still benefit from:

- **Hassle-free booking with no booking fees and foreign currency deposits.**
- **Comprehensive Travel Pack.**
- **Peace of mind: site fees paid in advance, with your pitch reserved for you.**

FULL DETAILS IN OUR 64 PAGE 2005 COLOUR BROCHURE CALL
0870 405 4055

book on-line and save money

www.alanrogersdirect.com is a website designed to give you everything you need to know when it comes to booking your Alan Rogers inspected and selected campsite, and your low cost ferry.

Our glossy brochure gives you all the info you need but it is only printed once a year. And our friendly, expert reservations team is always happy to help on **0870 405 4055** – but they do go home sometimes!

Visit www.alanrogersdirect.com and you'll find constantly updated information, latest ferry deals, special offers from campsites and much more. And you can visit it at any time of day or night!

alan rogers direct.com

book on-line and save

Campsite Information

- ✓ Details of all Travel Service campsites - **instantly**
- ✓ Find latest special offers on campsites - **instantly**
- ✓ Check campsite availability - **instantly**

Ferry Information

- ✓ Check ferry availability - **instantly**
- ✓ Find latest ferry deals - **instantly**
- ✓ Book your ferry online - **instantly**
- ✓ Save money - **instantly**

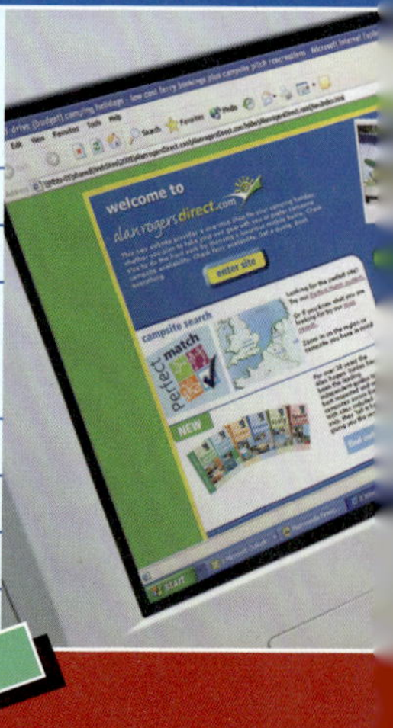

Save Money!

BOOK YOUR CAMPSITE AND FERRY - INSTANTLY

Perfect Match

Find the campsite that's right for you

With so many sites to choose from it can be difficult to find a short-list. With the unique Alan Rogers Perfect Match system you can quickly find a campsite that meets your requirements. This powerful and searchable database of top campsites, all Alan Rogers inspected and selected, means you can quickly find an ideal site, book it on-line and relax in the knowledge that your holiday is safely reserved.

have you visited www.alanrogers.com yet?

INSPECTED CAMPSITES & SELECTED

Thousands have already, researching their holiday and catching up with the latest news and special offers.

Launched in January 2004 it has fast become the first-stop for countless caravanners, motorhome owners and campers all wanting reliable, impartial and detailed information for their next trip.

Alan Rogers

It features a fully searchable database of the best campsites in the UK & Ireland, and the rest of Europe: over 2,000 campsites in 26 countries. All are Alan Rogers inspected and selected, allowing you to find the site that's perfect for you, with the reassurance of knowing we've been there first.

And now it has been re-launched for the 2005 season, with more than ever before.

Save up to 55% on your holiday

Camping Cheque©

Last year over 150,000 people used well over 1 million Camping Cheques and enjoyed half-price holidays around Europe. Make sure you don't miss out this year.

Huge off peak savings

511 quality campsites, in 18 European countries, including the UK, all at just £9.95 per night for pitch + 2 adults, including electricity. Go as you please and save up to 55% off normal site tariffs.

ferry savings

Ask about our famous special offers

- Caravans/trailers Go **FREE**
- Motorhomes Priced As Cars

Conditions apply – ask for details

For full information visit
www.campingcheque.co.uk
Buy Cheques, check ferry availability, book everything on-line AND SAVE!

Alan Rogers

CALL NOW for a free copy of how to save up to 55% on your holiday

0870 405 4057

Crossing the Channel

One of the great advantages of booking with the Alan Rogers Travel Service is the tremendous value we offer. Our money-saving Ferry Deals have become legendary: see below. As agents for all the cross-Channel operators we can book all your travel arrangements with the minimum of fuss and at the best possible rates.

Just call us for an instant quote

0870 405 4055

or visit

www.alanrogersdirect.com

Book on-line AND SAVE

Short Sea Routes

Hop across the Channel in the shortest possible time and you can be on your way. We offer all main routes at great prices (when you book a pitch + ferry 'package' through us). And why not take advantage of our Ferry Deals? Caravans and trailers can go **FREE** on Dover – Calais with P&O Ferries.

SEAFRANCE DOVER-CALAIS FERRIES

P&O Ferries
Dover - Calais

hoverspeed
Dover – Calais
Newhaven - Dieppe

EURO TUNNEL
Folkestone – Calais

Stena Line
Harwich – Hook of Holland

Short Sea Routes **SPECIAL OFFERS**

Caravans **Go FREE** - Trailers **Go FREE** - Motorhomes **Priced as Cars**

SEAFRANCE DOVER-CALAIS FERRIES P&O Ferries **Dover – Calais**

Caravans Go FREE*

Available all year between 1 May 2005 – 31 Oct 2005 excluding high season weekends.

Motorhomes Priced as Cars*

Available between 1 May 2005 – 31 Oct 2005 on midweek, low season sailings and apply at all times of the day.

High season is 26-28 May and 15/7-31/8 outward and 4-5 June and 23/7-4/9 inward. Weekends are Fri/Sat outward, Sat/Sun inward.

* Applies to certain sailings only. Over-length supplements may apply. Please ask for details.

EURO TUNNEL **Folkestone – Calais/Coquelles**

FREE Caravans between midnight and 06:00.
Low caravan supplements on off peak crossings.

Don't delay – this offer is strictly subject to availability and will be first come, first served.

Just call us for an instant quote **0870 405 4055**
or visit **www.alanrogersdirect.com** BOOK ON-LINE AND SAVE

Longer Routes

Sometimes it pays to take a longer crossing: a more leisurely journey perhaps. Or a chance to enjoy dinner on board ship, followed by a night in a comfortable cabin, awaking refreshed and ready for the onward drive. Either way there are still savings to be had with our super Ferry Deals (when you book a pitch and ferry 'package' through us).

Brittany Ferries

Portsmouth – St Malo/ Caen/Cherbourg
Plymouth – Roscoff/Santander
Poole – Cherbourg
Portsmouth – Le Havre

P&O Ferries

Portsmouth – Bilbao
Hull – Rotterdam/Zeebrugge

Condorferries

Poole – St Malo
Weymouth – St Malo

Longer Routes SPECIAL OFFERS

Motorhomes **Priced as Cars** - Caravans **FROM JUST £13** each way

Brittany Ferries Portsmouth – Le Havre**

Motorhomes Priced as Cars* on 'special sailings' from Portsmouth in low season (midweek AND weekend). Le Havre is now just £4 each way supplement over Dover-Calais on lead-in sailings for cars. Caravan supplement starts at just £13 each way on Portsmouth - Le Havre.

Many supplements for high season have reduced – **call us for an instant quote.**

Condorferries Poole/Weymouth – St Malo

Motorhomes Priced as Cars on all crossings direct to St Malo and via the Channel Islands. Travel must be on a Tuesday or Wednesday (either direction). Offer excludes high season (27/5-29/5 and 15/7-24/8 out, 3/6-5/6 and 22/7-4/9 in).

* Applies to certain sailings only. Over-length supplements may apply. Please ask for details.
** At the time going to press Portsmouth – Le Havre crossings are operated by P&O Ferries. This route may, in time, be operated by Brittany Ferries, subject to the outcome of negotiations.

1st time abroad?

PREPARATIONS FOR THAT FIRST TRIP CAN BE DAUNTING. BUT DON'T WORRY - WE'RE WITH YOU ALL THE WAY.

Don't delay – **this offer is strictly subject to availability and will be first come, first served.**

Just call us for an instant quote **0870 405 4055**
or visit **www.alanrogersdirect.com** BOOK ON-LINE AND SAVE

SPAIN

One of the largest countries in Europe, with glorious beaches, a fantastic sunshine record, vibrant towns and laid back sleepy villages, plus a diversity of landscape, culture and artistic traditions, Spain has all the ingredients for a great holiday.

Spain has a huge choice of beach resorts to choose from. With charming villages and attractive towns, the Costa Brava boasts spectacular scenery with towering cliffs and sheltered coves. There are plenty of lively resorts, including Lloret, Tossa and Calella, plus several quieter ones. Further along the east coast, the Costa del Azahar stretches from Vinaros to Almanzora, with the great port of Valencia in the middle. Orange groves abound. The central section of the coastline, the Costa Blanca, has 170 miles or so of silvery-white beaches. Benidorm is the most popular resort. The Costa del Sol lies in the south, home to more beaches and brilliant sunshine, whilst in the north the Costa Verde is largely unspoiled, with clean water, sandy beaches and rocky coves against a backdrop of mountains.

Beaches and sunshine aside, Spain also has plenty of great cities and towns to explore, including Barcelona, Valencia, Seville, Madrid, Toledo and Bilbao, all offering an array of sights, galleries and museums.

Population: 39.5 million

Capital: Madrid

Climate: Spain has a very varied climate. The north is temperate with most of the rainfall; dry and very hot in the centre; subtropical along the Mediterranean

Language: Castilian Spanish is spoken by most people with Catalan (northeast), Basque (north) and Galician (northwest) used in their respective areas

Currency: The Euro (€).

Banks: Mon-Fri 09.00-14.00. Sat 09.00-13.00

Telephone The country code is 00 34

Shops: Mon-Sat 09.00-13.00/14.00 and 15.00/16.00-19.30/20.00. Many close later

Public Holidays: New Year; Epiphany; Saint's Day 19 Mar; Maundy Thurs; Good Fri; Easter Mon; Labour Day; Saint's Day 25 July; Assumption 15 Aug; National Day 12 Oct; All Saints Day 1 Nov; Constitution Day 6 Dec; Immaculate Conception 8 Dec; Christmas Day

Tourist office:

Spanish National Tourist Office
22/23 Manchester Square, London W1U 3PX

Tel: 020 7486 8077
Fax: 020 7486 8034
E-mail: info.londres@tourspain.es
Internet: http://www.tourspain.es

CANTABRIA
PAIS VASCO-EUSKADI
ASTURIAS
FRANCE
GALICIA
NAVARRA
ANDORRA
LA RIOJA
CATALUNYA
CASTILLA Y LEON
NORTH
ARAGON
MADRID
BEIRAS
LISBON AND
VALE DO TEJO
EXTREMADURA
CASTILLA-LA-MANCHA
COMUNIDAD
VALENCIANA
ALENTEJO
MURCIA
ANDALUCIA
ALGARVE

Cataluña-Catalunya

Flanked by the Pyrenees mountains and bathed by the Mediterranean Sea, Catalunya occupies the north eastern part of the peninsula. It has a strong identity, with a unique culture and language all of its own.

Catalunya is comprised of four provinces: Barcelona, Tarragona, Lleida and Girona

The regional capital is Barcelona

Barcelona is the historical capital of Catalunya and Spain's second leading city in both size and importance, after Madrid. The beautiful city has an impressive architectural heritage that includes the Gothic Quarter, with its cathedral, the old City Hall Building, the Episcopal Palace and the splendid Palace of the Generalitat. The city also boasts the work of the incomparable modernist architect Antonio Gaudí. In the centre of the fertile plain of the river Segre sits Lleida, capital of the province of the same name. Prominent atop a hill in the historic quarter of the city is the old cathedral or Seu Vella, symbol of the capital. The Costa Brava is the coastal zone that begins about 40 km. north of Barcelona and includes the entire shoreline of the province of Girona. It is an area of great natural beauty, formed by a succession of steep cliffs and small coves with finely grained sand. Some of its towns have been massively exploited for tourism but others, such as Tossa de Mar, still maintain their original size and fishing-village charm. The principal tourist centres on the coast include Roses, Sant Pere Pescador, L´Escala, L´Estartit, Palamos, Palafrugell, Platja d´Aro, S´Agaro, Sant Feliu de Guixols, Lloret de Mar and Blanes. There are daily boat services which operate along the coast for most of the year.

Cuisine of the region

Mediterranean influence with lots of tomatoes, garlic, fresh herbs, olive oil, onions, fish. Wild mushrooms in the autumn. Locally produced wines from Penedés, Conca de Barberá, Pla de Bages and Alella

Calçots: green onions grilled on a barbecue

Cod esqueixada: cod soaked in cold water then mixed with tomatoes, olives and onion

Escalivada: vegetable stew with roasted aubergine and peppers

Fuet, llonganisa, butifarra: local sausages

Suquet: seafood casserole

Recao de binefar: rice cooked with white beans, potatoes and chorizo

Places of interest

Empuries: Greco-Roman city

Figueres: birthplace of Salvador Dali, museum displaying his finest work

Girona: one of the oldest and most beautiful Catalan cities, 14th century cathedral

La Costa Dorada: stretches south from the Costa Brava to Tarragona, with beautiful, open, well maintained beaches

Parque Natural de Aigüamolls de L'Empordà: park made up of three reserves, with wildlife and over 320 bird species

Sitges: attractive beach town, museum of Cau-Ferrat featuring paintings by El Greco

Tarragona: Roman remains of Tarraco, the original Roman city

Alan Rogers tip

FOR FREE TRAVEL ON PUBLIC TRANSPORT PLUS REDUCED ENTRY FEES INTO MANY MUSEUMS, SHOPS AND RESTAURANTS BUY A 1-3 DAY BARCELONA CARD FROM TOURIST OFFICES.

ES8005 Camping Cadaques

Ctra de Port Lligat 17, 17488 Cadaques (Girona)

Picturesque Cadaqués is only accessible by a long winding road over the hills behind Roses and has an air of isolation. The attractive promenade is lined with restaurants and you can sit and watch the fishermen land their catches. Camping Cadaqués overlooks Port Lligat where Salvador Dali constructed his famous home which has recently been opened to the public (spot the house from the terrace). This site is ideal as a stopover if you want to be able to walk to this magnificent house in a most unusual setting. Camping Cadaques is basic and mainly used by transit campers for short stays to visit the Dali attraction. Not recommended for holidays, it is included to give an easier overnight visit to this difficult location. There are 200 pitches of 60-70 sq.m, some with a slight slope, and a separate area for tents.

Facilities

Restaurant/bar. Good, well stocked supermarket producing its own bread. Swimming pool (high season). Laundry service and ironing. Dogs are not accepted. Off site: Fishing 2 km. Golf 12 km. Riding 5 km. Bicycle hire 2 km.

Open

Easter - 15 September.

At a glance

Welcome & Ambience	✓✓✓✓	Location	✓✓✓✓✓
Quality of Pitches	✓✓✓	Range of Facilities	✓✓✓

Directions

From the A7 (Figueres - Girona) exit 4 take C260 to Roses and on to Cadaqués. It is a long, winding road and the return journey is along the same route.

Charges guide

Per adult	€ 4,30
pitch and car	€ 8,00 - € 9,30
electricity	€ 3,10

Reservations

Not generally necessary. Tel: 972 258 126.

ES8015 Camping Caravaning La Laguna

Apdo. de Correos 55, 17486 Castelló d'Empúries (Girona)

La Laguna is a relaxed, spacious site on an isthmus within a Catalan national maritime park. It has direct access to the sandy beach and estuary of the river Muga. The new owners are continuing to spend much time and effort on improvements, including the large lagoon from which it takes its name. The approach is by a long (4 km), and more or less private road. This is quite an unusual site for this area, being laid out informally among mature pine trees. The 750 pitches (just 10 occupied by mobile homes) are clearly marked on grass and sand, all with 5A electricity (long leads may be useful). An attractive bar/restaurant overlooks the lagoon and there is a pool (July/Aug) and a disco across the road from reception. A large riding school operates on site (May-Sept). The beach frontage is large and has a sailing school. It is said to be possible to cross over to Empuria Brava when the tide is out. The river Muga running along one side of the site is hidden by a high bank with a path along the top and there are many pleasant walks in this area. With the ongoing improvements this is becoming a pleasant site for family holidays.

Facilities

Five toilets blocks, placed to avoid long walks, are simple in design. Three have been completely rebuilt (the others will follow); all hot water is free. Plenty of dishwashing sinks. Well equipped laundry. Bar, restaurant and takeaway (all 15/3-20/10). Supermarket. Swimming pool (15/5-30/9). Tennis (free in low seasons). ATM. Minigolf. Sailing school (July/Aug). Fishing. Mini club. Bicycle hire. Riding. Dinner dance Thursday. 24 hour photo service. Animation programme. Off site: Bicycle hire 3 km. Golf 15 km.

Open

17 March - 23 October.

At a glance

Welcome & Ambience	✓✓✓	Location	✓✓✓✓
Quality of Pitches	✓✓✓	Range of Facilities	✓✓✓✓

Directions

Site is signed from Castello d'Empuries bypass (C260 Figures - Roses) and is on the junction with the road for Sant Pere Pescador (signs for Camping). Follow approach road for approx. 4 km.

Charges 2004

Per person	
child (3-10 yrs)	€ 3,10 - € 5,05
pitch	€ 7,20 - € 13,10
electricity	€ 3,10

Discounts for longer stays and pensioners.
No credit cards.

Reservations

Contact site. Tel: 972 45 05 53.
E-mail: info@campinglaguna.com

ES8012 Camping Mas Nou

Ctra Figueres - Roses, km 38, 17486 Castelló d'Empúries (Girona)

Some two kilometres from the sea on the Costa Brava, this is a surprisingly tranquil site. Split into two parts, one contains pitches and sanitary blocks and the other houses the impressive leisure complex. There are 450 neat, level and marked pitches on grass and sand, a minimum of 70 sq.m. but most 80-100 sq.m, and 300 with electrical connections (6/10A). The leisure complex is 80 metres from the main site across a very quiet road and features a huge L-shaped swimming pool with a paddling area. A formal restaurant has ajoining bar, pleasant terrace crêperie and rotisseria under palms. Another barbeque/rotisseria in another part of the site offers takeaway meals (in season). The site owns the large souvenir shop on the entrance road. There are many traditional bargains here and it is worth having a good look around as the prices are extremely good. Lots of time and money goes into the cleanliness of this site and it is good very for families. Ask about the origin of the site coat of arms. The Bay of Roses and the Medes islands have a natural beauty and a visit to Dali's house or the museum (the house is fascinating) will prove he was not just a surrealist painter.

Facilities

Three excellent, fully equipped sanitary blocks include baby baths, good facilities for disabled visitors. These are amongst the best we have seen. Dishwashing and laundry sinks. Washing machines. Supermarket and other shops close by. Bar/restaurant. Takeaway. Swimming pool with life guard (from 1/6). Tennis. Minigolf. Basketball. Volleyball. Football. Mini club in dedicated building(July/Aug). Table tennis. Children's playground. Electronic games.
Off site: Riding 1.5 km. Fishing or bicycle hire 2 km. Beach 2.5 km. National Park. Aquatic Park. Romanica tour of famous local churches.

Open

12 April - 28 September.

At a glance

Welcome & Ambience	✓✓✓✓✓	Location	✓✓✓✓✓
Quality of Pitches	✓✓✓✓✓	Range of Facilities	✓✓✓✓✓

Directions

From A7 use exit 3. Mas Nou is 2 km. east of Castelló d'Empúries, on the Roses road, some 10 km. from Figueres.

Charges 2005

Per person	€ 3,75 - € 5,95
child (4-11 yrs)	€ 3,15 - € 4,20
caravan or tent	€ 3,75 - € 5,95
car or motorcycle	€ 3,75 - € 5,95
motorcaravan	€ 7,50 - € 11,90
electricity	€ 2,75 - € 3,20

All plus 7% VAT.

Reservations

Write to site. Tel: 972 454 175.
E-mail: info@campingmasnou.com

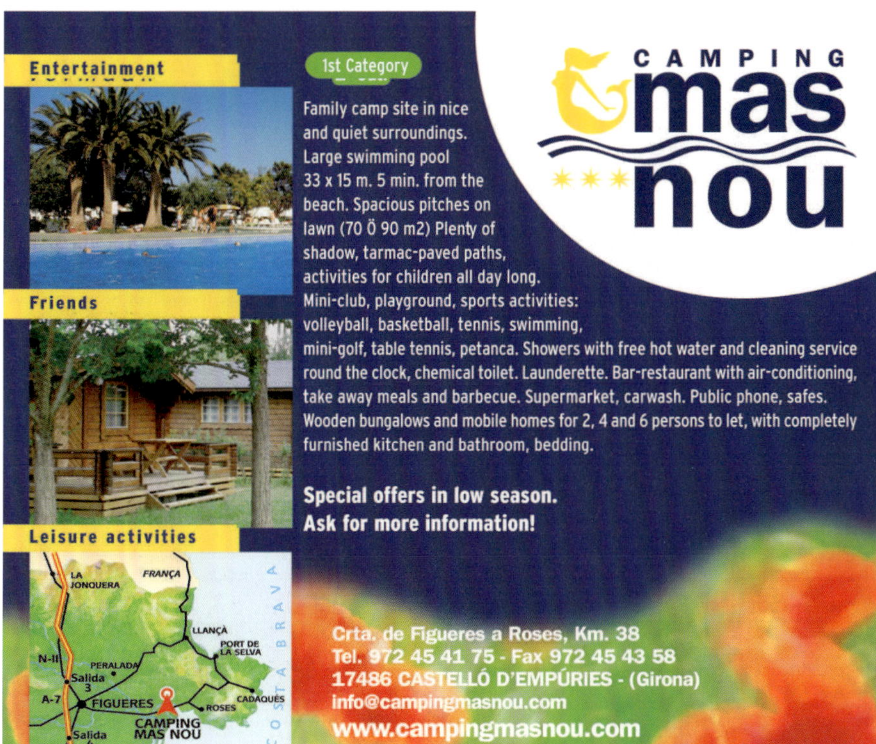

ES8030 Camping Nautic Almata

Ctra Sant Pere Pescador, km 11.6, 17486 Castelló d'Empuries (Girona)

Situated in the Bay of Roses, south of Empuria Brava and beside the Parc Natural dels Aiguamolls de l'Empordá, this is a site of particular interest for nature lovers (especially bird watchers). Beautifully laid out, it is arranged around the river and waterways, so will suit those who like to camp close to water or and those who enjoy watersports and boating. It is worth visiting because of its unusual aspects and the feeling of being on the canals, as well as being a high quality beach-side site. As you drive through the natural park to the site watch for the warning signs for frogs on the road and enjoy the wild flamingos alongside the road. It is a large site with 1,109 well kept, large, numbered pitches, all with electricity and on flat, sandy ground. There are some pitches right on the beach. The name no doubt derives from the fact that boats can be tied up at the small marina within the site and a slipway also gives access to a river and thence to the sea. Throughout the season there is a varied entertainment programme for children and adults. The facilities on this site are impressive. Some tour operators use the site.

Facilities

Sanitary blocks all of a high standard, attractively decorated. include some en-suite showers with basins, taps to draw hot water for dishwashing, laundry sinks and baby baths. Good facilities for disabled visitors and ramps where necessary. Washing machines. Gas supplies. Excellent supermarket. Restaurant and bar (recently refurbished), rotisserie and pizzeria near pool. Two separate bars by beach where discos held in main season. Water-ski and windsurfing schools. 300 sq. m. swimming pool. Tennis, squash, volleyball, fronton all free. Minigolf. Games room with pool and table tennis. Extensive riding tuition with own stables and stud. Children's play park (near river). Car, motorcycle and bicycle hire. Hairdresser. Torches are useful near beach. Off site: National Park and wetlands around site. Canal trips 18 km. Aquatic Park 20 km. Adventure sports 40 km. Excursions to Barcelona, Monserrat, Andorra and Dahli's museum.

At a glance

Welcome & Ambience	✓✓✓✓✓	Location	✓✓✓✓✓
Quality of Pitches	✓✓✓✓✓	Range of Facilities	✓✓✓✓✓

Directions

Site is signed at 26 km. marker on C252 between Castello d'Empuries and Vildemat, then 7 km. to site. Alternatively, on San Pescador - Castello d'Empuries road head north and site is signed on right.

Charges 2005

Per pitch	€ 18,00 - € 36,00
person (over 3 yrs)	€ 1,65 - € 3,30
dog	€ 3,85 - € 4,90
boat or jetski	€ 6,30 - € 8,50

All plus 7% VAT. No credit cards.

Reservations

Write to site. Tel: 972 454 477.
E-mail: info@almata.com

Open

14 May - 18 September, including all facilities.

ES8010 Camping Castell Mar

Platja de la Rubina, 17486 Castelló d'Empúries (Girona)

This friendly site is 350 metres from one of the very pleasant Gulf of Roses beaches, and within the large Aiguamolls de l'Emporda nature reserve. It is also convenient for (but quite separate from) the latest tourist development and facilities at Empuria Brava. With some 300 pitches, it is smaller than many sites in this part of Spain and is particularly suitable for families. There is a heated outdoor pool, a restaurant and bar and an large open-air auditorium where a varied entertainment programme is provided. A roof-top, terraced area is used for special occasions and enjoys pleasant views of the surrounding area. The pitches, most with electricity, are of average size for the Costa Brava and are on level ground with some artificial shade mainly for tents, and natural shade from the trees and hedges. There are opportunities for most watersports nearby and reception can arrange excursions by canoe through the nature reserve. Security is very good - if you want to leave before 8 am. you must make prior arrangements. There are several tour operators (100 pitches) and a further 50 pitches have mobile homes to rent.

Facilities

The large, well maintained, modern toilet block is of a high standard. It provides some washbasins in cabins, facilities for disabled visitors and dishwashing with hot water. Washing machines. Bar, restaurant/pizzeria and takeaway (all season). Supermarket. Large screen satellite TV/video. Play area. Table tennis. Swimming pools (all season). Many organised activities and entertainment over a long season. Riding and children's donkey rides with cart. Exchange facilities. ATM. Torches required in some areas. Off site: Riding 1 km. Bicycle hire 3 km. Golf 10 km.

Open

14 May - 25 September.

At a glance

Welcome & Ambience	✓✓✓	Location	✓✓✓✓
Quality of Pitches	✓✓✓	Range of Facilities	✓✓✓✓

Directions

From A7 motorway exit 3 (Figueres N/Roses) take N11 south and exit onto C260 Figueres - Roses road; site is signed on the right at km. 40.5, just after the second turn for Empuriabrava; follow road for approx. 1.5 km.

Charges 2005

Per person	€ 3,00
child (3-10 yrs)	€ 2,00
pitch incl. electricity	€ 9,00 - € 32,00

VAT included. No credit cards.

Reservations

Necessary for July/Aug. and made with deposit (€ 12,02) for a min. of 8 days between 9/7-15/8. Tel: 972 450 822. E-mail: cmar@campingparks.com

3 km of beach in "Els Aiguamolls de l'Empordà" nature reserve
Nautic Almata
Camping Caravaning
Private jetty with direct access to the sea
50% DISCOUNT LOW SEASON
15% DISCOUNT MEDIUM SEASON
Camping Nautic Almata
E-17486 Castelló d'Empúries (Girona) Spain
Tel.(34)972 454477-Fax (34) 972 454686
E-Mail: info@almata.com
Internet: http://www.almata.com
1st CLASS
La Jonquera
Figueres
Castelló d'Empúries
Sant Pere Pescador

ES8020 Camping Internacional de Amberes

Playa de la Rubina, 17487 Empúria-brava (Girona)

Situated in the 'Venice of Spain', Empuria Brava is interlaced with inland waterways and canals, where many residents and holiday-makers moor their boats directly outside their homes on the canal banks. Internacional Amberes is a large friendly site 50 m. from the wide, sandy beach, which is bordered on the east and west by the waterway canals (no access into them from the beach, only by car on the main road). The site can arrange temporary moorings for boats at Empuria Brava on request. The sea breeze here appears regularly during the afternoon so watersports are very good and hire facilities are available. Amberes is a surprisingly pretty and hospitable site where people seem to make friends easily and get to know other campers and the staff. The site has 798 touring pitches, most enjoying some shade from strategically placed trees. All have electricity and water connections. The restaurant and bar are close to the site entrance and the cuisine is so popular that locals use it too. Unusually the swimming pool is on an elevated terrace, raised out of view of most onlookers with sunbathing areas and a small children's pool adjoining. A shallow river runs through the site and the children can amuse themselves catching the colourful crawfish that abound here. A 'secret garden' style minigolf course is special to this site.

Facilities

Toilet facilities are in five fully equipped and recently renovated blocks. Washing machines. Motorcaravan services. Supermarket. Restaurant/bar. Disco bar and restaurant. Takeaway. Pizzeria. Watersports - windsurfing school. Boat moorings. Organised sports activities, children's programmes and entertainment. Swimming pool. Playgrounds. Football. Table tennis. Tennis. Volleyball. Apartments. Off site: Bicycle hire, riding and fishing 500 m. Golf 12 km.

Open

1 April - 15 October.

At a glance

Welcome & Ambience	✓✓✓✓	Location	✓✓✓✓✓
Quality of Pitches	✓✓✓✓	Range of Facilities	✓✓✓✓

Directions

Empuria Brava is reached by the C260 Figueres - Roses road. Site is signed from main roundabout leading into Empuria Brava but it is easier to continue to second roundabout, turn towards Empuria Brava and follow road for some distance. Watch for site entrance (hidden by trees) on left on one of the many bends.

Charges 2005

Per person over 3 yrs	€ 3,00
pitch incl. electricity (55 sq.m.)	€ 7,80 - € 20,00
pitch 70 sq.m.	€ 10,00 - € 23,20
pitch 85 sq.m.	€ 11,80 - € 25,10
pitch 100 sq.m.	€ 13,00 - € 28,00

Less 20% for pensioners for stays of 15 days or over in low seasons.

Reservations

Contact site for booking form. Tel: 972 450 507.
E-mail: info@inter-amberes.com

ES8033 Camping Las Palmeras

Ctra de la Platja, 17470 Sant Pere Pescador (Girona)

A very polished site, the pleasant experience begins as you enter the palm bedecked site and are greeted at the air conditioned reception building. The 230 pitches are flat, very clean and well maintained, with shade and 5A electricity. A few pitches are complete with water and drainage. Some smart mobile homes are placed unobtrusively around the site. A very pleasant pool complex has a lifeguard and the brightly coloured play areas are clean and safe. There is a huge array of activities including some very exotic activities which are booked at the site resulting in visits to the various locations to indulge (known as 'active holidays' - extra charge). A full animation programme allows parents a break during the day and there is organised fun in the evenings in high season. Juan Alcantara, the owner is a kind gentleman who is very keen for you to enjoy your time at his family site. You will enjoy a stay here as there is a very happy atmosphere. The very pleasant beach is a 200 m. walk through a gate at the rear of the site.

Facilities

Two excellent toilet blocks are very clean, including first class facilities for disabled campers plus two well equipped baby rooms (key at reception). Facilites may become a little busy at peak periods and the family cabins are sought after. Washing machines. Motorcaravan services. Supermarket. Restaurant/bar (children's menu). Swimming pools (heated). Play areas. Table tennis. Tennis. Gym. Boule. Electronic games. Barbecue. Bicycle hire. Mini-club. Animation. Active holiday programme (ask at reception). Torches useful.
Off site: Fishing. Beach 200 m. Boat launching 1 km. Riding 3 km. Golf 20 km.

At a glance

Welcome & Ambience	✓✓✓✓✓	Location	✓✓✓✓
Quality of Pitches	✓✓✓✓✓	Range of Facilities	✓✓✓✓

Directions

From A7/E15 Perpignan - Girona road take Figueres exit and N11/C31 towards L'Escala. Turn for town of San Pescador and site is well signed around the town.

Charges 2005

Per person	€ 2,00 - € 3,20
child (under 10 yrs)	€ 1,50 - € 2,00
pitch	€ 11,80 - € 29,10
electricity	€ 2,70
animal	€ 2,00 - € 3,50

Reservations

Made for min. 1 week with deposit (€ 100).
Tel: 972 520 506.
E-mail: info@campinglaspalmeras.com

Open

1 April - 31 October.

ES8035 Camping L'Amfora

Avenida Josep Tarradellas 2, 17470 Sant Pere Pescador (Girona)

This is a large, friendly family site with a Greek theme, which is manifested mainly in the restaurant and pool areas. The site is clean and well kept and the owner is keen to operate in an environmentally friendly way. There are 850 pitches (730 for touring), all with 10A electrical connections and most with a water tap, on level grass with small trees and shrubs. Of these, 64 pitches are large (180 sq.m.) and made for two units per pitch, each with an individual sanitary facility (toilet, shower and washbasin). Some 200 more recently developed pitches have limited shade as yet. An inviting terraced bar and self-service restaurant overlook three large swimming pools (one for children) and a new one with two water slides. Ambitious evening entertainment (pub, disco, shows) and children's animation are organised in season and a choice of watersports activities is available on the beach.

Facilities

In addition to the individual units, the two main sanitary blocks (one heated) offer free hot water, washbasins in cabins, hairdryers and baby rooms. There is extra provision near the pool area. Access is good for disabled visitors. Laundry facilities. Supermarket. Terraced bar, self service and waiter service restaurants, takeaway and pizza service. Restaurant and bar on the beach with limited menu (high season). Disco-bar for the young. Swimming pools (1/5-30/9). Table tennis. Tennis courts. Bicycle hire. Minigolf. Football. Volleyball. Playground. Entertainment and organised activities for children. Evening shows. Windsurfing school. Sailing. Fishing. Doctor daily in season. Exchange facilities. Internet point. Car wash. Torches required in beach areas. Off site: Boat laumching 1 km. Riding 6 km. Golf 15 km.

Open

19 March - 30 September.

At a glance

Welcome & Ambience	✓✓✓✓	Location	✓✓✓✓✓
Quality of Pitches	✓✓✓✓	Range of Facilities	✓✓✓✓✓

Directions

From A7 motorway take exit 3 (Figueres/Roses) on N-11 towards Girona/Barcelona. Exit on C260 for Figueres/Roses towards Roses and, at roundabout near Castello d'Empuries turn right to Sant Pere Pescador. Site is signed through town.

Charges 2005

Per person	€ 3,32 - € 4,28
child (2-9 yrs)	free - € 3,42
pitch (100 sq.m.)	€ 13,05 - € 33,12
with individual sanitary facilities	€ 19,00 - € 48,00
dog	€ 1,30 - € 3,60

Electricity (10A) included. Plus 7% VAT. Discounts for pensioners for longer stays. No credit cards.

Reservations

Made with deposit (€ 61) and fee (€ 15.03); write to site. Tel: 972 520 540. E-mail: info@campingamfora.com

TRAVEL SERVICE SITE

TO BOOK CALL 0870 405 4055 OR www.alanrogersdirect.com

ES8040 Camping Las Dunas

Ctra Sant Marti d'Empuries - Sant Pere, 17470 Sant Pere Pescador (Girona)

Las Dunas is an extremely large, impressive and well organised site with many on site activities and an ambitious programme of improvements. It has direct access to a superb sandy beach that stretches along the site for nearly one kilometre with a windsurfing school and beach bar. There is also a much used swimming pool with large double children's pools. Las Dunas is very large, with 1,500 individual hedged pitches of around 100 sq.m. laid out on flat ground in long, regular parallel rows. Electrical connections are provided on all pitches and shade is available in some parts of the site. Much effort has gone into planting palms and new trees here and the results are very attractive (find the 600 year old olive tree - it is easier than you think). Pitches are usually available, even in the main season. The large restaurant and bar have spacious terraces overlooking the pools and you can enjoy a very pleasant more secluded cavern styled pub. A magnificent disco club is close by in a soundproof building (although people returning from this during the night can be a problem for pitches in the central area of the site). With free quality entertainment of all types in season and positive security arrangements, this is a great site for families with teenagers. Everything is provided on site so you don't need to leave it during your stay.

Facilities

Five excellent large toilet blocks (with cleaners 07.00-21,00) have British style toilets, controllable hot showers and washbasins in cabins. One block has underfloor heating and automatic doors for cooler weather. Excellent facilities for youngsters, babies and disabled people. Laundry facilities. Motorcaravan services. Extensive supermarket with bakery, good butcher and other shops. Large bar with terrace. Large restaurant. Takeaway. Ice-cream parlour. Beach bar in main season. Disco club. Swimming pool (30 x 14 m) with children's pool. Playgrounds. Tennis. Minigolf. Football and rugby pitches. Basketball. Boule. Volleyball. Sailing and windsurfing school and other watersports. Organised programme of events - sports, children's games, evening shows, partly in English (15/6-31/8). Exchange facilities .ATM. Safety deposit. Torches required in some areas.

At a glance

Welcome & Ambience	✓✓✓✓	Location	✓✓✓✓✓
Quality of Pitches	✓✓✓✓	Range of Facilities	✓✓✓✓✓

Directions

From A7 take exit 5 towards L'Escala (G1623) and turn north 2 km. before reaching L'Escala at sign to Sant Marti d'Ampurias. Site well signed on this road.

Charges 2004

Per person	€ 3,00
child (2-10 yrs)	€ 2,50
standard pitch incl. electricity	€ 13,00 - € 38,00
water and drainage	€ 1,00 - € 3,00
dog (one section only)	€ 3,00 - € 4,00

All plus 7% VAT.

Reservations

Made for numbered pitches with deposit and fee. Address for information: Apdo. de Correus 23, 17130 La Escala (Girona). Tel: 972 521 717.
E-mail: info@campinglasdunas.com

Open

9 May - 25 September.

ES8060 Camping La Ballena Alegre 2

17470 Sant Pere Pescador (Girona)

La Ballena Alegre 2 is partly in a lightly wooded setting, partly open, and with some 1,800 m. of frontage directly onto an excellent beach of soft golden sand (which is cleaned daily). They claim that none of the 1,629 pitches is more than 100 m. from the beach. The site has won Spanish tourist board awards and is keen on ecological fitness. The grass pitches are individually numbered and of decent size (over 200 are 100 sq.m.). Electricity (5A) is available in all parts and there are 70 fully serviced pitches. Restaurant and bar areas are beside the pleasant terraced pool complex (four pools including a children's pool). For those who wish to drink and snack late there is a pub open until 03.00 hrs. The soundproof disco has a covered approach and is firmly managed - a discount card doubles for easy identification of customers. A little train ferries people along the length of the site. Activities include a well managed watersports centre, with sub-aqua, windsurfing and kite surfing, where equipment can be hired and lessons taken. A comprehensive open air fitness centre is near the beach and there is a full entertainment programme all season. An area across the road provides extra parking and sports activities. A great site for families.

Facilities

All seven toilet blocks have been refurbished to a very high standard and are well maintained. These feature large pivoting doors for showers, wash cabins, etc, special low facilities for children, baby baths and facilities for disabled campers. Launderette. Motorcaravan services. Gas supplies. Supermarket. Chemist. Bar and self-service restaurant. Full restaurant (evenings all season). Takeaway. 'Croissanterie'. Pizzeria and beach bar in high season. Swimming pool complex (all season). Three tennis courts. Table tennis. Watersports centre. Fitness centre. Bicycle hire. Playgrounds. Sound proofed disco. Dancing twice weekly and organised activities, sports, entertainment, etc. all season but it is generally a quiet site. Safe deposit. Cash point. Resident doctor and site ambulance. Car wash. Internet point. Torches useful in beach areas. Off site: Go-karting nearby with bus service. Fishing 300 m. Riding 2 km.

At a glance

Welcome & Ambience	✓✓✓✓	Location	✓✓✓✓✓
Quality of Pitches	✓✓✓✓	Range of Facilities	✓✓✓✓✓

Directions

From A7 Figueres - Girona autopista take exit 5 to L'Escala GI 623 for 18.5 km. At roundabout take sign to Sant Marti d'Empúries and follow camp signs. Access has now been entirely asphalted.

Charges 2004

Per person	€ 3,30
child (3-9 yrs)	€ 2,50
pitch incl. electricity	€ 14,90 - € 35,00
serviced pitch plus	€ 6,00 - € 11,00
dog (one section only)	€ 2,10 - € 4,00

All plus 7% VAT. Discount of 10% on pitch charge for pensioners all season. No credit cards.

Reservations

Made with deposit (€ 200), min. 10 days 10/7-10/8. Winter address: Ave. Roma 12, 08015 Barcelona.
Tel: 902 510 520. E-mail: infb2@ballena-alegre.com

Open

15 May - 27 September.

www.alanrogers.com for latest campsite news

ES8050 Camping Aquarius

Mobile homes page 168

Ctra de la Platja s/n, 17470 Sant Pere Pescador (Girona)

A smart and efficient family site, Aquarius has direct access to a quiet sandy beach that slopes gently and provides good bathing (the sea is shallow for quite a long way out). The site is ideal for those who really like sun and sea, with a quiet situation. One third of the site has good shade with a park-like atmosphere with the great variety of plants here being carefully labelled (Mr Rupp the owner is an enthusiast). An extension with less shade provided an opportunity to enlarge the pitches and they are now all at least 70-100 sq.m. which is good for Spain. There are 447 numbered pitches, all with electrical connections (6A). Only five pitches are not for touring. The owner has an architectural background and a wealth of knowledge on the whole Catalan area and culture. He has written a booklet of suggested tours (from reception). The whole family is justifiably proud of their most attractive site and they continually make improvements. The fountain at the entrance, the fishponds and the water features in the restaurant are soothing and pleasing. A small stage close to the restaurant is used for live entertainment in season. The spotless beach bar complex with shaded terraces and minigolf has marvellous views over the Bay of Roses. The 'Surf Center' with rentals, school and shop is ideal for enthusiasts and beginners alike.

Facilities

Attractively tiled, fully equipped, large toilet blocks provide some cabins for each sex. Excellent facilities for disabled people, plus baths for children and hot water for sinks. A superb new block has under-floor heating and features family cabins with showers and basins. Laundry facilities. Gas supplies. Car wash. Motorcaravan services. Full size refrigerators. Supermarket with butcher. Pleasant restaurant and bar with terrace. Takeaway. Children's play centre (with qualified attendant), playground near the beach and games hall. TV room with giant screen and ample comfortable seating. 'Surf Center'. Table tennis. Volleyball. Minigolf. Bicycle hire. Football field. Boules. Barbecue and dance once weekly when numbers justify. Security boxes. Exchange facilities. ATM. Electronic games. Dogs are accepted in one section. (Note: no pool). Off site: Fishing and boat launching 3 km. Riding 6 km. Golf 15 km.

At a glance

Welcome & Ambience	✓✓✓✓	Location	✓✓✓✓✓
Quality of Pitches	✓✓✓	Range of Facilities	✓✓✓

Directions

From A7 motorway take exit 3 (Figueres/Roses) and take N11 south to join C260 towards Roses. At roundabout near Castello d'Empuries take road to and through Sant Pere Pescador. Site signed to left shortly after bridge south of town.

Charges 2005

Per person	€ 2,75 - € 3,30
child (2-12 yrs)	free - € 2,40
pitch acc. to season and facilities	€ 6,80 - € 33,35
electricity	€ 2,50
animal	€ 2,50 - € 3,00

All plus 7% VAT. Discounts for pensioners on longer stays. No credit cards.

Reservations

Made for any length with £50 deposit and £15 fee. (you are strongly advised to book early for any pitch near the beach). Tel: 972 520 003. E-mail: camping@aquarius.es

Open

All year except 11 January - 14 March.

ES8070 Camping L'Escala

Cami Ample, 17130 L'Escala (Girona)

Under the same ownership as Las Dunas (no. ES8040), but a complete contrast in terms of size, this is a small, traditional site with limited facilities. It takes just five minutes to walk to either the very pleasant beach or to the centre of this modestly sized, lively, yet historic holiday resort. Here you will find most of the usual seaside attractions. The site has a canopy of fir trees giving excellent shade. There are 140 pitches of which 90 are for touring units, so reservation is essential. All pitches have electricity, water and drainage. In season there is a bar and restaurant offering very good food with a pleasant enclosed terrace with a retractable candy-striped canopy. There is some road noise despite the very high wall between the site and the busy road alongside.

Facilities

The central toilet block is basic but clean, with British style toilets, washbasins (two in cabins for ladies), free hot water and 25 free showers. Dishwashing and laundry sinks with hot water. Shop, bar and restaurant (all high season). Basic play area. Off site: Fishing 100 m. Bicycle hire 500 m. Riding 3 km. Golf 15 km.

Open

Easter - 25 September.

At a glance

Welcome & Ambience	✓✓✓	Location	✓✓✓
Quality of Pitches	✓✓✓	Range of Facilities	✓✓✓

Directions

Site lies on the north side of the town and the beach. Follow road for beach, then fork immediately left into Cami Ample to site on the right in 200 m. (watch for site name on wall and gate in high wall).

Charges guide

Per person	€ 2,10
child (2-10 yrs)	€ 1,80
pitch incl. electricity	€ 11,45 - € 16,00
dog	€ 2,10 - € 2,70

All plus 7% VAT.

Reservations

Essential in high season. Tel: 972 770 084.
E-mail: info@campinglescala.com

ES8074 Camping Paradis

Avenida de Montgó 260, 17130 L'Escala (Girona)

If you prefer a quieter site out of the very busy resort of L'Escala then this site is an excellent option. This large, friendly, family run site has a dynamic owner Marti, who is a most pleasant man with excellent English and very keen to help. The site is divided by the beach access road and has its own private access to the very safe and unspoilt beach. The site has 646 pitches, all with electricity (10A), some on sloping ground although the pitches themselves tend to be flat. Established pine trees provide shade for most places with more coverage on the western side of the site. Non-stop maintenance ensures that all facilities at this site are of a high standard. There are three swimming pools, the largest with an idyllic and most unusual setting on the top of a cliff overlooking the Bay of Roses. The site operates its own well equipped sub-aqua diving school and campers can experience a free diving experience in the pool or more adventurous coastal diving where appropriate. A CCTV security system monitors the pools and general security from a purpose built centre.

Facilities

Modern, fully equipped sanitary blocks are kept very clean. Washing machines and dryers. Shop (1/4-30/9). Extensive modern complex of restaurants, bars and takeaways (1/4-30/9). Takeaway(1/4-15/9). Swimming pools (1/5-20/10). Pool bar. Play areas. Fishing. Basketball, volleyball and badminton. Kayak hire. Sub aqua school. Organised activities for children in high season. ATM machine. Private access to beach. Off site: Cala Montgo beach 100 m. with a charming bay of soft sand offering all manner of watersports, pretty restaurants and a disco in season. Road train service to town centre from outside site. Riding 2 km. Golf 10 km.

At a glance

Welcome & Ambience	✓✓✓✓✓	Location	✓✓✓✓✓
Quality of Pitches	✓✓✓✓✓	Range of Facilities	✓✓✓✓✓

Directions

Leave autopista A7 at exit 5 heading for Viladimat, then L'Escala. Site is well signed from town centre.

Charges 2004

Per person	€ 2,70 - € 4,58
child (3-9 yrs)	€ 1,92 - € 3,22
pitch	€ 10,40 - € 21,58
electricity	€ 3,27

Plus 7% VAT. No credit cards.

Reservations

Advisable in high season. Tel: 972 770 200.
E-mail: info@campingparadis.com

Open

17 March - 20 October.

ES8072 Camping Les Medes

Paratge Camp De L'Arbre, 17258 L'Estartit (Girona)

Les Medes is different from some of the 'all singing, all dancing' sites so popular along this coast and the friendly family of Pla-Coll are rightly proud of their award winning site. Set back from busy L'Estartit itself, it is only 800 metres to the nearest beach and a little train runs from near the site (June - Sept) to the town. With just 172 pitches, the site is small enough for the owners to know their visitors and, being campers themselves, they have been careful in planning their top class facilities. The level, grassy pitches range in size from 60-80 sq.m. depending on your unit. All have electricity and the larger ones (around half) also have water and drainage. All are clearly marked in rows, but with no separation other than by the deciduous trees which provide summer shade. A cheery children's pool with fountains is behind the unusually shaped pool ringed by palms. This is part of an attractively landscaped feature with a false island, producing a relaxing atmosphere in front of the old Catalan farmhouse buildings. The open air dance floor has music twice weekly (in season). A classy indoor pool (heated) with sauna and solarium and good access for disabled campers is a great option out of high season. The Medes islands are very pretty and worth exploring or a bad weather day could be used to visit Salvador Dali's amazing house.

Facilities

Two modern, spacious sanitary blocks, can be heated and are extremely well maintained, providing washbasins in private cabins, top class facilities for disabled people and baby baths. Washing machines and dryer. Dishwashing and laundry sinks. Motorcaravan services. Bar with TV and snacks (all year). Restaurant (1/4-31/10). Shop (all year, but only basics in winter). Outdoor swimming pool and paddling pool (15/6-15/9) with drinks stall. Indoor pool with sauna, solarium (15/9-15/6). Masseur. Play area. Indoor children's area. TV room. Internet terminals. Excursions organised in July/Aug. Diving activities arranged. Giant chess. Table tennis. Volleyball. Boules. Quality information folder on arrival. Bicycle hire. Tours arranged. Dogs accepted in parts of two low season periods - check with the site. Environmentally friendly. Torches are useful. Off site: Riding 400 m. Fishing 800 m. Nearest beach 800 m. Medes Natural Reserve 1.5 km. Estartit 2 km. Golf 8 km.

At a glance

Welcome & Ambience	✓✓✓✓✓	Location	✓✓✓✓✓
Quality of Pitches	✓✓✓✓✓	Range of Facilities	✓✓✓✓✓

Directions

Site is signed from the main Torroella de Montgri - L'Estartit road GE641. Turn right after Camping Castel Montgri, at Joc's hamburger/pizzeria and follow signs.

Charges 2005

Per person	€ 6,00
child (0-10 yrs)	€ 4,30
pitch	€ 13,50
electricity	€ 3,50

All plus 7% VAT. Discounts outside high season and special offers for low season longer stays. No credit cards.

Reservations

Advised for July/Aug. Write to site with € 31 deposit. Tel: 972 751 805.
E-mail: info@campingslesmedes.com

Open

All year except November.

lesmedes
camping - caravaning
bungalows

Only 2 km from L'Estartit, one of the most beautiful and ecological-minded villages of the Costa Brava, only 800m from the Beach. On our family site you will enjoy a fabulous holiday in the midst of nature. We have high quality installations: modern sanitary instal. With baby-baths, install. for the handicapped and free hot water, swimming pool (also indoors heated) bar, restaurant and supermarket... Leisure activities for the whole family: children's playground, watersports, bicycles for rent and a large programme of activities for all ages. And to relax a dive in our swimming pool with solarium and sauna.

TÜV UNE ISO 9001: 2000 Nº 0.04.03194
TÜV UNE EN ISO 14001: 1996 Nº 3.00.00002
EMAS GESTIÓ AMBIENTAL VERIFICADA

telf.+34 972 751 805 - fax.+34 972 750 413 - www.campinglesmedes.com - info@ campingslesmedes.com
paratge Camp de l'Arbre, apartado de correos, 140 - 17258 l'ESTARTIT, Girona COSTA BRAVA

ES8007 Camping Castell Montgri

Ctra Toroella - L'Estartit, km 4.7, 17258 L'Estartit (Girona)

This is a large bustling site with all the modern paraphernalia of holiday-making. With over 50% of the site dedicated to catering for tour operators, it may come as a surprise that we should choose to feature it in a guide for independent campers and caravanners. However, the site does include three designated areas for independent campers and these provide 590 terraced and flat pitches, some shaded but all with electricity. On arrival you are invited to find your own place. There is a busy bar/restaurant and terrace overlooking an attractive swimming pool with a pair of water slides (one large with attendant) close to these areas. The remainder of the site offers a very wide range of amenities and attractions, including one further, large pool with restaurant/bar and terrace areas higher on the site, and a new pool, bar and live music area at the very top with fantastic views. There are also two mini-pools for toddlers around the site along with various play areas, disco, sports facilities and a live entertainment programme. This site could be of interest to families with teenagers, offering the possibility for parents to rest whilst the youngsters enjoy their own type of holiday within the confines of the site.

Facilities

Toilet facilities are quite adequate, if not that luxurious, each area of the site having its own block, with dishwashing (H&C) and laundry facilities. Cleaning is continual (06.00-22.00 hrs) but with the numbers on site, litter may be a problem at times. Bars and restaurants. Pizzeria. Takeaway. Swimming pools. Supermarket and souvenirs. Football field. Tennis. Table tennis. Billiards. Volleyball. Minigolf. Play area. Large screen TV and videos. Disco. Entertainment programme and excursions. Exchange and safe deposit facilities. Car wash. Gas supplies. Free site bus to L'Estartit Torches required in some areas. Off site: Fishing 300 m. Riding 500 m. Bicycle hire 1 km. Golf 10 km. Seaside entertainment in Estartit.

At a glance

Welcome & Ambience	✓✓✓	Location	✓✓✓
Quality of Pitches	✓✓✓	Range of Facilities	✓✓✓✓✓

Directions

Site is on the main Torroella de Montgri - L'Estartit road GI 641 just north of the town on the left, just after town sign.

Charges 2005

Per person	€ 3,00
child (3-10 yrs)	€ 2,00
pitch incl. car and electricity	€ 8,00 - € 34,00

Prices include VAT. Minimum 7 day stay 6/7-18/8. Good discounts in low season. No credit cards.

Reservations

Made with non-returnable deposit (€ 12.02), to guarantee admission only. Tel: 972 751 630. E-mail: cmontgri@campingparks.com

Open

14 May - 9 October.

ES8080 Camping El Delfin Verde

Ctra de Torroella de Montgri, 17257 Torroella de Montgri (Girona)

A large, popular and high quality site in a quiet location, El Delfin Verde has its own long beach stretching along its frontage which campers have to themselves. A feature of the site is an attractive large pool in the shape of a dolphin with a total area of 1,800 sq.m. This has two island areas, one containing a huge fountain which can be lit at night. In the main season an elevated area with a large bar, full restaurant and a separate takeaway give wonderful views over the huge pool. There is a further restaurant with slightly cheaper, good value food in the main complex with an open air arena. This is a large site with nearly 6,000 visitors at peak times, well managed with friendly staff. Level grass pitches nearer the beach are marked and many are separated by small fences and newly planted hedging. All have electrical connections and access to water points and a stream runs through the centre of the site. There is shade in some of the older parts and a particularly pleasant area of pine trees in the centre provides marked but not separated pitches (sandy and not so level). El Delfin Verde is a large and cheerful holiday site with many good facilities, sports and a free family entertainment programme in season. It is well worth considering for your Costa Brava holidays. Used by British tour operators (60 pitches).

Facilities

Six excellent large toilet blocks plus a seventh smaller block, all with resident cleaners, have fully controllable showers using desalinated water and of good, comfortable size, and some washbasins in cabins. Laundry facilities. Motorcaravan services. Supermarket and other shops. Swimming pools (with lifeguard). Two restaurants, grills and pizzerias. Three bars - the main one closes 11 pm, pool bar open until 1 am; small bar by beach open in season. 'La Vela' barbecue and party area. Large sports area, football, volleyball, 8 tennis courts. 2 km. exercise track. Dancing and floor shows weekly in season. Disco. Excursions organised. General room with TV. Video room. Games room. Bicycle hire. Minigolf. Playground. Trampolines. Badminton. Fishing. Hairdresser. Car repairs, servicing and washing. Gas supplies. Dogs are not accepted in high season (11/7-14/8). Off site: Golf 4 km (20% discount). Riding 4 km.

At a glance

Welcome & Ambience	✓✓✓	Location	✓✓✓✓
Quality of Pitches	✓✓✓	Range of Facilities	✓✓✓✓✓

Directions

Site is at end of very long approach road leading off the C31 Torroella de Montgri - Palafrugell road (east of Girona). Watch out for white dolphin and flags by road side.

Charges 2005

Per person	€ 3,50
child (2-9 yrs)	€ 3,00
pitch incl. electricity	€ 13,00 - € 38,00
dog (excl 11/7-14/8)	€ 3,00

All plus 7% VAT. Special offers on long stays in low season.

Reservations

Only a guarantee to admit - no specific pitch allocated. Write (all year) with deposit (€ 91) to Apdo. 43, 17257 Torroella de Montgri. Tel: 972 758 454. E-mail: info@eldelfinverde.com

Open

19 March - 16 October, incl. all amenities.

www.alanrogers.com for latest campsite news

ES8075 Camping Estartit

Calle Villa Primavera 12, 17258 L'Estartit (Girona)

This friendly, Belgian run site has limited facilities, but is only 300 metres from Estartit town. A short walk down the hill brings you into the heart of the town which is extremely popular and very commercialised, although you can find authentic tapas bars and street entertainment. The site itself is surprisingly quiet, considering its proximity to the town. Set amongst tall pine trees (which provide complete shade), in a narrow valley, it has 173 terraced pitches (132 for touring units), all with electrical connections (2/6A). These are best suited for campers with tents as there are some very steep drops between the terraces. However, there are two sand/gravel areas for a small number of motorcaravans and caravans (booking essential in high season). The local beaches are extremely good but if the town is too frenetic the site has a very small swimming pool plus a sunbathing area with loungers. An attractive shaded area has a terrace beside the bar. Access around the site could be difficult for disabled people.

Facilities

The modern, fully tiled sanitary block is kept very clean and provides hot and cold showers (small fee for hot water), small laundry with washing machines and a separate baby area. Gas supplies. Bar/restaurant (1/6-15/9). Shop (1/6-15/9). Swimming pool (all season). Limited, small play area. Children's activities and adult social events (barbecue, bingo, etc). Excursions can be booked. Site is guarded day and night. Torches are necessary in the more remote parts of the site. Dogs are not accepted in high season (20/6-20/8). Off site: Fishing, bicycle hire and riding within 1 km. Golf 7 km.

Open

Easter/1 April - 1 October.

At a glance

Welcome & Ambience	✓✓✓✓	Location	✓✓✓
Quality of Pitches	✓✓✓	Range of Facilities	✓✓✓

Directions

L'Estartit is approached on the E1641 which leaves the C31 road at Torroella de Montgri. Site is signed from Estartit town centre; follow the one-way system.

Charges guide

Per person	€ 4,25
child (2-10 yrs)	€ 2,75
caravan or family tent	€ 4,70
car	€ 4,00
motorcaravan	€ 7,80
motorcycle	€ 2,80

Plus 7% VAT. Less 10-30% outside high season (10/6-31/8). No credit cards.

Reservations

Contact site. Tel: 972 751 909.

ES8090 Camping Cypsela

Ctra de Pals - Platja de Pals, 17256 Platja de Pals (Girona)

This impressive, de-luxe site with lush vegetation and trees has many striking features, one of which is the sumptuous complex of sport facilities and amenities near the entrance. This provides a fine large swimming pool, a good children's pool and playgrounds, two excellent squash courts, a tennis court, fitness room, and other entertainment rooms. These include a children's playroom with mini-club and organised entertainment (including video screen), an amusements room with pool tables, football tables, video games, and a luxurious air conditioned lounge. The 'Les Moreres' is a pleasant al fresco restaurant offering a varied menu plus good wines (it can become very busy). Another indoor restaurant offers a similar excellent service. You have the choice of a smart bar or the air conditioned cocktail bar. The main part of the camping area is pinewood, with 661 clearly marked touring pitches of varying categories on sandy gravel, all with electricity and some with full facilities. The 202 'Elite' pitches of 120 sq.m. are impressive. If you wish to travel to the beach there is a regular free bus service from the site. Cypsela is a busy, well administered site, only two kilometres from the sea, which we can thoroughly recommend, especially for families. It is very efficiently run, with good quality fixtures and fittings, all kept clean and maintained to a high standard, all your needs will be catered for here. The gates are closed at night. Several tour operators use the site (299 pitches).

Facilities

Four stylish sanitary 'houses' are of excellent quality with comprehensive cleaning schedules. Using solar heating, three have washbasins in cabins and three have amazing children's rooms with a battery of baby baths and larger ones for older children. Facilites for disabled people are superb. Serviced launderette. Ironing. Supermarket and other shops. Restaurant, cafeteria and takeaway. Bar. Hairdresser. Swimming pools. Tennis. Squash. Table tennis. Football field. Minigolf. Fitness room. Air conditioned social/TV room. Barbecue and party area. Children's club. Comprehensive animation programme for children and adults in season. Organised sports and games activities. Games room with pool tables, electronic games etc. Air conditioned telephone parlour. Business and internet centre. Doctor always on site; well equipped treatment room. Car wash. Gas supplies. ATM. Dogs are not accepted. Off site: Bicycle hire 150 m. Golf 1 km. Fishing 2 km.

At a glance

Welcome & Ambience	✓✓✓✓✓	Location	✓✓✓✓
Quality of Pitches	✓✓✓✓	Range of Facilities	✓✓✓✓✓

Directions

Cypsela is on the EN6502 road to Platja de Pals, leaving the C31 (Figueres - Palamos) road at roundavout near Pals.

Charges 2004

Per person	€ 5,30
child (2-10 yrs)	€ 4,25
pitch acc. to season and services	€ 16,47 - € 47,69

Reservations

Contact site. Tel: 972 667 696.
E-mail: info@cypsela.com

Open

15 May - 26 September.

www.alanrogers.com for latest campsite news

ES8101 Camping Playa Brava

Avda. del Grau, 1, 17256 Platja de Pals (Girona)

This is a pleasant site with an open feel which has access to a large sandy beach (200 metres) and a freshwater lagoon. On both you can enjoy watersports and you may launch your own boat. The ground is level and very grassy with shade provided for the 500 pitches by a mixture of conifer and broad-leaf trees. Electricity is provided (5A) and about a third of the pitches (75-85 sq.m.) have water and drainage. The air of spaciousness continues around the large swimming pool and children's pool (life-guard). There are no fences but huge grass sunbathing areas, the whole being overlooked by the restaurant and bar terrace. The restaurant is very pleasant and offers a most reasonable menu of the day including wine. An energetic entertainment programme runs during July and August. There are many interesting things to explore in the area including La Bisbal – famous for the ceramics, Dali's Museum the Roman ruins at Empuries Girona and many more. A green and pleasant family site.

Facilities

Five modern, fully equipped toilet blocks include facilities for disabled visitors. Dishwashing facilities under cover. Washing machines and dryers. Bar/restaurant. Takeaway. Supermarket. Swimming pool. Tennis. Volleyball. Minigolf. Play area on grass. Fishing. Watersports on river and beach, including sheltered lagoon for windsurfing learners. Gas supplies. Torches required in some areas. Dogs are not accepted. Off site: Two 18 hole golf courses 1 km. Bicycle hire 3 km. Riding 5 km.

Open

14 May - 18 September.

At a glance

Welcome & Ambience	✓✓✓✓	Location	✓✓✓✓✓
Quality of Pitches	✓✓✓✓	Range of Facilities	✓✓✓✓

Directions

Platja de Pals is reached via EN6502 road which leaves the C31 Figueres - Palamos road near Pals just north of Palafrugell. Site is well signed approaching village, then follow road for 3 km. (keeping golf course on your right) to site and beach.

Charges 2005

Per person	€ 1,75 - € 2,50
child (2-9 yrs)	free - € 2,00
senior	free - € 2,50
75 sq.m. pitch incl. electricity	€ 22,00 - € 31,50
85 sq.m.	€ 25,00 - € 36,50

All plus 7% VAT. Discount for longer stays in low season. No credit cards.

Reservations

Write to site. Tel: 972 636 894.
E-mail: info@playabrava.com

ES8100 Camping Inter-Pals

Avenida Mediterrania, 17256 Platja de Pals (Girona)

Sister site to no. ES8170 and set on sloping ground, with tall pine trees providing shade and about 500 metres from the beach, this site has 625 terraced pitches (including 280 for touring units and 250 for tents), on terraces and levelled plots, mostly with shade. Some of the terraced pitches have views of the sea through the trees. The main entrance and its drive resembles a pretty village street as the bungalows are set on both sides of the street, lined with traditional lampposts. Continuing the village theme is a row of shops where you will find most camper's needs. The site is close to Platja de Pals which is a long sandy unspoilt stretch of beach, a discreet area, part of which is now an official naturist beach. The formal restaurant with good value menu and choice of takeaway overlooks the pools. The pretty town of Pals is close by along with a good golf course. The site will assist with touring plans of the area.

TRAVEL SERVICE SITE

TO BOOK CALL 0870 405 4055 OR www.alanrogersdirect.com

Facilities

Three well maintained toilet blocks include individual washbasins, dishwashing and laundry sinks and facilities for disabled campers. Washing machines and dryers. Gas supplies. Fridge/TV rental. Medical centre. Excursions. ATM. Diving and watersport arranged. Shops. Restaurant/bar with Pizzeria/croissenterie with dancing and entertainment area. Cafe/bar by entrance. Swimming pool. Basketball, volleyball and badminton courts. Tennis. Children's playground and organised activities and entertainment in high season. Electronic games. Pool tables. Some breeds of dog are excluded -; check with site. Torch useful. Off site: Fishing 200 m. Bicycle hire 500 m. Golf 1 km. Riding 10 km.

Open

1 April - 30 September.

At a glance

Welcome & Ambience	✓✓✓✓✓	Location	✓✓✓✓
Quality of Pitches	✓✓✓✓✓	Range of Facilities	✓✓✓✓✓

Directions

Site is on the road leading off the Torroella de Montgri-Bagur road north of Pals and going to Playa de Pals (Pals beach).

Charges 2004

Per person	€ 3,50 - € 4,95
child (3-10 yrs)	€ 2,50 - € 2,90
pitch	€ 15,50 - € 26,90
small tent and car	€ 13,50 - € 18,60
dog	€ 2,60

Plus 7% VAT. Discounts for long stays in low season. No credit cards.

Reservations

Made in the sense of guarantee to admit only, without deposit. Tel: 972 636 179.
E-mail: interpals@interpals.com

ES8102 Camping Mas Patoxas

Mobile homes ▶ page 168

Ctra Palafrugell-Pals, km 339, 17256 Pals (Girona)

This is a mature and well laid out site for those who prefer to be apart from, but within easy travelling distance of the beaches (5 km.) and town (1 km). It has a very easy access and is set on a slight slope with wide avenues on level terraces providing 400 grassy pitches of a minimum 72 sq.m. All have electricity (5A) and water, many have drainage as well. There are some very pleasant views and shade from a variety of mature trees. An air-conditioned restaurant/bar provides both waiter service meals and take-away food to order (weekends only mid Sept - April) and entertainment takes place on a stage below the terraces during the high season. Both bar and restaurant terraces give views over the pools and distant hills. The restaurant menu is varied and very reasonable. We were impressed with the children's mini-club activity when we visited. There is a large, supervised irregularly shaped swimming pool with triple flume, a separate children's pool and a generous sunbathing area of the poolside and surrounding grass. Used by tour operators (40).

Facilities

Three modern sanitary blocks provide controllable hot showers, some washbasins with hot water, baby bath and three children's cabins with washbasin and shower. No specific facilities for disabled people, although access throughout the site looks to be relatively easy. Dishwashing facilities under cover (H&C). Laundry facilities. Restaurant/bar (1/4-30/9). Pizzeria. Takeaway. Well stocked shop (1/4-30/9). Swimming pool (15/6-30/9). Tennis. Table tennis. Volleyball. Football field. Entertainment in high season. Fridges for rent. Gas supplies. Torches useful in some areas. Off site: Bus service from site gate. Bicycle hire or riding 2 km. Fishing or golf 4 km.

At a glance

Welcome & Ambience	✓✓✓✓	Location	✓✓✓✓
Quality of Pitches	✓✓✓✓	Range of Facilities	✓✓✓✓

Directions

Site is east of Girona and approx. 1.5 km. south of Pals at km. 339 on the C31 Figueres-Palamos road, just north of Palafugel.

Charges 2004

Per person	€ 3,60 - € 5,00
child (1-10 yrs)	€ 2,50 - € 3,00
caravan pitch	€ 17,00 - € 24,00
tent pitch with car	€ 14,00 - € 21,00
dog	€ 2,10

Plus 7% VAT. Special low season offers.

Reservations

Write to site. Tel: 972 636 928.
E-mail: info@campingmaspatoxas.com

Open

All year, except 19 December - 13 January.

ES8103 Camping El Maset

Playa de Sa Riera, 17255 Begur (Girona)

A delightful little gem of a site in lovely surroundings, El Maset has 116 pitches, of which just 20 are for caravans or motorcaravans (the site reports there are some larger pitches for 2005), the remainder suitable only for tents. The owner of some 40 years, Senor Juan Perez is delightful, as is his secretary Josaphine, and longer stay customers may be presented with a memento of their visit. The site entrance is steep and access to the caravan pitches can be quite tricky. However, a new road has been cut out of the hillside and the owner's son will tow your caravan to your pitch. All these pitches have electricity, water and drainage with some shade. Access to the tent pitches, which are more shaded on attractive rock-walled terraces on the hillside, seems quite straightforward, with parking for cars not too far away - of necessity the pitches are fairly small. All steep terraced pitches are safely fenced for children. For a small site the amenities are quite extensive, including an unusual elliptical shaped swimming pool. A bar and very homely restaurant offering excellent food, with a terrace giving very pleasant views over the pool and towards the other side of the valley. This small site provides the standard of service normally associated with the very best of the larger sites. It is situated in the tiny resort of Sa Riera with access to the beach (300 m), in a beautiful protected bay with traditional fishing boats taking up one end of the sand. There is a naturist beach (via a longer uphill path). Begur, with its beautiful, small, quite unspoilt bay and beach, is 10 minutes by car.

Facilities

Sanitary facilities are superb with marble tops, hair and hand dryers and soap. In three small blocks and very clean, they include baby facilities. Top quality washing up area (H&C), industrial washing machines and dryers. Unit for disabled campers. Bar/restaurant, takeaway (all season). Shop (from May). Swimming pool (all season). Solarium. Play area on astroturf. Area for football and basketball. Excellent games room. Internet point. Dogs are not accepted. Off site: Fishing 300 m. Golf and bicycle hire 1 km. Riding 8 km.

Open

2 April - 25 September.

At a glance

Welcome & Ambience	✓✓✓✓	Location	✓✓✓✓
Quality of Pitches	✓✓✓	Range of Facilities	✓✓✓

Directions

From the C31 Figueres - Palamos road south of Pals, north of Palafrugell, take GI653 to Begur. Site is 2 km. north of the town; follow signs for Playa de Sa Riera and site (steep entrance).

Charges 2005

Per person	€ 4,30 - € 6,00
child (1-10 yrs)	€ 3,00 - € 4,30
caravan	€ 5,40 - € 7,60
tent	€ 3,30 - € 7,00
car	€ 4,00 - € 5,30
motorcycle	€ 2,60 - € 3,90

Plus 7% VAT. Discount in low season for 7 day stay.

Reservations

Write to site. Tel: 972 623 023.
E-mail: info@campingelmaset.com

ES8104 Camping Begur

Ctra D'Esclanya, km 2, 17255 Begur (Girona)

The new owners here have made a massive investment in making the site a pleasant place to spend some time. Begur has some good supporting facilities including a pleasant swimming pool and paddling pool at its centre. The bar and snack bar are part of this new pool complex and it has been well designed with terraces and sunbathing area. The touring areas are protected from the sun by mature trees and the 317 pitches are informally arranged on sloping sandy ground (chocks useful). Most pitches have electrical connections (10A), water and drainage. A few mobile homes and apartments are scattered around the slopes. Environmental activities are encouraged including visits to the revolutionary water cleansing plant deep in the woods. There are many sporting facilities including a well equipped weight training room (free). A huge supermarket is just outside the gate, used by locals and the new restaurant here is now open. The bays of the Costa Brava are just 1.5 km. away.

Facilities

Two modern toilet blocks are fully equipped and include really large showers. Excellent facilites for disabled campers. Baby bath. Washing machines and dryers. Motorcaravan services. Bar and snacks. Restaurant and supermarket just outside gate. Swimming pools (all season). Table tennis. Boules. Weight training room. Play area. Volleyball. Football. Some animation in high season. Area for children with playground and entertainment and games in high season. Little farm with ponies, goat and chickens. Internet access. Off site: Village and beaches 1.5 km. Fishing 3 km. Golf 10 km. Riding 15 km.

At a glance

Welcome & Ambience	✓✓✓✓	Location	✓✓✓✓
Quality of Pitches	✓✓✓✓	Range of Facilities	✓✓✓✓✓

Directions

From Girona take road east to La Bisbal and Palafrugell then Begur. Turn south towards Fornells, the site is well signed 3 km. south of Begur.

Charges 2004

Per adult	€ 2,00 - € 3,50
child (3-10 yrs)	€ 1,30 - € 1,80
pitch	€ 7,40 - € 16,50
with electricity	€ 9,50 - € 23,30
animal	€ 3,10 - € 3,50

Reservations

Possible with € 100 deposit. Tel: 972 623 201.
E-mail: info@campingbegur.com

Open

25 April - 28 September.

ES8150 Camping Internacional de Palamos

Apto. Correus 100, 17230 Palamós (Girona)

First impressions of this site are that it is unusual with a long perimeter wall covered with bright graffiti style murals. The site's strong point is the large swimming pool, plus children's pool, with attractive palms. It has a grass sunbathing area and its own modest white-washed bar/terrace in season. It might have space when others are full and has over 450 moderate sized, level, terraced pitches on a gentle slope. All pitches have a sink and variable shade, with electrical connections (6A) available in most parts. Access roads are gravel and may suffer in the case of heavy rain. Used by a tour operator (20 pitches). This is an improving site which is clean, welcoming and useful for exploring the local area from a peaceful base although it is pricey in high season.

Facilities

Three refurbished toilet blocks are fully equipped and include facilities for disabled people. Laundry room with washing machines, irons, etc. Small shop. Bar. Snack bar serving simple food and takeaway (from 1/6). Swimming pool (36 x 16 m.) with paddling pool. Torches necessary. Off site: Nearest beach 400 m. Fishing 500 m. Town 1 km. with hourly bus service. Bicycle hire or riding 1.5 km.

Open

19 March - 30 September.

At a glance

Welcome & Ambience	✓✓✓✓✓	Location	✓✓✓✓✓
Quality of Pitches	✓✓✓✓✓	Range of Facilities	✓✓✓✓

Directions

Cars can approach site from central Palamós, but town streets are too narrow for caravans which should turn off C255 road just outside Palamós continue north by large garage, signed to Kings Camping and La Fosca, turn right just before Kings and from there follow Camping Internacional Palamos signs. Do not be confused by another site close by called Camping Palamos.

Charges guide

Per person	€ 2,70 - € 2,98
child (under 10 yrs)	€ 1,98 - € 2,18
pitch for car and tent/caravan	€ 15,15 - € 31,37
tent pitch (motorcycle but no car)	€ 5,65 - € 12,51
electricity	€ 4,21

All plus 7% VAT. No credit cards.

Reservations

Write to site with € 31 deposit. Tel: 972 314 736.

ES8125 Camping Relax-Nat

Mont-Ras, 17230 Palamós (Girona)

Enclosed by a perimeter wall, this extremely well maintained, small naturist site affords complete privacy. Set in pleasant countryside, eight hectares provide 310 pitches, (all with 2A electricity) amongst a large variety of trees, spaced in such a manner as to provide sun and shade. Entering the site through the electronic security gate, you will find English spoken at reception. From this point you overlook the terraces fronting the bar, shop and pools. Although the site does not have a restaurant, there are many in the area offering good Spanish cuisine. A small picturesque bay, typical of those to be found along the Costa Brava and only five kilometres away, is for use by naturists. Naturism is increasingly popular in Spain and reservation is advised.

Facilities

The main toilet block, completely refurbished to a high standard, provided partitioned hot showers (free), facilities for babies and a unit for disabled visitors. Shop. Bar. Snack bar. Swimming pools, one 30 x 12 m. from mid-May, a smaller, heated one open all season with sun loungers, and a children's pool. Table tennis, boule, volleyball, basketball, football. Tennis (charged). Water activities. Minigolf. Two play areas. High season entertainment. Off site: Bicycle hire 2 km. Fishing and riding 5 km. Golf 20 km.

Open

31 March - 30 September.

At a glance

Welcome & Ambience	✓✓✓	Location	✓✓✓
Quality of Pitches	✓✓✓✓	Range of Facilities	✓✓✓✓

Directions

Travelling along road C31 Palafrugell - Palamos (formerly C255), site is to east near km. 330 (opposite Mercamat store). If approaching from Palafrugell, use loop in front of store to turn across road.

Charges 2004

Per person	€ 4,95
child (under 10 yrs)	€ 3,90
pitch	€ 10,00 - € 17,60
electricity	€ 2,00
dog	€ 2,80

Plus VAT.

Reservations

Contact P.B. 19, 17230 Palamos (Girona) for details. Tel: 972 300818. E-mail: info@campingrelaxnat.com

ES8120 Kim's Camping

Font d'en Xeco 1, 17211 Llafranc (Girona)

This attractive, terraced site is arranged on the wooded slopes of a narrow valley leading to the sea and there are many trees including huge eucalyptus. A steep lower area rises to a very pleasant plateau where all the amenities are located. There are 350 grassy and partly shaded pitches, all with electric hook-ups (6A). Many of the larger pitches are on the plateau from which great views can be enjoyed, whilst those on the terraces are connected by winding drives, narrow in places. The site has an excellent swimming pool (with lifeguard) and children's pool, a bar, and a pleasant restaurant with 'al fresco' eating. There are high standards of cleanliness and efficiency. The site is under 1 km. from the resort of Llafranc. This is a pleasant place for holidays where you can enjoy the bustling atmosphere of the village and beach, while staying in a quieter environment. The site provides an entertainment programme in high season and it is possible to organize a visit to the local sub aqua schools for all levels of diving. There is an outstanding view along the coastline and of the Pyrenees from Cap Sebastian close by. English is spoken by the very friendly management and staff.

Facilities

Sanitary provision is adequate and includes a small brand new block and toilet facilities for disabled visitors. Laundry facilities. Motorcaravan services. Car wash. Gas supplies. Well stocked shop. Bar. Bakery and croissanterie. Cafe/restaurant (15/6-20/9). TV room. Swimming pools. Tickets sold for the Girona bullfights. Excursions arranged - bus calls at site. Play areas and kid's club. Torches required. Off site: Fishing, Glass bottomed boat in Llafranc. Bicycle hire 500 m. Riding 4 km. Golf 9 km.

Open

Easter - 30 September.

At a glance

Welcome & Ambience	✓✓✓✓	Location	✓✓✓✓
Quality of Pitches	✓✓✓	Range of Facilities	✓✓✓✓

Directions

Llafranc is southeast of Palafrugell. Turn off the Palafrugell - Tamariu road at turn (GIV 6542) signed 'Llafranc, Club de Tennis'. Site is on right 1 km. further on.

Charges 2004

Per person	€ 2,50 - € 6,00
child (3-10 yrs)	free - € 3,00
pitch incl. electricity	€ 12,00 - € 25,00

Plus 7% VAT. Discounts for long stays and for senior citizens.

Reservations

Made with deposit (€ 90). Tel: 972 301 156. E-mail: info@campingkims.com

ES8140 Camping Treumal

Ctra 253, km 47.5, 17250 Calonge (Girona)

This very attractive terraced site has been developed on a hillside around the attractive gardens of a large, spectacular estate house which is close to the beach. The house is the focus of the site's excellent facilities, including a superb restaurant with terraces that overlook two tranquil beaches protected in pretty coves. The beaches are connected by a tunnel carved through solid rock through which you may safely walk. A multi-coloured, flower bedecked, and landscaped hillside leads down to the sea from the house with pretty paths and fishponds. There is a constant supply of fresh plants and flowers from the greenhouses which belonged to the house in yesteryear. In summer the house area is a blaze of colour and very appealing. The site which reaches back to the road has 582 pitches on well shaded terraces. Of these 447 are accessible to tourers and there are some 50 pitches on flat ground alongside the sea - the views are stunning and you wake to the sounds of the waves. 135 pitches are occupied by mobile homes and chalets to rent. There is a small (10 m) round swimming pool in the lower areas of the gardens, if you prefer fresh water. Cars may not park by tents or caravans in high season, but must be left on car parks or roads. Electrical connections are available in all parts, (5A for tents, 10A for caravans). Dogs are no longer accepted.

Facilities

Three well maintained sanitary blocks have free hot water in the washbasins (with some private cabins) and controllable showers, and a tap to draw from for the sinks. Washing machines. Motorcaravan services. Gas supplies. Supermarket, bar and takeaway (19/3-30/9). Restaurant (15/6-15/9). Table tennis. Fishing. Play area and sports area. Games room. Off site: Bicycle hire 2 km. Riding, golf 5 km.

Open

19 March - 30 September.

At a glance

Welcome & Ambience	✓✓✓✓	Location	✓✓✓✓✓
Quality of Pitches	✓✓✓	Range of Facilities	✓✓✓✓

Directions

Site is on C253 (at km 47.5) Playa de Aro – Palomós coast road, 3 km south of Palomós. Avoid the town centre by using C31 (Girona – Palomós) road, leaving at km 320, dropping down to Sant Antóni de Calonge and turning right onto C253.

Charges 2005

Per person	€ 3,60 - € 6,60
child (4-10 yrs)	€ 2,05 - € 3,70
caravan, car and electricity	€ 13,50 - € 24,00
motorcaravan and electricity	€ 13,00 - € 23,00
tent, car and electricity	€ 13,00 - € 23,00

Plus 7% VAT. Discounts in low seasons. No credit cards.

Reservations

Made to guarantee admission (needed more for caravans than for tents) with deposit. Contact site at Aptdo Correos 348, 17250 Playa de Aro. Tel: 972 651 095. E-mail: info@campingtreumal.com

ES8130 Camping Internacional de Calonge

Ctra S Feliu/Guixols - Palamos, 17251 Calonge (Girona)

This spacious, well laid out site has access to the fine beach by a footbridge over the coast road, or you can take the little road train as the site is on very sloping ground. Calonge is a family site with two good sized pools on different levels, a paddling pool plus large sunbathing areas. These are overlooked by the restaurant terrace which has great views over the mountains. The site's 800 pitches are on terraces and all have electricity (5A) with 167 available for winter use. A large proportion are suitable for touring units (the remainder for tents) being set on attractively landscaped terraces. Access to some pitches may be a little difficult. There is good shade from the tall pine trees and some views of the sea through the foliage, although the views from the upper levels are taken by the tour operator and mobile home pitches. A nature area within the site is used for walks or picnics. A separate area within the site is set aside for visitors with dogs (including a dog shower!)

Facilities

Generous sanitary provision in new or renovated blocks include some washbasins in cabins. One block is heated for winter use. Laundry facilities. Motorcaravan services. Gas supplies. Shop (19/3-31/10). Bar/restaurant (19/3-23/10). Patio bar (pizza and takeaway). Swimming pools with lifeguard (19/3-30/9). Playground. Electronic games. Rather noisy disco two nights a week (but not late). Bicycle hire. Table tennis. Tennis. Volleyball. Hairdresser. ATM. Internet. Security boxes. Torches necessary in some areas. Good security. Off site: Fishing 300 m. Golf 3 km. Riding 10 km. Supermarket 500 m.

Open

All year.

At a glance

Welcome & Ambience	✓✓✓✓✓	Location	✓✓✓✓✓
Quality of Pitches	✓✓✓✓✓	Range of Facilities	✓✓✓✓✓

Directions

Site is on the inland side of the coast road between Palamos and Platja d'Aro, take the C31 south to the 661 at Calonge. At Calonge follow signs to the C253 towards Platja d'Aro and on to site which is well signed.

Charges 2005

Per adult	€ 3,40 - € 6,25
child (2-10 yrs)	€ 1,75 - € 3,45
pitch for caravan or tent with car incl. electricity	€ 11,75 - € 22,00
motorcaravan incl. electricity	€ 11,10 - € 18,50
dog	€ 3,00 - € 3,10

All plus 7% VAT. Discounts for longer stays Oct - end May. No credit cards.

Reservations

Write with deposit (€ 37). UK contact: Mr J Worthington (0161) 799 9562. Tel: 972 651 233. E-mail: info@intercalonge.com

ES8160 Camping Cala Gogo

Ctra S Feliu-Palamos, km 46.5, 17251 Calonge (Girona)

Cala Gogo is a large traditional campsite with a pleasant situation on a wooded hillside with mature trees giving shade to most pitches. A small cove of considerable natural beauty has a coarse sand beach and there is access to a further two small beaches along the sand. If you prefer fresh water there are two pools on the site (one heated in low season). The site facilities are contained in terraced buildings which have a supermarket, shops, small restaurant and a bar all with an adjoining terrace enjoying views over the pools down to the sea. A second floodlit bar, pleasant restaurant and a takeaway are on the beach and open in high season. The 619 shaded touring pitches varying in size are in terraced rows, some with artificial shade, all have 10A electricity and 250 have water and drainage. There may be road noise in eastern parts of the site. Some pitches are right by the beach, the remainder are up to 800 metres uphill, but the 'Gua gua' (South American Spanish for bus) tractor train, operating all season, takes people between the centre of the site and the beach adding to the general sense of fun. The management aim to make the site attractive to families. It is an active, bustling place, with over 2,500 campers when full. A huge aqua-park close by offers amazing waterslides, waves and all manner of water enjoyment and there is a bus from the site. Used by tour operators (60 pitches), 170 mobile homes and chalets to rent.

Facilities

Seven toilet blocks are of a high standard and are continuously cleaned. Some washbasins are in private cabins. Laundry. Motorcaravan services. Gas supplies. Supermarket. General shop. Restaurants and bars. Swimming pools (25 x 12 m.) and paddling pool (lifeguards). Playground. Crèche and babysitting service for smaller children (extra charge). Sports centre with tennis, volleyball, basketball, etc, plus a mini-club. Programme of animation including sports, TV and video programmes daily, tournaments, entertainment. Bicycle hire. Limited table tennis. Kayaks (free). Fishing. Bureau de change. Medical service; nurse daily, doctor alternate days. Good 24 hr security service including video surveillance. Sponsored bus to local disco. Dogs are not accepted from mid June - end August. Off site: Bicycle hire and golf 4 km. Riding 10 km. Huge Aqua Park nearby with bus from site.

At a glance

Welcome & Ambience	✓✓✓✓	Location	✓✓✓✓
Quality of Pitches	✓✓✓✓	Range of Facilities	✓✓✓✓

Directions

Site is on inland side of coast road between Palomos and Platja d'Aro on the C253 at km 46.5 (4 km. south of Palomos). Avoid town centre by using C31 (Girona - Palomos) road, leaving at km 320, dropping down to Sant Antoni de Calonge, and turning right on C253.

Charges 2005

Per person	€ 3,25 - € 6,00
child (3-12 yrs)	€ 1,00 - € 2,70
caravan or trailer tent	€ 12,10 - € 24,50
motorcaravan	€ 10,55 - € 23,60
tent	€ 10,10 - € 19,50
dog	€ 2,00

Electricity (5A) included. All plus 7% VAT. Low season discounts. No credit cards.

Reservations

Made for min. 1 week with deposit (€ 150). Tel: 972 651 564. E-mail: calagogo@calagogo.es

Open

29 April - 25 September.

ES8225 Camping La Masia

C/Colon, 44, 17300 Blanes (Girona)

A large resort site, La Masia has 757 pitches with 300 for touring units. These pitches are flat, shaded by trees and in rows with some tour operater mobile homes inserted here and there. Two pools are in separate areas of the site, one having the restaurant terrace which also serves as the area for watching the entertainment programme. A large, central building houses the main bar and restaurant, which offers a varied menu, including a menu of the day and full English breakfast – good prices! The jewel in the crown of the site is below this complex where you can enjoy spas, massage, plunge pools, exercise pools and pamper yourself in luxury in a Roman Bath type setting (extra charge). The tops of the buildings are for sunbathing or watching fireworks in the town. There is something for everyone in La Masia and the resort town is just outside the gate, as is the fine beach.

Facilities

Five mature toilet blocks provide clean facilities with facilities for disabled campers and a well equipped baby room (key at reception). Motorcaravan services. Car wash. Washing machines and dryers. Supermarket. Bakery. Restaurants. Snack bars. Swimming pools. Spa centre. Play areas. Football. Boules. Basketball. Table tennis. Electronic games. Bicycle hire. Barbecue area. Entertainment programme. Internet. ATM. Exchange service. Security boxes. Torches useful. Off site: Resort town and beach outside the gate with usual attractions. Fishing. Boat launching 200 m. Bicycle hire 1 km. Riding 3 km. Golf 5 km.

At a glance

Welcome & Ambience	✓✓✓✓	Location	✓✓✓✓
Quality of Pitches	✓✓✓✓	Range of Facilities	✓✓✓✓✓

Directions

From A7, A19 or N11 take an exit to the coast for Blanes. Once at Blanes take Malgrat de Mar road and follow signs in town centre towards the beach. Site is very well signed in the town.

Charges 2005

Per person	€ 4,30 - € 5,80
child (2-10 yrs)	€ 3,70 - € 4,95
pitch	€ 6,85 - € 22,60

Reservations

Contact site. Tel: 972 331013.
E-mail: info@campinglamasia.com

Open

1 May - 30 September.

ES8170 Camping Valldaro

Aptdo 57, Avda. Castell d'Aro, 17250 Platja d'Aro (Girona)

Valldaro is 600 metres back from the sea at Platja de Aro, a small, bright resort with a long, wide beach and plenty of amusements. It is particularly pleasant out of peak weeks and is popular with the British. Like a number of other large Spanish sites, Valldaro has been extended and many pitches have been made larger, bringing them up to 80 or 100 sq.m. There are now 1,200 pitches with 660 available for tourers. The site is flat, with pitches in rows divided up by access roads. You will probably find space here even at the height of the season. The newer section has its own vehicle entrance (the nearest point to the beach) and can be reached via a footbridge; it is brought into use at peak times. It has some shade and its own toilet block, as well as a medium-sized swimming pool of irregular shape with grassy sunbathing area and adjacent bar/snack bar and take-away. The original pool (36 x 18 m.) is adjacent to the good Spanish-style restaurant which also offers takeaway fare. There are 400 permanent Spanish pitches and 150 mobile-homes and chalets to rent, but these are in separate areas and do not impinge on the touring pitches.

TRAVEL SERVICE SITE

TO BOOK CALL 0870 405 4055 OR www.alanrogersdirect.com

Facilities

Sanitary facilities are of a good standard and are well maintained. Children's size toilets. Washbasins (no cabins) and adjustable showers (temperature perhaps a bit variable). Two supermarkets and general shops. Restaurant. Large bar. Swimming pools. Tennis. Table tennis, minigolf with snack bar. Playgrounds. Sports ground with football and basketball. Organised entertainment in season. Hairdresser. Air conditioned telephone/internet parlour. Gas supplies. Keen interest in environmental issues with many recycling bins. Off site: Fishing, bicycle hire and golf 1 km. Riding 4 km.

At a glance

Welcome & Ambience	✓✓✓✓✓	Location	✓✓✓✓
Quality of Pitches	✓✓✓✓	Range of Facilities	✓✓✓✓✓

Directions

Site is off the C31 Girona-Palamós road; follow signs for Platja de Aro.and site is signed off roundabout.

Charges 2005

Per person	€ 3,25 - € 5,20
child (2-10 yrs)	€ 2,20 - € 3,05
pitch incl. electricity	€ 15,00 - € 25,00
dog	€ 2,30

All plus 7% VAT. Discounts in low seasons.

Reservations

Made only in the sense of guaranteeing admission without deposit. Tel: 972 817 515.
E-mail: info@valldaro.com

Open

18 March - 2 October.

ES8232 Camping Bella Terra

Platja de S'Abanell, 17300 Blanes (Girona)

Camping Bella Terra is a very Spanish site, set in a shady pine grove facing a white sandy beach on the Mediterranean coast. There are 870 pitches with 590 for touring units, the rest taken by bungalows to rent (80) and by Spanish 'residents' (200). All pitches have 5/6A electricity and 24 are fully serviced. The site is in two sections, each with its own reception, on either side of a road which leads only to another campsite. The older part, with direct access to the beach, always fills up first and has the small supermarket with its own bakery, and the bar in front of which the children's activities and the evening entertainments take place. Main reception is on the right of the road as you approach, as are the restaurant with its own bar and the swimming pool, both of which (though already good) are due to be completely refurbished for 2004. This site has a real Spanish feel.

Facilities

The older sanitary blocks are quite adequate and fully equipped with provision for disabled visitors and laundry. The block on the newer side is much more modern and spacious, and an unusual feature is the suite of half-size showers, toilets and washbasins for young campers on both male and female sides. Shop, restaurant, bar and takeaway and outdoor swimming pool (all May - Sept). Playground. Fishing. Off site: Bicycle hire 500 m. Golf and riding 5 km.

At a glance

Welcome & Ambience	✓✓✓✓	Location	✓✓✓✓
Quality of Pitches	✓✓✓	Range of Facilities	✓✓✓✓

Directions

Site is south of Blanes. Follow signs from the town centre and site is just after Camping Blanes.

Charges 2004

Per person	€ 4,15 - € 4,50
child (3-10 yrs)	€ 3,40 - € 3,70
pitch	€ 12,80 - € 24,15
dog	€ 2,60 - € 4,20

Reservations

Contact site. Tel: 972 348017.
E-mail: cbellaterra@cbellaterra.com

Open

5 April - 30 September.

ES8200 Camping Cala Llevadó

Ctra de Tossa a Lloret, km. 3, 17320 Tossa de Mar (Girona)

For splendour of position Cala Llevadó can compare with almost any in this book. A beautifully situated cliff-side site, it has fine views of the sea and coast below. It is shaped something like half a bowl with steep slopes. There are terraced, flat areas for caravans and tents on the upper levels of the two slopes, with a great many individual pitches for tents scattered around the site. Some of these pitches (without electricity) have fantastic settings and views. There is usually car parking close to these pitches, although in some areas cars may be required to park separately. Electrical connections cover all caravan sectors and one tent area. High up in the site with a superb aspect, is the attractive restaurant/bar with a large terrace overlooking a play area and the pleasant swimming pool. One beach is for all manner of watersports within a buoyed area and there is a sub-aqua diving school. Some other pleasant little coves can also be reached by climbing down on foot (with care!). The steepness of the site would make access difficult for disabled people or those with limited mobility. Cala Llevadó is luxurious and has much character and the atmosphere is informal and very friendly. Only 204 of the 575 touring pitches are accessible for caravans, so reservation in high season is essential. There are a few tour operator pitches (45). It is peacefully situated but only five minutes away from the busy resort of Tossa - take a look at the town where the castle is beautifully lit by night or if you visit in July enjoy the many lively fiestas. The owner has recently added a botanic garden on the site with many of the plants, flowers and trees of the region, an explanation of its history and including a historic windmill.

Facilities

Four very well equipped toilet blocks are well spaced around the site, built in an attractive style and immaculately maintained, with some washbasins in cabins, well equipped showers, and baby baths. Washing machines and dryer. Laundry service. Motorcaravan services. Gas supplies. Fridge hire. Large, well stocked supermarket. New restaurant/bar with terrace (5/5-28/9). Swimming pool (20 x 10 m.) and semi-circular children's pool. Three play areas. New garden. Entertainment for children (4-12 yrs). Sailing, water ski and windsurfing school. Fishing. Scuba diving. Excursions. Torches are definitely needed in some areas. Off site: Bicycle hire 3 km. The site is alongside a larger complex where all manner of sophisticated sports and adventure activities are available. Campers can also use the other pools here

At a glance

Welcome & Ambience	✓✓✓✓✓	Location	✓✓✓✓✓
Quality of Pitches	✓✓✓	Range of Facilities	✓✓✓✓✓

Directions

Cala Llevadó is signed off the G1682 Lloret - Tossa road at km 18.9, about 3 km. from Tossa.

Charges 2005

Per person	€ 4,85 - € 7,60
child (4-12 yrs)	€ 3,00 - € 4,15
car or motorcycle	€ 4,85 - € 7,60
tent	€ 4,85 - € 7,60
caravan	€ 5,60 - € 8,10

Plus 7% VAT.

Reservations

Accepted with deposit and fee. Tel: 972 340 314.
E-mail: info@calallevado.com

Open

1 May - 30 September, including all amenities.

TRAVEL SERVICE SITE
TO BOOK CALL 0870 405 4055 OR www.alanrogersdirect.com

www.alanrogers.com for latest campsite news

ES8230 Beach Camp El Pinar

Avenida Villa de Madrid, 17300 Blanes (Girona)

This is a pleasant, family orientated site adjoining a good beach. The name sums up the direction in which the owners are developing the site, with an emphasis on a more participatory approach to camping with an increase in the amount of activities and facilities offered - mostly directed towards sports. It is situated at the southern edge of Blanes beach, with direct access, and is about 2 km. from the town. The 587 touring pitches (250 on the new side), all with electricity and a minimum of 60 sq.m. are in two sections separated by the road, with both sides having direct access to the beach. The older side is mostly shaded by pine or broad leaf trees, the newer part has young trees that do not yet offer a great deal of shade. The newer side has its own modern sanitary block, plus a large swimming pool with a generous sunbathing area, and a children's pool (only used in July and August). This site will particularly appeal to families seeking easy access to a long beach (which shelves quite steeply) and the attractions of a major resort.

Facilities

The sanitary blocks are tiled, have controllable hot showers, baby baths and open plan washbasins (all with hot water). The facilities on the original site have recently been refurbished. Dishwashing under cover. Laundry services. Motorcaravan services. Gas supplies. Bar/restaurant and takeaway. Small supermarket. Secure children's play area on grass. Swimming pool (small deposit for pass). Volleyball. Table tennis. Activities for adults and children organised in season (2/5-16/9) including dancing, bicycle excursions, aquagym. Excursions. Watersports near. No jetskis accepted. Regular bus service into the centre of Blanes.
Off site: Bicycle hire 1.5 km. Boat launching 2 km. Riding 8 km. Golf 15 km.

At a glance

Welcome & Ambience	✓✓✓	Location	✓✓✓✓✓
Quality of Pitches	✓✓✓	Range of Facilities	✓✓✓

Directions

Site is the last travelling south from Blanes town centre. Follow camping signs in Blanes until you see the El Pinar sign.

Charges 2004

Per person	€ 4,20 - € 5,00
child	€ 3,40 - € 4,40
pitch incl. electricity	€ 12,60 - € 15,80

Plus 7% VAT. Discounts for pensioners and low season longer stays.

Reservations

Write or phone site (no deposit). Tel: 972 331 083.
E-mail: camping@elpinarbeach.com

Open

31 March - 30 September.

ES8180 Camping Sant Pol

Ctra Doctor Fleming No.1, 17220 Sant Feliu de Guixols (Girona)

Sant Pol is a small, family owned site and Anna Genover speaks excellent English, with a good understanding of campers needs. On the Costa Brava, this hillside site is on the edge of Sant Feliu, only 350 metres from the beach (there may be some road noise on one side of the site). An attractive pool, bar and restaurant are the central focus of the site with shaded terraces and pitches of differing sizes curving down the slope. Higher terraces have the chalets and bungalows. There are only a few pitches for large units, but pleasant small terraces take tents and smaller units. The on site restaurant features regional dishes based on the best local produce available. San Feliu is an attractive seaside village with lots of cafés, restaurants and a crescent shaped white sandy beach. The local area has museums and archaeological sites. Dali's house is within driving distance (book ahead). A great site for short stays, not for exploring the area.

Facilities

The clean and modern sanitary block has British style WCs and hot water. WC for disabled campers, but no shower (terrain would be difficult for wheelchairs). Washing machines and dryer. Motorcaravan services. Small supermarket for basics. Restaurant/bar. Swimming pools. Play area. Animation for children in high season. Minigolf. Library. Internet point. Electronic games. Excursions. Torches needed in some area. Off site: Large supermarket 300 m. Beach 350 m. Regular bus service into town.

Open

12 March - 30 November.

At a glance

Welcome & Ambience	✓✓✓	Location	✓✓✓✓
Quality of Pitches	✓✓✓	Range of Facilities	✓✓✓✓

Directions

San Feliu is southeast of Girona and is reached via the C65/C31 (Girona - Palomos) road. Leave this at km 312 signed S'Agaró. At roundabout take first exit signed to Sant Feliu and site, which is on left in a short distance.

Charges 2004

Per person	€ 3,40 - € 7,10
child (5-10 yrs)	€ 2,15 - € 4,60
pitch	€ 7,70 - € 16,50
pitch incl. electricity and water	€ 12,00 - € 23,70
electricity	€ 2,95 - € 4,00

Discounts for stays in excess of 21 days.
Low season special offers for senior citizens.

Reservations

Contact site. Tel: 972 327 269.
E-mail: info@campingsantpol.com

www.alanrogers.com for latest campsite news

ES9122 Camping Montagut

Ctra Montagut-Sadernes, km 2, 17855 Montagut (Girona)

This is a delightful, small family site where everything is kept in pristine condition. Jordi and Nuria, a brother and sister team, work hard to make you welcome and maintain the superb appearance of the site. Flowers and shrubs abound, with 90 pitches on attractively landscaped and carefully constructed terraces or on flat areas overlooking the pool. A tranquil atmosphere pervades the site and drinks on the pleasant restaurant terrace are recommended, along with sampling the authentic menu as you enjoy the views over the Alta Garrotxa. There is much to see in the local area between the Pyrenees and the Mediterranean, for example a trip to the stunning village of Castellfollit de la Roca perched seemingly precariously on a precipice 60 m. above the Fluvia river. Or, on a different scale, the pretty Pont del Llierca which is a bridge in a most pleasant setting which the site has chosen to use on its logo. Walking and outdoor pusuits abound and the team will assist with bookings. This is a super site for relaxing and enjoying the peaceful situation and wonderful scenery.

Facilities

The modern sanitary block has free hot showers, washing and laundry facilities plus a modern section for babies and disabled campers; everything was spotless when seen. Motorcaravan services. Restaurant and bar (1/3-31/10; weekends only in low season). Supermarket. Medium sized swimming pool with large sunbathing area and children's pool (1/5-30/9). Playground. Soccer. Petanque. Volleyball. Barbecue area. Torches are useful in some areas.

Open

12 March - 16 October.

At a glance

Welcome & Ambience	✓✓✓✓	Location	✓✓✓✓✓
Quality of Pitches	✓✓✓✓	Range of Facilities	✓✓✓✓✓

Directions

Going west from Figueres on N260 Olot road, approx. 10 km. past Besalu at km. 75, turn right towards Montagut. At end of village turn left towards Sadernes and site entrance is 2 km.

Charges 2005

Per person	€ 5,30
child (under 10 yrs)	€ 4,50
caravan or tent	€ 5,80
small tent	€ 4,65
motorcaravan	€ 8,75
car	€ 4,95

Plus 7% VAT. No credit cards.

Reservations

Contact site. Tel: 972 287 202.
E-mail: info@campingmontagut.com

ES9143 Camping Pirineus

Ctra Guils de Cerdanya, km 2, 17528 Guils de Cerdanya (Girona)

This is a sister site to nos. ES8420 and ES9144, with a well organized entrance and an immediate impression of space, green trees and grass – there is always someone watering and clearing up to maintain the high standards here. From the restaurant terrace you have fine views of the mountains in the background and the pool in the foreground. There is an open fire inside for cooler evenings and a huge mural of the mountains in case you cannot see the real thing out of the window. The pitches are neat, marked, of average size and organized in rows. Generally flat with some on a gentle incline, a proportion have water at their own sink on the pitch. There are many trees offering shade but watch overhanging branches if you have a high unit. There is much to see in the area but we do recommend a trip to the only cog railway in Spain which opened in 1931 (runs 15/7-11/9). It leaves Ribes de Fresser and climbs 2,000 m. to the Sanctuary de Nuria where cars cannot go! It is a breathtaking trip. Try also the famous Catalonian gastronomy and experiment with the local wines and Cava.

Facilities

Two fully equipped, sanitary blocks of top quality and decorated with boxes of bright flowers, are kept spotlessly clean and can be heated. Smart washing machines and dryers. Motorcaravan service point. Shop (open all season). Bar/restaurant (all season). TV room and well-equipped games room. Snooker. Heated swimming pool and circular paddling pool. Boules. Table football. Tennis. Table tennis. Basketball and five-a-side courts. Outdoor sports. Play area and clubhouse where youngsters can paint and play under supervision. Excursions. Entertainment (high season). Drinks machines. Dogs are not accepted. Off site: River fishing. Bicycle hire 2 km. Riding 4 km. Golf 6 km. French border and Andorra close by for duty free shopping.

At a glance

Welcome & Ambience	✓✓✓✓	Location	✓✓✓✓
Quality of Pitches	✓✓✓✓✓	Range of Facilities	✓✓✓✓✓

Directions

From Perpignan take N116 to Prades and Andorra. Exit at Piugcerda taking N-250 signed Le Seu d'Urgell and almost immediately take second right for Guils de Cerdanya. Follow for 2 km. to site on right.

Charges 2004

Per person	€ 4,80
child (3-10 yrs)	€ 4,20
pitch	€ 17,00
incl. water	€ 21,00
electricity (7.5A)	€ 3,20

All plus 7% VAT. No credit cards.

Reservations

Advisable in July and August. Tel: 972 881 062.
E-mail: guils@stel.es

Open

18 June - 12 September.

www.alanrogers.com for latest campsite news

ES9144 Camping Stel

Ctra N-152 Ramal-Llivia s/n, 17520 Puigcerdà (Girona)

Sister site to ES8420 and ES9143, this is an extremely efficient if pricey site. Part of a large, attractive building at the spacious entrance houses a modern reception (English is spoken). From here you will quickly be on your way to one of the flat, terraced pitches. Many of the pitches have shade and all are marked, clean and organized in rows with a water tap for each row. There is some road noise so, in order to avoid this and have views of the Cerdanya valley and the eastern Pyrenées, take one of the pitches on the upper terraces. It is worth the trouble. The terrace closest to the facility block is occupied by bungalows. The rectangular pool with easy access is overlooked by the restaurant terrace, where you can enjoy a menu with local food, or the very reasonable menu of the day. You are very close to the French border here and thus you can enjoy sampling the two different cultures with ease. Visit Llivia, a Spanish village located on French soil where the oldest pharmacy in Europe is located and enjoy a trip to Andorra, famous for duty free shopping.

Facilities

Sanitary facilities in the main building are of very high standard with all the little luxuries and are kept very clean. A small, smart block serves the upper terraces. Both can be heated. Separate modern unit with facilities for disabled campers. Washing machines and dryer in main block. Shop, Bar/restaurant (all season). Swimming pool (July-Sept). Boules. Table football. Snooker. Novel adventure style play frame for children (supervision needed). Adventure club organizes all manner of watersports, and outdoor activities such as biking, tours, climbing, hang gliding, indoor archery and many others. Animation in high season. Drinks machines. Animals accepted in separate area. Off site: Boat rental 2 km. Riding 5 km. Fishing and golf 7 km.

At a glance

Welcome & Ambience	✓✓✓✓	Location	✓✓✓✓
Quality of Pitches	✓✓✓✓	Range of Facilities	✓✓✓✓✓

Directions

From Perpignan take N116 to Prades and Andorra. At roundabout at the border crossing at Puigcerdà take first right for Llivia (almost a turn back on yourself). Site is on left after 1 km.

Charges 2004

Per person	€ 4,80
child (3-10 yrs)	€ 4,20
pitch	€ 17,00
electricity	€ 3,20

All plus 7% VAT. No credit cards.

Reservations

Advisable in July and August. Tel: 972 882 361.
E-mail: puigcerda@stel.es

Open

28 May - 26 September.

ES8063 Camping El Llac

Ctra Circumval.lació de l, 17820 Banyoles (Girona)

This is a cool, unassuming site which is is open most of the year and is close to an attractive lake. The 240 touring pitches are under many mature trees giving good shade and they are generally flat, with some very large pitches for big motorhomes (no full drainage). The bungalows, mobile homes and permanent units do not encroach on the touring pitches and the site is very restful. The pools are atop a large bar/restaurant and there are terraces for sunbathing. The supermarket is also in this central unit and pretty patios are at one end for relaxing with a cool drink. A novel barbecue unit is provided close to the pool and, whilst Dad is cooking, children can enjoy the wide variety of animals in the 'estany' (animal enclosure). This is a clean, peaceful site for exploring the area or as a transit stop.

Facilities

Four sanitary blocks provide clean facilities plus separate units for disabled campers (key at reception). Motorcaravan services. Supermarket. Restaurant/bar. Swimming pools. Play area. Table tennis. Tennis courts. Basketball. Gas. Medical centre. Barbecue. Torches useful.

Open

15 January - 15 December.

At a glance

Welcome & Ambience	✓✓✓✓	Location	✓✓✓✓
Quality of Pitches	✓✓✓✓	Range of Facilities	✓✓✓

Directions

From A7 at Girona take C66 to Banyoles and then west to Olot. Look for campsite signs and directions to the lake. At lake look carefully for signs as only one of the many one-way streets lead to the site entrance.

Charges guide

Per person	€ 3,15 - € 3,70
child (4-10 yrs)	€ 2,00 - € 2,80
pitch	€ 2,00 - € 7,00
electricity	€ 3,50
animal	€ 2,00

Reservations

Contact site. Tel: 972 570 305.
E-mail: c.llac@retemail.es

ES8135 Eurocamping

Ctra Palamós a Platja d'Aro, km. 49.2, 17252 Sant Antoni de Calonge (Girona)

This very large campsite on the Costa Brava near Girona is attractively landscaped, with lawns, flowers and pretty features around the site, and 708 grass and gravel pitches. The size of the pitches varies, with some of good size and others that would struggle with larger units. Older areas of the campsite are shaded by tall trees creating a cooler zone, while the new areas have good size trees but are not yet under the same shade canopy. There are two pool complexes, one near the entrance with an unusual feature where one large pool cascades into another at a slightly lower level. Nearby are a paddling pool, outoor chess and a large grassy area. Central to the site, the larger lagoon style pool with its huge entertainment area also has a garden like atmospere. This can also be enjoyed at night when the pool is closed as there is a large restaurant with views over the pool and animation area. A small road train, popular with children, takes campers to the nearby beach. This family oriented site is very popular with visitors from Holland and Germany so it is a good idea to book ahead for busy periods.

Facilities

Four refurbished, clean toilet blocks vary in size and are well positioned. Almost all WCs are British style in comfortably sized cabins with shower and basin. Facilities for disabled visitors are very good as are baby rooms and many family rooms. Washing machines. Gas supplies. Supermarket just outside gate. Pleasant bars and good restaurant. Swimming pools. Playgrounds. TV in bar. Football field. 5 a-side. Volleyball. Basketball. Netball. Weight training room. Full animation programme including children's entertainment. Internet. ATM. Excursions. Beach train (July/Aug). Animal owners in two areas. Torches useful. Off site: Nearest beach 300 m. Fishing 300 m. Golf 6 km. Riding 15 km. Bicycle hire 100 m.

At a glance

Welcome & Ambience	✓✓✓✓	Location	✓✓✓✓
Quality of Pitches	✓✓✓✓	Range of Facilities	✓✓✓✓✓

Directions

From N11 (Girona – Barcelona) take Palafrugal road and continue to St Antoni de Calogni where site is well signed (huge arched entrance on the main road of the town).

Charges 2005

Per person	€ 2,15 - € 5,30
child (3-9 yrs)	€ 1,90 - € 3,65
pitch	€ 15,15 - € 24,85
dog	€ 3,00

Reservations

Made with deposit. Tel: 972 650 879.
E-mail: info@euro-camping.com

Open

Easter and 30 April - 25 September.

ES8210 Camping Tucan

Ctra de Lloret - Blanes, 17310 Lloret de Mar (Girona)

Situated on the busy, densely populated Costa Brava near Lloret de Mar, Camping Tucan is well placed to access all the attractions of the area. Views over the mountains are mixed with views of the development in the town. The 200 good size pitches all have electricity, and are laid out in a herring-bone pattern with areas dedicated to singles, families with young children and couples who enjoy the quiet. Pitches are on terraces, flat surfaced with gravel and some are shaded. Activities on the site centre around the pleasant pool, bar, restaurant and terrace all of which are close to reception allowing staff to keep a watch on things. Tucan is a lively site with a wide variety of activities including an animation program for children and some entertainment at night. There is a separate, largely independent facility for young people at the rear of the site.

Facilities

The single toilet block. includes washbasins with hot water and facilities for disabled visitors, although access is difficult. All very clean when seen, we suspect the showers would be busy at peak periods. Washing machine. Gas supplies. Shop. Busy bar and good restaurant. Takeaway. Swimming pools. Playground. TV in bar. Volleyball. Basketball. Bicycle hire. Animation in season. Mini-club. Off site: Town 500 m. Nearest beach 600 m. Riding 1 km. Golf 4 km.

Open

1 April - 30 September.

At a glance

Welcome & Ambience	✓✓✓	Location	✓✓✓
Quality of Pitches	✓✓✓✓	Range of Facilities	✓✓✓✓

Directions

From A7/E4, A19 or N11 Girona – Barcelona roads take an exit for Lloret de Mar. Site is 1 km. west of the town, well signed and is high on the hill off the main road. The entrance can get congested in busy periods.

Charges 2004

Per person	€ 4,30 - € 6,10
child (1-9 yrs)	€ 3,30 - € 4,20
pitch	€ 4,30 - € 6,10
motorcaravan	€ 7,40 - € 10,50
electricity	€ 3,40 - € 4,40
animal	€ 1,60

Reservations

Contact site. Tel: 972 369 965.
E-mail: info@campingtucan.com

Cataluña-Catalunya

ES9123 Camping El Solsones

Ctra Sant Llorenc, km 2, 25280 Solsona (Lleida)

Situated on a hillside, two kilometres from Solsona, this all year site has pleasant views of the hills on three sides and lots of mature trees giving a pleasant green shady appearance. With a lovely Spanish feel, it would be a pleasant spot for a short stay during any season. There are many weekend units here, and although only 72 of the 269 pitches are available for touring (22 for caravans or motorcaravans and 50 for tents), we were told that finding a pitch was unlikely to be a problem. They are in separate sectuions of the site and are slightly sloping, with very little shade and 4/6A electricity. The restaurant with its attractive stained glass screens and menu featuring Catalan style food is complemented by the large bar and casual eating area. A feature of the bar area is the central open fireplace. A large children's play area is provided, however parents are advised to supervise little ones as some of the equipment is of the older metal frame style which is not as child friendly as newer plastic play equipment. For winter visitors, the 'Ski Port del Conte' is 18 km. away. and there are facilities for riding, golf and walking in the vicinity. A friendly welcome is provided by the owner's daughter who speaks English, or sometimes by the owner himself who has no English, but good French.

Facilities

Modern sanitary facilities are in two buildings, with free hot water to the showers, washbasins, laundry and dishwashing sinks. Motorcaravan services. Large supermarket with fresh food. Restaurant and bar (24/6-15/9 and winter weekends). Simple meals and snacks are served indoors and outside on the terrace overlooking the pool. Swimming pool with lifeguard (24/6-16/9). Excellent sports complex and minigolf. Bicycle hire. Play area (see above). Petanque. Fronton. Aviary. Off site: Golf, riding and skiing nearby.

Open

All year.

At a glance

Welcome & Ambience	✓✓✓✓	Location	✓✓✓
Quality of Pitches	✓✓✓	Range of Facilities	✓✓✓✓

Directions

Sologna is 45 km. northwest of Manresa, along the C55 and is on the C26 Lleida/Andorra - Barga road. Site is 2 km. out of town on the LV4241 signed to Sant Llorenc de Morunys and Ski Port del Comte.

Charges guide

Per person	€ 4,60
child (2-10 yrs)	€ 4,30
caravan or tent	€ 4,60
motorcaravan	€ 8,25
electricity (4A)	€ 2,45
car	€ 4,60

Plus 7% VAT.

Reservations

Contact site for high season (in French).
Tel: 973 482 861. E-mail: info@campingsolsones.com

ES9121 Camping de la Vall d'Ager

Ctra Afores, s/n, 25691 Ager (Lleida)

Ager is not on a through route to anywhere – hence the very peaceful situation – so if you are coming here it is likely to be for a specific reason. One of the main reasons could be that it is a hang-glider's paradise. The Montsec mountain range (1,677 m.) towers over the site in the Catalan pre-Pyrenees. Site activities revolve around flying – one of the launch points is just outside the perimeter and even the beer pump is in the form of a hang-glider! When you also consider that climbing, walking, mountain biking, canoeing and other water sports are all available in the vicinity, you may well wish to visit this pleasant site. There are 132 during pitches on slightly sloping ground, marked out by trees and with some shade. Electricity (10A) is available to all. There is a pleasant large bar with snack area and a restaurant which offers local fare at good prices. The pool is very pleasant and most welcome as it is hot and a little dusty hereabouts in high summer.

Facilities

A central sanitary building provides good facilities, including large showers (with divider and lots of room to change). Separate rooms for disabled visitors, facilities for dishwashing (hot water) and laundry (cold), plus a washing machine and dryer downstairs. Bar, snack bar and restaurant (all year). Shop (July/Aug). Bicycle hire. Delta-wing store. Swimming pools (high season). Boule. Barbecue. Play area. Torches are required. Off site: Village 300-400 m. Summer parties in the village. Riding 500 m. Fishing 7 km.

Open

All year.

At a glance

Welcome & Ambience	✓✓✓✓	Location	✓✓✓✓
Quality of Pitches	✓✓✓✓	Range of Facilities	✓✓✓✓

Directions

Site is on northern edge of Ager village, at km. 201 on the C12 from Balaguer (which is 28 km. NNE of Lleida) to Tremp. From 2004 this will be the easiest access as major road works will have been completed. Alternatively, use the excellent C13 Lleida/Tremp road and turn west near km 67 onto the C12 (formerly L904) which has not been modernised and has old, narrow sections requiring attention.

Charges guide

Per person	€ 4,20
child (under 10 yrs)	€ 3,80
tent or caravan	€ 4,20
motorcaravan	€ 8,10
electricity (10A)	€ 5,30
car	€ 4,20

Reservations

Unlikely to be needed. Tel: 973 455 200.
E-mail: iniciatives@valldager.com

ES9142 Camping Solana del Segre

Ctra N260, km 198, 25720 Bellver de Cerdanya (Lleida)

The Sierra del Cadi offers some spectacular scenery and the Reserva Cerdanya is very popular with Spanish skiers. This site is situated in an open, sunny lower valley beside the River Segré where the far bank is a National Park (unfenced so children will need supervision). The immediate area is ideal for walkers and offers many opportunities for outdoor sports enthusiasts. The site is in two sections, the lower one nearer the river being for tourists, mainly flat and grassy with 200 pitches of 100 sq.m. or more, shaded by trees with 15A electricity. The upper area is taken by permanent units and the site can be busy at weekends. The climb to the disabled facilities on the upper level is steep and may be difficult for infirm campers. The plain restaurant offers a 'menu del dia' and the bar is co-located. Both have terraces where barbecue food may be bought in high season. A fair-sized swimming pool is overlooked from the terrace. A new air-conditioned heated indoor pool have been added.

Facilities

Modern sanitary facilities are in a central building on the lower level, with extra 'portacabin' style units (unisex toilets/showers). Facilities for disabled campers are on the upper level (wheelchair users will experience problems). Hot water to most sinks. Modern area with washing up machine (€ 1) and deep sinks. Laundry with modern machines. Motorcaravan services. Shop, bar and restaurant (1/6-15/9). Swimming and paddling pools (1/6-5/9). Indoor pool. Two play areas. Games room. River fishing. Dance area. Volleyball and petanque. Barbecue areas. Internet. Torches are required. Off site: Village has a range of shops bars and restaurants. Riding 2 km. Bicycle hire and golf 10 km. Skiing. Superb walking area. Butterflies abound for enthusiasts. The Romanica tour of churches in the area.

At a glance

Welcome & Ambience	✓✓	Location	✓✓✓✓
Quality of Pitches	✓✓✓	Range of Facilities	✓✓✓✓

Directions

Site is on left at the 198 km. marker on the N260 road from Puigcerda to La Seu d'Urgell, well signed just beyond Bellver le Cerdanya.

Charges 2004

Per person	€ 4,68
child	€ 2,81
pitch incl. electricity	€ 17,29
dog	€ 2,81

Plus 7% VAT.

Reservations

Write to site. Tel: 973 510 310.
E-mail: sds@solanadelsegre.com

Open

1 June - 15 September.

ES8240 Camping Botánic Bona Vista Kim

Ctra N-II, km 665, 08370 Calella de la Costa (Barcelona)

While Calella itself may conjure up visions of mass tourism, this site is set on a steep hillside some three kilometres out of the town. Apart from perhaps some noise from the nearby coast road and railway, it is a quite delightful setting with an abundance of flowers, shrubs and roses (1,700 in total, all planted by the knowledgeable owner Kim, who has won several top Catalonian prizes for his roses). The site design successfully marries the beautiful botanic surrounds with the attractive views of the bay. Of the 160 pitches, all with electricity, 130 are available for tourers, they are 60-80 sq.m. or more and are situated on flat terraces on the slopes, with some shade. On arrival, park at the restaurant and choose a pitch – Kim is most helpful with siting your van. The access road is steep, with many of the pitches enjoying lovely views. The bar/restaurant is close to reception at the bottom of the site and is unusual in the attractive choice of Spanish décor and in having a circular, central open-hearth fire/cooker. There are two roof top terraces, the first terrace has service from the restaurant and bar and above that (for over 16 year olds), is the computer controlled sauna, jacuzzi with pool sized filter, a well equipped gymnasium and a sunbathing area, all enjoying views over the sea. There are quite good beaches just across the road and railway, accessible via a tunnel and crossing (including a naturist beach). The site has recently won environmental awards.

Facilities

The standard of design in the three sanitary blocks is quite outstanding for a small site (indeed for any site). Some washbasins in cabins in the newest block. Baby room. Dishwashing under cover. Washing machines. Motorcaravan services. Bar/restaurant, takeaway and shop (1/4-1/10). Large children's playground. Recreation park. Satellite TV. Internet point. Games room. Barbecue and picnic area. No cycling allowed on site. Off site: Fishing 100 m. Bicycle hire 1 km. Riding and golf 3 km. Watersports near.

Open

All year.

At a glance

Welcome & Ambience	✓✓✓✓	Location	✓✓✓✓
Quality of Pitches	✓✓✓✓	Range of Facilities	✓✓✓

Directions

From N11 coast road site is signed travelling south of Calella (at km. 665), and is on right hand side of road - care is needed as road is busy and sign is almost on top of turning (entrance shared with Camping Roca Grossa). Entrance is very steep. From Barcelona, after passing through Sant Pol de Mar, go into outside lane shortly after 'Camping 800 m.' sign and keep signalling left. Site entrance is just before the two lanes merge. (From C32 toll motorway, leave at exit 22 for Calella to join N11 south, then as above).

Charges 2005

Per person	€ 5,15
child (3-10 yrs)	€ 4,40
car	€ 5,15
tent or caravan	€ 5,15
motorcaravan	€ 10,30

All plus 7% VAT. No credit cards.

Reservations

Write to site. Tel: 93 769 24 88.
E-mail: info@botanic-bonavista.net

www.alanrogers.com for latest campsite news

ES8242 Camping Roca Grossa

Ctra N-II, km 665, 08370 Calella de la Costa (Barcelona)

Translating from the Catalan as 'big rock', Roca Grossa celebrated its 50th year of business in 2004. The owners, the Bachs family, are very friendly and there is a very happy atmosphere in the campsite. Very steep slopes predominate at this site and there is a 100 metre climb from reception to the swimming pool set at the top of the site. A road train runs all day to ferry you to the amenities, but the site is unsuitable for disabled campers and the infirm. The bonus is some great views over the sea from most of the terraced, but flat and reasonably sized pitches. Landrovers are used to site your unit. The permanent section of pitches is separated from the touring pitches and everything is kept very smart and clean. Clean and crisp, the pleasant pool enjoys fabulous views and the small restaurant/bar there is open all day. The sports facilities are also at this lofty point and if you wish to shop or use the main bar and restaurant, catch the train to the lower area near reception. The beach is just 50 m. across the road and the town is a short walk.

Facilities

An amazing array of clean sanitary blocks means there is not far to walk from any area of the site. Large and small, all blocks are well kept with hot water throughout. Washing machines. Gas supplies. Shop. Pleasant bar and restaurant. Swimming pools (May - Sept). Playground.
TV in bar. Road train. Football field. 5-a-side. Volley ball. Two tennis couts. Animation programme including children's entertainment. Excursions. ATM. Torches useful. Off site: Beach, boat launching and fishing 50 m. Town 100 m. Riding 1 km. Golf 2 km. Watersports nearby.

Open

1 April - 15 October.

At a glance

Welcome & Ambience	✓✓✓✓	Location	✓✓✓✓
Quality of Pitches	✓✓✓✓	Range of Facilities	✓✓✓✓✓

Directions

From A7 (Girona -; Barcelona) take exit 9 or 10 for Malgrat del Mar on the N11. Turn south towards Calella and site is at 665 km. marker sharing an entrance with another campsite. Caravans are placed on pitches with site Landrover.

Charges guide

Per person	€ 4,11 - € 4,40
child (under 10 yrs)	€ 3,64 - € 3,89
pitch	€ 4,11 - € 8,80
electricity	€ 3,97 - € 4,25
dog	€ 2,94 - € 3,15

Reservations

Made without deposit. Tel: 937 691 297.
E-mail: rocagrossa@rocagrossa.com

ES9140 Camping Repos del Pedraforca

Ctra B400, km 13.5, 08699 Saldés (Barcelona)

Looking up through the trees in this steeply terraced campsite in the area of the Cadi-Moixero Natural Parc, you see the majestic Pedraforca mountain. A favourite for Catalan climbers and walkers, its amazing rugged peak in the shape of a massive stone fork gives it its name. The long scenic drive through the mountains to reach the site is breathtakingly beautiful. The natural beauty of the area, pretty villages, wild flowers, wonderful walks, and interesting local attractions including sea salt mountain and historic coal mines are what attract people to this area. The campsite owner, Alicio Font, is a charming hostess who speaks English. She has created excellent summer and winter facilities including an indoor heated pool, sauna, jacuzzi and gym complex, a large outdoor pool, rooftop relaxation area, upstairs social room, excellent restaurant and popular bar, plus some log cabins to rent. This is generally a very environmentally conscious campsite. Access to the site is via a steep, curving road which could challenge some units. Pitches vary in size and accessibility, although there are excellent pitches for larger units.

Facilities

Two clean, modern sanitary blocks are fully equipped (but at peakperiods there may be queues). Facilities for disabled campers. Separate family room with baby baths, showers, etc. Washing machines and dryer. Restaurant/bar and small supermarket for basic items (both w/ends all year, then 15/5-30/9). Heated indoor swimming pool, gym and spa. Outdoor pool (15/5-30/9). Play areas. Animation for children and adults in high season. Games and social rooms. Rooftop relaxation area. Table tennis. Electronic games. Torches required. Off site: Motorcaravan service point close but not within site. Itinerary suggestions for excursions in the area. Mountain biking. Artigas gardens designed by Gaudi. Museum of mines.

Open

All year.

At a glance

Welcome & Ambience	✓✓✓✓	Location	✓✓✓✓✓
Quality of Pitches	✓✓✓	Range of Facilities	✓✓✓✓✓

Directions

Site is approx. 90 minutes from Barcelona. Access to the site is gained from the C-16 Burga road. 2 km. south of Guardiola de Bergued́á turn west to Saldes and site is well signed. It is 13.5 km. to site from the C-16.

Charges 2005

Per person	€ 4,85
child (1-10 yrs)	€ 3,90
pitch	€ 12,20
electricity (3-5A)	€ 3,50 - € 4,40
dog	€ 1,80

Discounts for stays of more than 3 nights and other offers for long stays (excluding high season).

Reservations

Contact site for details. Tel: 938 258 044.
E-mail: pedra@campingpedraforca.com

www.alanrogers.com for latest campsite news

ES8390 Camping Vilanova Park

Mobile homes ▶ page 169

Ctra de l'Arboc, km 2.5, 08800 Vilanova i la Geltru (Barcelona)

Sitting on the terrace of the bustling but comfortable restaurant at Vilanova Park, it is difficult to believe that back in 1908 this was an old Catalan farm and then, quite lacking in trees, it was known as 'Rock Farm'. If you find this hard to believe look at the old photos in the restaurant. Since then imaginative planting has resulted in there being literally thousands of trees and gloriously colourful shrubs making a most attractive large site, with an impressive range of high quality amenities and facilities open all year. These now include a second pool higher up in the site with marvellous views across the town to the sea. By 2005 this area will have a second, more intimate restaurant for that romantic dinner. The original pool has water jets and a coloured floodlit fountain playing at night time, which complement the dancing and entertainment taking place on the stage in the coutyard overlooking the pool. An unusual attraction is a Nature Park and mini-zoo with deer and bird-life, which has very pleasant picnic areas and views. At present there are 865 pitches with many occupied by bungalows and chalets carefully designed to fit into the environment There are 248 pitches for touring units in separate areas with 133 having a water supply. Marked and of 70-100 sq.m, all have 6A electricity and some larger pitches (100 sq.m.) also have water and drainage. The terrain, hard surfaced and mostly on very gently sloping ground, has many trees and considerable shade. Plans include an indoor pool, sauna and gym which will be appreciated by winter visitors. There is a transfer service from Barcelona and Reus airports.

Facilities

All toilet blocks are of excellent quality, can be heated and have washbasins (over half in cabins) with free hot water, and others of standard type with cold water. Serviced laundry. Motorcaravan services. Supermarket (Easter - 30/9). Souvenir shop. Restaurants. Bar with simple meals (both all year). Swimming pools with lifeguards (Easter - 15/10). Play areas. Sports field for football, basketball and volleyball. Games room. Tennis. Bicycle hire. Tennis. ATM and exchange facilities. Off site: Fishing 4 km. Golf 5 km. Barcelona is easily accessible - hourly buses in the main season or train from Vilanova i la Geltru every 20 minutes. Vilanova town and beach 4 km.

Open

All year.

At a glance

Welcome & Ambience	✓✓✓✓	Location	✓✓✓✓
Quality of Pitches	✓✓✓✓✓	Range of Facilities	✓✓✓✓✓

Directions

Site is 4 km. northwest of Vilanova i la Geltru towards L'Arboc (BV2115). From Barcelona on A16/1C32 take exit 26 towards El Vendrall (C31), then take L'Arboc exit (km. 153) and narrow road uphill to site on right. From Tarragona use exit 16 signed L'Arboc but go right under autopista for 2 km. to site on left.

Charges 2004

Per person	€ 4,15 - € 6,70
child (4-12 yrs)	€ 2,50 - € 4,20
pitch incl. electricity	€ 12,30 - € 17,60
with water	€ 14,90 - € 20,00
dog	€ 2,24 - € 4,50

All plus 7% VAT. Excellent deals for retired people on longer stays.

Reservations

Made with deposit; contact site. Tel: 93 893 34 02. E-mail: info@vilanovapark.es

TRAVEL SERVICE SITE

TO BOOK CALL 0870 405 4055 OR www.alanrogersdirect.com

ES8238 Camping Caballo de Mar

Passeig Maritim 52 - 54, 08397 Pineda de Mar (Barcelona)

This is definitely a site for lovers of the seaside with its direct access to a lovely, sandy beach. Actually divided into two parts by the railway and dual-carriageway, the main part of the site is neatly arranged off a central access road with plenty of colourful shrubs and trees providing shade. In total there are 400 pitches, 200 taken by seasonal visitors and a few bungalows. On the beach side of the site the pitches are generally smaller (60-70 sq.m.) with less shade (some artificial shade is provided) but there is a bar and a toilet block on this side. All pitches have electricity (5/6A). A bar/restaurant fronts the main road (also open to the public). The site's rectangular pool is of a good size with lifeguards and an entertainment team organises activities (every day in high season, weekends at other times). This site has been owned by the same family for over 30 years, the sons now having campsites of their own and many visitors return year after year. There is a security barrier and guard at the main entrance and the beach gate is locked at night. An underpass leads under the railway but care is needed crossing the dual-carriageway when going from one part of the site to the other.

Facilities

Two toilet blocks, one in each area, are fully equipped and well maintained. En-suite units to rent (main side) with units for disabled visitors. Facilities for babies. Dishwashing and laundry sinks. Washing machines. Motorcaravan services. Shop (limited hours in low season). Main bar and restaurant (all season). Swimming pool. Play area. Entertainment organised. Off site: Beach activities. Town with bars and restaurants within walking distance. Bicycle hire 500 m. Riding 3 km.

Open

1 April - 30 September.

At a glance

Welcome & Ambience	✓✓✓✓	Location	✓✓✓✓
Quality of Pitches	✓✓✓✓	Range of Facilities	✓✓✓✓✓

Directions

Site is between Pineda and Calella with access off dual-carriageway linking the two places and runs parallel to the railway.

Charges 2004

Per person	€ 4,20 - € 5,30
child (1-9 yrs)	€ 3,80 - € 4,60
pitch incl. car	€ 6,70 - € 10,60
electricity (3/6A)	€ 3,10 - € 4,90
water	€ 3,10
dog	€ 2,00

Reservations

Advised for high season (min. 6 nights).
Tel: 937 671 706. E-mail: info@caballodemar.com

ES8392 Camping El Garrofer

Ctra C31 km 39, 08870 Sitges (Barcelona)

This large, pine covered site, alongside fields of vines, is 800 m. from the beach, close to the pleasant town of Sitges. It has over 500 pitches of which 380 with 6A electricity are for tourers, including 28 with water used for large motorcaravans. Everything is kept clean and the pitches are tidy and shaded, all with electricity. Dino is the young, dynamic, English speaking manager who has a vast programme of improvements which will make this a most attractive site. The permanent pitches are grouped in a completely separate area and the amenity buildings are along the site perimeter next to the road which absorbs most of the road noise. A varied menu is offered in the cosy restaurant with a small terrace. Everything is cooked to perfection and complemented with the wines of the Penedes DO made hereabouts (the restaurant has a local reputation and is used by non campers - the menu of the day is great value). A traditional bar is alongside and from here you can see the pretty mosaic clad play area (the 'Gaudi touch' which is also evident elsewhere). An ambitious animation programme is conducted for children in summer. Late evening Salsa classes were offered for adults when we visited. A small swimming pool with sunbathing areas is welcome on the hot summer days or you can walk to the very pleasant beach (ten minutes from a gate at the back of the site). The town of Sitges is an attractive resort with seaside entertainments and is well worth exploring. Open most of the year the site offers all manner of adventure activities (extra charge) which may be organized through reception and there are many things to see here - we especially recommend a visit to Monserrat.

Facilities

Two of the three sanitary blocks have been refurbished and provide roomy showers and special bright facilities for children. Separate baby room with bath. Good facilities for disabled campers. Laundry. Bar/restaurant. Shop (reception in low season). Swimming pool. Golf packages. Practice golf. Tennis. Play area for older children and fenced play area for toddlers. Bicycle hire. Boules. Car wash. Bus link from outside site to Barcelona airport and city.
Off site: Golf, riding and fishing 0.5 km.

Open

17 January - 17 December.

At a glance

Welcome & Ambience	✓✓✓✓	Location	✓✓✓✓
Quality of Pitches	✓✓✓✓	Range of Facilities	✓✓✓✓✓

Directions

Sitges is roughly 30 km. southwest of Barcelona. From A16/C32 autopista take exit 26 towards Vilanova/St Pere Ribes. From Tarragona direction, go under autopista, and around roundabout and back to roundabout on the other side to pick up site sign (towards Sitges). Follow C-246 to km. 39; site entrance is not too easy to see beside old large tree.

Charges 2004

Per person	€ 2,50 - € 4,40
child (1-9 yrs)	€ 1,70 - € 3,40
pitch incl. electricity	€ 13,40 - € 17,30
water point	€ 1,20 - € 2,95
dog	€ 1,95 - € 3,95

Plus 7% VAT.

Reservations

Contact site. Tel: 938 941 780.
E-mail: info@garroferpark.com

ES8502 Camping Caravaning Montblanc Park

Mobile homes ▶ page 169

Ctra Prenafeta, km 1,8, 43400 Montblanc (Tarragona)

Taking current trends into account, Montblanc Park may be described as a campsite of the future. Purpose designed, there are 213 terraced pitches for touring units and about 60 for wooden chalets, with more being developed, on the upper terraces. Visitors have first class facilities, including a very high quality restaurant serving typically Spanish dishes along with dishes to suit any palate and a terrace area for those who would choose a less formal atmosphere. Both the restaurant and terrace enjoy views of the exceptionally large, lagoon-style pool and further across the valley, over the autoroute towards the town of Montblanc and the Prades mountains of the Sera del Prades. The pitches are on terraces so take advantage of the mountain views and gentle cooling afternoon breezes. They vary in size, with hedging but little shade yet, and are sloping (chocks useful). There is much emphasis on activities for children and an animation team keep children amused during the day in July and August so parents can have a break. There is organised sport and live entertainment on Saturday night. This is a very professional operation, ideal for a relaxing holiday or exploring the many attractions of the local area. Medieval Montblanc itself is worth exploring and nearby Poblet with its monastery.

Facilities

Two purpose built toilet blocks feature en-suite facilities including superb facilities for disabled campers and a well equipped baby room. Washing machines and dryers. Supermarket. Restaurant. Snack bar. Swimming pool and large paddling pool. Play areas. Football. Boules. Basketball. Table tennis. Electronic games. Bicycle hire. Entertainment for children (wwekends and main holiday season). Tents for hire. Off site: Riding 4 km. Beach or golf 35 km. Mountain activities: climbing, caving, canyoning and orienteering. Paint ball. Quad biking and trips by 4x4.

Open

All year.

At a glance

Welcome & Ambience	✓✓✓✓	Location	✓✓✓✓
Quality of Pitches	✓✓✓✓	Range of Facilities	✓✓✓✓✓

Directions

Site is 3 minutes off the autopista. From A2 (Barcelona - Lleida) take exit 9 and follow N240 (Reus - Tarragona), then road to Prenafeta and site stands out on the left. It is 1.8 km. out of Montblanc and signed in the town.

Charges 2004

Per person	€ 3,00 - € 5,00
child (0-10 yrs)	free
pitch incl. electricity	€ 12,00 - € 18,00
water	€ 2,00
dog	€ 1,00 - € 2,00

Reservations

Contact site. Tel: 977 862544.
E-mail: info@montblancpark.com

ES8235 Camping Bon Repos

Malgrat de Mar, 08398 Santa Susana (Barcelona)

If you enjoy the hustle and bustle of the Costa Brava in summer, then Bon Repos is ideal. It is a long, narrow coastal site with many pitches along the length of the attractive fine sandy beach with direct access and no fence. The 500 pitches are of reasonable size, flat with a sand surface and lots of shade, and with 10A electricity. The beach is a strong point of the site having rocky outcrops and close by is the bar/restaurant with huge terrace. The pool is overlooked from here through perspex screens and the terrace was buzzing when we visited. Afternoon entertainment was in full swing with the hosts of Dutch campers enjoying the music and 'happy hour'. The railway runs close along one side of the site, which is good for train spotters but does create a noise problem. The play area is basic and there were some breakages when seen, so children would need supervising. There is a separate paddling pool beside the main pool. This is a good site for a short visit or transits but the beach pitches are great and will need booking in high season.

Facilities

The two sanitary blocks are dated but clean. The number of showers is low and we suspect they are extremely busy at peak periods. Cold water at washbasins. Units for disabled campers. Well equipped baby room (key at reception). Washing machines and dryers. Motorcaravan services. Supermarket. Restaurant. Chicken bar. Giant TV in bar. Swimming pools (with lifeguard). Play area with some broken toys. Internet. Barbecue area. Tennis courts. Table tennis. Electronic games. Bicycle hire. Animation and happy hour. ATM. Security boxes. Torches useful. Off site: Resort town very close by. Boat launching 200 m. Bicycle hire 1 km. Riding 3 km. Golf 5 km.

At a glance

Welcome & Ambience	✓✓✓✓	Location	✓✓✓✓
Quality of Pitches	✓✓✓✓	Range of Facilities	✓✓✓

Directions

From A7 exit 9 (A19 exit 22) take road to Malgrat de Mar. Then turn south on coast road for Santa Susanna. Follow obvious campsite signs – they lead to site through a high tunnel under the railway line on a minor beach road.

Charges guide

Per adult	€ 4,15
child	€ 3,50
pitch incl. electricity	€ 22,00

Reservations

Contact site. Tel: 937 678 475.
E-mail: info@campingbonrepos.com

Open

All year.

ES8312 Camping Tres Estrellas

C-31, km 186,2, 08850 Gavá (Barcelona)

The name translates as the 'three stars' and this beach site lives up to its name. The 407 pitches are mostly flat with 5A electricity, informally placed under trees, with no permanent units. Many pitches are along the beach front, those closer to the beach having little shade, but they are very pleasant with great views - beach access is through a security fence. Amenities, including a large pool, are in a separate area of the site, nearer to but shielded from the road, keeping noise away from the pitches. Although busy, the site has a pleasant open feel. The bar and restaurant are close to the beach enjoying cool breezes in the evening. The bar is lively at times with everyone having great fun and it is located where there is little or no noise impact on the pitches, ideal in a site popular with all age groups. English is spoken and the staff are efficient and friendly. A modest entertainment programme is provided in high season. Tour operators use the site but have a separate area. This is a great site for visiting Barcelona as the bus stops outside the gate.

Facilities

Four traditional style toilet blocks provide clean facilities including neat facilities for disabled campers and a well equipped nursery room (key at reception). Washing machines and dryers. Motorcaravan services. Car wash. Supermarket. Restaurant. Bar. Snack bar. Swimming pool. Play areas. Football. Boules. Basketball. Internet. Animation. Table tennis. Electronic games. Bicycle hire. Entertainment programme. ATM. Security boxes. Torches useful.
Off site: Bus outside gate into town. Fishing. Boat launching 200 m. Bicycle hire 1 km. Riding 3 km. Golf 7 km.

At a glance

Welcome & Ambience	✓✓✓✓	Location	✓✓✓✓
Quality of Pitches	✓✓✓✓	Range of Facilities	✓✓✓✓✓

Directions

On C31 south of Barcelona go towards Castelldefels and the site is at the 186 km. marker directly off the main road.

Charges guide

Per adult	€ 4,31 - € 5,80
child (3-10 yrs)	€ 3,38 - € 3,84
pitch	€ 5,46 - € 13,19
electricity (5A)	€ 4,04
animal	€ 2,65 - € 3,32

Reservations

Contact site. Tel: 936 330637.
E-mail: fina@camping3estrellas.com

Open

15 March - 15 October.

ES8506 Camping Serra de Prades

Sant Antoni, s/n, 43439 Vilanova de Prades (Tarragona)

On the edge of the village of Vilanova, nestling in granite foothills with superb views from its elevation of 950 m, this is a welcoming and peaceful site. The 215 pitches are on terraces formed with natural stone and with good access. The upper tent pitches have wonderful views although you have a trek to the sanitary facility on the lower level. Hedges and trees separate pitches providing a pleasant green environment and some shade, and 90% of the pitches have electricity (176 with 6A, 13 with 10A). The site has won awards for its approach to ecology and solar power is used to heat water for the showers and the pool, and recycling bins are used. The swimming pool (supervised) is attractively set, with grass surrounds and a terrace for sunbathing overlooked by the lower bar (mainly used in the winter). The bar/restaurant offers a limited range of meals including some regional dishes. The strength of this site is the range of adventure and outdoor activities on offer. These are most professionally organized and climbing is a favourite followed by abseiling, paint ball, cycling, archery and a host of others. There is a horse riding area within the site and guided treks are offered at Whitsun and in July/August. The helpful staff will organize any activity and if it is not on offer here they have contracts with outside agencies for further extensive activities. On site, less arduous activities are also organised for children and adults in season. From here it is possible to enjoy the wonderful Prades mountains or go to the beach an hour's drive away, returning to sleep well in the mild, sunny climate 900 m. above sea level.

Facilities

The modern, heated, well equipped toilet block has washbasins in cabins and is well maintained. Facilities for disabled visitors and babies. Laundry facilities. Motorcaravan service point. Shop. Bar/restaurant. Swimming and paddling pools (open and heated 1/4-15/10). Satellite TV. Archery. Basketball. Volleyball. Quad bike and 4x4 hire. Paint ball. Tennis. Riding with guided treks. Activities organised. Sports area. Entertainment organised in season. Safety deposit. Exchange facilities. Gas supplies. Torches required in some areas. Off site: Follow the Cistercian Way – 65 towns full of history and tradition; Poblet is of particular interest with its community of monks.

Open

All year.

At a glance

Welcome & Ambience	✓✓✓✓✓	Location	✓✓✓✓✓
Quality of Pitches	✓✓✓✓	Range of Facilities	✓✓✓✓✓

Directions

From Tarragona on autopista A2 take exit 9 (Montblanc) and continue towards Lleida on N240. At km. 48 just west of Vimbodi, turn left towards Vallclara and Vilanova de Prades. Site is on roundabout at entrance to village. From Lleida leave A2 at exit 8 towards Tarragona on N240, then as above from km. 48 just before Vimbodi.

Charges 2004

Per person	€ 4,95
child (under 10 yrs)	€ 4,20
pitch incl. car	€ 9,50
electricity (6A)	€ 4,20

Plus 7% VAT.

Reservations

Write to site. Tel: 977 869 050.
E-mail: info@serradeprades.com

ES8508 Camping Poboleda

Placa de les Casetes s/n, 43376 Poboleda (Tarragona)

Time stands still at this unique site hidden away in a corner of the village, watched over by La Morera de Montsant, a peak of the Serra del Montsant. Situated among olive groves, yet almost in the heart of the lovely old village of Poboleda, it is an idyllic site for tents, small caravans and motorcaravans. Large units may have problems negotiating the narrow village streets. The young manager is enthusiastic and proud of the facilities offered which are quite unexpected and special. Behind the modern reception is a traditional, comfortablly furnished room with piano and TV, which doubles as a peaceful cool area for relaxing if it is too hot on the terrace. Here you can have breakfast or order a drink. The village is on the doorstep for other needs. The mellow terraced pool area is a lovely surprise and very welcome, as is the tennis court. The 151 pitches of 80 sq. m. are set under olive and almond trees. Fairly level and 70 with 4A electricity, they provide a peaceful haven broken only by the peal of church bells or bird song. There is plenty to do, walking or climbing, visiting the region's vineyards and enjoying the local cuisine. A must to visit is the monastery of Poblet nearby.

Facilities

One small block, open all year, is fully equipped, as is a larger block open for high season. Shower for children. Facilities for disabled people (key). Dishwashing and laundry sinks. Laundry service. Breakfast can be ordered. Bar. Swimming pool (24/6-11/9). Tennis. Boules. Reception has tourist information, postcards and basic bits and pieces. Off site: Beach and Port Aventura 30 km. Fishing 12 km. Bicycle hire 10 km.

Open

All year.

At a glance

Welcome & Ambience	✓✓✓✓	Location	✓✓✓✓
Quality of Pitches	✓✓✓✓	Range of Facilities	✓✓✓✓

Directions

Bypass Reus (west of Tarragona) on N420. After Borges del Camp pick up C242, signed Alforja. Continue over Coll d'Alforja (the road is OK and the views magnificent). Watch out for left turn (T702) for Pobodeda. Continue for 6 km. until village. Watch for tent signs and follow carefully through narrow village streets. Not recommended for large units.

Charges 2004

Per person	€ 4,00
child	€ 3,50
pitch incl. car	€ 7,50 - € 8,00
electricity	€ 4,00

Reservations

Contact site. Tel: 977827197.
E-mail: poboleda@campingsonline.com

www.alanrogers.com for latest campsite news

ES8410 Camping Playa Bara

Ctra N340, km 1183, 43883 Roda de Bará (Tarragona)

This is a most impressive, family owned site near the beach, which has been carefully designed and developed. On entry you find yourself in a beautifully sculptured, tree-lined drive with an accompanying aroma of pine and woodlands and the sound of waterfalls close by. Considering its size, with over 850 pitches, it is still a very green and relaxing site with an immense range of activities. It is well situated with a 50 metre walk to a long sandy beach via a tunnel under the railway (some noise) to a new promenade with palms and a quality beach bar and restaurant. Much care with planning and in the use of natural stone, palms shrubs and flowering plants gives a pleasing tropical appearance to all aspects of the site. The owners have excelled themselves in the design of the impressive terraced Roman-style pool complex, which is the central feature of the site. This complex is really amazing. Sunbathe on the pretty terraces or sip a drink whilst seated at the stools submerged in one of the pools or enjoy the panorama over the sea from the rooftop spa or the upper Roman galley bar surrounded by stylish friezes. A very well equipped gym with a dedicated instructor and a massage service. An attractive amphitheatre seats 2,000 and is used to stage ambitious entertainment in season. Pitches vary in size, the older ones terraced and well shaded with pine trees, the newer ones more open, with a variety of trees and bushes forming separators between them. Arrive early to find space in peak weeks.

Facilities

Excellent, fully equipped toilet blocks are of different sizes and types. Private cabins in some blocks, children's baths, basins and toilets and superb facilities for disabled visitors. Good private sanitary facilities for hire. Washing machines and dryers. Motorcaravan services. Supermarket. Butcher, bakery, papers, fruit, tabac and souvenir shops. Full restaurant and larger bar with simpler meals and takeaway, other bars, pleasant bar/restaurant on beach. Swimming pools. Jacuzzi/hydro-massage. Fronton and tennis (floodlit). Roller skating. Football. Junior club. Sports area. Doctor (24 hrs high season). Windsurfing school. Volleyball. Basketball. Gym. Petanque. Minigolf on a giant map of Europe. Fishing. Entertainment centre: amphitheatre with stage and dance floor. Animation in several languages. Large games room; video room, films. satellite TV, cocktail bar/disco room open 11 to 4 am. (weekends only in low season). ATM. Deposit boxes. Hairdresser. Internet points. Flights/excursions/tours booked. Off site: Bicycle hire 2 km. Riding 3 km. Golf 4 km.

At a glance

Welcome & Ambience	✓✓✓✓✓	Location	✓✓✓✓✓
Quality of Pitches	✓✓✓✓✓	Range of Facilities	✓✓✓✓✓

Directions

From the A7 take exit 31. Site entrance is at the 1183 km. marker on the N340 just opposite the Arco de Bara monument from which it takes its name.

Charges 2004

Per person	€ 3,11 - € 8,90
child (1-9 yrs)	€ 2,17 - € 6,20
large tent or caravan	€ 8,90
small tent	€ 6,20
car	€ 8,90
motorcycle	€ 6,20

All plus 7% VAT. Low season reductions for pensioners and all sports charges reduced by 90%.

Reservations

Contact site for details. Tel: 977 802 701.
E-mail: info@barapark.es

Open

11 March - 25 September, with all amenities.

ES8420 Camping Stel

Ctra N340, km 1182, 43883 Roda de Bará (Tarragona)

Camping Stel is situated between the pre-Littoral mountains and the sea. The rectangular site is between the N340 road and the excellent beach, with the railway running close to the bottom of the site. Beach access is gained through a gate and under the railway - there is rail noise on the lower pitches. The main facilities are grouped around the pools which are very pleasant with a large flume to an extension of the main pool (heated all season), an octagonal paddling pool and pleasant grass area carefully set out with palms. The central complex containing all the services is impressive with a large bar, terrace and snack area overlooking the pools. A small restaurant is behind the bar. The pitches are generally in rows with hedges around the rows but at the lower end of the site the layout is less formal. Many pitches have individual sinks. There is a separate area where no radio or TV is allowed ensuring peace and quiet. Just outside the gate is the famous Roman Arc de Bara which sits astride the original road.

Facilities

Four clean, fully equipped, sanitary blocks. One totally refurbished (2002) with facilities for children, excellent facilities for disabled campers and four high standard private cabins. Baby baths in the ladies' sections of blocks. One block in the chalet area is available to campers. Laundry. Motorcaravan service area. Supermarket and tourist shop. Bar/restaurant and snack bar. Swimming pools.(4/4-28/9) Outdoor sports area. Gym. Animation for children and some adult entertainment in high season. Electronic games. Internet bar. Hairdresser. ATM. Overnight area for late arrivals. Dogs are not accepted. Torch useful. Off site: Fishing from beach. Golf, riding and bicycle hire 4 km. Travel to the area's many attractions is simple by the nearby autopista.

At a glance

Welcome & Ambience	✓✓✓✓	Location	✓✓✓✓✓
Quality of Pitches	✓✓✓✓✓	Range of Facilities	✓✓✓✓✓

Directions

Site is at 1182 km. marker on the N340 near Arc de Bara, between Tarragona and Vilanova.

Charges 2004

Per adult	€ 6,10
child (3-10 yrs)	€ 4,70
pitch incl. electricity	€ 18,90 - € 19,60
with water and drainage	€ 22,70 - € 23,50

All plus 7% VAT.

Reservations

Advisable in July/August. Tel: 977 802 002.
E-mail: rodadebara@stel.es

Open

9 April - 28 September.

ES8395 Camping Arc de Bara

CN 340, km 1182, 43883 Roda de Bará (Tarragona)

In comparison to the gigantic sites along this coastline, this smaller site has only 300 pitches of which most are taken up with static holiday caravans. The site is 200 m. from the impressive Roman monument, Arc de Bara, and 60 m. from the superb beach. The beach is accessed by a rear gate in the site perimeter and is soft sand shelving gently into the waves. The 30 pitches for tourers are generally shaded, are of average size (60-70 sq.m.) and are somewhat set apart from the very extensive permanent pitches but there is a distinct feeling of compression. The unusual feature of this site, perpetrated by one of the owners, is the modernistic design theme used on many of the camp building exteriors and interiors. This theme is continued at the attractive large heated swimming pool and children's pool elevated above the site's ground level and forming a curved arrowhead shape. The shop, bar and restaurant close to the entrance are open every day between July and September and at weekends only all other times of the year, as is the bar near the beach access (the site is open all year).

Facilities

Three very clean toilet blocks are of various designs (one a most unusual elevated circular building) and a fourth without showers. These offer free hot water to washbasins (some in cabins) and showers. Units for disabled visitors. Limited facilities for babies. Dishwashing and laundry (cold water only). Washing machines and dryers. Swimming pools. Bars. Restaurant. Snack bars. Supermarket. Small play area. Some animation in season. Torches required in some areas.

Open

All year.

At a glance

Welcome & Ambience	✓✓✓	Location	✓✓✓✓
Quality of Pitches	✓✓✓	Range of Facilities	✓✓✓✓

Directions

From A7 autopista take exit 31 towards Tarragona. Site is on CN340 Barcelona - Tarragona road at 1182 km. marker just 50 m. downhill from the Roman Arc which spans the road. Use the approach turn for Camping Stel.

Charges 2004

Per person	€ 2,90 - € 4,68
child (3-9 yrs)	€ 1,78 - € 2,90
pitch	€ 4,68 - € 7,95
electricity	€ 2,62 - € 3,00
dog	€ 0,66 - € 1,97

Minimum charge € 23,40 per day for pitch and persons (1/7-31/8). All plus 7% VAT.

Reservations

Contact site. Tel: 977 800 902.
E-mail: camping@campingarcdebara.com

ES8480 Camping & Bungalow Park Sanguli

Mobile homes page 170

Prolongacion Calle, Apdo de Correos 123, 43840 Salou (Tarragona)

Sanguli is a superb site boasting excellent pools and ambitious entertainment. Owned, developed and managed by a local Spanish family, it provides for all the family with everything open when the site is open. It lies little more than 100 metres from the good sandy beach, across the coast road and a small railway level crossing (some train noise at times). Sister site to ES8481, although large, Sanguli manages to maintain a quality family atmosphere due to the efforts of the very keen and efficient staff. There are three very attractive pool areas, one (heated) near the entrance with a grassy sunbathing area partly shaded and a second deep one with water slides that forms part of the excellent sports complex (with fitness centre, tennis courts, minigolf and football practice area). The third pool is the central part of the amphitheatre area at the top of the site which includes an impressive Roman style building with huge portals, containing a bar and restaurant with terraces. An amphitheatre seats 2,000 campers and treats them to very professional free nightly entertainment (1/5-30/9). All the pools have adjacent amenity areas and bars. Located near the centre of Salou, the site can offer the attractions of a busy resort while still being private and it is only 3 km. from Port Aventura. The owners are striving to achieve the 'Garden of Eden' that is their dream. There are 1,220 pitches of varying size (75-90 sq.m) and all have electricity with about 160 used by tour operators and 140 with bungalows. A wonderful selection of trees, palms and shrubs provides natural shade. A real effort is made to cater for young people with a 'Hop Club' (entertainment for 13-17 year olds), along with an internet room. This is a large, professional site providing something for all the family, but still capable of providing peace and quiet for those looking for it.

Facilities

The quality sanitary facilities are constantly improved and are always exceptional, including many individual cabins with en-suite facilities. A new block also has excellent facilities for babies. All are kept very clean. Launderette with service. Motorcaravan services. Bars and restaurant with takeaway. Swimming pools. Jacuzzi. Fitness centre. Sport complex with tennis, football practice ground, Sports area and fitness room (charged). Playgrounds including adventure play area. Mini club, teenagers club. Internet room. Upmarket minigolf. First-aid room. Gas supplies. Off site: Fishing and bicycle hire 100 m. Riding 3 km. Golf 6 km. Resort entertainment.

Open

11 March - 1 November.

At a glance

Welcome & Ambience	✓✓✓✓✓	Location	✓✓✓✓✓
Quality of Pitches	✓✓✓✓✓	Range of Facilities	✓✓✓✓✓

Directions

On west side of Salou about 1 km. from centre, site is well signed from the coast road to Cambrils and from the other town approaches.

Charges 2005

Per person	€ 5,00
child (4-12 yrs)	€ 3,00
pitch incl. electricity	€ 12,00 - € 35,00
incl. water	€ 14,00 - € 37,00

All plus 7% VAT. Less 25-45% outside high season for longer stays. Special long stay offers for senior citizens.

Reservations

Advised for July/Aug. and made up to 1 March with sizeable booking fee. Tel: 977 381 641.
E-mail: mail@sanguli.es

ES8402 Camping Vendrell Platja

Avda. del Sanatori, s/n, 43880 Cond-Rugd - El Vendrell (Tarragona)

In the bustling Calafell area, this site is set back from the beach across a minor road. Popular with tourists for many years, the area has apartment buildings, bars and restaurants. An avenue of palms greets you on arrival here, and the pool with more tall palms and grassy areas, has two slides that delight children and adults alike. Around one side of the pool red umbrellas provide shade where cool drinks and snacks can be enjoyed. A large thatched area used in the evenings for entertainment, provides extra shade away from the pool. The very Spanish restaurant serves paella, pizza and family style meals. The site is bustling with activity and crowded during high season. The small pitches (60 sq.m.) are partially shaded by trees yet to reach their full potential. Access to all the pitches is through one narrow central road which is busy with foot and vehicle traffic. As the pitches are very tightly packed this is not the site for campers who enjoy their privacy.

Facilities

Two well located toilet blocks provide clean facilities with a new unit for disabled campers and well equipped baby rooms. The numbers of showers and toilets are low - we think they would be stressed at peak periods. Washing machines. Motorcaravan services. Supermarket. Restaurant. Snack bar. Swimming pools and pool bar. Play areas. Football. Boules. Basketball. Table tennis. Electronic games. Bicycle hire. Very modest animation programme. ATM. Security boxes. Torches useful. Off site: Resort town and beach outside the gate with usual attractions. Fishing. Bicycle hire 200 m. Riding 2 km. Golf 3 km.

At a glance

Welcome & Ambience	✓✓✓✓	Location	✓✓✓✓
Quality of Pitches	✓✓✓	Range of Facilities	✓✓✓✓

Directions

From A7 or A16 take exits for El Vendrel. Then go east to Sant Salvador, and north on coast road towards Platja Calafell. Site is well signed on this road west of the town centre.

Charges 2005

Per adult	€ 2,10 - € 6,20
child (3-11 yrs)	€ 1,00 - € 5,20
pitch	€ 3,50 - € 12,40
electricity	€ 3,50 - € 4,20

Reservations

Contact site no deposit required. Tel: 977 694 009.
E-mail: vendrell@camping-vendrellplatja.com

Open

18 March - 16 October.

Parc de Vacances
Sangulí Salou
CAMPING & BUNGALOW PARK
Prolongació carrer E, s/n
Apartat de Correus 123
43840 SALOU • Costa Daurada
Tarragona • España
tel. +34 977 38 16 41
fax +34 977 38 46 16
Better is Impossible...
mail@sanguli.es • www.sanguli.es
Salou • Costa Daurada • Catalunya • España

ES8481 Camping Cambrils Park

Mobile homes page 170

Apartado de Correos 123, 43850 Salou (Tarragona)

This is a superb site for a camping holiday providing for all family members, whatever their age. A drive lined with palm trees and flowers leads from a large, very smart round reception building at this impressive modern site. Sister site to ES8480, it is set 500 metres back from the excellent beach in a generally quiet setting with outstanding facilities. The 684 slightly sloping, grassy pitches of around 90 sq.m. are numbered and separated by trees. All have 10A electricity, 55 have water and waste water connections, some having more shade than others. The marvellous central lagoon pool complex with three pools and water slides is the main focus of the site with a raised wooden 'poop deck' sunbathing area with palm surrounds that doubles as an entertainment stage at night. There is a huge bar/terrace area for watching the magnificent floodlit spectacles, along with an excellent restaurant in the old farmhouse with an adjacent takeaway. By day there is a small bar at a lower level in the pool where you can enjoy a cool drink from submerged stools, plus a dryer version on the far side of the bar or just relax on the spacious grass sunbathing areas. There are a number of tour operator pitches and attractive thatched chalets. A fabulous jungle theme children's pool is nearer the entrance - they love it, especially the elephants! An extra pool for adults has been added here, along with a snack bar.

Facilities

Four excellent sanitary buildings provide some washbasins in cabins, superb units for disabled visitors and immaculate, decorated baby sections. Dishwashing and laundry sinks. Huge serviced laundry. Motorcaravan services. Car wash. Restaurant. Takeaway. Huge supermarket, souvenir shop and 'panaderia' (fresh-baked bread and croissants). Swimming pools with lifeguards. Minigolf. Tennis Football. Multi-games court. Basketball. Volleyball. Petanque. Animation and entertainment all season. Mini-club. Internet café. Doctor on site daily all season. ATM. Gas supplies. Dogs are not accepted. Off site: Beach 500 m. Fishing, bicycle hire 400 m. Riding 3 km. Port Aventura theme park 4 km. Golf 7 km.

Open

18 March - 9 October.

At a glance

Welcome & Ambience	✓✓✓✓	Location	✓✓✓✓
Quality of Pitches	✓✓✓✓✓	Range of Facilities	✓✓✓✓✓

Directions

Site is about 1.5 km west of Salou. From the A7 take exit 35 and at roundabout take signs for Cambrils. Follow new dual-carriageway around the back of Salou and site is signed at last roundabout towards Cambrils (you can see the bungalos from the dual-carriageway).

Charges 2005

Per person	€ 5,00
child (4-12 yrs)	free - € 3,00
pitch incl. electricity	€ 12,00 - € 35,00
incl. water and waste water	€ 14,00 - € 37,00

All plus 7% VAT. Special offers, plus low season discounts for pensioners.

Reservations

Contact site. Tel: 977 351 031.
E-mail: mail@cambrilspark.es

'My Sweet Camping'

This was the name of a unique photographic exhibition held at Cambrils Park and Camping Sanguli during the July and August 2004. In all, 90 poster-sized photographs were displayed around the two sites, all of which had been taken by the world renowned Portuguese photographer Aldo Soares. The images are all of holidaymakers who had spent their 2003 holidays at Cambrils and Sanguli, and each succeeded superbly in capturing the essence of each family's holiday experience.'

Ctra. Salou – Cambrils, Km. 1 • Apartat de Correus 123
43840 SALOU • Tarragona • España
tel. +34 977 35 10 31 • fax +34 977 35 22 10
The only luxury Camping on the Costa Daurada
Cambrils • Costa Daurada • Catalunya • España
PARC DE VACANCES
Cambrils-Park
CAMPING - BUNGALOW
mail@cambrilspark.es • www.cambrilspark.es

www.campinglapineda.com PARK & POOL & SPA

DIFFERENT, NATURAL, CULTURAL, UNFORGETTABLE HOLIDAYS

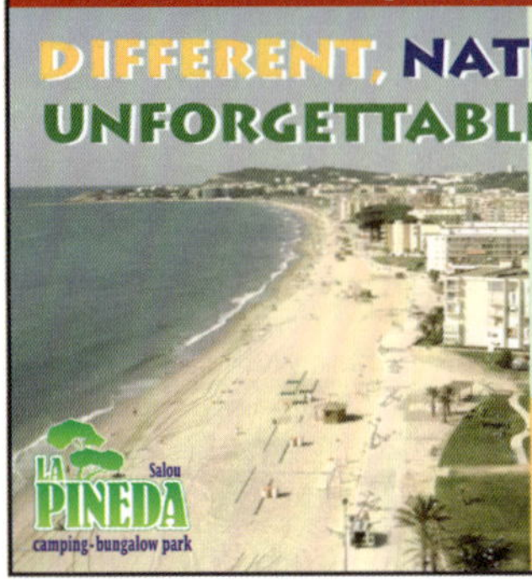

CAMPSITE & BUNGALOWS OPEN ALL YEAR ROUND

Check out our web site for rates, SPECIAL OFFERS, how to find us and to make on-line bookings via our secure server.

CAMPING LA PINEDA DE SALOU

Ctra. de la Costa de Tarragona a Salou, km 5, E-43481 LA PINEDA (Tarragona) - Costa Daurada - Tel. (00-34) 977 37 30 80
Fax (00-34) 977 37 30 81 info@campinglapineda.com

ES8482 Camping La Pineda de Salou

Mobile homes page 171

Ctra Costa Tarragona - Salou km 5, 43481 La Pineda (Tarragona)

La Pineda is just outside Salou towards Tarragona and this site is just 300 metres from the Aquapark and 2.5 kilometres from Port Aventura, to which there is an hourly bus service from outside the site entrance. There is some noise from this road. The site has a fair-sized swimming pool adjoining a smaller, heated one, open from mid June, behind large hedges close to the entrance. A large terrace has sun loungers, and various entertainment aimed at young people is provided in season. The 366 flat pitches are mostly shaded and of about 70 sq.m. All have 5A electricity. The beach is about 400 metres The simple restaurant/bar is shaded and has a large cactus garden to the rear. This is a plain, friendly and convenient site, with reasonable rates, probably best used for visiting Tarragona and Port Aventura, or exploring the local area, rather than for extended stays. Note: the site is reasonably close to a large industrial centre.

Facilities

Sanitary facilities are mature but clean with baby bath, dishwashing and laundry sinks. Facilities for disabled visitors. Two washing machines in each block. The second building is opened in high season only. Gas supplies. Shop (1/7-31/8). Restaurant and snacks (1/7-31/8). Swimming pools (1/7-31/8). Bar (all season). Five-a-side soccer pitch. Small TV room. Bicycle hire. Games room with videos and drink and snack machines. Playground (3-12 yrs). Entertainment (1/7-30/8). Torches may be required.
Off site: Fishing 500 m. Golf 12 km.

Open

All year except 1 January - 22 March.

At a glance

Welcome & Ambience	✓✓✓	Location	✓✓✓
Quality of Pitches	✓✓✓	Range of Facilities	✓✓✓✓

Directions

From A7 just southwest of Tarragona take exit 35 and follow signs to La Pineda and Port Aventura then campsite signs appear.

Charges 2004

Per person	€ 3,70 - € 5,40
child (1-10 yrs)	€ 2,50 - € 4,00
pitch incl. car	€ 8,80 - € 17,50
electricity	€ 3,30
dog	€ 1,60 - € 0,27

All plus 7% VAT.

Reservations

Made for high season (min. 7 nights).
Tel: 977 37 30 80.
E-mail: info@campinglapineda.com

CAMPING & BUNGALOW PARK
PLAYA CAMBRILS
(DON CAMILO)

E-43850 CAMBRILS (Tarragona)
(Postcode) Ap. Correos 315.
Tel. (34) 977 36 14 90
Fax (34) 977 36 49 88
www.playacambrils.com
camping@playacambrils.com

Access: Autopista A-7, exit 37, driving then towards Cambrils Puerto and Salou along the coast.

Well-shaded family campsite fronting the sea and the beach boulevard along the beach, in privileged surroundings for walking, leisure and sports activities, etc. All pitches with electr. supply. Fully equipped bungalows (also with TV). Modern and complete sanitary installations with free hot water.Bar-Restaurant, superrmarket. Animation activities in July and August. Large adult swimming pool and children's pool. Tennis court, (windsurf, catamaran, kayak,...)
Only 5 km from theme park Port Aventura (direct bus).

ES8483 Camping Tamarit Park

N340 km 1172, Tamarit, 43008 Tarragona (Tarragona)

This is a marvellous, beach-side site, attractively situated at the foot of Tamarit castle at one end of a superb one kilometre long beach of fine sand. Parts are landscaped with lush Mediterranean palms and shrubs, other areas have natural pine shade, all home to mischievous red squirrels. The 734 pitches, 50 of which are virtually on the beach, are marked out on hard sand and grass and some are attractively separated by green vegetation which provides good shade. There are about 120 tour operator pitches, a number of seasonal pitches and about 120 bungalows. All pitches have electricity (6A) and are 70-100 sq.m. in area. Long electricity leads and metal awning pegs may be required in places but wide internal roads give good access for even the largest of units (American motorhomes are accepted). Catering includes a beach-side waiter service restaurant with superb views and a terrace with tables just a few metres from the sea. A vast, attractively designed, lagoon-type swimming pool with bar and sun terrace has recently been added. The site is approached by a long access road, rather narrow but with passing places, reached across a bridge (6 m.) over the railway line (there is train noise on the site). Security is provided but the very low wall which is the site beach boundary must be viewed with caution. Tamarit would be a good choice for windsurfing enthusiasts or a family holiday by the sea. The early morning sun shining on the blue sea and the golden stone of Tamarit castle high above is a memorable sight! It is only 9 km. from Tarragona and 16 km. from Port Aventura.

Facilities

Sanitary blocks (one heated) are modern and tiled, providing good facilities. An unfortunate economy feature in the showers is the introduction of push-button controlled hot water with tap controlled cold, leading to a confusing mixture of temperatures. Private bathrooms to rent. Dishwashing under cover with hot water. Laundry facilities including washing machines. Motorcaravan services. Gas supplies. Shop, bar/restaurant and takeaway service (all until 15/10). Swimming pool (15/5-15/10). Tennis. Volleyball. Petanque. Minigolf. Table tennis. Playground. Animation programme in season. Fishing. Exchange facilities and ATM. Internet access. Barbecues not permtted on pitches.
Off site: Riding 1 km. Bicycle hire 2 km. Golf 8 km.

Open

All year.

At a glance

Welcome & Ambience	✓✓✓✓✓	Location	✓✓✓✓✓
Quality of Pitches	✓✓✓✓✓	Range of Facilities	✓✓✓✓✓

Directions

From A7 take exit 32 towards Tarragona and continue for 4.5 km. At roundabout (km. 1172) turn back on yourself towards Atafulla/Tamarit and after just 200 m. turn right to Tamarit (beside Caledonia Bungalow Park). Take care over railway bridge, then turn immediately sharp right. Site entrance is on left after 1 km.

Charges 2004

Per person	€ 4,25
child (1-12 yrs)	€ 3,25
pitch acc. to size and season	€ 15,00 - € 40,00
dog	€ 1,00 - € 3,00

All plus 7% VAT. Discounts for students, pensioners, large families and longer stays in low season.

Reservations

Contact site. Tel: 977 650 128.
E-mail: tamaritpark@tamarit.com

ES8479 Camping Playa Cambrils - Don Camilo

Mobile homes page 171

Ctra Cambrils - Salou km 1.5, 43850 Cambrils (Tarragona)

Almost completely canopied by trees which provide welcome shade on hot days, the site is 300 m. from the beach across a busy road. It is mature and has had some recent renovations (2003). The small (60 sq.m.) pitches are on flat ground, divided by hedges, there are many permanent pitches and half the site is given up to chalet style accomodation. Large units are placed in a dedicated area where the trees are higher. The pool complex includes a functional glassed restaurant and bar with a distinct Spanish flavour reflected in the menu and tapas available all day. The pool is long and narrow with separate children's pool and a large paved area for soaking up the sun. There is children's entertainment organised by a good animation team. A big building at one end of the site consists of the supermarket, an attended electronic games room and a large play room. As this is a popular site with Spanish families it is a good place to practice your language.

Facilities

One modern sanitary building, and one large plus one small refurbished block offer reasonable facilities with British style WCs and free showers in separate buildings. Washing machines, dishwashing (some hot some cold) and laundry sinks (cold only) are at the end of the block under cover. Facilities for disabled campers near the swimming pool. Supermaket hop (Apr -Sep). Bar/snacks and separate restaurant (April-Sept). Playground. Animation in high season. Mini club. Huge electronic games room with attendant. Torches useful. Off site: Resort town has a range of shops, bars and restaurants. Bicycle hire 500 m. Fishing and golf 1 km. Riding 1.5 km.

At a glance

Welcome & Ambience	✓✓✓✓	Location	✓✓✓✓
Quality of Pitches	✓✓✓	Range of Facilities	✓✓✓

Directions

Leave A7 autopista at exit 37 and head for Cambrils and then to the beach. Turn left along beach road. Site is 1 km. east of Cambrils Playa and is well signed as you leave Cambrils marina.

Charges 2004

Per pitch	€ 10,00 - € 23,00
adult	€ 1,50 - € 4,00
child (1-10 yrs)	€ -2,00 - € 3,00

Reservations

Write to site. Tel: 977 361 490.
E-mail: camping@playacambrils.com

Open

15 March - 12 October.

ES8470 Camping La Siesta

Mobile homes page 172

Calle Ctra Norte 37, 43840 Salou (Tarragona)

The palm bedecked entrance of La Siesta is only 250 metres from the pleasant sandy beach and close to the life of the resort of Salou. The town is popular with British and Spanish holidaymakers and has just about all that a highly developed Spanish resort can offer. For those who do not want to share the busy beach, there is a large, free swimming pool which is elevated above pitch level. La Siesta is divided into 470 individual pitches which are large enough and have electricity (10A), with smaller ones for tents. Many pitches are provided with artificial shade and within some pitches there is one box for the tent or caravan, and a shared one for the car. There is considerable shade from the trees and shrubs that are part of the site's environment. In high season, the siting of units is carried out by the management, who are friendly and helpful. Young campers are located separately to the rear of the site. The restaurant, which overlooks the good-sized pool, has a comprehensive menu and wine list, competing well with the town restaurants. A bar is alongside with TV and a large terrace, part of which is given over to entertainment in high season. A suprisingly large supermarket caters for most needs in season.

Facilities

Three bright and clean sanitary blocks provide very reasonable facilities. Motorcaravan services. Supermarket. Various vending machines. Self-service restaurant and bar with cooked dishes to take away. Dancing some evenings till 11 pm. Swimming pool (300 sq.m; open all season). Playground. Medical service daily in season. ATM point. Torches may be required. Off site: Huge numbers of shops, restaurants and bars near. Port Aventura is close. Bicycle hire 200 m. Fishing 500 m. Riding amd golf 6 km.

Open

14 March - 3 November.

At a glance

Welcome & Ambience	✓✓✓✓	Location	✓✓✓✓
Quality of Pitches	✓✓✓✓	Range of Facilities	✓✓✓✓✓

Directions

Leave A7 at exit 35 for Salou. Site is signed off the Tarragona/Salou road and from the one way system in the town of Salou. The site is in the town so keep a sharp eye for the small signs.

Charges 2004

Per person	€ 3,70 - € 6,80
child (4-9 yrs)	€ 3,00 - € 3,80
pitch and car	€ 7,40 - € 13,60
electricity	€ 2,50 - € 2,95

All plus 7% VAT. No credit cards.

Reservations

Advised 1 July - 20 Aug. and made in sense of guaranteeing a shady place, with electricity if required. Deposit required. Tel: 977 380 852. E-mail: info@camping-lasiesta.com

E-43840 SALOU
(Tarragona)
C/ Norte, 37
Tel. (34) 977 38 08 52
Fax (34) 977 38 31 91
www.camping-lasiesta.com
info@camping-lasiesta.com

A real holiday site, situated in the centre of the elegant, intern. holiday resort of SALOU, in the always sunny prov. of Tarragona. Excellent installations as swimming pool and paddling pool, free hot water, electr. conn. f. tent and caravan, supermarket, restaurant, bar, cafeteria, etc. At only 100m from a large, magnificent beach and at 900m from the theme-leisure park "PORT AVENTURA".

MOBILE HOMES FOR HIRE.
OPEN: 14.03 - 03.11.

Very reasonable of-season fees and 10% P/N reduction from 14.03 - 16.06 and 01.09 - 03.11

ES8486 Camping Torre de la Mora

CN 340, km 1171, 43080 Tarragona (Tarragona)

Located on a promontory in a pleasant corner of the Costa Daurada with a village like atmosphere, Torre de la Mora takes advantage of its wonderful location, offering some pitches with beautiful views over the white sandy beaches and rocky promontories of the coastline. The hinterland is pine forest and there are areas where you can pitch a tent, access electricity (6A) and feel close to nature. The 200 touring pitches vary in just about every way, some are on the lower flat area, including a few with beach frontage, others are on steep terraces around the promontory. Many of the higher pitches around the old coastal defence fort and building have amazing views. It is important to select a pitch related to your level of fitness as the higher pitches and some of the lower terraces require an energetic approach (children should be supervised). We spoke to some campers who enjoyed Torre de la Mora so much they had been happily returning to the site for years. Some areas of the site reflect its age, however we are told a program is underway to renovate the sports area, across a small road, which has a pleasant large pool in a garden-like setting.

Facilities

Two large and three small sanitary blocks are mature but the facilities within are clean with a unit for disabled campers. Careful selection of pitch is required for disabled campers or infirm visitors. There is a mixture of washing facilities some of which have hot water, others not and most are dated. Washing machine. Motorcaravan services. Supermarket. Restaurant. Chicken bar (high season). Swimming pool and sports area (to be renovated in 2004). Play area. Table tennis. Electronic games. Animation programme 5 nights a week. Torches useful. Off site: Pretty beach town outside the gate. Fishing. Bicycle hire 1 km. Golf 2 km. Riding 3 km. Boat launching 8 km.

Open

18 March - 31 October.

At a glance

Welcome & Ambience	✓✓✓✓	Location	✓✓✓✓
Quality of Pitches	✓✓✓✓✓	Range of Facilities	✓✓✓✓

Directions

From A7 Barcelona – Tarragona autopista take exit 32, then N340 towards Tarragona. Turn off for Punta del la Mora and site is well signed approaching the village. The final approach is via some narrow streets so watch for one way signs and there is an unusual entry through a high wire fence alongside road.

Charges 2004

Per unit incl. 1 person	€ 11,00 - € 20,00
extra person	€ 4,00 - € 6,20
child (under 10 yrs.)	€ 3,00 - € 4,35
electricity	€ 3,45
dog	€ 0,50

Reservations

Contact site. Tel: 977 650277.
E-mail: info@torredelamora.com

ES8520 Camping Marius

Ctra N340, km 1137, 43892 Miami-Playa (Tarragona)

Quiet, well tended and not too huge, this agreeable site has a family atmosphere and a personal touch. One perimeter is on a good sandy beach with direct access and no roads to cross - you can almost fall out of bed and onto the beach and a large beach bar will provide resuscitation when required! The site is divided into 345 individual pitches of adequate size so it does not become too overcrowded. They are quite shady and all have electrical connections, 8 pitches with water and drainage. Dog owners go on one half of the site which is split down the centre by a wall and large storm drain gully (clean). The lively fishing port of Cambrils, where you can buy freshly caught fish, is about seven kilometres. It is an excellent watersports venue in high season. The use of TV sets outside your unit and the riding of bicycles on site is not permitted. Some train noise may be expected.

Facilities

Two of the sanitary blocks are quite elderly but clean and well maintained, with a third of excellent standards. Free hot water in the showers and half the washbasins, plus 21 private cabins. Facilities for babies and disabled campers. Laundry room. Motorcaravan services. Bar and restaurant (1/6-30/9). Supermarket (15/4-30/9). Souvenir shop. Gas supplies. Children's club and playground. Hairdresser. Fishing. Table tennis. Torches required at night.
Off site: Windsurfing, water ski and pedaloes nearby. Riding 4 km. Golf 10 km.

At a glance

Welcome & Ambience	✓✓✓✓	Location	✓✓✓✓✓
Quality of Pitches	✓✓✓	Range of Facilities	✓✓✓

Directions

The site entrance is 28 km. from Tarragona on the Valencia road (N340).

Charges 2004

Per person	€ 5,00 - € 7,00
child (1- 10 yrs)	€ 2,50 - € 3,50
pitch incl. electricity	€ 12,00 - € 17,00
dog	€ 2,50 - € 3,50

Plus 7% VAT. Less 10-20% for longer stays.

Reservations

Contact site. Tel: 977 810 684.
E-mail: schmid@teleline.es

Open

1 April - 15 October.

www.alanrogers.com for latest campsite news

ES8530 Playa Montroig Camping Resort

Aptdo 3, N340 km 1136, 43300 Montroig (Tarragona)

What a superb site! Playa Montroig is about 30 kilometres beyond Tarragona set in its own tropical gardens with direct access to a very long soft sand beach. Bathing, windsurfing, surfboarding two diving rafts and many beach sports are available. The main part of the site lies between the sea, road and railway (as at other sites on this stretch of coast, there is some train noise) and there is a huge underpass. The site is divided into spacious, marked pitches with excellent shade provided by a variety of lush vegetation including very impressive palms set in wide avenues. There are 1,950 pitches, all with electricity and 330 with water and drainage. Some 48 pitches are directly alongside the beach – they are somewhat expensive and extremely popular. The site has many outstanding features. There is an excellent pool complex near the entrance with two pools (one heated for children). A quality restaurant serves traditional Catalunian fare (seats 150) and overlooks an entertainment area where you may watch genuine Flamenco dancing and buffet food is served (catering for 1,000). A large terrace bar dispenses drinks or if you yearn for louder music there is a disco and smaller bar. If you prefer international food there is yet another eating option in a very smart restaurant (seats 500). Above this is the 'Pai-pai' Caribbean cocktail bar where softer music is provided in an intimate atmosphere. Activities for children are very ambitious – there is even a ceramics kiln (multi-lingual carers). 'La Carpa', a spectacular open air theatre, is an ideal setting for daily keep fit sessions and the professional entertainment provided. If you are 5-11 years old you can explore the 'Tam-Tam Eco Park', a 20,000 sq.m. forest zone where experts teach the natural life of the area. You can even camp out for a night (supervised) to study wildlife (a once weekly activity). Adults are also allowed in to barbecues and other evening fun. This is an excellent site and there is insufficient space here to describe all the available activities. We recommend it for families with children of all ages and there is much emphasis on providing activities outside the high season.

Facilities

Fifteen sanitary buildings, some small, but of very good quality with toilets and washbasins, others really excellent, air conditioned larger buildings housing large showers, washbasins (many in private cabins) and separate WCs. Facilities for disabled campers and for babies. A 24 hour cleaning service operates. Water points around site (water said to be very pure from the site's own wells). Several launderettes. Motorcaravan services. Good shopping centre with supermarket, greengrocer, butcher, fishmonger, tobacconist and souvenir shops. Restaurants and bars. The 'Eurocentre', with 250 person capacity and equipped for entertainment and activities, large screen videos, films, shows and meetings (air conditioned). Fitness suite. Eco-park (see above). TV lounges (3) incl. satellite. Beach bar. Playground. Free kindergarten with multi-lingual staff. Skate-boarding. Jogging track. Sports area for volleyball, football and basketball. Tennis. Minigolf. Table tennis. Organised activities for children and adults including pottery and gardening classes. Windsurfing and water skiing courses. Surfboards and pedaloes for hire. Boat mooring. Hairdressers. Bicycle hire. Bureau de change. Safety deposit boxes. Telephone service. Internet café. Gas supplies. Dogs are not accepted. TVs are not allowed outside your vehicle. Off site: Riding and golf 3 km.

At a glance

Welcome & Ambience	✓✓✓✓	Location	✓✓✓✓✓
Quality of Pitches	✓✓✓✓✓	Range of Facilities	✓✓✓✓✓

Directions

Site entrance is off main N340 nearly 30 km. southwest from Tarragona. From motorway take Cambrils exit and turn west on N340 at 1136 km marker.

Charges 2004

Per unit incl 2 persons and electricity	€ 15,00 - € 56,00
premium pitch	€ 22,00 - € 80,00
extra person	€ 5,00
child (1-9 yrs)	free - € 4,00

All plus 7% VAT. Discounts for longer stays and for pensioners.

Reservations

Are possible and made with refundable booking fee (€ 30). Contact Dept. de Reservas, Apdo 3. at site address. Tel: 977 810 637. E-mail: info@playamontroig.com

Open

1 March - 31 October.

ES8540 Yelloh! Village La Torre del Sol

Mobile homes page 172

Ctra N340, km 1136, 43300 Montroig (Tarragona)

A pleasant banana tree-lined approach road gives way to avenues of palms as you arrive at Torre del Sol, a member of the French Airotel chain and of the 'Yelloh' group of sites. Sister site to Templo del Sol (ES8537N), Torre del Sol is a very large site occuping a good position with direct access to the clean, soft sand beach, complete with a beach bar. Strong features here are 800 m of clean beach-front and entertainment is provided all season. There is a separate area where the 'Happy Camp' team will take your children to camp overnight in the Indian reservation, plus they can amuse them two days a week with other activities. The cinema doubles as a theatre to stage shows all season. A complex of three pools, thoughtfully laid out with grass sunbathing areas and palms has a lifeguard. There is good shade on a high proportion of the 1,500 individual, numbered pitches. All have electricity and are mostly of about 70-80 sq.m. There is usually space for odd nights but for good places between 10/7-16/8 it is best to reserve (only taken for a stay of five nights or more). Part of the site is between the railway and the sea so there is train noise. We were impressed with the provision of season-long entertainment and to give parents a break whilst children were in the safe hands of the animation team.

Facilities

Four very well maintained, fully equipped, toilet blocks include units for disabled people and babies, and some tiled units at three blocks with cabins with washbasins and hot showers. Washing machines. Gas supplies. Fridge hire. Large supermarket, bakery, and souvenir shops at entrance, open to public. Full restaurant with soft-toy playpen area. Takeaway. Bar with large terrace where entertainment held daily all season. Beach bar. Coffee bar and ice cream bar. Pizzeria. Open roof cinema with seating for 520; TV lounges (satellite); separate room for films or videos shown on TV. Well-soundproofed disco. Swimming pools (two heated). Solarium. Sauna. Tennis. Table tennis. Squash. Volleyball. Language school (Spanish). Minigolf. Multi purpose hardcourt. Sub aqua diving. Bicycle hire. Fishing. Windsurfing school; sailboards and pedaloes for hire. Playground and crèche. Library. Hairdressers. Car repair and car wash. No animals permitted. No jet skis. Off site: Theme parks. Beach fishing. Riding 3 km. Golf 4 km.

At a glance

Welcome & Ambience	✓✓✓✓✓	Location	✓✓✓✓✓
Quality of Pitches	✓✓✓✓✓	Range of Facilities	✓✓✓✓✓

Directions

Entrance is off main N340 road by 1136 km. marker, about 30 km. from Tarragona towards Valencia. From motorway take Cambrils exit and turn west on N340.

Charges 2005

Per pitch incl. 2 adults and electricity	€ 19,50 - € 55,00
extra person	€ 3,20 - € 8,50
child (0-10 yrs)	free - € 6,75

All plus 7% VAT. Discounts in low season for longer stays.

Reservations

Made with booking fee (€ 20); contact site first. Tel: 977 810 486. E-mail: info@latorredelsol.com

Open

15 March - 20 October.

ES8535 Camping-Pension Cala d'Oques

43890 Hospitalet del Infante (Tarragona)

This peaceful and delightful site has been developed with care and dedication by Elisa Roller over 30 years or so and she now runs it with the help of her daughter Kim. Part of its appeal lies in its situation beside the sea with a wide beach of sand and pebbles, its amazing mountain backdrop and the views across the bay to the town and part by the atmosphere created by Elisa, and staff - friendly, relaxed and comfortable. The restaurant with its homely touches has a super menu and a reputation extending well outside the site (the excellent cook has been there for many years) and the family type entertainment is in total contrast to that provided at the larger, brasher sites of the Costa Daurada. There are 255 pitches, mostly level and laid out beside the beach, with more behind on wide, informal terracing. Odd pine and olive trees are an attractive feature and provide some shade. Electricity is available although long leads may needed in places. Gates provide access to the pleasant beach with useful cold showers to wash the sand away. Torches are needed at night. For those interested, there is a naturist beach of fine sand around the little headland just south of the site. This is a pretty place to stay and Elisa gives a pleasant personal service but do not expect 'Costa' type entertainment. Ask how the nearby village of Hospitalet del Infante got its name - it's a royal riddle! The village itself is well worth exploring and if you are here in June watch for the fabulous fireworks of the celebration of St John. It is interesting to note that Cala d'Oques (Goose Bay) was where migrant geese landed on return from wintering in South Africa, hence the geese on the site logo and the guard goose that watches the entrance.

Facilities

The main toilet facilities are in the front part of the building housing the restaurant, reception and the family home on the first level. Clean and neat, there is hot water to showers (hot water by token but free to campers - a device to guard against unauthorized visitors from the beach). New heated unit with toilets and washbasins for winter use. Additional small bock with toilets and washbasins at the far end of the site. Motorcaravan service point. Restaurant/bar and shop (1/4-30/9). Play area. Kim's kids club. Five-a-side soccer. Fishing. Internet point. Gas supplies. Torches required in some areas Off site: Village facilities, incl. shop and restaurant 1.5 km. Bicycle hire or riding 2 km.

Open

All year.

At a glance

Welcome & Ambience	✓✓✓✓✓	Location	✓✓✓✓✓
Quality of Pitches	✓✓✓✓	Range of Facilities	✓✓✓✓

Directions

Hospitalet del Infante is south of Tarragona, accessed from the A7 (exit 38) or from the N340. From the north take first exit to Hospitalet del Infante at the 1128 km. marker. Follow signs in the village, site is 2 km. south, by the sea.

Charges 2004

Per person	€ 4,85 - € 7,20
child (0-10 yrs)	€ -2,00
pitch incl. car	€ 6,95 - € 15,00
electricity	€ 3,35
dog	€ 2,50 - € 2,85

Discounts for seniors and for longer stays.
No credit cards.

Reservations

Contact site. Tel: 977 823 254.
E-mail: eroller@nil.fut.es

ES8537 Camping Naturista El Templo del Sol

43890 Hospitalet del Infante (Tarragona)

El Templo del Sol is a large, luxurious terraced naturist site with a distinctly Arabesque style and superb buildings in Moorish style. The owner has designed the magnificent main turreted building at the entrance with fountains and elaborate Moorish arches. Three large, tiered pools are wonderful with water cascading from one to the other and are part of a supporting complex containing a huge luxurious Jacuzzi with cracking views over the sea, a large bar with snacks, a games area, plus a sunbathing area on the roof. Also included is a 'Solar Park' where visitors may learn how solar energy is used and applied. The main building contains an impressive reception area and has an elegant restaurant and an elegant mosaic central, open area with a fountain. The site has 435 pitches, mainly rather small (60/70 sq.m), but 85 fully serviced. Pitches are on terraces giving rewarding views over the sea and ready access to the sandy beach. There is some shade. Site lighting is provided from pleasing serpent shaped light assemblies. The site is under French management and English is spoken. There is some daytime rail noise especially in the lower areas of the site where the larger pitches are located.

Facilities

The sanitary blocks are amongst the best you will find in Spain providing everything you could require and extensive services for disabled campers. Washing machines. Well stocked supermarket. Health shop. Souvenir shop. Bars. Restaurant and snack bar (1/4-10/10).Swimming pools (20/3-15/10). Jacuzzi. Cinema. Games area. Volley ball. Boule. Separate children's pool and play area. Miniclub. Doctor available. Library. Safety deposit boxes. Professional entertainment includes genuine Flamenco dancing. Hairdresser. Bicycle hire. ATM. Animals are not accepted. No jet skis. Off site: Fishing 100 m. Golf 2 km. Bicycle hire and boat launching 3 km. Riding 7 km. Theme parks.

At a glance

Welcome & Ambience	✓✓✓✓✓	Location	✓✓✓✓✓
Quality of Pitches	✓✓✓✓✓	Range of Facilities	✓✓✓✓✓

Directions

From N340 south of Tarragona, exit at km. 1123 in the direction of L'Hopitalet and follow signs.

Charges 2004

Per person	€ 3,00 - € 6,50
child (under 10 yrs)	€ 1,80 - € 5,00
pitch incl. electricity	€ 11,00 - € 21,00

Plus 7% VAT. Discounts for longer stays.

Reservations

Min. stay July/Aug. 5 nights, otherwise 3 nights. Naturist licence required. Contact site for details. Tel: 977 823 434. E-mail: info@eltemplodelsol.com

Open

20 March - 20 October.

www.alanrogers.com for latest campsite news

ES8536 Camping Caravanning Ametlla Village Platja

Apdo. Correus 240, Paraje Santes Creus, 43860 Ametlla de Mar (Tarragona)

This site within a protected area is new (2000), has been well thought out and is startling in the quality of service provided, the finish and the materials used in construction. The 373 pitches are on a terraced hillside above colourful coves with shingle beaches and two small associated lagoons (with a protected fish species). The site is environmentally correct, local planning regulations are extremely tight including the types of trees that may planted. The many bungalows here have been tastefully incorporated. There are great views, particularly from the friendly restaurant (which has a very good chef). Animation is organised for children in high season and there is a well equipped fitness room (free). There are good quality pools (with lifeguard) and a sub-aqua diving school operates on the site in high season and beginners may try a dive. This is a most attractive small site in an idyllic situation near the picturesque fishing village of L'Ametlla de Mar, famous for its fish restaurants, and within the Ebro Delta nature reserve. It is about 20 minutes from Europe's second largest theme park, Port Aventura, but as there is no regular bus service your own transport is required (the owners arrange free buses to the local disco each Wednesday). No transit traffic is allowed within the site in high season. Used by tour operators (30 pitches). This is a very good site for families or for just relaxing. There is some train noise.

Facilities

Three really good toilet blocks provide free hot water throughout, British style WCs, washbasins and some private cabins with WC and washbasin, plus others with WC, basin and shower. The showers are very clean, roomy and have hot water. Motorcaravan services. Gas supplies. Supermarket (1/4-30/9; small shop incl. bread at other times). Good restaurant with snack menu and bar. TV room (1/4-15/10). Swimming pool. Sub aqua diving. Kayaking. Fishing. Children's club and play area. Fitness room. Bicycle hire. Football. Basketball. Volleyball. Entertainment July/Aug. Barbecue area. Bicycle hire. Fishing. English is spoken.
Off site: Boat launching 3 km. Golf 15 km. Riding 20 km. Theme parks.

Open

All year.

At a glance

Welcome & Ambience	✓✓✓✓	Location	✓✓✓✓
Quality of Pitches	✓✓✓✓	Range of Facilities	✓✓✓✓

Directions

From A7/E15 (Barcelona - Valencia) take exit 39 for L'Ametlla de Mar. Follow numerous large white signs on reaching village and site is 2.5 km. south of the village.

Charges guide

Per person	€ 2,06 - € 5,00
child (under 10 yrs)	€ 1,69 - € 4,10
tent or caravan	€ 2,18 - € 5,30
car	€ 2,18 - € 5,30
motorcaravan	€ 3,86 - € 9,40
electricity	€ 3,00 - € 3,50

All plus 7% VAT. Less for longer stays, especially in low season.

Reservations

Contact site. Tel: 977 267 784.
E-mail: info@campingametlla.com

This Mediterranean region is famous for its magnificent orange groves and beautiful long, sandy beaches. Centuries of Moorish presence have resulted in a profound Hispano-Moorish heritage.

Valenciana is made up of the provinces of Castellon, Valencia and Alicante

The capital of the region is Valencia

La Costa del Azahar (Orange-blossom Coast) stretches from Vinaros to Almanzora, with the great port of Valencia in the middle. Orange groves grow right down to the coast, particularly in the northern section. Good beaches can be found around Benicassim and Peñíscola. South of Valencia, the Costa Blanca derives its name from its 170 miles or so of silvery-white beaches – some of the best beaches are to be found on this coast, especially between Gandía and Benidorm. As a result it is one of the most popular tourist areas in Spain

The capital city of Valencia boasts a great nightlife and plays host to numerous festivals held throughout the year, including the unique fiesta of *Las Fallas de Saint Joseph*, when enormous papier-mache sculptures are set ablaze. Throughout it all are bullfights, music and fireworks. Alicante, the capital of the province of the same name, is dominated by the great Moorish castle of Santa Barbara, which offers marvellous views of the entire city. It also has several beaches in and around the town.

Cuisine of the region

Rice is the dominant ingredient, grown locally in paddy fields; the most famous dish is the *Paella Valenciana*. Soups and stews known locally as *ollas* are popular and seafood is readily available. Tiger nut milk is a soft drink exclusive to this region, usually accompanied by *fartons* (local pastries).

Arnadí: dessert with pumpkin and sweet potato

Arroz al horno: rice, baked with chickpeas

Arroz con costra: meat-based paella topped with baked egg crust

Arroz negro: rice cooked with squid

Bajoques farcides: stuffed peppers

Olla recapte: with potatoes and pork

Turrón: made of nuts and honey, either soft and flaky or hard like nougat

Places of interest

Castellón de la Plana: Santa Maria cathedral

El Puig: monastery, Museum of Print and Graphics (world's smallest book)

La Albufera: vast lagoon, home to 250 species of bird

Morella: medieval fortress town, dinosaur musuem

Oropesa: 16th century Tower of the King

Peñiscola: medieval castle

Alan Rogers tip

JOIN IN THE FUN AT THE TOMATO-THROWING FESTIVAL OF BUÑOL (AUG). THE SPECTACULAR *LA TOMATINA* SEES SOME 30,000 PEOPLE HURL 120,000 TONNES OF TOMATOES AT EACH OTHER!

ES8560 Camping Playa Tropicana

Playa Tropicana, 12579 Alcossebre (Castelló)

Playa Tropicana is the living dream of the owners Vera and Charlie. It has been given a tropical theme with scores of 'Romanesque' white statues around the site including in the sanitary blocks. It has a delightful position away from the main hub of tourism, alongside a good sandy beach which shelves gently into the clean waters. There is a shingle beach for fishing nearby and a pretty promenade in front of the site, with statues. It is in a quiet position and it is a drive rather than a walk to the centre of the village resort. The site has 300 marked pitches separated by lines of flowering bushes under mature trees. The pitches vary in size (50-100 sq.m), most are shaded and there are electricity connections throughout (some need long leads). There are 50 places for motorcaravans with water and drainage and there is a scale of charges for the different pitches. The site has several large water features by the high quality restaurant (some are very cheeky!), aviaries and small monkeys. Visit the restaurant and enjoy the pictures of the owners with famous people.

Facilities

Two sanitary blocks delightfully decorated, fully equipped and of excellent standard, include 16 washbasins in private cabins. Baby baths, some units with WC, basin and shower, and facilities for disabled people. Washing machine. Motorcaravan services. Gas supplies. Large supermarket (all season). Superb restaurant, a little expensive. (Easter - late Sept). Drinks served on terrace. Swimming pool (18 x 11 m.) and children's pool. Playground. Volleyball. Table tennis. Bicycle hire. Fishing. Torches necessary in some areas. No TVs allowed in July/Aug. Dogs are not accepted (but cats are). Off site: Fishing and watersports on the beach. Riding and boat launching 3 km. Golf 25 km.

Open

1 January - 31 December.

At a glance

Welcome & Ambience	✓✓✓✓✓	Location	✓✓✓✓✓
Quality of Pitches	✓✓✓✓✓	Range of Facilities	✓✓✓✓✓

Directions

Alcoceber (or Alcossebre) is between Peniscola and Oropesa. Turn off N340 at 1018 km. marker towards Alcossebre on CV142. Just before entering town proceed through the traffic lights to main road at next junction, turn right and follow coast road to site in 2.5 km.

Charges 2005

Per person	€ 3,00 - € 6,00
child (1-10 yrs)	€ 2,00 - € 5,00
pitch	€ 10,00 - € 43,00

Electricity and VAT included.
Discounts up to 45% out of season.

Reservations

Made for min. 10 days with deposit (25%).
Tel: 964 412 463. E-mail: info@playatropicana.com

ES8558 Camping Vinaros

Ctra N340 km 1054, 12500 Vinaros (Castelló)

Taking its name from the seaside town nearby, this uncomplicated site now has 179 numbered pitches of average size on flat ground. Mature trees provide shade and neat hedges separate the pitches, all of which have an individual sink. The site entrance is directly off the N340, with a spacious drive and lots of outside parking, but there is traffic noise. A pleasant small swimming pool has a sunbathing area and a paddling pool. The restaurant is nicely decorated, has a reasonable menu and serves snacks all year. Large blocks of natural stone have been used for decoration in the site and the theme is continued in the spotless sanitary block. Petanque is played and indoor games are available in the bar. This site is ideal as an all year stopover site and normally has several long stay British customers enjoying the peace and good discounts in low season. Nathalie, the chirpy manager speaks good English and has a keen sense of humour. This area reputedly enjoys 300 days of sunshine a year.

Facilities

Exceptionally clean, fully equipped, toilet block with clever use of marble and tiling creating a light crisp environment enhanced by potted shrubs. Some washbasins are in cabins. Washing machines and irons. Motorcaravan services. Camping essentials sold (tent pegs etc) and milk and bread can be ordered. Bar/restaurant (all year). Play area. Swimming pools (1/4-30/10). Petanque. Musical entertainment in season. Large aviary. Fax machine. Ice for sale. Off site: Beach 800 m. Bus service outside gate. Rail station close by. Vinaros 500 m. with extensive choice of bars and restaurants. Golf 7 km.

At a glance

Welcome & Ambience	✓✓✓✓✓	Location	✓✓✓✓
Quality of Pitches	✓✓✓✓✓	Range of Facilities	✓✓✓✓✓

Directions

Take exit 43 (Ulldecona) from the A7. Switch to the N340 and head towards Barcelona. Site is at 1054 km. marker directly off N340.

Charges 2005

Per unit, all inclusive	€ 13,40

All plus 7% VAT.
Stay over 7 days in low season € 7.20 + 7% VAT.

Reservations

Contact site. Tel: 964 402424.
E-mail: info@campingvinaros.com

Open

All year.

ES8570 Camping Torre La Sal 2

Cami L'Atall, 12595 Ribera de Cabanes (Castelló)

Torre La Sal 2 is a large site split in two by a fairly busy road, with a reception on each side. There are two pool complexes (one can be covered and heated) which are both on the west side, whilst the beach (shingle and sand) is on the east. Both sides have a restaurant (expensive) - the beach restaurant has two air conditioned wooden buildings and a terrace, but no views of the sea. Sports activities are on the western side, as is a children's park and a large disco. The pools and the park are locked for certain periods during the day. The 240 flat pitches vary in size, some very large with their own sinks, and most have either shade from trees or very high artificial shading rigged on frames. All have 10A electricity and are on sand, a few being close to the sea, but none with views. There is a plethora of bungalows, mobile homes, chalets and permanent pitches around the two areas. Many activities are organised in high season and the various amenities are scattered around the two locations - be sure to consult the lists and use your map to find your way around them all.

Facilities

Toilet facilities are of a good standard in both sections, four to the west and two to the east, with facilities for disabled campers in both. Baby rooms. Hot water to some sinks. British style toilets. Washing machines. Motorcaravan services. Shop, bars and restaurants (all year). Swimming pools and paddling pools - one heated and covered. Large play area. Games room. Disco. Football. Tennis. Volleyball. Basketball. Petanque. Fronton. Car wash. Security boxes. Medical room. Torches are required. Off site: Village has a range of shops bars and restaurants. Riding 10 km. Golf 20 km.

At a glance

Welcome & Ambience	✓✓✓	Location	✓✓✓✓
Quality of Pitches	✓✓✓✓	Range of Facilities	✓✓✓✓

Directions

From A7/E15 take exit 45 for Oropesa onto the N340. Move north to 1,000 km. marker and take road to the coast and town of Camil'atall. Site is well signed from here.

Charges 2004

Person	€ 5,10
child (1-9 yrs)	€ 4,60
pitch	€ 7,80
electricity	€ 4,60

Reservations

Write to site. Tel: 964 319 744.
E-mail: camping@torrelasal2.com

Open

All year.

ES8580 Bonterra Park

Avenida de Barcelona 47, 12560 Benicasim (Castelló)

If you are looking for a town site which is not too crowded and has good facilities, this one may be for you, as there are few quality sites in the local area and this is open all year. It is a 300 metre walk to a good, shady beach – and parking is not too difficult. Good beach for scuba diving or snorkelling - hire facilities are available at Benicasim. The site has 375 pitches (70-90 sq.m), all with electricity and a variety of bungalows on site. Bonterra has a clean and neat appearance with reddish soil, palms, grass and a number of trees which give good shade. There is a little road and rail noise. This is a well run, Mediterranean style site useful for visiting local attractions such as the Carmelite monastery at Desierto de las Palmas, six kilometres distant or the historic town of Castellon.

Facilities

Four attractive, well maintained sanitary blocks sensibly laid out, providing some private cabins, washbasins with hot water, others with cold. Showers have solar heating and include baby showers. Facilities for disabled campers. Laundry and motorcaravan services. Restaurant/bar. Shop (all year). Swimming pool, covered pool and children's pool. Playground (some concrete bases). Tennis. Multi-sport court. Table tennis. Disco. Bicycle hire. Off site: Town facilities. Fishing 500 m. Riding 3 km. Boat launching 5 km. Golf 10 km.

Open

All year.

At a glance

Welcome & Ambience	✓✓✓✓✓	Location	✓✓✓✓✓
Quality of Pitches	✓✓✓✓	Range of Facilities	✓✓✓✓

Directions

Site is east of Benicasim village, with entrance off the old main N340 road running a little back from the coast. Coming from the north, turn left at sign 'Benicasim por la costa'. On the A7 from the north use exit 45, from the south exit 46.

Charges 2005

Per adult	€ 3,10 - € 4,10
child (3-9 yrs)	€ 2,60 - € 3,60
pitch acc. to type and season	€ 9,10 - € 24,90
electricity	€ 3,10 - € 5,15

All plus 7% VAT. Less in low season and special long stay rates excl. July/Aug.

Reservations

Made if you write at least a month in advance.
Tel: 964 300 007. E-mail: info@campingbonterra.com

ES8590 Camping Monmar

Ctra Serratelles s/n, 12593 Moncofa (Castelló)

This purpose built, very neat site is situated in the small town of Moncofa, just 400 metres from the sea and right beside a water park with pools and slides. There are 170 gravel based pitches arranged in rows off tarmac, kerb-edged access roads. They all have 6A electricity connections, water and a drain and each pair shares a small, cold water sink. Hedges have been planted to separate the pitches but these are still small so there is little shade (canopies can be rented in high season if required). The site's facilities and amenities are all very modern but small stone reminders of the area's Roman and Arab history are used to decorate corners of the site. The attractive pool on the site remains open all year and in high season there is a shop, bar and restaurant. Shops and other local amenities are within walking distance. There may be some noise from children enjoying themselves at the water park next door. This would be a good base for touring the beautiful inland region from a seaside base.

Facilities

Three modern toilet blocks are well placed and provide good, clean facilities. Free hot showers. Facilities and good access for disabled visitors. Chemical disposal point. Laundry with washing machines, dryer and ironing board. Shop (1/7-31/8). Bar and restaurant (weekends and high season). Swimming pool (all year). Good play area. Boules. Volleyball. Dogs and other pets are not accepted. Off site: Water complex. Local amenities within walking distance. Beach 400 m.

Open

All year.

At a glance

Welcome & Ambience	✓✓✓✓✓	Location	✓✓✓✓
Quality of Pitches	✓✓✓✓✓	Range of Facilities	✓✓✓✓✓

Directions

Turn off the N340 Castellon - Valencia road onto CV2250 signed Moncofa. Follow sign for tourist information office in town and then signs for site. Pass supermarket and turn left to site in 600 m.

Charges 2004

Per unit incl. 2 persons and electricity	€ 22,50
extra person	€ 5,50
child	€ 3,50

VAT included. Discounts in low season and for longer stays.

Reservations

Contact site. Tel: 964 588 592.
E-mail: campingmonmarmoncofa@wanadoo.es

ES8620 Camping L'Alqueria

Mobile homes page 173

46730 Gandia (Valencia)

Recommended by our agent, we plan to conduct a full inspection of this site in 2005. Alqueria is a popular site to the south of Valencia and 1 km from a sandy beach. The 242 pitches are well shaded and most are equipped with electrical connections. This is a lively site in peak season with a varied activity and entertainment programme. Chalets are available for rent.

Facilities

Swimming pool, covered pool, bar, restaurant, takeaway meals, shop, sports field, children's playground, entertainment programme in high season, children's club. Off site: Nearest beach 1 km, golf 8 km, shops, restaurant etc. within 1 km.

Open

All year.

Directions

Leave the A7 at junction 60, joining the N332 (Valencia - Alicante road). At Gandia follow signs to Grao de Gandia. From here the site is well signed.

Charges year

Per person	€ 4,00 - € 7,00
child	€ 2,60 - € 3,60
pitch	€ 3,46 - € 4,27
electricity	€ 3.04

Reservations

Advised for high season; contact site.
Tel: 96 284 04 70. E-mail: info@campinggandia.com

L'ALQUERIA Gandia

A-7, exit 60, than N-332 till Gandia
E-46730 Grao-GANDIA (Valencia)
Tel. (34) 96 284 04 70
Fax (34) 96 284 10 63
www.lalqueria.com

Special fees out of-season • Fully renovated • Holiday Park with excellent installations and free hot water • Organised leisure • Swimming pools and sports • Wooden bungalows for hire • Reservations possible • Small present on presentation of this advert

Open throughout the year

ES8615 Kiko Park Oliva

46780 Oliva (Valencia)

Kiko Park is a smart site nestled behind protective sand dunes, alongside a 'blue flag' beach. There are sets of attractively tiled steps over the dunes or a long boardwalk near the beach bar (good for prams and wheelchairs) to take you to the fine white sandy beach and the sea. There is an award-winning restaurant with architecture that reminds one of a ship near the tropical style beach-bar, both overlooking the marina, beautiful beach and sea. The 200 large pitches all have electricity and the aim is to progressively upgrade all these to serviced 'super' pitches. There are plenty of flowers, hedging and trees adding shade, privacy and colour. This is an excellent site for watersport enthusiasts, as it is beside a marina for boat launching. A variety of entertainment is provided all year. The children's club area has a mini zoo, with healthy looking animals (the 'burro' is popular, as are rabbits and the strange Chinese duck that dances rather than walks). Spanish lessons are held along with dance class and aerobics during the winter. The site is run by the second generation of a family involved in camping for 30 years and their experience shows. They are supported by a friendly, efficient team who speak many languages. The narrow roads leading to the site can be a little challenging for very large units but it is worth the effort.

Facilities

Four modern sanitary blocks are very clean and fully tiled with free hot water, large showers, washbasins (a few in cabins), British style WCs and excellent facilities for disabled visitors (who will find a large part of this site flat and convenient). Laundry facilities. Motorcaravan services. Gas supplies. Restaurant. Bar with TV. Beach-side bar and restaurant (all year). Supermarket (all year, excl. Sundays). Playground. Watersports facilities. Diving school in high season (from mid-June). Mini club. Entertainment for children from mid-June. Petanque. Bicycle hire. Beach volleyball. Exchange facilities. Off site: The yacht club also offers its facilities of swimming pool, bar, restaurant and TV room to campers at Kiko. The footpath to the marina leads into the town - about a 10 minute walk. Indoor pool 1 km. Golf 5 km. Riding 7 km.

At a glance

Welcome & Ambience	✓✓✓✓✓	Location	✓✓✓✓✓
Quality of Pitches	✓✓✓✓	Range of Facilities	✓✓✓✓

Directions

From A7 north of Benidorm take exit 61 to the town and then the beach; site is at the northwest end.

Charges 2005

child (under 10 yrs)	€ 2,20 - € 4,80
pitch acc. to services and season	€ 10,90 - € 29,00
dog	€ 0,60 - € 2,20
electricity (per kw)	€ 0,30

Reservations

Write to site. Tel: 962 850905.
E-mail: kikopark@kikopark.com

Open

All year.

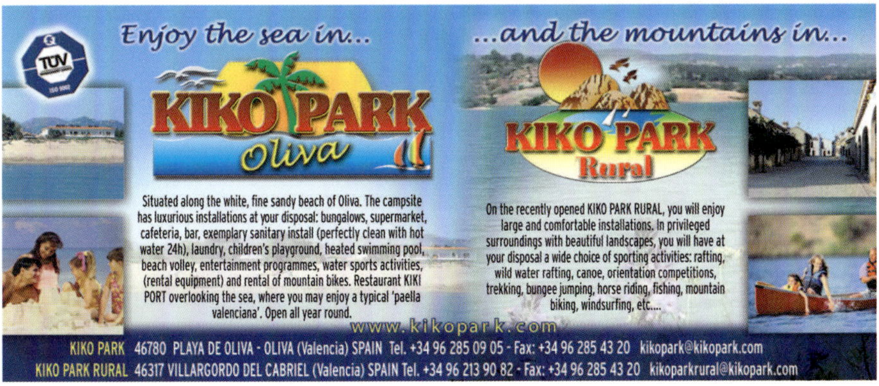

ES8612 Euro Camping

Playa de Oliva, 46780 Oliva (Valencia)

This English owned site is located beside the Playa de Oliva's golden sands. To reach it, you travel through the famous Valencia orange orchards. However be warned the final approach road to the site is very narrow and large units will find it necessary to drive through over-hanging foliage. The rectangular site has tarmac and gravel roads. The gravel pitches are on the small side but are well maintained and eucalyptus trees provide shade for many. The mature sanitary blocks are well maintained, although you will need to take a torch as the lighting is on a push-button timer and inevitably one is plunged into darkness which can be alarming (particularly in the disabled campers bathroom). The reception staff are helpful, speak excellent English and maintain a book swap library. A well stocked supermarket is on site and the restaurant complex looks over the sand dunes leading to the beach. Here you can enjoy food from the excellent menu including some delicious local delicacies and a good selection of regional wines. The bar and terrace area alongside the restaurant is a popular spot early in the evening to enjoy a drink with the sound of the waves in the background. Later in the evening entertainment is provided for adults while the children play happily on the adventure equipment nearby.

Facilities

Two mature sanitary blocks (and a third under construction) are well maintained. British style WCs, preset hot water in showers. Push-button lighting in sanitary blocks. Toilet facilities for disabled campers. Washing machines and dryer. Motorcaravan services. Well stocked supermarket. Restaurant/bar. Play area. Volleyball. Pentanque. Animation in high season. Refrigerator hire. Electronic games. Torches essential inside all sanitary blocks.

At a glance

Welcome & Ambience	✓✓✓✓	Location	✓✓✓
Quality of Pitches	✓✓✓✓	Range of Facilities	✓✓✓

Directions

From Alicante - Valencia autopista A7 take exit 61 onto N332 to Oliva. Exit at km. 213 or 210 and follow campsite signs.

Charges 2005

Per adult	€ 3,90
child (2-10 yrs)	€ 2,70
pitch	€ 15,15 - € 26,60
electricity	€ 3,20

Reservations

Contact site. Tel: 962 854 098.
E-mail: info@eurocamping-es.com

Open

All year.

ES8625 Kiko Park Rural

46317 Villargordo del Cabriel (Valencia)

Approaching Kiko Park Rural, you will see a small hilltop village appearing in a landscape of mountains, vines and a jewel-like lake. Kiko was a small village and farm and the village now forms the campsite and accomodation. Amenities are contained within the architectually authentic buildings, some old and some new. The restaurant serves delicious food that would compete favourably in any Spanish setting. Kiko Rural is run by four cousins from a family with 30 years of camping experience - a passionate and enthusiastic team with a vision of excellence. The 103 pitches (with 6A electricity) all have stunning views. Hundreds of trees planted in 2003 are yet to provide shade due to their size, although this will soon remedy itself. Generous hedge plantings have been made which already afford some privacy. There are swimming pools for adults and children, again with superb views. Kiko Rural is an ideal site for those folk, young and old, who enjoy adventurous activites, communing with nature, or relaxing with an occasional sightseeing excursion. A sister site to Kiko Park in Oliva Valencia (ES8615) Kiko Rural is like no other campsite. Old and new have combined to create an environment that is, within its catergory, outstanding.

Facilities

Three new sanitary blocks are very well equipped, including hot water throughout, preset showers and excellent facilities for disabled people.. Gas supplies. Motorcaravan services. Excellent restaurant. Well stocked shop with reasonable prices. Pleasant bar with TV. Swimming pool and paddling pool. Very good playground. Bicycle hire. Many adventurous activities can be undertaken here, including white water rafting, gorging, orienteering, trekking, bungee and riding. Special programmes organised on application. Large families and groups catered for. Animation for children and adults in high season.
Off site: All the arranged activities. Fishing, boating, canoening and windsurfing on the lake. Boat launching. Village 3 km. with usual facilites. Tours to 'bodegas'. Tours to Valencia.

At a glance

Welcome & Ambience	✓✓✓✓✓	Location	✓✓✓✓✓
Quality of Pitches	✓✓✓✓	Range of Facilities	✓✓✓✓

Directions

From autopista A7/E15 on Valencia ring road (near the airport) take N111 to the west. Villagordo del Cabriel is about 18 km. towards Motilla. Take the village exit and follow the signs which lead through the village and over a hill -; spot the village on a hill just 2 km. away. That village is the campsite!

Charges guide

Per pitch	€ 5,00 - € 10,00
person	€ 3,60
child up to 10 yrs	€ 2,80

Reservations

Contact site. Tel: 962 139 082.
E-mail: kikoparkrural@kikopark.com

Open

All year.

ES8675 Camping Vall de Laguar

C/Sant Antonio 24, La Vall de Laguar, 03791 Campell (Alacant)

Near the pretty mountain-top village of Campell, this new campsite is perched high on the side of a mountain with breathtaking views of hilltop villages, the surrounding hills and distant sea. The pitches, pool, terrace and restaurant all share the views. Enrique and Consuello and their children Nico and Neus efficiently run this charming country site. Consuello cooks the most wonderful food and Nico is a font of information about the local area. A good time to be here is at the end of October when campers join in the festivities in the local village after the 'walk with history' when over a thousand people dine on paella. There are fascinating historic features in the area like the old (now disused) leper colony just a few hundred metres away and the ancient Moorish walk with over 6,500 carved rock steps (from a distance it looks like the Great Wall of China)! The 68 average size gravel pitches are on terraces and all have electricity and water. Trees and hedges have been planted but are yet to reach their potential. This is a great site to get away from the coastal hustle, bustle and high rise of the beaches. The restaurant has a pretty terrace and the pool is served by a small pool bar. There is a tight steep turn at the entrance although there is room to manoeuvre. This is a new site showing great promise for the future.

Facilities

Two new sanitary blocks have excellent clean facilities including some for disabled campers. Washing machines and dryers. Shop. Restaurant. Bar and pool bar. Swimming pool. Small entertainment programme in high season. Barbecue area with sinks. Torches useful. Off site: Attractive town close by. Donkey excursions 1 km. Golf and beach 18 km.

Open

All year.

At a glance

Welcome & Ambience	✓✓✓✓	Location	✓✓✓✓
Quality of Pitches	✓✓✓✓	Range of Facilities	✓✓✓

Directions

Site is about 20 km. west of Xabia/Javea. From A7/E15 take exit 62 and head to Beniarbeig on minor road. From there go to Sanet, Benidoleig and finally Vall de Laguar. Site is well signed from the town and sits above it. There are some winding and narrow sections on the way.

Charges guide

Per unit	€ 8,42 - € 12,02
person	€ 3,61 - € 3,61
child (over 3 yrs)	€ 3,00
electricity	€ 2,00

Minimun charge Easter week and July - August € 19.23

Reservations

Contact site. Tel: 699 773 509. E-mail: info@campinglaguar.com

ES8680 Camping Armanello

Avenida de la Communidad Valenciana, 03500 Benidorm (Alacant)

This small, uncomplicated site is in a slightly scruffy area a kilometre back from the eastern Benidorm beach (the one on the other side of the town is less crowded), Armanello is quietly situated just far enough away from the main coast road to avoid excessive noise. It is a plain and mature site, with small pitches (60 sq.m.) marked out in bays of ten or twelve in former citrus and olive groves. There is a small and much-used swimming pool. About 103 units are taken on flat ground with electricity available throughout (10A). The site is popular with long stay units in winter. The approach road from the main N332 is narrow. The facilities here are rather basic and we see this as a site for transit stops and short stays, rather than as a holiday site, but the rates are very good.

Facilities

Two heated toilet blocks (arranged back to back) have washing and shower facilities with hot and cold water, British style toilets and some washbasins in cabins. Hot water for laundry and dishwashing. Facilities near reception include a washroom, shower and WC for disabled people. Washing machines and dryer. Gas supplies. Motorcaravan services. Well stocked shop (all year). Bar. Restaurant (high season). Swimming pool. Aviary. Off site: Fishing, bicycle hire or riding within 1.5 km. Golf 10 km.

Open

All year.

At a glance

Welcome & Ambience	✓✓✓	Location	✓✓✓
Quality of Pitches	✓✓	Range of Facilities	✓✓✓

Directions

From new bypass (N332) take Levante Beach road into Benidorm; watch for site signs after 1 km. directly off this road. From autopista junction 65 take Benidorm exit and at second traffic lights turn left. Site approach road is 1 km. on right. As you leave the site turn right not left for the main road as the road becomes impossibly rough and narrow.

Charges 2004

Per unit incl. 2 persons	€ 22,00
electricity	€ 3,00

Plus 7% VAT. Reductions in low season, plus special winter prices.

Reservations

Contact site for details (it also has much winter trade when reservation is advisable). Tel: 965 853 190. E-mail: arenablanca@ctv.es

www.alanrogers.com for latest campsite news

ES8681 Camping Villasol

Avda. Bernat de Sarria, 03500 Benidorm (Alacant)

Benidorm is increasingly popular for winter stays and Villasol is a genuinely excellent, purpose built modern site. There is a small indoor pool, heated for winter use, and a very attractive, large outdoor pool complex (summer only) featuring a lovely, sheltered free-form pool in a beautifully landscaped, grassy sunbathing area where palm trees and Mediterranean shrubs and flowers create a colourful and exotic atmosphere. The pool is overlooked by the bar/restaurant and restaurant terrace. Many of the 309 well separated pitches are arranged on wide terraces which afford views of the mountains surrounding Benidorm. All pitches (80-85 sq.m.) have electricity and satellite TV connections, with 160 with full services for seasonal use. Shade is mainly artificial as yet. The town and Levante beach are 1.3 km. within easy walking distance leaving your car on site. If you are looking for first class amenities in Benidorm, in pleasant and fairly quiet surroundings, this site would make an excellent choice. Reservation is advised even in winter. We hear that part of the site will be lost to a road widening scheme.

Facilities

Modern, well fitted sanitary blocks provide free, controllable hot water to showers and washbasins and British WCs. Good facilities for disabled campers. Laundry facilities. Good value restaurant. Bar. Shop. Swimming pools, outdoor and indoor. Playground. Evening entertainment programme. Dogs are not accepted. Off site: Fishing and bicycle hire 1.3 km. Golf 8 km.

Open

All year.

At a glance

Welcome & Ambience	✓✓✓✓	Location	✓✓✓✓
Quality of Pitches	✓✓✓✓	Range of Facilities	✓✓✓✓✓

Directions

From autopista take Benidorm exit (no. 65) and turn left at second set of traffic lights. After 1 km. at another set of lights turn right, then right again at next lights. Site is on right in 400 m. From northern end of N332 bypass follow signs for Benidorm Playa Levante. In 500 m. at traffic lights turn left, then right at next lights. Site is on right after 400 m.

Charges 2004

Per person	€ 4,65 - € 6,10
child (1-9 yrs)	€ 3,60 - € 4,50
pitch incl. car	€ 9,50 - € 16,50
electricity	€ 3,60

All plus 7% VAT. Good discounts for longer stays in winter.

Reservations

Only accepted for 3 month min. stay, starting 1 Oct. Write to site. Tel: 965 850 422.
E-mail: camping-villasol@dragonet.es

ES8682 Camping Villamar

Carre Del Albir, 03503 Benidorm (Alacant)

A new all year site with all the amenities a camper could desire, Villamar is a superb site, operating to high standards and rules. The central Lake style pools and amenities complex with its extensive grassed areas, dotted with palms, is cleverly designed and very smart. Sit on the terraces looking over the tropical scenery as you enjoy an English breakfast or dinner later in the day, and you will find it difficult to remember the teeming town of Benidorm is close by. The 650 pitches are occupied by a myriad of foreign guests and we are told the owners hoped to create a small camping area. The pitches are very big, flat, with some shade from young trees. The entertainment programme and indeed the whole site is aimed at a mature population though there are few things for children to do (at present there is no children's play area, although one is planned for the future). The sports area has many courts for boules and other sedate activities such as darts, centred in the restaurant area. The restaurant is attractively decorated and has lounges and terraces for relaxation along with internet terminals and electronic games. All round this is a great site. There are no tour operator pitches.

Facilities

The four new sanitary blocks include open style washbasins (some partitioned), free controllable hot showers, baby areas and units for disabled campers. Dishwashing and separate laundry sinks outside each block. Well stocked shop with reasonable prices. Restaurant. Snack bar. Motorcaravan services. Car wash. Two outdoor swimming pools (one heated for the winter guests), one indoor pool (lifeguards in high season). Small play area. TV room, games room and leisure area. Boules. ATM. Internet point. Entertainment in the restaurant area. Dogs are not accepted. Off site: Resort town and beach close with usual attractions. Golf, riding, bicycle hire and boat launching 2 km. Excursions.

At a glance

Welcome & Ambience	✓✓✓✓✓	Location	✓✓✓✓
Quality of Pitches	✓✓✓✓✓	Range of Facilities	✓✓✓✓

Directions

Site is northeast of Benidorm at Platja de L'abril. From the A7, A19 or N11 take the exit for Benidorm (Platja de L'Abril). Once at the end of the exit road from the autoroute look for the very obvious camping signs.

Charges guide

Per person	€ 4,50 - € 6,90
child ((1-3 yrs)	€ 3,50 - € 4,30
pitch	€ 9,20 - € 16,00
electricity	€ 3,50

Reservations

Contact site. Tel: 96 681 1255.
E-mail: camping@campingvillamar.com

Open

All year.

ES8683 Camping Benisol

Avda. de la Comunidad Valenciana s/n, 03500 Benidorm (Alacant)

Camping Benisol is a well developed and peaceful site with lush, green vegetation and a mountain background. Mature hedges and trees afford privacy to each pitch and some artficial shade is provided where necessary. There is an excellent restaurant serving traditional spanish food at great prices, with a pretty, shaded terrace overlooking the pool with its palms and thatched pool bar. There are 298 pitches of which around 115 are for touring units (60-80 sq.m). All have electrical hook-ups (4/6A) and 75 have drainage. All the connecting roads are now surfaced with tarmac and the large internationally themed minigolf area is very popular with children. Amenities include a good-sized, pleasant swimming pool which is open late (22.00 in summer), with tall palms, a tropical ambience, cascades and small water slides. The pool has a pleasant sunbathing area. Some day-time road noise should be expected.

Facilities

Modern sanitary facilities with free hot water in the showers, heated in winter and kept very clean, have free, solar heated hot water to the washbasins, showers and sinks for laundry and dishwashing. Laundry facilities and clothes lines. Car wash. Gas supplies. Restaurant with terrace and bar (all year, closed 1 day a week). Shop. Swimming pool (Easter - Nov). Sports ground. Small, old-style play area. Minigolf. Table tennis. Jogging track. Tennis. Golf driving range. Doctor's room. ATM. Car wash. Off site: Riding 1 km. Bicycle hire 3 km. Fishing (sea) 3 km. Golf 14 km. Bus route.

At a glance

Welcome & Ambience	✓✓✓✓	Location	✓✓✓✓
Quality of Pitches	✓✓✓✓	Range of Facilities	✓✓✓✓

Directions

Site is northeast of Benidorm. Exit N332 at 152 km. marker and take turn signed Playa Levant. Site is 100 m. on left off the main road, well signed.

Charges guide

Per pitch	€ 11,45 - € 15,65
person	€ 4,20 - € 4,50
child (1-10 yrs)	€ 3,60 - € 3,90
electricity	€ 2,40

All plus 7% VAT. Less 15-60% in low seasons. No credit cards.

Reservations

Contact site. Tel: 965 851 673.
E-mail: campingbenisol@yahoo.es

Open

All year.

ES8685 Camping Caravaning El Raco

Avda. Doctor Severo Ochoa, s/n, 03500 Benidorm (Alacant)

This purpose built site (opened in '96) with excellent facilities and very competitive prices provides about 1,000 pitches (180 for touring units). There is wide access from the Rincon de Loix road. The site is quietly situated 1.5 km. from the town, Levante beach and promenade. The road has both footpaths and a cycle track. There are wide tarmac roads and pitches of 80 sq.m. or more, separated by low, clipped cypress hedging and some trees which provide some shade. Free satellite TV connections are provided to each pitch and there are 94 with all services with (10A) electricity available. The whole site is on a slight downward slope away from the entrance and affords excellent views of the rugged mountains in the hinterland, although this open aspect could be a disadvantage in windy weather. The good value restaurant, bar and elegant outdoor and indoor pools are all at the entrance, some distance from the touring pitches. There are large numbers of permanent pitches and many seasonal pitches are occupied by wintering campers (lots of British) and the site has a mature, cheerful atmosphere. This is a popular, clean and tidy site of good quality.

Facilities

Four large toilet blocks are well equipped. Facilities for disabled people. Dishwashing sinks. Laundry facilities. Gas supplies. Motorcaravan services. Restaurant. Bar. Well stocked shop with reasonable prices. Busy bar with TV also open to public and good value restaurant. Outdoor swimming pool, no slides or diving board (1/4-31/10). Indoor heated pool (1/11-31/3). Playground. ATM. Off site: Beach 1 km. Bicycle hire 2 km. Golf 6 km. Theme parks.

Open

All year.

At a glance

Welcome & Ambience	✓✓✓✓	Location	✓✓✓✓
Quality of Pitches	✓✓✓✓	Range of Facilities	✓✓✓✓✓

Directions

From autopista take Benidorm (Levante) exit 65 and at second set of traffic lights turn left on N332 (main route to Altea and Valencia). After 1.5 km. turn right at lights (signed Levante Playa), then straight on at next lights for 300 m. to site on right. From north on N332 follow signs for Playa Levante (or Benidorm Palace). At traffic lights turn left (Playa Levante), straight on at next lights to site on right in 300 m.

Charges 2004

Per person	€ 4,80 - € 5,00
child (1-9 yrs)	€ 3,50 - € 3,70
tent	€ 5,50 - € 5,80
caravan	€ 6,50 - € 7,00
car	€ 5,50 - € 5,80
motorcaravan	€ 10,00 - € 11,00

Discounts for longer stays.
VAT included. No credit cards.

Reservations

Not accepted. Tel: 96 586 8552.
E-mail: campingraco@inicia.es

www.alanrogers.com for latest campsite news

ES8755 Camping Caravanning Moraira

Camino Paellero 50, 03724 Moraira-Teulada (Alacant)

This small hillside site with some views over the town and marina is quietly situated in an urban area amongst old pine trees and just 400 metres from a sheltered bay. Terracing provides shaded pitches of varying size (access to some of the upper pitches may be difficult for larger units). A few pitches have water and waste water facilities and a few have sea and marina views. There are electricity connections (6/10A). A large, painted water tower stands at the top of the site. An attractive irregular shaped swimming pool with paved sunbathing terrace is below the small bar/restaurant with terrace. The pool has observation windows where you can watch the swimmers, and is used for sub-aqua instruction. The site runs a professional diving school for all levels (the diving here is good and the water warm, even in winter). A sandy beach is 1.5 km. There are plans to extend the reception building to provide a range of new facilities.

Facilities

The high quality toilet block, with polished granite floors and marble fittings, is built to a unique and ultra-modern design with extra large free hot showers. Washing machine and dryer in separate room. Motorcaravan services. Bar/restaurant and shop (1/7-30/9). Small swimming pool (all year). Sub-aqua with site boat and instruction. Tennis. Electronic games. Comprehensive security system. Torches may be required. Off site: Shops, bars and restaurants within walking distance. Beach 1.5 km. Fishing 400 m. Bicycle hire 1 km. Golf 8 km.

Open

All year.

At a glance

Welcome & Ambience	✓✓✓	Location	✓✓✓
Quality of Pitches	✓✓✓	Range of Facilities	✓✓✓

Directions

Site is best approached from Teulada. From A7 take exit 63 onto N332. In 3.5 km. turn right signed Teulada and Moraira. In Teulada fork right to Moraira. At junction at town entrance turn right signed Calpe and in 1 km. turn right into road to site on bend immediately after Res. Don Julio. Do not take the first right as the signs seem to indicate otherwise you will go round a loop.

Charges 2004

Per person	€ 4,50
child (4-9 yrs)	€ 3,50
pitch incl. car	€ 10,00 - € 12,00
electricity	€ 3,00

All plus 7% VAT. Less 15-60% in low seasons.

Reservations

Write to site for details. Tel: 965 745 249.
E-mail: campingmoraira@campingmoraira.com

ES8754 Camping Jávea

Ctra Cabo de la Nao, km 1, 03730 Jávea (Alacant)

The 200 metre access road to this site is a little unkempt as it passes some factories, but all changes on the final approach with palms, orange and pine trees, the latter playing host to a colony of parakeets. English is spoken at reception. The boxed hedges and palms surrounding this area with a backdrop of hills dotted with villas presents an attractive setting. Three hectares provides space for 246 numbered pitches with 146 for touring units. Flat, level and rectangular in shape, the pitches vary in size 60-80 sq.m. (not advised for caravans or motorhomes with an overall length exceeding 7 m). All have a granite chip surface and 8A electricity. Being a typical Spanish site, the pitches are not separated so units may be close to each other. Some pitches have artificial shade, although for most the pruned eucalyptus and pepper trees will suffice. The area has a large number of British residents so a degree of English is spoken by many shopkeepers and many restaurants provide multi language menus. Besides being popular for a summer holiday, Camping Javea is now open all year and could be of interest to those that wish to 'winter' in an excellent climate. Discounts can make an extended stay extremely viable.

Facilities

Two very clean, fully equipped, sanitary blocks include two children's toilets plus a baby bath, dishwashing and laundry sinks. Two washing machines. Fridge hire. Small bar and restaurant where in high season you purchase bread and milk. Large swimming pool and paddling pool with lifeguard and sunbathing lawns. Play area. Table tennis. Boules. Five-a-side football. Basketball. Electronic barriers (deposit for swipe card). Caravan storage. Off site: Sandy beach 3 km. Old and New Javea within easy walking distance with supermarkets and shops catering for all needs.

Open

All year.

At a glance

Welcome & Ambience	✓✓✓	Location	✓✓✓
Quality of Pitches	✓✓✓	Range of Facilities	✓✓✓

Directions

Exit N332 for Javea on A134, continue in direction of Port (road number changes to CV 734). On reaching roundabout and Lidl supermarket turn right signed Arenal Platges and Cabo de la Nao (also camping sign). Straight on at next roundabout to camping sign and slip road in 100 m. If you miss slip road go back from next roundabout.

Charges 2004

Per adult	€ 3,82 - € 4,50
child	€ 3,61 - € 4,25
pitch	€ 9,86 - € 15,45
electricity	€ 3,00
dog	€ 1,50 - € 2,00

Reservations

Necessary for high season. Tel: 965 791 070.
E-mail: info@campingjavea.com

ES8687 Camping Cap Blanch

Playa de Cap Blanch 25, 03590 Altea (Alacant)

This well run site, in a coastal location, is open all year and very popular for winter stays. It is alongside the beach road and has direct access to the pebble beach and is within a few hundred yards of all Albir's shops and restaurants. Campers can join in a host of activities organised by the site, from physical ones such as tennis and walking to gentler ones such as painting or lessons in Spanish in the pleasant classroom. The site tends to be full in winter and is very popular with several nationalities, especially the Dutch. For winter stays, it would pay to get there before Christmas as January and February are the peak months. Although it is on the coast, the site is well sheltered and something of a sun-trap, the 250 pitches on flat, hard gravel are of a good size and well maintained with 5A electricity. There is much to see in the Levant (this area takes its name from the Spanish word 'lavantarse' which means get up - as in sun!) and a visit to the mountains is recommended to sample traditional foods and the wonderful Jumilla and Yecla wines.

Facilities

The refurbished sanitary block can be heated and provides good facilities including some washbasins in cabins, baby facilities, a new shower room for children and a room for disabled visitors (both these accessed by key). Motorcaravan services. Gas supplies. Laundry. Bar and restaurant. Takeaway. Playground. Tennis. Boules. Fitness centre. Organised entertainment and courses. ATM.
Off site: Restaurants, shops and commercial centre close. Golf 0.5 km. Bicycle hire 1 km. Riding 5 km.

Open

All year.

At a glance

Welcome & Ambience	✓✓✓✓✓	Location	✓✓✓✓✓
Quality of Pitches	✓✓✓	Range of Facilities	✓✓✓✓

Directions

Site is on Albir - Altea coast road and can be reached from either end. From N332, north or south, watch for sign Playa del Albir and proceed through Albir until you reach the coast road. Site is on north side of Albir, well signed.

Charges 2004

Per person	€ 5,50
child (3-12 yrs)	€ 4,50
pitch incl. car	€ 8,50 - € 12,00
electricity	€ 5,50

VAT included. Less 10-35% for low season stays 7-30 days, special rates for long stays.

Reservations

Contact site. Tel: 965 845 946.
E-mail: capblanch@ctv.es

ES8686 Excalibur Medieval Camping

Camino Viejo del Albir s/n, 03580 Alfaz del Pi (Alacant)

This is a site you could either love or loathe. Unlike other campsites, it has a theme of medieval times. An American theme park approach has been attempted here and we saw lots of families enjoying themselves. However, we also saw that there was a constant struggle to keep up with the high maintenance demands a site with as many guests as this has. There are 386 level pitches with bitumen access roads and gravel surfaces and some shade; 128 of these are for tourers. There are also 150 chalets to rent. The large pseudo-medieval dining room has a self-service menu, as has the breakfast room. Meals can be included in the daily rate here and many visitors take an inclusive package. At peak times amenities appear to be stressed. However, some campers may find the circus-like chaos, the medieval dinner and show with its knights in shining armour on horseback, the giant Excalibur looming above the pool area with its large playground, sauna, gym and underground indoor pool, enough compensation. This is a site where close attention needs to be paid to children's welfare as the unfenced pools and giant play areas are side by side - there are slippery areas and steps without rails all in the same area.

Facilities

Four matching sanitary blocks are showing signs of heavy usage and the breakages within are extensive; this extends to the facilities for disabled campers. Washing machines. Motorcaravan services. Large multiple pool complex with jacuzzis. Sauna. Roman style indoor pool below main pool complex. Snack bar. Self service restaurants. Basic shop with souvenirs. Football. Boules. Basketball. Huge outdoor play areas. Inside play area with American style games (everything is free). Table tennis. Electronic games. Bicycle hire for children. ATM. Internet terminal. Security boxes. Torches useful. Off site: Resort town and beach near with usual attractions. Riding 100 m. Bicycle hire 1 km. Fishing 3 km. Golf 20 km. Excursions.

At a glance

Welcome & Ambience	✓✓✓	Location	✓✓✓
Quality of Pitches	✓✓✓✓	Range of Facilities	✓✓✓

Directions

Site is northwest of Benidorm in Playa de L'Albir. From A7/E15 or N332 roads from the north leave at first exit for Benidorm. At end of the exit road there are numerous signs for Excalibur.

Charges 2004

Per person	€ 4,65 - € 6,10
child (1-9 yrs)	€ 3,60 - € 4,50
pitch	€ 9,50 - € 17,00
electricity	€ 3,13

Reservations

Contact site. Tel: 966 866 928.
E-mail: c-m@camping.medieval.com

Open

All year.

www.alanrogers.com for latest campsite news

ES8742 Camping Internacional La Marina

Ctra N332 km 76, 03194 La Marina (Alacant)

Efficiently run by a friendly Belgian family, La Marina has 370 pitches of seven different types and size of pitch ranging from about 50 sq.m. for tents to 100 sq.m. with electricity (10A), TV, water and drainage. Artificial shade is provided and the pitches are extremely well maintained on level, well drained ground with a special area allocated for tents in a small orchard. The Lagoon swimming pool complex is absolutely fabulous and has something for everyone (with lifeguards). The quality restaurant and bustling terraces overlook the Lagoon making for a most relaxing meal. A fine fitness centre and covered, heated pool (14 x 7 m) are close by. A pedestrian gate is at the rear of the site to give access to the long sandy beach through the coastal pine forest that is a feature of the area. You can be assured of quality at La Marina and we recommend it very highly whatever type of holiday camper you may be.

Facilities

The elegant sanitary blocks offer the very best of modern facilities. Heated in winter, they include private cabins and facilities for disabled visitors. These facilities are amongst the best we have seen on the Mediterranean coast. Laundry facilities incl. irons. Modern motorcaravan services. Gas supplies. Supermarket. Bar/restaurant serving traditional Spanish dishes (all year). Swimming pools (1/4-15/10). Indoor pool. Fitness centre with massage. Sauna. Extensive activity and entertainment programme. New sports area. Tennis. Table tennis. Huge playground. Hairdresser. Good security. Off site: Fishing 800 m. Boat launching 5 km. Golf 7 km. Bicycle hire 8 km. Riding 15 km. Hourly bus service from outside the gate if you wish to explore Alicante or Murcia. Theme parks.

Open

All year.

At a glance

Welcome & Ambience	✓✓✓✓✓	Location	✓✓✓✓✓
Quality of Pitches	✓✓✓✓✓	Range of Facilities	✓✓✓✓✓

Directions

Site is 2 km. west of La Marina. Leave N332 Guardamara de Segura - Santa Pola road at the 75 km. marker if travelling north, or the 78 km. marker if travelling south. Site is well signed.

Charges 2005

Per person	€ 5,00 - € 7,20
child (under 10 yrs)	€ 3,50 - € 4,80
pitch acc. to type and season	€ 16,00 - € 37,20
electricity	€ 2,40 - € 3,00
dog	€ 1,00 - € 2,00

Plus 7% VAT. Seven grades of pitch. Less in low season, plus good discounts for longer stays 16/9-14/6, excluding Easter.

Reservations

Made with deposit (€ 50), min. 5 days Easter and Aug. Tel: 965 419 200. E-mail: info@campinglamarina.com

ES8689 Camping Playa del Torres

Partida Torres Norte 11, Apdo. Correus 243, 03570 Villajoyosa (Alacant)

Jacinto and Mercedes have a pretty beachside site with the lower part set under eucalyptus trees. Reception is placed in one of the site's tasteful wooden buildings close to the beach (excellent English is spoken). The 85 lower pitches, some large, are on flat ground with shade. 10 good pitches are right alongside the beach fence (book early). All have electricity (16A), some are fully serviced and there are ample water fountains around the site along with efficient, modern lighting. The upper levels of the site have chalets and mobile homes. A modest sized pool with a sunbathing area is set in the centre part of the site between the building housing the bar, cafeteria and shop and the separate clean sanitary block (a short walk from the beachside pitches). Boats can be launched from the sand and shingle beach, sub-aqua diving and other watersports can be organised. Benidorm with its beaches is close, along with many tourist activities including the Fuentes del Algar waterfall and the huge exiting new 'Terra Mittica' theme park. If you prefer small sites away from the 'high rise' and bustle of Benidorm which is of high quality this could be for you.

Facilities

The sanitary building is of a high specification, as are the fittings within, including excellent showers. Laundry. Bar. Cafeteria. Shop. Swimming pool. Children's play area. Petanque. Fishing. Barbecues. Freezer. Fridge hire. Reception will assist with all tourist activities. Off site: Riding 100 m. Golf 18 km. Serious or recreational walking and climbing is possible about 20 minutes away from the site. Benidorm is very close.

Open

All year.

At a glance

Welcome & Ambience	✓✓✓✓✓	Location	✓✓✓✓✓
Quality of Pitches	✓✓✓✓✓	Range of Facilities	✓✓✓

Directions

From Villajoyosa on N332, 1 km. after town, 300 m. past traffic lights, sign on right, follow road 800 m. to site. From Benidorm after 3 km. site on left, but left turn prohibited. Proceed 400 m. to traffic lights, circle onto other carriageway, then as above. From autoroute leave at Benidorm or Villajoyosa on N332, then as above. Do not confuse with two older sites (Hercules and Sartorium), adjacent beach sites.

Charges guide

Per person	€ 3,44 - € 3,82
child (4-13 yrs)	€ 2,57 - € 2,85
pitch	€ 3,22 - € 7,15
caravan	€ 3,57 - € 3,97
tent	€ 3,44 - € 3,82
car	€ 3,44 - € 3,83

Plus 7% VAT. Less 5-50% for low season stays of 7 days or more.

Reservations

Contact site. Tel: 966 810 031. E-mail: capto@ctv.es

Do as the sun does, spend your holidays at...
Welcome
RECOMENDED BY THE BEST EUROPEAN GUIDES
VACANCE-PARK
Camping Internacional
La Marina
CARAVANING - BUNGALOW PARK
1ª CATEGORIA
www.campinglamarina.com
Located at the Elche coastline, in the middle of nature, close to a beautiful beach of fine sand, distinguished with the ECC blue flag for optimal water quality. We offer luxurious installations: 3.000 m² thematic swimming complex, heated swimming-pool, fitness center, very high quality sanitary, entertainment to the highest level for children, young and adults. All free of charge for our clients. Prices in accordance with season and duration of the stays. Open all year.
TNESS CENTER
d New Sport Complex
The Leading Camping & Caravaning Parks of Europe
CERTIFIED IQNet MANAGEMENT SYSTEM
AENOR
ER
Empresa Registrada
ER-1694/2001
CERTIFIED IN ISO 9001
CALIDAD TURISTICA
CV COMUNITAT VALENCIANA
Costa Blanca
www.costablanca.org
Information and reservations
Ctra. N-332a Km.76 - E-03194 LA MARINA (Alicante) SPAIN
Telf.: (34) 96 541 92 00 - Fax: (34) 96 541 91 10
info@campinglamarina.com

ES8743 Complejo Ecoturistico Marjal

Ctra N-332, km 73.4, 03140 Guardamar del Segura (Alacant)

MarJal is located beside the estuary of the Segura river, alongside the pine and eucalyptus forests of the Dunas de Guardamar natural park. It is a new site with a huge lagoon-style pool and a superb sports complex. Reception is housed within a delicately coloured building complete with a towering Mirador, topped by a weather-vane depicting the 'Garza Real' (heron) bird which frequents the local area and forms part of the site logo. There are 212 pitches on this award winning site, all with water, electricity, drainage and satellite TV points, the ground covered with crushed marble, making the pitches clean and pleasant. There is some shade and the site has an open feel with lots of room for manoeuvring. The large leased restaurant overlooks the pools and the river that leads to the sea in the near distance. This situation is shared with the taperia (high season) and bar with large terraces fringed by trees, palms and pomegranates. The impressive pool/lagoon complex (1,100 sq.m) has a water cascade, an island bar plus bridge, one part sectioned as a pool for children and a jacuzzi. The extensive sports area is also impressive with qualified instructors who will customise your fitness programme whilst consulting the doctor. No effort has been spared here, the quality heated indoor pool, light-exercise room, sauna, solarium, beauty salon, fully equipped gym and changing rooms, including facilities for disabled visitors, are of the highest quality. Aerobics and physiotherapy are also on offer. All activities are discounted for campers. A programme of entertainment is provided for adults and children in season by a professional animation team. The fine sandy beach can be reached through the forest (800 m).

Facilities

Three excellent heated toilet blocks have free hot water, elegant separators between sinks, spacious showers and some cabins. Each block has high quality facilities for babies and disabled campers, modern laundry rooms with washing machines, dryers, ironing boards and dishwashing rooms. Car wash. Well stocked supermarket. Restaurants. Bar. Large outdoor pool complex (1/6-31/10). Heated indoor pool (low season). Fitness suite and gym. Jacuzzi. Sauna. Solarium. Aerobics and aquarobics for the more mature camper. Play room for children. Minigolf. Floodlit tennis and soccer pitch. Volleyball. Bicycle hire. Games room. TV room. ATM. Business centre. Internet access.
Off site: Beach 800 m. Riding or golf 4 km.

At a glance

Welcome & Ambience	✓✓✓✓✓	Location	✓✓✓✓
Quality of Pitches	✓✓✓✓✓	Range of Facilities	✓✓✓✓✓

Directions

On N332 40 km. south of Alicante, site is on the sea side between 73 and 74 km. markers.

Charges 2004

Per person	€ 4,00 - € 6,00
child	€ 2,50 - € 4,00
pitch	€ 16,00 - € 28,00
dog	€ 2,00 - € 3,00
electricity (per kw, monitored by computer)	€ 0,25

All plus 7% VAT.

Reservations

Contact site. Tel: 966 725 022.
E-mail: camping@marjal.com

Open

All year.

ES8741 Camping Florantilles

03193 San Miguel de Salinas (Alacant)

Florantilles is an unassuming site, some four kilometres behind the coast, with some views over the top of the neighbouring citrus groves to a distant salt lake. It is open all year and in winter and spring the delicious scent of orange blossom fills the air. Mimosa trees provide shade for the 271 good-sized pitches (around 90 sq.m.) which are laid out on wide terraces; some very large pitches are available at extra cost. Electricity connections (10A) are provided for each pitch, together with water and a raised drain. There are many long stay customers including lots of British. The entrance has a large parking area with car wash facilities, with the entrance to the camping area fitted with a barrier. Amenities include a good sized pool and a children's pool. There is a restaurant with a standard tourist menu. Some light entertainment may be organized in season. Many watersports are possible in the nearby noisy beach resort of Torrevieja and walking clubs are popular, also bird watching, cycling and golf (discounts available). There is noise from the new motorway on the north side of the site. We see this as a transit site or for short visits to explore the area, rather than for family holidays.

Facilities

Two main toilet blocks provide controllable hot showers. Several smaller blocks dotted around the site have toilets and showers but no hot water. All of these facilities were showing signs of wear and tear. Laundry facilities. Bar (all year). Restaurant (summer only). Shop (limited hours in low seasons). Swimming pool (supervised in peak season, closed in winter). Tennis. Boules. Children's playground. Only 20 dogs are accepted on the site so a call is advised to ascertain acceptability. Torches required in some areas.
Off site: Golf 4 km. Fishing, bicycle hire 5 km. Major resort entertainment in Torrevieja.

Open

All year

At a glance

Welcome & Ambience	✓✓✓	Location	✓✓✓✓
Quality of Pitches	✓✓✓✓	Range of Facilities	✓✓✓✓

Directions

Leave A7 Valencia - Alicante autopista at Crevillente exit 724 on to recently upgraded and renumbered A37 Alicante - Cartegena autopista. The exit for the camping is immediately after the first toll, exit 758 for Torrevieja (Sur). A the roundabout turn right (site is now signed), at 300 m. turn first right. Site is on left.

Charges guide

Per unit	€ 9,02
adult	€ 3,61
child (1-12 yrs)	€ 3,01
electricity	€ 2,70

All plus 7% VAT. Special low season discounts.

Reservations

Contact site. Tel: 965 720 458.

www.alanrogers.com for latest campsite news

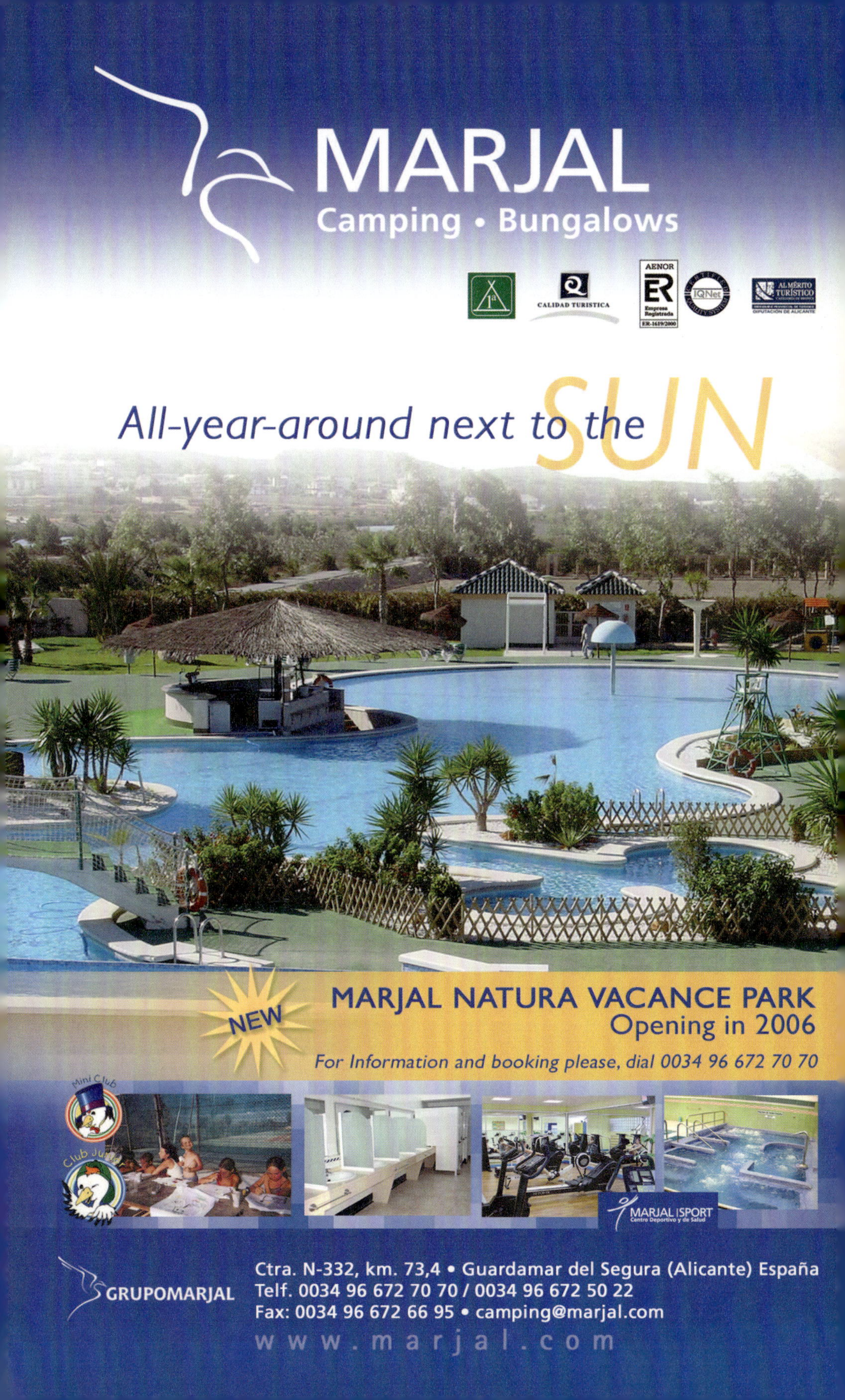
MARJAL
Camping • Bungalows
CALIDAD TURISTICA
AENOR
ER
Empresa Registrada
ER-1619/2000
IQNet
AL MÉRITO TURÍSTICO
All-year-around next to the SUN
NEW
MARJAL NATURA VACANCE PARK
Opening in 2006
For Information and booking please, dial 0034 96 672 70 70
Mini Club
MARJAL SPORT
GRUPOMARJAL
Ctra. N-332, km. 73,4 • Guardamar del Segura (Alicante) España
Telf. 0034 96 672 70 70 / 0034 96 672 50 22
Fax: 0034 96 672 66 95 • camping@marjal.com
www.marjal.com

In the province of Murcia you'll find sandy beaches, dunes and unspoilt coves along the coast; inland hills and valleys plus the regional parks of Sierra de Carche, Sierra de la Pila, Sierra de Espuña, and Carrascoy and El Valle.

The capital of the region is Murcia

Murcia, the capital of the region, was founded in the ninth century by the Moors on the banks of the Río Segura. The square of Cardinal Belluga houses two of the town's architectural gems, the Episcopal Palace and the Cathedral, and there are a range of museums and exhibitions to visit. With narrow medieval streets, the characterful town of Cartagena has lots of bars and restaurants plus two nautical museums: the National Museum of Maritime Archaeology and the Naval Museum. Also on a nautical theme, the International Nautical Week is celebrated here in June. Along the coast there are numerous beaches offering a wide range of water sports: sailing, windsurfing, canoeing, water skiing and diving. And the area between the coastal towns of Águilas and Mazarrón is a breeding ground for tortoises and eagles.

Inland are the historic towns of Lorca and Caravaca de le Cruz. The former is known as the 'baroque city' with its examples of baroque architecture, seen in the parish churches, convents, and houses; the latter too is home to beautiful churches, including El Santuario de Vera Cruz.

Cuisine of the region

Vegetables are important and found in nearly every dish. Fish is also popular, cooked in a salt crust or *a la espalda* (lightly fried and baked), and usually accompanied by rice. Fig bread is a speciality of the region.

Bizcochos borrachos: sponge soaked in wine and syrup

Cabello de Ángel: pumpkin strands in syrup

Caldero: made of rice, fish and the hot ñora pepper

Caldo con pelotas: stew made of turkey with meatballs

Chuletas de cordero al ajo cabañil: suckling lamb chops served with a dressing of garlic and vinegar

Tocino de cielo: dessert made with egg yolks and syrupYemas de Caravaca: cake made with egg yolks

Places of interest

Águilas: seaside town with good beaches

Moratalla: pretty village, castle offering stunning views of the surrounding countryside and forests

Puerto de Mazarrón: Enchanted City of Bolnuevo - a small area of eroded rocks, nature reserve and lagoon at La Rambla de Moreras

San Pedro del Pinatar: seaside resort, La Pagan beach is renowned for its therapeutic mud, which reputedly relieves rheumatism and is good for the skin

Santiago de la Ribera: upmarket resort with sailing club

Alan Rogers tip

MANY PLACES OF INLAND MURCIA ARE NOT EASILY ACCESSIBLE BY PUBLIC TRANSPORT; A CAR IS THE MOST CONVENIENT WAY TO VISIT THE AREA.

ES8748 Camping Los Madriles

Ctra de la Azohia, km 4.5, 30868 Isla Plana (Murcia)

An extraordinary site with super facilities, Los Madriles is run by a hard working team, with constant improvments being made. Twenty kilometres west of Cartegena, the approach to the site and the surrounding area is fairly unremarkable, but the site is not. It provides huge rectangular and lagoon style pools with water sprays and jacuzzis which are fed by thermal waters used by the ancient Romans. Unbelievably the pools are emptied every night after they close at 10 pm. and are refilled by morning with fresh water, thus doing away for the need for chlorination. A fairly steep access road leads to the 311 flat, good to large size terraced pitches. Some have shade from large trees, with others in the newer area having less shade but panoramic views of the sea and behind to the mountains (ideal for winter visits). Private cabins are available. Simple snacks and prepackaged meals are served in the bar and attractive area near the pools. The campsite is immaculately clean and has excellent sports facilities. The guests we spoke to were really enjoying their stay. Local excursions can be made to the Campillo de Adrentro now a picnic spot, but once a military base. There are lots of walks in the region, and the ancient Roman city of Cartegena with its Roman ampitheatre, ancient bullring and port (once admired by Napoleon) is well worth a visit.

Facilities

Five sanitary blocks provide excellent facilities, including facilities for disabled campers. Washing machines and dryers. Motorcaravan services. Car wash. Restaurant/snack bar. Bar. Shop. Swimming pools with jacuzzi. Five-a-side football. Boules. Basketball. Table tennis. Play areas. Electronic games. Bicycle hire. ATM. Dogs and other animals are not accepted. Torches useful. Off site: Town close by. Fishing. Beach and boat launching 600 m. Riding 6 km. Golf 20 km. Excursions.

At a glance

Welcome & Ambience	✓✓✓✓	Location	✓✓✓✓
Quality of Pitches	✓✓✓✓	Range of Facilities	✓✓✓✓✓

Directions

From A7/E15 take km. 627 exit to Mazarron (southeast of Murcia) and go east on coast road towards Cartegena. Site is well signed before entering town of La Azohia.

Charges 2004

Per person	€ 4,00 - € 5,00
child (1-7)	€ 3,50 - € 4,50
pitch	€ 12,00 - € 15,00

Reservations

Contact site. Tel: 968 152 151.

Open

All year.

ES8752 Camping Naturista El Portus

El Portus, 30393 Cartagena (Murcia)

Set in a secluded, mountain fringed, south facing bay, El Portus is a fairly large naturist site with direct access to a sand and shingle beach and enjoying magnificent views. With its own micro-climate, this part of Spain enjoys almost all year round sunshine; mid-day temperatures which seldom drop below 20 degrees. There are some 400 pitches, half for tourers, ranging from 60-100 sq.m, all but a few having electricity (6A), mostly on fairly level, if somewhat stony ground. El Portus has a reasonable amount of shade from the trees and every pitch has views. Permanent units are situated on the hill-side above the site. A large, supervised swimming pool and paddling pool are sheltered and landscaped with grass areas for sunbathing. At other times there may be a smaller heated pool above the camping area. One of the bar/restaurants is open all year. This is relaxed site with welcoming, English speaking reception staff.

Facilities

Five toilet blocks of varying styles are fully equipped. Opened as required, they are clean and bright, some are unisex. Open plan dishwashing and laundry facilities. Showers all with hot water,. Facilities may be a little busy in peak season. Unit for disabled visitors, key from reception. Washing machines. Motorcaravan services. Three drinking water points clearly marked near the steps to restaurant. Non-drinking water points well spaced around site. Well stocked shop. Bar with TV and libary. Restaurant with 'menu del dia' high season, snack bar by beach acts as restaurant low season. Swimming pools. Play area. Tennis. Volleyball. Table tennis. Petanque. Yoga. Scuba-diving club (high season). Windsurfing. Spanish lessons. Small boat moorings. Disco and entertainment (high season). Off site: Fishing from beach. Riding and golf 40 km.

At a glance

Welcome & Ambience	✓✓✓✓✓	Location	✓✓✓✓✓
Quality of Pitches	✓✓✓✓	Range of Facilities	✓✓✓✓✓

Directions

Site is on the coast, 10 km. west of Cartagena. Follow signs to Mazarron then take E22 to Canteras. Site is well signed for 4 km. to El Portus.

Charges 2004

Per person	€ 5,49
child (3-9 yrs)	€ 4,04
pitch	€ 12,31
pitch incl. 6A electricity	€ 17,20
dog	€ 3,73

Plus 7% VAT. Special discounts for longer stays and in low season.

Reservations

Made with € 181 deposit. Tel: 968 553 052.
E-mail: elportus@elportus.com

Open

All year.

ES8753 Caravaning La Manga

Autovia Cartagena-La Manga exit 15, 30370 La Manga del Mar Menor (Murcia)

The site is a very large well equipped, 'holiday style' site with its own beach and pool. With a good number of typical Spanish long stay units, the length of the site is impressive (1 kilometre) and a bicycle is very helpful for getting about. La Manga is a 22 km. narrow strip of land, bordered by the sea on one side and by the Mar Menor on the other. There are sandy beaches on both sides and considerable development in terms of hotels, apartments, restaurants, night clubs, etc. in between – a little reminiscent of Miami Beach! You cannot drive all round this narrow strip of land as there is a gap in the centre, however, the very end of the southern part is great for 'getting away from it all' (take a picnic for the beach and be sure to go over the little bridge for privacy). The campsite is situated on the approach to 'the strip' and enjoys the benefit of its own semi-private beach alongside the Mar Menor, with a sailing, canoeing and windsurfing school and the site's excellent restaurant (traditional Spanish Tapas and food) and bar right beside the beach. The beach is dotted with tall palm trees and the sea is very shallow and warm, so it is ideal for families with small children or choose between the outdoor or indoor pools. There are some 1,000 touring pitches of two sizes (84 or 110 sq.m), regularly laid out in rows on slightly sloping gravel. They are smart, separated and shaded by high hedges, all have electricity and water. This site's excellent facilities are ideally suited for holidays in the winter when the weather is very pleasantly warm.

Facilities

Seven clean toilet blocks of standard design include washbasins with hot water in five blocks. Laundry. Gas supplies. Large well stocked supermarket. Restaurant. Bar. Snack bar. Swimming pool complex (April - Sept). Indoor pool, gym, sauna and jacuzzi. Open air cinema (April - Sept). Tennis. Petanque. Minigolf. Basketball. Volleyball. Football area. Play area. Watersports school. Off site: Golf 2 km. Bicycle hire or riding 5 km.

Open

All year.

At a glance

Welcome & Ambience	✓✓✓✓✓	Location	✓✓✓✓✓
Quality of Pitches	✓✓✓✓✓	Range of Facilities	✓✓✓✓✓

Directions

From MU312 dual-carriageway take exit 15 towards Cabo de Palos, signed Playa Honda (site signed also). Cross road bridge and double back. Site entrance is beside dual-carriageway with many flags flying.

Charges 2004

Per pitch incl. 2 persons	€ 17,00 - € 26,75
3 persons	€ 19,00 - € 29,75
4 persons	€ 21,50 - € 33,00

Electricity (10A) included. All plus 7% VAT. Discounts in low season.

Reservations

Contact site. Tel: 968 563 014.
E-mail: lamanga@caravaning.es

CARAVANING LA MANGA COSTA CALIDA

Ctra. de El Algar a Cabo de Palos, km 12.
E-30370 La Manga del Mar Menor
Cartagena (Murcia)
Tel.: (34) 968 56 30 19
(34) 968 56 30 14
Fax: (34) 968 56 34 26

www.caravaning.es • lamanga@caravaning.es

A paradise between two seas. Come for a lovely, warm winter to the borders of the Mar Menor, there where you can enjoy the sun 3000 hours per year. Not far from the historical towns Cartagena and Murcia. In winter in-door swimming pool, jacuzzi, sauna and gym and up till 50% reduction.

ES8745 Camping La Fuente

Camino de La Bocamina, 30626 Banos de Fortuna (Murcia)

Located in an area known for its thermal waters since Roman and Moorish times and with just 62 pitches, La Fuente is a gem. The main attraction here is the huge pool complex where the water is constant at 22 degrees for 365 days of the year. Fed from thermal springs this is really good for old bones! Importantly there is a long gentle ramp into the pool for the not so agile. The site is in two sections, one where pitches are in standard rows and the other where they are in circles around blocks. The flat pitches have 10A electricity, some with shade, and unusually all have their own modern mini-sanitary block.

Facilities

All pitches have their own high quality facilities including a unit for disabled campers. Washing machines and dryers. High quality restaurant. Pool (small charge). Snack bar by pool. Supermarket. Bicycle hire. Communal barbecues.

Open

All year.

At a glance

Welcome & Ambience	✓✓✓✓	Location	✓✓✓✓✓
Quality of Pitches	✓✓✓✓✓	Range of Facilities	✓✓✓

Directions

From A7/E15 (Alicante - Murcia) take C3223 to Fortuna then signs to Banos de Fortuna, then site.

Charges 2004

Per person	€ 2,25
pitch (with private sanitary facilities)	€ 9,50
electricity (per kw/h on meter)	€ 0,19

Reservations

Contact site. Tel: 968 685125.
E-mail: campingfuente@terra.es

Andalucia

Famous for its sun, its beautiful traditions, its poets, original folklore, age-old history and magnificent heritage left behind by the Moors, Andalucía is one of the most attractive regions in Spain.

This comprises eight provinces:
Almeria, Cadiz, Cordoba, Granada, Huelva, Malaga, Jaen and Seville

The regional capital is Seville

With the River Guadalquivir running through it, the charming city of Seville is one of the most visited places in the region. The old city, with its great monuments; the Giralda tower, Cathedral and the Alcázar, plus the narrow, winding streets of Santa Cruz, is particularly popular. Also on the Guadalquivir, Cordoba is located northeast of Seville. It too has a picturesque Jewish Quarter along with a rich Moorish heritage. Indeed, the Mezquita is one of the grandest mosques ever built by the Moors in Spain.

Located further east on the foothills of the Sierra Nevada Mountain Range, Granada is home to the impressive Alhambra, a group of distinct buildings including a Royal Palace, splendid gardens, and the fortress of Alcazaba. The Sierra Nevada, Spain's highest range, offers good skiing and trekking. Further south, you'll find the fine beaches and tourist areas of the Costa Tropical and the Costa del Sol, including the developed resort of Malaga. There are more beaches on the west coast plus one of the oldest settlements in Spain, the bustling port of Cádiz.

Cuisine of the region

Andalucía has more tapas bars than anywhere else in Spain. Sea food in abundance, fresh vegetables and fruit: oranges from Cordoba; persimmons, pomegranates, figs, strawberries from Alpujarra; avocados, mangos, guavas, papayas from the coast of Granada and Malaga. Locally produced wine and sherry.

Alboronía: vegetable stew

Alfajors: almond and nut pastry

Gazpacho ajoblanco: cold soup with garlic and almond

Gazpacho salmorejo: much thicker and made with tomatoes only

Pestiños: honey coated pastries

Tocinillo de cielo: pudding made with egg yolks and syrup

Places of interest

Almeria: preserved Moorish heritage with greatest purity. Located on a beautiful bay

Casa-Museo Pablo Ruiz Picasso: art museum including collection of originals by Pablo Picasso

Jaen: medieval fortress, Renaissance cathedral, 11th century Moorish baths, Santa Catalina castle

Jerez de la Frontera: birthplace of sherry and Spanish brandy, site of renowned equestrian school

Mijas: enchanting village, with narrow streets bordered by brilliantly white-washed houses

Parque Natural de las Sierras de Cazorla y Segura: largest park in Spain with mountains, river gorges, forests and wildlife

Ronda: beautiful town on the edge of an abrupt rocky precipice

Alan Rogers **tip**

JOIN IN THE FERIA DE ABRIL. HELD IN SEVILLE SHORTLY AFTER THE HOLY WEEK FESTIVITIES, IT IS A WEEK-LONG PARTY OF FOOD, DRINK AND FLAMENCO.

ES8749 Camping Sopalmo

Sopalmo, 04638 Mojacar (Almeria)

This is a tiny, homely, site run by a cheerful man called Simon and his charming mother Isabel. They are full of fun and determined that you will enjoy your stay. The site is on two levels, the upper site (be prepared for a fairly steep gravel track to the gates) for 20 tourers and the lower section for 12 tents. All pitches are marked, level and on gravel with electricity. It is unspoilt and has much rustic charm with the family house providing the focal point of the site. The attractive trees and shrubs around the site include olives, figs, mimosa and cacti. Reception is a pretty little room in the front section of the quaint house and a few steps take you into a small but typically Spanish bar. There are informal 'al fresco' gatherings and late barbecues on the lovely 'barbacoa' (terrace), especially at Christmas! We recommend the site for the more mature camper who wishes to get away from it all and be very much within a family atmosphere. Lots of British campers winter here! Ask to see the baby tortoises that Simon rescues and then releases back into the wild when mature.

Facilities

The small sanitary block is very clean and fully equipped. Facilities for disabled campers. Hot showers assisted by solar power. Basic laundry and dishwashing facilities in a pleasant roofed area near reception. Bar. Breakfast available in summer. Baker calls daily. Torch useful. Off site: The beach is 2 km. (naturism permitted) and the nearest serious shops are 5 km. Riding and bicycle hire 10 km.

Open

All year.

At a glance

Welcome & Ambience	✓✓✓✓✓	Location	✓✓✓✓
Quality of Pitches	✓✓✓✓✓	Range of Facilities	✓✓✓

Directions

Exit from main coast road (N340) at junction 520 (northeast of Almeria). Take the AL152 (formerly A150) to Mojacar Playa and continue south towards Carboneras. Site is 6 km south of Mojacar Playa, signed off the road

Charges 2005

Per person	€ 4,00
child	€ 3,00
pitch	€ 7,40
electricity	€ 2,40

Plus 7% VAT. Reductions for low season and longer stays. No credit cards.

Reservations

Contact site. Tel: 950 478413.

ES8751 Camping Cuevas Mar

Cuevas del Almanzora, 04618 Palomares (Almeria)

The site opened in '95 is managed by Pedro, a friendly Frenchman and is gaining a reputation for its excellent service, comfortable facilities and immaculate appearance. Cuevas Mar is a welcome addition in a region very popular with British visitors who appreciate its year-round dry, sunny climate. Quietly situated just back from the coast road (a little road noise on the site) and 500 m. across the road from the beach, the site offers 200 large, smart pitches (80-100 sq.m), all with electricity connections (6A) and firm dry surfaces. The newer section for large motorhomes is closest to the road. The older pitches are screened by hedges and young trees which afford some shade and have easy access from wide roads (some artificial shade is provided). The most attractive sheltered, tiled, oval-shaped pool (14 x 9 m) is surrounded by a grassy sunbathing area and has a thoughtfully provided long ramp to help the elderly or infirm to enter the water. Although there are few additional facilities here it is a most pleasant site and there are good restaurants within easy walking distance.

Facilities

The well designed neat central sanitary block is generous in size, adequate and fully equipped. Good laundry and dishwashing facilities under cover. Washing machines and dryer. Two drinking water points on site (note: in common with many other sites in this very dry area, drinking water is supplied from tanks refilled by tanker delivery and the remainder of the water on site is non-potable). Shop. Bar with terrace by pool. Snacks may be offered in high season. Swimming pool (May - Sept). Jacuzzi. Off site: Restaurants 200 m. Fishing from beach 200 m. Bicycle hire 3 km. Golf 4 km. Mojaca 7 km. for seafood and lively bars.

Open

All year.

At a glance

Welcome & Ambience	✓✓✓✓✓	Location	✓✓✓✓
Quality of Pitches	✓✓✓✓✓	Range of Facilities	✓✓✓

Directions

From N340 (Murcia -; Almeria) leave at 537 km. for Cuevas del Amanzora, then follow the road to Vera and Palomares. Site is signed from Vera.

Charges guide

Per person	€ 4,20
child	€ 3,20
caravan or tent	€ 4,20
car	€ 4,20
motorcaravan	€ 8,42
motorcycle	€ 3,01

Generous discounts for longer winter stays. No credit cards.

Reservations

Contact site. Tel: 950 467 382.
E-mail: cuevasmar@arrakis.es

ES8765 Camping La Garrofa

Ctra Nacional 340 - km 435,4, Direccion a Aguadulce via Litoral, 04002 Almeria (Almeria)

One of the earliest sites in Spain (dating back to 1957), La Garoffa is a simple site nestled into a cove with a beach that is virtually private. The shingle beach cannot be accessed other than by sea or through the campsite. It is rather dramatic with the tall mountain cliffs behind. Many of the rather small 102 flat and sloping sandy pitches here are shaded, some are virtually on the beach, most very close to the water. An old fortress looks down on the campsite - you can walk to it via a valley at the back of the site and across an old Roman bridge. These are all on land owned by the family who also own the campsite. La Garoffa was let for many years and is now back in the hands of the family who are working hard to return the site to its full potential. Sites in this area are generally poor and this is good by comparison. The impact of the high road bridges to the back of the site is minimal and the sound you are most likely to hear is the noise of the waves or the circadas (cricket like insects) singing in the many eucalyptus trees. There is a small restaurant that served delicious food in a rather relaxed way. It's all very relaxed here and that is part of its rather unique rustic, simple charm.

Facilities

A single sanitary block is mature but clean. No facilities for disabled campers. Restaurant/snack bar. Shop. Play area. Torches useful. Fishing. Off site: Town close by. Walks. Sub aqua diving. Bicycle hire 2 km. Golf 8 km. Excursions - tickets to attractions sold.

Open

All year.

At a glance

Welcome & Ambience	✓✓✓✓	Location	✓✓✓✓
Quality of Pitches	✓✓✓	Range of Facilities	✓✓✓

Directions

Site is west of Almeria From N340 take exit 438 exit and follow the camping signs. The site is below the minor road on the beach side and easy to find.

Charges 2005

Per person	€ 4,00
child	€ 3,70
motorcaravan	€ 6,70
caravan	€ 4,70
tent	€ 4,50
car	€ 4,00

Reservations

Contact site. Tel: 950 235770.
E-mail: info@lagarrofa.com

ES9270 Camping Suspiro del Moro

Ctra Bailén-Motril, km 145., Puerto Suspiro del Moro, 18630 Granada (Granada)

Suspiro Del Moro is 11 kilometres south of Granada just off the Motril road or, alternatively, can be approached on the scenic mountain road from Almunecar. Based high in the Sierra Nevada mountain range, the area offers spectacular views from just outside the site, with trees and fences inhibiting the views inside. The site is small and rectangular with a cool and peaceful atmosphere and noise from the road is reduced by a high wall. Many locally made colourful pottery items are on sale in the rear of reception. Family run, it is well kept with gravel paths leading to the flat, grass pitches which benefit from the shade of the mature trees. The site is part of a business which includes a very attractive large swimming pool and there is a direct access from the site. Above this is a huge restaurant and bar both with terraces. The restaurant has a most extensive menu with waiter service.

Facilities

Clean and tidy, small toilet blocks are situated around the camping area with British style WCs and free hot showers. Laundry and dishwashing facilities. Small basic shop. Small simple restaurant/bar (high season). Small play area on gravel. Off site: Swimming pool and restaurant adjacent. Sierra Nevada and Granada within reasonable distance to explore.

Open

All year.

At a glance

Welcome & Ambience	✓✓	Location	✓✓✓
Quality of Pitches	✓✓✓	Range of Facilities	✓✓✓

Directions

Leave the Granada to Motril road (E902/A44) at junction 144 if from the south or 139 from the north and follow the un-named campsite signs. At roundabout go towards Suspiro but then tun left (signed after turn). Site is about 600 m. on right beside large restaurant. There is only one site here.

Charges 2004

Per person	€ 3,61
child	€ 2,40
pitch	€ 7,81
electricity	€ 2,40

Less 20% in low season.

Reservations

Contact site. Tel: 958 555 411.
E-mail: suspirodelmoro@eresmas.com

www.alanrogers.com for latest campsite news

ES9280 Camping Sierra Nevada

Avenida Madrid 107, 18014 Granada (Granada)

This is a good site either for a night stop or for a stay of a few days while visiting Granada and for a city site it is surprisingly pleasant. Quite large, it has an open feeling and, to encourage you to stay a little longer, an irregular shape pool with a smaller children's pool open in high season. There is some traffic noise around the pool as it is on the road boundary. Granada has much to offer for sightseeing, including the amazing La Alhambra. We recommend that you allow a minimum of a full day to explore the palaces, but longer is needed to cover everything. Granada also has some interesting shops and there are usually one or two excellent shows. With 148 pitches for touring units, the site is in two connected parts with more mature trees and facilities to the northern end. Artificial shade is available throughout the site if required (but may be quite low). Electrical connections (10/20A) are available. There is a small tour operator presence but it is not intrusive. English is spoken by the friendly staff.

Facilities

Two very modern sanitary blocks, with excellent facilities, including cabins, very good facilities for disabled people and babies. Additional high standard sanitary facilities by the pool made available at peak times. Washing machines. Motorcaravan services. Gas supplies. Shop (15/3-15/10). Swimming pools with lifeguards and charge of € 1.5 (15/6-15/9). Bar/restaurant by pool. Tennis. Table tennis. Petanque. Large playground. Doctor lives on site.
Off site: Fishing 10 km. Golf 12 km. Bus station 50 m. from site gate giving access to everywhere.

Open

1 March - 31 October.

At a glance

Welcome & Ambience	✓✓✓✓✓	Location	✓✓✓✓✓
Quality of Pitches	✓✓✓✓	Range of Facilities	✓✓✓✓

Directions

Site is just outside the city to north, on road to Jaén and Madrid. From autopista, take Granada North - Almanjayar exit 123 (close to central bus station). Follow road back towards Granada and site is shortly on the right, well signed. From other roads join the motorway to access the correct exit.

Charges 2005

Per person	€ 5,00
child (3-10 yrs)	€ 4,25
pitch	€ 11,40
electricity (10A)	€ 3,45

VAT included.

Reservations

Made for camping or motel. Tel: 958 150 062.
E-mail: campingmotel@terra.es

ES9275 Camping Los Avellanos de Sierra Nevada

Ctra de la Fábrica s/n, 18152 Dilar (Granada)

This is a fascinating tiny business with a philosophy of peace and tranquillity, a world apart from other sites in southern Spain. This has been achieved by Pilar and her brother Idvier. The site is also called Camping Cortijo which loosely translates from the Spanish as a big house in grounds with animals, birds and produce where 'people work towards people'. There is a fabulous old house and 20 beautifully terraced pitches (mainly for tents) with amazing views enjoying the sound of water tinkling through the ancient irrigation channels on its way to the crops (cars are parked separately). You can pick fruit from the scores of fruit trees (just take what you can eat though!) and collect the 'huevos corral' – free range eggs or pick your own vegetables from the plot (small charge). There is a shaded area with a spring set aside for reading and dreaming and as you walk to the sanitary block, birds fly out of holes in the bank. The vine-covered patio overlooks the small raised pool and commands wonderful views of the mountains. The narrow approach roads are interesting for larger units and a few motorhomes may be accepted in an informal lower area where electricity can be supplied. A phone call is a good idea if you are driving a large unit; ask for Pilar as her English is very good. Expect a different experience here but we stress this is mainly for tents and better for summer visits.

Facilities

Toilet facilities are modern and clean. Pretty bar/restaurant serves typical local fare and sells basic supplies (very limited in low season). Kitchen for hire. Restaurant/bar. Swimming pool (high season only). Table tennis. Darts. Bicycle hire. Riding. Fishing in river Dilar. Details of walks from reception. Torches essential. Excellent rooms to let. Off site: Tours of Granada (20 minutes away), especially the Alhambra, organised. Site also useful for skiing in Sierra Nevada in season.

Open

All year.

At a glance

Welcome & Ambience	✓✓✓✓✓	Location	✓✓✓✓✓
Quality of Pitches	✓✓✓✓	Range of Facilities	✓✓

Directions

From Granada going south take the A323, then the GR05 road to Otura. Go through the town following signs for Dilar where you will find signs for the site. Note: Do not stray from the route indicated by the signs through town, as the roads are extremely narrow.

Charges guide

Per person	€ 3,16
child	€ 2,70
tent	€ 3,61
car	€ 3,01
motorcycle	€ 2,70

Electricity and larger units- price on application.
All plus 7% VAT. No credit cards.

Reservations

Contact site. Tel: 958 596016.
E-mail: Avellano@Teleline.es

ES9285 Camping Las Lomas

Ctra de Sierra Nevada, 18160 Güejar-Sierra (Granada)

This site is high in the Güéjar Sierra and looks down on the Patano de Canales reservoir. After a wonderful drive to Güéjar-Sierra, you are rewarded with a site boasting excellent facilities. It is set on a slope but the pitches have been levelled to a great degree and are quite private, with high separating hedges and with many mature trees giving good shade (some pitches are fully serviced, with sinks and most have electricity). Development will mean that for 2005 there will be 120 pitches in all. The large bar/restaurant complex has a patio with wonderful views over the lake and an impressive huge central fire that is lit in winter. The pools also share this view and have a grassed area for sunbathing that runs down to the fence looking over the long drop to the lake below (safe fencing). A new feature is luxury rooms for rent, including one with a superb spa which is for hire by the hour. Any infirm visitors will need a car to get around as the inclines are extreme.

Facilities

Pretty blue tiled sanitary blocks (heated in winter) provide clean facilities. First class facilities for disabled campers and well equipped baby room (key at reception). Spa for hire. Motorcaravan services. Supermarket. Restaurant/bar. Swimming pool. Play area. Table tennis. Minigolf. Basketball. Many other activities available including parascending. Barbecue. Internet connection in reception. Torches useful. Off site: Buses run from outside site to village and Granada (15 km). Tours of the Alhambra organised with guides supplied if required. Useful site for winter skiing.

Open

All year.

At a glance

Welcome & Ambience	✓✓✓	Location	✓✓✓✓
Quality of Pitches	✓✓✓✓	Range of Facilities	✓✓✓✓

Directions

Using A323 (Jaén - Motril) take exit 135 at Granada to Sierra Nevada which brings you to the A395. At 4 km. marker take exit 5B for Sierra Nevada. Pass 7 km. marker and turn immediately right towards Cenes de la Vega and Güéjar-Sierra and right again after 200 m. onto GR420, then left to Güéjar-Sierra. Site is signed – drive uphill past the dam and enjoy the views to the site. Its easier than it sounds!

Charges 2004

Per person	€ 3,50
child	€ 2,40
pitch	€ 9,00

VAT included. No credit cards.

Reservations

Contact site. Tel: 958 484 742.
E-mail: laslomas@campings.net

ES9296 Camping Castillo de Baños

Ctra. 340, km 360, La Mamola, 18750 Granada (Granada)

This is a smaller sister site to Don Cactus (ES9295). It is located right on the beach (the side gate leads straight onto a small pebble beach). Many pitches run along the sea with a bamboo fence providing some shade and from many pitches you can see and hear the sea. It is a peaceful and wonderful setting. There are 240 pitches of various sizes (mostly medium) shaded by a variety of trees. About 20% in one area are taken by static units. A family run site (with a little English spoken) facilities include a small shop, small restaurant and bar (with pool and table football). A small pool surrounded by painted concrete gives the chance to cool off. This is a good choice for those looking for a quieter site to just relax.

Facilities

One toilet block provides basic stainless steel double sink facilities with only cold water for dishwashing and laundry. British WCs and good showers. Small shop. Restaurant/bar (15/6-1/9).Internet. Barbecue area with sink. Off site: Bus stop 200 m.

Open

All year.

At a glance

Welcome & Ambience	✓✓✓	Location	✓✓✓✓
Quality of Pitches	✓✓✓	Range of Facilities	✓✓✓

Directions

From N340 Motril – Adra road turn south at km 360 (towards sea). At roundabout take second turn (small camping sign) and site is about 50 m. on right.

Charges 2004

Per person	€ 4,30
child (4-10 yrs)	€ 4,10
pitch	€ 8,00
electricity (5A)	€ 2,60

Reservations

Contact site. Tel: 82 95 28.
E-mail: info@campingcastillo.com

ES9295 Camping Don Cactus

CN 340 km 343, 18730 Carchuna-Motril (Granada)

Situated between the main N340 and the beach, this family run campsite is pleasantly suprising with clever planning and ongoing improvements. It is a comfortable site of 320 pitches. Many people come and winter here, with 70 permanent pitches providing a Spanish flavour (people commute from Granada in the hot summer prefering to sleep in cooler circumstances down near the beach). This quieter section of the coast is beautiful with coves and access to larger towns if wished. The friendly reception staff are very helpful with tourist advice and can arrange trips for you if needed. The flat pitches vary in size with electricity connections (5/12A), some providing water and satellite TV connections, and are arranged along avenues with eucalyptus trees (which keep the mosquitoes away apparently) for shade. One large toilet block provides all the facilities necessary. A swimming pool designed by the owner and his son is a unique shape – a wonderful place for children to play with plenty of water jets and a jacuzzi. Sports courts, a playground and a barbecue area where there is a summer disco are positioned near the front of the site so as not to disturb others. For winter visitors there are courses in the Spanish language and cookery. A bar and restaurant at the front of the site overlook the beach.

Facilities

The large toilet block provides British style WCs, showers (lights go on as you shut the door) and plenty of washbasins. Laundry facilities. Beach showers. Well stocked shop. Bar, restaurant and takeaway (all year). Swimming pool (in high season € 1.50 per day as only 200 people allowed in swimming pool area) with changing rooms. Football, basketball and tennis courts. Play area. Summer activities for children. Pets corner. Cash machine. Internet point. Dogs are not accepted in July/Aug. Barbecues only in special area. Caravan storage. Off site: Bus service 500 m. Nerja caves 40 minutes. Alpujarra mountains 50 minutes.

At a glance

Welcome & Ambience	✓✓✓✓	Location	✓✓✓
Quality of Pitches	✓✓✓✓	Range of Facilities	✓✓✓✓

Directions

From Motril - Carucha road (N340/E15) turn towards the sea at km 343. (site signed, but look at roof level for large green tent on the top of the building!). Travel about 600 m. then turn east to site on left.

Charges 2004

Per person	€ 4,50
child (4-10 yrs)	€ 4,00
pitch	€ 8,50 - € 9,50
electricity (5A)	€ 2,75

Low season discounts for longer stays.

Reservations

Contact site. Tel: 958 623 109.
E-mail: camping@doncactus.com

Open

All year.

ES9290 Camping El Balcon de Pitres

18414 Pitres (Granada)

A simple country site perched high in the mountains of the Alpujarras, on the south side of the Sierra Nevada, El Balcon de Pitres has its own rustic charm. Some 15 years ago the mountain top was terraced and many thousands of trees were planted around the site. These include cherry and apple trees and many of these trees provide shade. There are stunning views from some of the 175 level grassy pitches. The garden is kept green by spring waters, which you can hear and sometimes see, tinkling away in places. It is a wonderful relaxing place to cool down, away from the heat of the coast. On Saturday evenings in summer there is a wide variety of live entertainment around an exotic Morrocan tent, which serves as a bar and which is far enough away from the pitches not to disturb sleeping campers. Local visitors often add to the 'hot august night' ambience. The large restaurant serves excellent, typically Spanish meals. The pool is very popular in summer with locals as well as campers. The Lopez family, have built this site from barren mountain top to cool oasis in the mountains in just fifteen years. The area is famous for its mineral water and there are many local artisans working in the mountains. There are wonderful walks and lots of attractions including mountaineering sports such as canyoning, parascending, and trekking in the area.

Facilities

Two toilet blocks provide adequate facilities but the steeply sloping site is unsuitable for disabled campers and thus there are no facilities for them. Restaurant/snack bar. Bar. Shop. Swimming pools (extra charge, € 2.40 adult € 1.50 child). Bicycle hire. Torches useful. Off site: Town close by. Fishing. Canyoning. Trekking. Parascending. Quad bikes. Village sports centre providing football.

Open

All year.

At a glance

Welcome & Ambience	✓✓✓✓	Location	✓✓✓✓
Quality of Pitches	✓✓✓	Range of Facilities	✓✓✓

Directions

Site is about 30 km. northeast of Motril. From coastal N340 take N323 and E902 north to Lanjaron. On E348 proceed towards Orgiva and just before town turn left to Soportuja, Pampaneira and finally Pitres where site is signed. From Orgiva the roads are very winding so allow plenty of time.

Charges guide

Per person	€ 3,31
child	€ 2,50
electricity	€ 1,95

Reservations

Contact site. Tel: 958 766111.
E-mail: info@balcondepitres.com

ES8782 Camping Caravaning Laguna Playa

Prolongacion Paseo Maritimo, 29740 Torre del Mar (Málaga)

Camping Laguna Playa is a pleasant and peaceful site run by a father and son team (the son speaks excellent English) and they give a personal service, alongside one of the Costa del Sol beaches. Trips are organised to the famous Alhambra Mosque in Granada on a weekly basis and the site is well placed for visits to Malaga and Nerja. The pitches are flat, of average size and with good artificial shade supplementing that provided by the many established trees on site. All pitches have electricity (5/10A). The busy restaurant with a terrace offers good value for money and many locals use it. The site has a distinctly Spanish flavour in August but in low season you will find lots of European 'snow birds' enjoying the warmth here. Animation is organised for children in high season and you could visit the new cinema near reception. Various competitions including petanque are organised in summer. Good off peak discounts are available.

Facilities

Two well equipped, modern, sanitary blocks, both recently refurbished, include baby baths and good facilities for disabled campers. Laundry facilities. Supermarket. Bar and busy restaurant also used by locals (all open all year). Swimming pools (open high season). Play area. Drinks machine. Children's entertainment. Off site: Beach promenade 200 m. Bicycle hire 500 m. Regular bus service 700 m. outside site. Golf 1.5 km. Riding 2 km.

Open

All year.

At a glance

Welcome & Ambience	✓✓✓✓	Location	✓✓✓✓
Quality of Pitches	✓✓✓	Range of Facilities	✓✓✓✓

Directions

Site is on the sea front west of the town of Torre del Mar, off the main N340 Malaga - Nerja road. Follow signs and take care not to enter the first camp site you meet on the beach as this is inferior and will be demolished in new development in the near future.

Charges 2004

Per person	€ 4,10
child	€ 3,20
tent	€ 4,10
caravan	€ 4,60
car	€ 4,10
motorcaravan	€ 8,70

Reservations

Write to site. Tel: 952 540 631.
E-mail: info@lagunaplaya.com

ES8783 Camping Naturista Almanat

Carril de la Torre Alta s/n, 29749 Almayate (Málaga)

With direct access to a one kilometre grey sand and shingle naturist beach, this established all year naturist site, set amongst agricultural land with mountain backdrop, is proving a firm favourite with many British seeking winter sun. English is spoken at the modern reception adjacent to the security barrier. The site also has a night guard. The entire 2-hectare site is flat with a fine shingle surface on dirt. A large number of trees planted when the site opened in 1998 have now matured, providing much needed shade in the summer months. The 160 touring pitches with 16A electricity, vary in size and shape with the majority demanding physical manoeuvring of a touring caravan. Some pitches are long and narrow which could prevent the erection of an awning and you may feel quite close to your neighbour. The facilities on site are to a very high standard.

Facilities

The large, unisex toilet is fully equipped, regularly cleaned and all under cover. Good facilities for disabled campers near reception (approach surface may cause minor difficulty for wheel chair users). Between the campsite and beach, a sheltered grass area ideal for sunbathing and a bar/restaurant with terrace overlooking the sea provides good food at acceptable prices. Small shop for basic provisions. Large unheated swimming pool. Play area. TV in bar. Sauna and fully equipped gym. Basketball, paddle tennis. Cinema (56 seats) showing VHS tapes or DVD. Weather permitting, one is expected to be nude which is obligatory in the swimming pool area and bar during the day. Off site: Torre del Mar is 2 km. with many shops, restaurants, a street market on Thursdays and internet café. Regular bus service from end of approach road (1 km). Fishing, riding nearby.

Open

All year.

At a glance

Welcome & Ambience	✓✓✓✓	Location	✓✓✓✓
Quality of Pitches	✓✓✓✓✓	Range of Facilities	✓✓✓✓✓

Directions

Approaching this site from the east (Torre del Mar) it is necessary to make a left turn to access the 600 m. single-track tarmac lane leading to the site entrance. It is currently illegal to make that left turn and you will be fined if caught by the authorities. We recommend that whether travelling from the east or west exit the N340 autovia at junction 265 signed Cajiz Iznate and Costa 340a. Take the Costa direction and on reaching the coast turn left onto 340a toward Torre del Mar. Site well signed in 4 km. on right shortly after passing 'Bull' hoarding.

Charges 2004

Per person	€ 3,90
child (2-10 yrs)	€ 3,10
pitch	€ 7,80 - € 8,30
electricity (16A)	€ 2,30

All plus 7% VAT. No credit cards.

Reservations

Contact site. Tel: 952 556 462.
E-mail: almanat@arrakis.es

www.alanrogers.com for latest campsite news

ES8800 Camping Marbella Playa

Ctra N-340, km 192,800, 29600 Marbella (Málaga)

This large site is twelve kilometres east of the internationally famous resort of Marbella with public transport available to the town centre and local attractions. A sandy beach is about 150 m. away with direct access. There are 430 individual pitches of up to 70 sq.m. with natural shade (additional artificial shade is provided to some), and electricity (10/20A) available throughout. A large swimming pool complex with a restaurant/bar with large patio, palm trees, banana plants and lush grass for sunbathing provides a very attractive feature. The site is busy throughout the high season but the high staff to customer ratio and the friendly staff approach ensures a comfortable stay. We can recommend excursions to Gibraltar (via La Linea), and although an hour's winding drive is awaiting, a trip to Ronda is well worth the effort.

Facilities

Four sanitary blocks of mixed ages, are fully equipped and well maintained. Three modern units for disabled visitors. Laundry and dishwashing areas in good order. Large supermarket with butcher and fresh vegetable counter. Bar, restaurant and café. All open all year. Supervised swimming pool (free - April/Sept). Children's playground (on gritty sand). Torches necessary in beach areas.

Open

All year.

At a glance

Welcome & Ambience	✓✓✓✓	Location	✓✓✓✓✓
Quality of Pitches	✓✓✓✓	Range of Facilities	✓✓✓✓✓

Directions

Site is 12 km. east of Marbella with access close to the 193 km. point on the main N340 road.

Charges guide

Per person	€ 3,55
child (1-10 yrs)	€ 3,01
car	€ 3,55
caravan or tent	€ 6,01
motorcycle	€ 3,25
motorcaravan	€ 8,41

All plus 7% VAT. Reductions (up to 50%) for long stays and senior citizens outside 16/6-31/8.

Reservations

Write to site. Tel: 952 833 998.

ES8803 Camping La Buganvilla

Ctra N340, km 188.8, 29600 Marbella (Málaga)

This site has a grand total of 1,000 pitches, of which 300 are for touring units. They are mostly on terraces so there are some views across to the mountains and hinterland of this coastal area. La Buganvilla is a large, uncomplicated site with mature trees providing shade to some pitches. The terrain is a little rugged in places and the buildings are older in style but all were clean when we visited. A pool near the bar and restaurant is ideal for cooling off after a day's sightseeing. The restaurant offers barbecue style meals. This is an acceptable base from which to explore areas of the Costa del Sol and an easy drive to the picturesque Ronda Valley. Adjacent to the campsite a large area of common land provides pleasant walks. A footbridge crosses the N340 road and there is a gradual 400 m. downhill walk to the beach, where there are some bars and restaurants. The staff are friendly and some English is spoken but you will get a chance to practice your Spanish. There is a multi-language book swap, and internet point in the small reception area.

Facilities

Three painted sanitary blocks are clean and adequate with laundry facilities. Large bar/restaurant with terrace overlooking the pool area. Extremely well stocked mini supermarket. Play area. Basketball and tennis in high season. Dogs are not accepted in July/Aug. Off site: Bus service close to site entrance. Fishing and watersports 400 m. Bicycle and scooter hire 1 km. Golf 5 km. Resort type entertainment close.

Open

All year.

At a glance

Welcome & Ambience	✓✓✓✓	Location	✓✓✓✓
Quality of Pitches	✓✓✓✓	Range of Facilities	✓✓✓

Directions

Site is between Marbella and Fuengirola off the N340. Access at 188.8km marker on the N340 can only be achieved when travelling in a westerly direction, i.e. from Fuengirola towards Marbella. If travelling in the opposite direction, it is necessary to continue past the site until reaching the 'cambio de sentido' signed Elviria. This enables a U-turn over the dual carriageway. Site is signed.

Charges guide

Per person	€ 3,50 - € 4,00
child (under 10 yrs)	€ 2,50 - € 3,50
tent	€ 4,00 - € 5,50
caravan	€ 4,00 - € 6,00
car	€ 3,50 - € 4,50
motorcaravan	€ 5,00 - € 7,00

All plus 7% VAT. Discounts in low season.

Reservations

Contact site. Tel: 952 831 973.
E-mail: info@campingbuganvilla.com

ES8809 Camping El Sur

Ctra Ronda - Algeciras, km 1,5, Apartado de Correos 127, 29400 Ronda (Málaga)

The generous manoeuvring area and delightfully decorated entrance to this site are a promise of something different which is fulfilled in all respects. The very friendly family who run the site have worked hard for many years combining innovative thinking with excellent service. The 114 terraced pitches have electricity (5A) and water, and are partially shaded by olive and almond trees. Most have relaxing views of the surrounding mountains but at an elevation of 850 m. the upper pitches (the very top 45 pitches are for tents only) allow a clear view of the fascinating town of Ronda. The various leisure facilities are very clean, well maintained and the personal touches of the owners are obvious which make using them more enjoyable. This is one of the best small sites we have seen in Andalucia with prices that are extremely competitive. Enjoy the breathtaking 130 metre deep El Tajo gorge (where prisoners were thrown during the civil war) from the lovely 18th century bridge which joins the old and new parts of town. Look out also for the much-feared soldiers in tasselled red Fez headgear and green tunics. These are Franco's old crack unit; the infamous Spanish Africa Legion who are billeted here.

Facilities

The immaculate sanitary block is fully equipped (toilet paper purchased from reception). Laundry facilities in little separate blocks. Gas supplies. Bar and very large, high quality restaurant serving excellent food at reasonable prices (closed 71 15/1). Kidney shaped pool most welcome in summer as the temperatures soar (1/6-30/9). Children's playground and adventure play area. Separate camping area for groups. Minigolf. Dogs on leads with site permission. Barbeques on pitch with site permission. Off road bicycle hire. Internet terminal. Off site: The famous town of Ronda with all its attractions. The coast is approximately one hour drive. National parks to the north.

Open

All year.

At a glance

Welcome & Ambience	✓✓✓✓✓	Location	✓✓✓✓✓
Quality of Pitches	✓✓✓✓✓	Range of Facilities	✓✓✓✓✓

Directions

Site is well signed from the town centre (do not stray off the signed route as there are some very narrow roads) and it is off the Algeciras road, 1.5 km. south of Ronda.

Charges 2005

Per person	€ 4,00
child (under 10 yrs)	€ 3,80
tent	€ 4,00 - € 8,00
car or motorcycle	€ 4,00
motorcaravan	€ 8,00 - € 12,00
electricity (5-10A)	€ 3,50 - € 5,00

Plus 7% VAT. Less 40% in low season.
No credit cards.

Reservations

Advised for July/Aug. Tel: 952 875 939.
E-mail: info@campingelsur.com

ES8802 Camping Cabopino

Ctra N340, km 194.7, 29600 Marbella (Málaga)

This large mature site is alongside the main N340 Costa del Sol coast road, 12 km. east of Marbella and 14 km. from Fuengirola. The Costa del Sol is also known as the Costa del Golf and fittingly there is a major golf course alongside the site. Just 600 metres from the beaches and dunes, a short walk over the road and down the hill brings you to a restaurant on the beach and an unofficial naturist area. A small yachting harbour with a range of restaurants and shops is a similar distance. The site is set amongst tall pine trees which provide shade for the sandy pitches (there are some huge areas for large units). The upper areas of the site are filled with permanent pitches and bungalows. The 400 touring pitches, a mix of leval and sloping, all have electrical connections (10A) and there is a separate area on the western side for groups of younger guests. At the other side of the site you will find a fenced swimming pool with a grass sunbathing area. Close to the entrance is an Italian restaurant serving good food and with a terrace that enjoys shade and is very pleasant.

Facilities

Four mature but clean sanitary blocks provide hot water throughout (may be under pressure at peak times). Washing machines. Bar/restaurant. Shop. Swimming pool (all season). Play area. Excursions can be booked. Torches necessary in the more remote parts of the site. Off site: Fishing, bicycle hire and riding within 1 km. Golf 7 km.

Open

All year.

At a glance

Welcome & Ambience	✓✓✓✓	Location	✓✓✓✓
Quality of Pitches	✓✓✓✓	Range of Facilities	✓✓✓✓

Directions

Site is 7 km. from Marbella. Approaching Marbella from the east, leave the N340 at the 194 km. marker (signed Cabopino). Site is off the roundabout at the top of the slip road.

Charges 2004

Per unit incl. 2 persons and electricity	15,55 - 26,15
extra person	€ 3,15 - € 5,25
child	€ 2,10 - € 4,25
dog	€ 2,25

Plus 7% VAT. Discounts outside high season and for over 7 days.

Reservations

Contact site. Tel: 952 834 373.
E-mail: info@campingcabopino.com

TRAVEL SERVICE SITE
TO BOOK CALL 0870 405 4055 OR www.alanrogersdirect.com

ES8850 Camping Paloma

Ctra Cadiz - Malaga, km 70, 11380 Tarifa (Cádiz)

A spacious, neat and tidy, family orientated site popular with Spanish families and young people of all nations in high season. Paloma is well established and the many tall palms around the site remind one of how close Africa and the romance of Tangier is. Paloma is 700 m. from a fabulous beach with white sands and enormous dunes, great for beachcombing, fishing and old fashioned seaside games. The area is famous for its ideal kite and windsurfing conditions. The site has 353 pitches on mostly flat ground, although the westerly pitches are sloping. They are of average size with some places for extra large units, some are separated by hedges and most are shaded by mature trees; around 200 pitches have electrical connections (10A). A large, smart restaurant serves excellent Spanish fare and the bar with large court-yard buzzes with activity, tapas and snacks are served here. There is a small swimming pool with a paved and grassed sunbathing area and an attractive thatched, stone bar.

Facilities

There are two sanitary blocks, one of a good size, although it is a long walk from the southern end of the site. The other block is smaller and open plan, serving the sloping areas of the site. The sanitary blocks have been refurbished to a high standard. WC's are British style with some Turkish, washbasins have cold water. Facilities for disabled visitors are in the smaller block with access from sloping ground, also a babies room. All very clean when seen. Washing machine. Gas supplies. Shop. Busy bar and good restaurant. Swimming pool with adjacent bar (high season only). Playground. TV in bar. Excursions (June-Sept).
Off site: Nearest beach 700m. Bicycle/scooter/quads hire 5 km. Riding 10 km. Tarifa 12 km. with lots of night life and bars. Golf 25 km.

At a glance

Welcome & Ambience	✓✓✓✓	Location	✓✓✓✓
Quality of Pitches	✓✓✓✓	Range of Facilities	✓✓✓✓

Directions

Site is signed off N340 Cadiz road at Punta Paloma, about 10 km. northwest of Tarifa, just west of km. 74 marker. Watch carefully for the site sign - no advance notice. Be sure to use the slip road to turn left if coming from Tarifa. Follow the signs down a sandy road for 300 m. and site is on the right.

Charges guide

Per person	€ 4,81
child	€ 3,91
car	€ 3,01
motorcycle	€ 2,70
tent	€ 3,31
caravan	€ 3,31

Reservations

Made for one part of site, for any length and without deposit. Tel: 956 684 203.

Open

All year.

ES8855 Camping Tarifa

Ctra N340, km 78.87, 11380 Tarifa (Cádiz)

The long, golden sandy beach is a good feature of this site being ideal for windsurfing and, adjacent to the site with a private access, it is also clean and safe for swimming. The site has a pleasant, open feel and is reasonably sheltered from road noise. It has been thoughtfully landscaped and planted out with an amazing variety of shrubs and flowers and is remarkably clean. There is a smart, modern reception area with an attractive water feature close by. The 265 level pitches are of varying sizes and are surrounded by pine trees which provide ample shade. All have electricity (5/10A) and there are adequate water points. A pleasant restaurant/bar area provides fast food and drinks. The pool is rather small and crowded in summer but has pleasant views of the distant mountain range. Tarifa is a little over five kilometres and is well worth a visit, also a drive inland to the traditional Pueblo Blancos (white villages) is rewarding.

Facilities

Two modern, fully equipped sanitary blocks include facilities for campers with disabilities and baby room. All spotless when seen. Motorcaravan services. Gas supplies. Supermarket and excellent bar/restaurant - fast food only, all open all year with patio. Swimming pool complex with bar. Large children's play area with modern activities. Drinks machines. Good security. Off site: Fishing 100 m. Riding 300 m. Bicycle hire 5 km. Excursions.

Open

All year.

At a glance

Welcome & Ambience	✓✓✓✓	Location	✓✓✓✓
Quality of Pitches	✓✓✓	Range of Facilities	✓✓✓

Directions

Site is on main N340 Cadiz road at the 78.87 km. marker, 7.5 km. northwest of Tarifa. There are large modern signs well ahead of the site with a deceleration lane if approaching from the Tarifa direction, large gaily coloured signs mark the approach to the site.

Charges guide

Per person	€ 4,81
child	€ 3,61
tent	€ 2,70
caravan	€ 3,01
car	€ 2,70
motorcycle	€ 2,40

Reservations

Advised for July/Aug. Tel: 956 684 778.
E-mail: camping-tarifa@camping-tarifa.com

ES8860 Camping Fuente del Gallo

Apto. 48, 11149 Conil de la Frontera (Cádiz)

Fuente del Gallo extends a warm welcome to British visitors, particularly as one half of the ownership is Irish. The attractive pool, restaurant and bar complex with its large, shaded terace, are very welcoming in the height of summer. The site is well maintained with 221 pitches allocated to touring units. Although the actual pitch areas are generally a good size, the majority are long and narrow. This could, in some cases, prevent the erection of an awning and your neighbour may feel close. In low season it is generally accepted to make additional use of an adjoining pitch. Each pitch has 10A electricity and a number of trees create shade to some pitches. Good beaches are relatively near at 300 m. with access gained by steps through new houses with palm-lined roads. Helpful, friendly staff will assist in booking discounted trips to nearby attractions or even further afield to Africa. Cadiz, probably the oldest town in Spain, is worth a visit and in particular the old part with its narrow streets (many pedestrianised) and numerous shops.

Facilities

Two modernised and very clean sanitary blocks include excellent services for babies and disabled visitors and hot water at all facilities. Two new blocks provide additional areas for washing dishes and clothes (cold water only). Laundry room with two washing machines. Motorcaravan services. Gas supplies. Well-stocked shop. Attractive bar and restaurant (breakfast served). TV and games rooms. Swimming pool (all season, lifeguard in high season when there is a small charge) with large grass area for sunbathing and children's pool. Play area. Excursions. Torches useful. Safety deposit boxes. Off site: Watersports on beach. Fishing 300 m. Riding 1 km. Bicycle and motor scooter hire 2 km. Golf 5 km.

At a glance

Welcome & Ambience	✓✓✓✓	Location	✓✓✓✓
Quality of Pitches	✓✓✓✓	Range of Facilities	✓✓✓✓

Directions

From Cadiz-Algeciras road (N340) at km. 23.00, follow signs to Conil de la Frontera town centre, then shortly right to Fuente del Gallo and 'playas' following signs.

Charges 2005

Per person	€ 4,50
child (3-10 yrs)	€ 4,00
caravan and car	€ 8,00
motorcaravan	€ 7,50
electricity	€ 4,00

All plus 7% VAT. Less 11-30% for longer stays (except Jul/Aug).

Reservations

Contact site. Tel: 956 440 137.
E-mail: camping@campingfuentedelgallo.com

Open

Easter - 3 September.

ES8865 Camping Playa Las Dunas de San Anton

P Maritimo de la Puntilla s/n, 11500 El Puerto de Santa Maria (Cádiz)

This site lies within the Parque Natural Bahia de Les Dunes and is adjacent to the long and gently sloping golden sands of Puntilla beach. A ten minute walk takes you into the bustling heart of Puerto Santa Maria which claims to be the birthplace of the 'Flamenco', (along with Cadiz). It is a traditional Spanish family resort with gastronomic delights in the local port area, supplemented by an abundance of local wines and sherries produced in the immense white-washed warehouses (bodegas) which are open to visitors. This is a pleasant and peaceful site (though very busy in August) with some 400 separate marked pitches, 140 for tourers, with much natural shade and ample electrical connections. Motorcaravans park in an area called the Oasis which is very pretty. The tent and caravan pitches, under mature trees, are terraced and separated by low walls. This is a spacious site with a tranquil setting and it is popular with people who wish to 'winter over' in peace. The proximity to the 'sherry triangle' is very useful if you are interested in this fascinating subject which has had considerable British influence in the past. Sir Francis Drake attacked Cadiz in 1587 and made off with 3,000 barrels of sherry along with firing most of the Spanish fleet! Indeed many of the wonderful bodegas were founded by British Catholic refugees in the sixteenth century - this explains the ancient English churches hereabouts and the very British sounding companies producing sherry to this day.

Facilities

Immaculate modern sanitary facilities with separate facilities for disabled campers and a baby room. Laundry facilities are excellent. Gas supplies. Bar/restaurant (all year). Supermarket (high season). Very large swimming pool (supervised) and toddlers pool (high season). Children's play areas. Night security all year. Off site: Fishing 500 m. Riding or golf 2 km. Municipal sports centre close by offers all manner of sporting activities and the beach provides additional free sports facilities such as volleyball. Local buses for town and cities visits and a ferry to Cadiz.

Open

All year.

At a glance

Welcome & Ambience	✓✓✓✓	Location	✓✓✓✓
Quality of Pitches	✓✓✓✓	Range of Facilities	✓✓✓✓

Directions

Site is 5 km. north of Cadiz off N1V route. Take road to Puerto Santa Maria, site is very well signed throughout the town (small yellow signs high on posts).

Charges 2005

Per person	€ 4,08
child	€ 3,49
tent	€ 4,08
car	€ 3,49
motorcycle	€ 2,83
motorcaravan	€ 5,86

Reservations

Advised for August; contact site. Tel: 956 872 210.
E-mail: info@lasdunascamping.com

www.alanrogers.com for latest campsite news

ES8889 Camping Los Alcornocales

11330 Jimena de la Frontera (Cádiz)

Camping Los Alcornocales takes its name from the surrounding Los Alcornocales Natural Park which is one of Europe's largest Mediterranean forests. A small and charming new site, it is off the beaten track in unspoilt countryside. The site has been well planned and the owners have been environmentally strict in its construction and situation. The result is a most pleasant experience of nature if you tire of the beaches. There are magnificent views over the Natural Park and the river Hozgarganta, which is the last virgin Spanish river. It runs through the lower reaches of the site within easy reach, and presents a superb walking adventure. Within minutes you are in 170,000 hectares of park containing amazing landscapes, flora and fauna and you may spot otters, polecats, deer, wild boar, vultures and snake-eating eagles and others too numerous to mention. The 97 pitches 27 for tourers) have been thoughtfully hedged and grassed and all have electricity (16A). Trees such as catalpa, maple and hibiscus ensure a tranquil feeling. Because of the layout of the site there is a long steep walk (300 m.) from the lower pitches to the toilet block. The administration building has a natural thatch roof (turf to us) and contains a superb restaurant with an open fire. The theme is continued throughout with a pretty bar using the natural wood and stone of the area and cleverly decorated with cork from the magnificent oaks, which abound. This is a superb site for those who love nature.

Facilities

The sanitary block is very much in keeping with the surroundings. It offers free hot water and the modern facilities include very large showers with excellent facilities for disabled campers. The mirrors used are genuine ships' portholes and are a pleasant touch. Cleaning may be variable in low season. Small shop sells essentials but we recommend you stock-up. Bar/restaurant (all year). Playground. Football pitch. Swimming pool. English is spoken. No transit traffic is allowed within the site in high season. Off site: Walking in National park. Fishing 1 km. Riding and bicycle hire 15 km. Golf 40 km.

Open

All year.

At a glance

Welcome & Ambience	✓✓✓✓✓	Location	✓✓✓✓✓
Quality of Pitches	✓✓✓✓✓	Range of Facilities	✓✓✓✓✓

Directions

From N340 San Roque - Algeciras take exit 115. Follow C369 for approx. 30 km. then turn left on C3331 to Ubrique. Turn left after 80 km. marker signed Jimena de la Fronterra. Site is on the right. Don't be put off if the gate is shut on arrival someone will appear.

Charges guide

Per person	€ 3,60
child (2-12 yrs)	€ 2,40
car	€ 3,00
tent or caravan	€ 3,60 - € 4,00
motorcaravan	€ 6,00
electricity	€ 3,00

All plus 7% VAT. No credit cards.
Discounts for longer stays over 1 month.

Reservations

Contact site. Tel: 956 640060.
E-mail: camping@arrakis.es

ES8873 Camping La Aldea

El Rocio, 21750 Almonte (Huelva)

This impressive site lies just on the edge of the Parque Nacional de Donana, southwest of Sevilla on the outskirts of El Rocio. The town hosts a fiesta at the end of May with over one million people attending the local shrine. They travel for days in processions with cow drawn or motorized vehicles to attend. If you want to stay this weekend book well in advance! The well planned, modern site is well set out and the 246 pitches have natural shade from trees or artificial shade and 10A electricity. There are 52 serviced pitches with water and sewerage. There are also pitches for tents and bungalows for rent. The facilities are new, large and very clean. A beautiful waiter service restaurant (where the Spanish eat) provides lovely local food. The staff are welcoming and helpful with plenty of tourist information to hand. Expeditions on horseback or by 4x4 vehicle can be arranged in the national park.

Facilities

Two sanitary blocks provide excellent facilities including provision for disabled visitors. Motorcaravan service point. Swimming pool (May - Oct). Restaurant and bar in separate new complex. Shop. Internet connection. Playground. Football/basketball court. Off site: Bus stop 5 minutes walk. Huelva and Sevilla are about an hour's drive. Beach 15 km.

Open

All year.

At a glance

Welcome & Ambience	✓✓✓✓✓	Location	✓✓✓✓
Quality of Pitches	✓✓✓✓✓	Range of Facilities	✓✓✓✓✓

Directions

From main Huelva – Sevilla road E1/A49 take exit 48 and drive south through Almonte to the outskirts of El Rocio. Site is on left just past the 25 km. marker. Go down to the roundabout and back up to be on the right side of the road to turn in.

Charges 2004

Per person	€ 3,75 - € 4,20
child	€ 2,80 - € 3,25
pitch incl. car	€ 4,20 - € 8,20
electricity	€ 3,75

Less 10-15% for low season stays over 3 days.

Reservations

Contact site. Tel: 95944 2677.
E-mail: info@campinglaaldea.com

www.alanrogers.com for latest campsite news

ES8871 Camping Giralda

Ctra Provincial 4117, 21410 Isla Cristina (Huelva)

The fountains at the entrance and the circular 'thatched' reception building set the tone for this very large, well managed and pleasant site. The 520 pitches are quite spacious on sand, most benefitting from the attractive mature trees which abound on the site. Most pitches have electricity (142 are for tents). Access to the excellent beach is gained by a short stroll, crossing the minor road alongside the site and passing through attractive pine trees. The many additional activities are listed below. There is a separate area within this huge site where organised groups come to enjoy the activities offered within a dedicated adventure area (low season only). A quiet site out of the main tourist area with good leisure and adventure facilities.

Facilities

Four large, modern, semi-circular 'thatched' sanitary blocks are very clean and fully equipped. Laundry. Shop and bar (all year). Restaurant and snacks (Apr – Sept). Swimming pools. Basketball. Archery. Volleyball. Petanque. Soccer. Mountain biking. Beach games. Table tennis. Watersports school. Play area. Organised activity area for groups low season. Excursions booked. Site contract security all year. Off site: Beach and fishing 200 m. Bicycle hire 1 km. Golf 4 km. Riding 7 km.

Open

All year.

At a glance

Welcome & Ambience	✓✓✓✓✓	Location	✓✓✓✓
Quality of Pitches	✓✓✓✓	Range of Facilities	✓✓✓✓✓

Directions

Leave E1/A49 motorway at exit 113 signed Lepe on N444. Turn right on N431, use Lepe bypass, then left to Le Antilla and then on to Isla Cristina. Site is on right (clearly signed) just as you reach Isla Christina (this route avoids Pozo del Camino and many speed bumps).

Charges 2005

Per person	€ 4,85
child (2-10 yrs)	€ 3,55
caravan and car	€ 9,25
motorcaravan	€ 9,00
electricity	€ 3,95
animal	€ 1,50

Plus 7% VAT. Winter discounts.

Reservations

Advised for July/Aug. Tel: 959 343 318.
E-mail: campinggiralda@infonegocio.com

ES9081 Camping Villsom

Ctra Sevilla-Cadiz, km 554.8, 41700 Sevilla (Sevilla)

This city site was one of the first to open in Spain and it is still owned by the same pleasant family. The administrative building consists of a peaceful and attractive bar with patio and satellite TV (where breakfast is served) and there is a pleasant, small reception area. There are no static caravans here, although there is an area for groups. It is a good site for visiting Seville with a frequent bus service to the centre (20 minutes, bus stop close by). Camping Villsom has around 180 pitches which are level and shaded. A huge variety of trees and palms are to be seen around the site and in summer the bright colours of the flowers are very pleasing. The site has a most inviting, palm surrounded pool which is quite secluded. A new hotel (in Spanish style) of nine rooms has been added for 2005 and new facilities for disabled visitors are planned. It is important to book if you intend to visit this site in peak weeks. It is not suitable for large motorhomes and there are few places for large caravans, but book.

Facilities

Sanitary facilities require modernisation in some areas. Some washbasins have cold water only. Laundry facilities. Small shop selling basic provisions. Bar with satellite TV (open July/Aug). Swimming pool (June-Sept). Putting. Table tennis. Drinks machine. Off site: Most town facilities including restaurant, supermarket, cinema and theatre.

Open

All year.

At a glance

Welcome & Ambience	✓✓✓	Location	✓✓✓
Quality of Pitches	✓✓✓	Range of Facilities	✓✓✓

Directions

On main Seville ñ Cadiz NIV road travelling from Seville take exit at km. 553 signed Dos Hermanos – Isla Menor. Go under concrete road bridge and turn immediately right (Isla Mentor) ad site is 80 m. on right. From Cadiz take same signed exit and at roundabout take fourth exit to go over main road and then down a slip road to go under bridege, then as above.Make sure you take the correct exit otherwise it is a lonfg drive along the main road before you can turn back.

Charges 2004

Per person	€ 3,60
child	€ 3,20
pitch incl. car	€ 5,00 - € 7,65
electricity	€ 2,40

All plus 7% VAT.

Reservations

Write to site. Tel: 954 720 828.
E-mail: camping.sevilla@turinet.es

www.alanrogers.com for latest campsite news

ES9082 Camping Sevilla

Ctra N-IV, km 534, 41007 Sevilla (Sevilla)

This site is ideal for visiting the fascinating city of Seville. It is just south of the perimeter of Seville airfield, by day with your ear defenders, you can practice your plane-spotting, but thankfully the usual mandatory respite exists at night, although you are fairly close to the main Seville - Madrid road. This is a flat, sandy site with 85 pitches of varying size for motorcaravans and caravans, plus 450 for tents. Electricity (6/10A) is available. Trees provide some pitches with shade, others have artificial shade. There is the constant change-over bustle of all nationalities coming and going to visit Seville. The kidney shaped pool and paddling pool area are very welcome in the summer heat. The city of Seville is a must for anyone visiting southern Spain. From here came Carmen, Figaro and Don Juan and if you can we recommend the two great Feiras (fiestas) of Seville, one the week before Easter and the other in the last week of April.

Facilities

Buildings housing the sanitary and supporting facilities are round in shape and a happy yellow colour. To reinforce the reality of the intense summer temperatures, half of the showers are cold water only. The remainder provide free hot (very) water, but only cold for all other washing functions. Blocks kept very clean. Supermarket, bar and restaurant (high season). Small bar/snack area (out of main season). Swimming pools (June - Sept; adult € 1,20, child € 0,50). Drinks machines. Electronic games. Two excellent motorhome service points. Off site: Bus service runs to city centre leaving from inside site (high season - low season a short walk to municipal bus stop is necessary). 'Magic Island' theme park 3 km.

Open

All year.

At a glance

Welcome & Ambience	✓✓✓✓	Location	✓✓✓
Quality of Pitches	✓✓✓✓	Range of Facilities	✓✓✓

Directions

From any route follow signs to the airport (very easy) and you will pick up signs for the campsite from any direction. Be sure to follow signs carefully If you miss the turn the quickest way to cross the autoroute is to go through the airport.

Charges 2004

Per person	€ 3,25
child (3-11 yrs)	€ 2,75
car	€ 3,25
caravan	€ 3,25
tent	€ 2,75 - € 3,25
motorcaravan	€ 4,50

Plus 7% VAT. No credit cards.

Reservations

Advised in July and August. Tel: 954 514 379.
E-mail: campingsevilla@wanadoo.es

ES9078 Camping Los Villares

Parque Periurbano, Avenida de l Fuen Santa 8, 14071 Córdoba (Córdoba)

This is a site with a difference. Unusually it is part of one of Spain's natural parks and the environmental rules must be strictly followed when you stay here. For peaceful, simple camping with no frills, there is an area with electricity for 30 units about five minutes walk from a toilet block, restaurant and reception. The 170 tent pitches are delightfully informal. Bountiful pine, olives, gums and other trees provide shade and, as the site is within the Parque, the setting is absolutely natural. Thoughtfully some natural stone tables and benches are scattered around. The natty little bar and restaurant provide a simple menu and drinks - practice your Spanish here! You will most certainly need torches as you find your way home through the strange noises emanating from the densely wooded area beyond the site. The friendly warden will assist as necessary and we played an interesting little game of hunt the chemical disposal for a while (it is there and we did say it was different!). This is great site with reasonable prices for those who have there own transport for visiting the amazing city of Cordoba, or it will suit those who do not need the artificial entertainment of bigger sites and just wish to relax at one with nature.

Facilities

The single toilet facility is centrally located, provides free hot water and is of good quality. Washing machines. Restaurant/bar. Shop. Five-a-side soccer. Off site: Natural Parque (protected) - walks and wildlife.

Open

All year.

Reservations

Contact site. Tel: 957 330145.
E-mail: campingvillares@latinmail.com

At a glance

Welcome & Ambience	✓✓✓✓	Location	✓✓✓✓
Quality of Pitches	✓✓✓	Range of Facilities	✓✓✓

Directions

Site is about 7 km. north of Cordoba on the north side of the river which bisects the city. It is simpler to go to the centre to find the small access road to Parque and site. Follow the Parador (state run hotel) signs if you cannot see the signs for the Parque Periurbano which have small camping sign inside the fairly large green edged signs. Also follow signs for municipal camping which help. All these will bring you past the municipal camping - then look for a major right turn and follow clear signs out of city. Site is a stiff climb of several thousand feet out of city - the views are great!

Charges 2004

Per person	€ 3,00
child	€ 2,50
pitch	€ 3,00 - € 6,00
car or motorcycle	€ 2,50
electricity	€ 3,00

No credit cards.

www.alanrogers.com for latest campsite news

ES9080 Camping Municipal El Brillante

Avenida del Brillante 50, 14012 Córdoba (Córdoba)

For a municipal site this is impressive. Cordoba is one of the hottest places in Europe - the 'frying pan' of Spain - and the superb pool here is more than welcome. This large site is on the north side of the river with a canal running through the centre (well fenced) and pleasant terraced gardens where you can sunbathe. If you really want to stay in the city, then this site is a good choice. It has 120 neat pitches of gravel and sand attractively spaced alongside the canal. The upper pitches are now covered by artificial and natural shade but the lower, newer area has little. Here there are 32 fully serviced pitches and an area for a few large motorhomes. The site becomes very crowded in high season. The entrance is narrow and may be congested so care must be exercised - there is a lay-by just outside and it is easier to walk in initially. The bar/restaurant is close to reception and there is a pleasant terrace bar/restaurant which overlooks the pool gardens in high season. Cordoba is a fascinating town and the Mosque/Cathedral is one of the great buildings of Europe and it is worth allowing two days here to investigate the area. Buses go from outside the site to town.

Facilities

The toilet blocks have been renovated and an impressive newer block has facilities for babies and disabled people. Motorcaravan services. Gas supplies. Bar and restaurant (1/4-30/9). Shop (all year). Swimming pool (15/6-15/9). Play area. Off site: Bus service to city centre from outside site. Commercial centre 300 m. (left out of site, right at traffic lights).

Open

All year.

At a glance

Welcome & Ambience	✓✓✓✓	Location	✓✓✓✓✓
Quality of Pitches	✓✓✓✓	Range of Facilities	✓✓✓✓

Directions

Site is on the north side of the river. From the NIV/E25 road from Madrid, take exit at km. 403 (the middle of three exits for Cordoba) and follow signs for Mosque/Cathedral into city centre. Pass it (on right) and turn right onto the main avenue. Continue and take right fork where the road splits, and follow signs for campsite and/or green signs for district of El Brillante. Site is on right up slight hill on this avenue.

Charges 2004

Per unit incl. 2 persons	€ 17,40
tent incl. 2 persons and car	€ 16,40
tent without car	€ 12,30
child (1-10 yrs)	€ 2,80
electricity	€ 2,80

No credit cards.

Reservations

Not made. It is essential to arrive early in high season. Tel: 957 403 836. E-mail: elbrillante@campings.net

ES9085 Camping Carlos III

Ctra Madrid-Cadiz, km 430, 14100 La Carlota (Córdoba)

This rural site lies 25 km. south of Cordoba, just off the main Cordoba – Sevilla road and may be a good alternative to staying in the city. A very large, busy site especially at weekends, it has many supporting facilities including sporting facilities, a good swimming pool and a pool, play area and animal corner for children. With the bar and catering services open all year, the site has a more open feel than the bustling municipal site in Cordoba. The touring areas are canopied by trees which offer considerable shade for the 300 separated pitches. On sandy, gently sloping ground, around two-thirds have electrical connections (5A). Permanent units, mobile homes and bungalows are in a separate area, where there are further sporting facilities. There may be some slight road noise.

Facilities

Modern toilet blocks provide a mix of British and Turkish WCs, with hot showers in the block near reception. Laundry service. Motorcaravan services. Bar/restaurant, shop (all year). Swimming pools (1/6-15/9). Aviary. Table tennis. Boules. Minigolf, Children's play area. Volleyball. Football. Hairdressers. Off site: Bus service outside site. Riding 500 m. Village 2 km.

Open

All year.

At a glance

Welcome & Ambience	✓✓✓	Location	✓✓✓
Quality of Pitches	✓✓✓✓	Range of Facilities	✓✓✓✓

Directions

From N-IV Cordoba-Seville motorway take La Carlota exit (at km. 429 point northbound or exit 432 southbound). Site is 500 m. and well signed.

Charges 2004

Per person	€ 4,30
child (3-12 yrs)	€ 3,20
pitch	€ 4,30
car	€ 5,90
electricity (5A)	€ 3,20

Plus 7% VAT. Discounts after 7 days.

Reservations

Probably necessary in July/Aug; contact site. Tel: 957 300 697. E-mail: campingcarlos@navegalia.com

ES9084 Camping La Campiña

Ctra Altea Quintana-Pte Genil, 14547 Santaella (Córdoba)

What a charming site – literally amongst the olive trees and set high on a hill to catch cool summer breezes. Everything is immaculately kept and we rarely see sites of this size with such excellent amenities and standards. There is a large pool in a garden setting with cool green lawn and the restaurant, with its traditional rustic charm, has a delightful menu of home made food. The 'menu del dia' was delicious and very good value. Fresh bread and croissants are cooked to order in the morning, or you can have an inexpensive breakfast on the terrace with the piquant smell of olive trees drifting from the fields. We wish we could take credit for finding La Campina, but the truth is that an Alan Rogers reader was so delighted with the site they wrote to us with such a glowing report we just had to see it for ourselves. The 35 pitches are level and most have shade, the surface is gravel and there are views over the olive fields to the surrounding hills. The area is famous for its natural beauty, wine and olives (excursions can be arranged to see olive oil made, and to a local 'bodega' for the wine making). The Martin-Rodriguez family are enthusiastic and work hard to make a visit here a delightful experience.

Facilities

Two small traditional sanitary blocks have clean services including facilities for disabled campers (key at reception). Washing machines. Restaurant. Snack bar. Shop. Swimming pool. Table tennis. Basketball. Torches useful. Off site: Bus from gate to Cordoba. Town 2 km. Riding 15 km. Golf 40 km.

Open

21 January - 19 December.

At a glance

Welcome & Ambience	✓✓✓✓	Location	✓✓✓
Quality of Pitches	✓✓✓✓	Range of Facilities	✓✓✓

Directions

Take exit 441 (La Rambla/Montilla) from the N-IV (E5) Sevilla to Cordoba road. Continue past Santaella towards La Victoria. La Campiña is tucked off this road behind high hedging. If approaching from Cordoba, take exit 424 (Aldea-Quintana/La Victoria) and on towards Santaella for 11.5 km. to the site.

Charges 2004

Per person	€ 3,70
child	€ 3,40
pitch with electricity	€ 10,45

Reservations

Contact site. Tel: 957 315 303.
E-mail: info@campinglacampina.com

ES9089 Camping Despeñaperros

Ctra Infanta Elena, 23213 Santa Elena (Jaén)

This site is on the edge of Santa Elena in a natural park with shade from mature pine trees. This is a good place to stay en-route from Madrid to the Costa del Sol or to just explore the surrounding countryside. Just to the north there are some stunning views of the narrow mountain gorge of Despeñaperros, definitely worth a visit. The site is run in a very friendly manner where nothing is too much trouble. Reception has a monitor link with tourist information and touch screen access to all the region's sites of interest. The 116 pitches are fully serviced including a satellite TV/internet link. In the interests of health and possible smells, all rubbish must be taken to large bins outside the site gates (a long walk from the other end of the site). The site shop is small but there are shops a few hundred yards away in the town. There is an excellent bar with TV and a classy restaurant. A large swimming pool and paddling pool surrounded by grass overlook the beautiful mountains.

Facilities

Two traditional, central sanitary blocks have Turkish style WCs and well equipped showers. One washing machine (launderette in the town). Shop. Excellent bar (all year) and charming restaurant (12/3-20/10). Swimming pools (15/6-15/9). Tennis. First aid room. Caravan storage. Night security. Off site: Walking, riding and mountain sprts nearby. The main road gives good access to Jaen and Valdepenas.

Open

All year.

At a glance

Welcome & Ambience	✓✓✓✓✓	Location	✓✓✓✓✓
Quality of Pitches	✓✓✓✓	Range of Facilities	✓✓✓✓

Directions

Site is signed from the N1V motorway between Bailén and Madrid. Take exit 259 and drive through the main street of Santa Elena to site on edge of town. Drive up slope and under arches (there is an alternative entrance for tall vehicles – ask at reception.

Charges 2004

Per person	€ 3,18
child	€ 2,71
pitch incl. car	€ 6,50 - € 6,87
electricity	€ 2,00

All plus 7% VAT.

Reservations

Contact site. Tel: 953 664 192.
E-mail: campingdesp@navegalia.com

This is one of the most beautiful, and perhaps least known, regions of inland Spain. Its beautiful cities, first Roman and Moorish, then medieval and aristocratic, gave birth to many of the conquistadors - conquerors of the New World.

Extremadura has two provinces: Badajoz and Cáceres

Extremadura is a large and sparsely populated region in the west of Spain, bordering central Portugal and consisting of two provinces, both of which bear the name of their main town. Cáceres, to the north, has a fascinating old quarter, ringed by old Moorish walls and superb watchtowers. Nearby Plasencia is home to a splendid Gothic cathedral, old medieval walls and beautiful Baroque and Renaissance palaces. And the attractive town of Trujillo, birthplace of Pizzaro, the conqueror of Peru, has palaces, churches and a bustling town square.

To the south is Badajoz, the second province and the largest in Spain. With its fortified main town and Alcazaba (citadel), the city of Badajoz is located on the *Vía de la Plata* (Silver Route), an old pilgrimage route to Santiago de Compostela used during the Middle Ages. Located on this route, Mérida is one of the best preserved archaeological sites in Spain. Indeed, the city boasts more Roman remains than any other city, including a Roman theatre and amphitheatre, a Roman Bridge spanning over 800 metres long, with 60 arches, Roman villas and a Museum of Roman Art.

Cuisine of the region

Local cuisine includes the Iberian cured ham and a variety of cheeses; *Torta del Casar, La Serena, Ibores, Gata* and *Cabra del Tietar*. Game abounds in this region (partridge, pigeon, turtledove, rabbit, hare, wild boar, deer) served with wild mushrooms, truffles or wild asparagus. Honey, thyme, heather, rosemary, lavender, lime and eucalyptus are used to prepare a great variety of desserts.

Alfeñiques: caramel dessert

Nuégados: egg yolk and orange buns

Perrunillas: small round cakes

Rosquillas: ring-shaped biscuits

Técula-mécula: cinnamon, almond and tea

Places of interest

Alcántara: six-arched Roman bridge, castle, mansions

Corio: quiet old town enclosed by 4th century Roman walls, cathedral

Cuacos de Yuste: town with 15th century Jeronimos Monastery

Guadalupe: old pilgrimage centre, church and monastery

Jerez de los Caballeros: birthplace of various conquistadores

Olivenza: town with strong Portuguese influence, castle, ethnographic museum, 17th century church

Pedroso de Acim: Convento del Palancar – said to be the smallest monastery in the world

Alan Rogers tip

VISIT THE MONFRAGÜE NATURE RESERVE; A PROTECTED AREA WITH FORESTS, MEADOWS, RIVERS AND RESERVOIRS, WITH OVER 200 ANIMAL SPECIES INCLUDING THE SPANISH LYNX.

ES9087 Camping Mérida

Ctra NV Madrid-Port, km 336.6, 06800 Mérida (Badajoz)

Mérida was the tenth city of the Roman Empire and it is purported that it contains the most Roman remains in all of Spain. The 60-arched Roman bridge, the amphitheatre and the National museum of Roman art are just some of the attractions that can be enjoyed here. In July and August the theatre festival stages classical Greek plays and Roman tragedies. Camping Mérida is situated alongside the main N-V road to Madrid, the restaurant, café and pool complex separating the camping site area from the road where there is considerable noise. The site has 80 good sized pitches, most with some shade and on sloping ground, with ample electricity connections (long leads may be needed) and hedges with imaginative topiary. No English is spoken, but try out your Spanish. Reception is open until midnight. Camping Mérida is ideally located to serve both as a base to tour the local area or as an overnight stop en route when travelling either north/south or east/west.

Facilities

The central sanitary facility includes hot and cold showers, British style WCs, dishwashing sinks (H&C) and laundry sinks (cold only) under cover. Gas supplies. Small shop for essentials. Busy restaurant/cafeteria and bar, also open to the public. Medium sized swimming pool and paddling pool with lifeguard (May-Sept). Bicycle hire. Play area (unfenced and near road). Caravan storage. Torches useful.
Off site: Town 5 km.

Open

All year.

At a glance

Welcome & Ambience	✓✓✓	Location	✓✓✓
Quality of Pitches	✓✓✓	Range of Facilities	✓✓✓

Directions

Site is alongside NV road (Madrid-Lisbon), 5 km. east of Mérida, at km. 336.6. From east take exit 334 and follow camping signs (doubling back). Site is actuallty on the 630 road that runs alongside the motorway.

Charges 2004

Per person	€ 3,80
child	€ 3,20
pitch incl. car	€ 5,10 - € 7,60
electricity	€ 3,00

All plus VAT.

Reservations

Write to site. Tel: 924 303 453.
E-mail: proexcam@jet.es

ES9027 Camping Parque Natural de Monfrague

Ctra Plasencia-Trujillo km 10, 10680 Malpartida de Plasencia (Cáceres)

Situated on the edge of the Monfrague National Park, this well managed site owned by the Barrado family, has fine views to the Sierra de Mirabel and delightful surrounding countryside. It would prove difficult to find a more suitable location for those that savour peace, quiet, study of yesteryear, flora and fauna. Created as a National Park in 1979, Monfrague is now recognised as one of the best locations in Europe for anyone with any degree of interest in birdwatching. During our visit we saw Griffon, Black and Egyptian Vultures, Black and Red Kites, Azure-winged Magpies, Purple Gallinule, Purple Heron, Black-eared Wheatear, Bee-eater, White and the more rare Black Storks to name but a few. Nearby Plasencia has a medieval aqueduct, fine cathedral (14th C.) and the town's original twin ring of walls containing 68 towers. To the south, the classic historical towns of Merida, Caceres and Trujillo. Many of the 128 good-sized pitches are grassed on slightly sloping terraced ground. Scattered trees offer a degree of shade, there are numerous water points and electricity is rated at 10A. Used by locals, the air-conditioned restaurant provides good quality food at acceptable prices. An evening meal on the veranda as the sunsets will install fond memories of a rewarding holiday. The stork's nest perched precariously on a 15-metre pole near to the site entrance provided only a landmark when we visited as none had taken up residence. On rare occasions a goods train travels along the nearby railway line.

Facilities

Large modern toilet blocks, fully equipped, are very clean. Facilities for disabled campers and baby baths. Laundry. Supermarket/shop. Restaurant, bar and coffee shop. TV room with recreational facilities and fire for cooler times. Swimming pools and children's pool (June - Sept). Children's play area. Tennis. Basketball. Bicycle hire. Riding. Animation for children in season. Barbecue areas. Off site: Large supermarket at Plasencia.

Open

All year.

At a glance

Welcome & Ambience	✓✓✓✓	Location	✓✓✓✓✓
Quality of Pitches	✓✓✓✓✓	Range of Facilities	✓✓✓✓

Directions

Approaching on the N630 - From the north take the EX-208 (previously C524) Plasencia - Trujillo; site on left in approx. 6km. From the south turn right just south of Plasencia onto EX-108 (previously C511) in direction of Malpartida de Plasencia. Right at main junction onto EX-208 to site.

Charges guide

Per person	€ 3,20
child	€ 2,50
tent or caravan	€ 3,20
car	€ 2,50
motorcaravan	€ 4,50
electricity	€ 2,50

VAT included.

Reservations

Write to site. Tel: 927 459 233.

ES9028 Camping Las Villueracas

Ctra Villanueva, 10140 Guadalupe (Cáceres)

This rural site nestles in an attractive valley northwest of Guadalupe. The pools and restaurant are of a very high standard (the locals eat there!) and the restaurant leads to a pretty patio with overhead vines and potted plants allowing elevated views of the pools. There is a separate patio across the village street which is pleasant for sitting out with drinks whilst the management provide a barbecue and more casual food. The 70 pitches are level and of a reasonable size; some are marked, although the logic of the numbering is difficult to follow in places and large units may experience difficulty in getting into the more central pitches. There is limited shade from young trees and a more shaded area in a 'spinney'. A river runs alongside the site and we are told that the ground can be muddy in very wet periods. The site is co-located with hostel accommodation. An ideal location for visiting the Monastery of Guadalupe, and the town of Guadalupe in the Sierra de Guadalupe, an attractive historic tourist town with plenty of bars and restaurants.

Facilities

The single toilet block is in the older style but very clean, one area for women and one for men, providing British type WCs, washbasins and free hot showers (although hot water is from a 40 litre immersion heater which could be overwhelmed in busy periods). No facilities for disabled campers as yet. Restaurant. Bar. Swimming pools. Shop. Tennis. Small playground. Barbecue area. Safe deposit. Medical post. Car wash. No English spoken.

Open

All year.

At a glance

Welcome & Ambience	✓✓✓	Location	✓✓✓
Quality of Pitches	✓✓✓	Range of Facilities	✓✓✓

Directions

From NV/E90 Madrid - Mérida exit at Navelmoral de la Mata. Follow south to Guadalupe on CC713 (approx. 83 km). Site is 2 km. from Guadalupe, near the Monastery. From further southwest take exit 102 off main E90/NV (northeast of Merida) and follow signs for Guadalupe. Go through a few villages and near 72 km. marker turn left to site, a hundred meters on right.

Charges 2004

Per person	€ 3,00
child (2-12 yrs)	€ 2,50
tent	€ 2,10 - € 2,40
electricity	€ 2,50

No credit cards.

Reservations

Write to site. Tel: 927 367 139.

ES9400 Camping Sierra de Gata

Ctra Ex-109 a Gata, km 4,100, 10860 Gata (Cáceres)

For a taste of the real, rural Spain this very Spanish site (no English was spoken when we visited) is situated just before the tiny village of Sierra de Gata, south of Ciudad Rodrigo and northwest of Plasencia. Situated in beautiful countryside with a small stream alongside the site, the pitches are on grass with plenty of shade from trees. We suspect that it is a popular site with Spanish people which would give the opportunity to practice the language and get an insight into the Spanish way of life. The village of Gata is small with only a few houses and if you continue along the road you will climb into the mountains and natural park, good for walks and picnics. The other side of the hill leads down into another town but this has very small streets and is probably best not driven through with a motor-caravan! This site is being refurbished with the addition of 12 beautiful new bungalows to sleep 4-6 people. A special area with huts for groups of children to stay is positioned in one corner of the site.

Facilities

Two toilet blocks with British style toilets also include child size toilets, a laundry room and dishwashing facilities. Medium sized shop for necessities in summer. Smart restaurant/bar complex provides good food. Two swimming pools. Good football/basketball court. Tennis. Table tennis. Play area. Fishing. Riding. Bicycle hire. Off site: Restaurant near campsite entrance.

Open

18 March - 3 November.

At a glance

Welcome & Ambience	✓✓✓	Location	✓✓✓✓
Quality of Pitches	✓✓✓	Range of Facilities	✓✓✓

Directions

Approach ONLY from the southwest from the Ciudad Rodrico - Coria no. 109 road. Where the 205 meets the 109 take turn 20–30 m. north signed Gata 10. Travel along this road until km. 4. Turn left (near restaurant and small bridge) and site is ahead.

Charges 2004

Per person	2,82
child (3-12 yrs)	2,52
pitch	7,81
electricity	2,28

Reservations

Contact site. Tel: 927 672168.
E-mail: sierradegata@campingsonline.com

www.alanrogers.com for latest campsite news

This region is located south of Madrid and occupies what was the southern part of the ancient kingdom of Castille, including the area known as La Mancha, universally famous as the setting for Miguel de Cervantes great novel *Don Quijote de la Mancha.*

Castilla-La Mancha has five provinces: Albacete, Ciudad Real, Cuenca, Guadalajara and Toledo

The capital of the region is Toledo

The terrain can be divided into two distinct parts: the plateau, an extensive flat land with very few mountains, and the mountainous areas, which encircle the plateau around the region's borders, including the foothills along the massifs of the Central mountain range, the Iberian mountain range and the Sierra Morena.

Toledo is crammed with monuments and nearly all the different stages of Spanish art are represented with Moorish-Mudejar-Jewish buildings; Gothic structures, such as the splendid cathedral; and Renaissance buildings. Toledo was also home to El Greco and many of his paintings are displayed in the Museum of El Greco. The region of Cuenca is surrounded by mountainous, craggy countryside, with the city itself home to extraordinary houses which hang over the cliff tops of the deep gorges. One of these has been converted into the Museum of Abstract Art. In the heartland of La Mancha, through the region of Ciudad Real, you can follow the Ruta de Don Quixote and see the famous windmills at Campo de Criptana.

Cuisine of the region

Local produce features heavily: aubergines, garlic, peppers, tomatoes, olive oil, meat, including both game and farm animals. Wine from La Mancha, Valdepeñas, Méntrida, Almansa, Dominio de Valdepusa and Finca de Elez

Alajú: an almond and nut pastry

Bizcochás de Alcázar: a tart soaked in milk with sugar, vanilla and cinnamon

Caldereta manchega: lamb stew

Morteruelo: paté made of pork and game birds

Pisto manchego: a type of ratatouille with tomatoes, red and green peppers, courgettes, served either hot or cold

Tiznao: filleted cod which is flame-grilled in an earthenware dish with pepper, tomatoes, onions and garlic.

Places of interest

Almagro: home of international theatre festival

Albacete: renowned for its knife-making industry, 16th century cathedral

Guadalajara: preserved Moorish walls, 10th century bridge, Santa Maria la Mayor, 15th century Duque del Infantado Palace

Alan Rogers tip

VISIT LA CIUDAD ENCANTADA IN CUENCA, AN AREA OF LIMESTONE OUTCROPS, AND SEE HOW EROSION HAS SCULPTED THE ROCK TO CREATE ANIMAL-LIKE AND ABSTRACT FORMS.

www.alanrogers.com for latest campsite news

ES9090 Camping El Greco

Ctra CM-4000 km 0,7, Puebla de Montalban, 45004 Toledo (Toledo)

Toledo was the home of the Grecian painter and the site that bears his name boasts a beautiful view of the ancient city from the restaurant, bar and superb pool. The friendly, family owners make you welcome and are proud of their site which is the only one in Toledo (it can get crowded). There is an attractive, tree-lined approach and ivy clad pergolas run down each side of the swimming pool. A large shaded terrace offers shelter from the sun which can be very hot here. The 150 pitches are of 80 sq.m. with electrical connections and shade from strategically planted trees. Most have hedges that separate and give privacy, with others in herring bone layouts that make for interesting parking in some areas. Access to some pitches may be tricky for caravans (narrow and at an angle) and some site roads are narrow. The river Tagus streches alongside the site but fishing in it is a better bet than swimming. This site makes a relaxing base to return to after a hard day visiting the amazing sights of the old city of Toledo or for something different visit the Warner Brothers Theme Park.

Facilities

Two sanitary blocks, both modernised include facilities for disabled campers and everything is modern and kept clean. Laundry. Motorcaravan services. Swimming pool (15/6-15/9; with charge). Restaurant/bar (1/4-30/9) with good menu and fair prices. Shop in reception. Volleyball. Playgrounds. Barbecues. Ice cube machine. Off site: Fishing in river. Golf 10 km. Riding 15 km. An hourly air-conditioned bus service runs from the gates to the city centre, touring the outside of the walls first. Warner Brothers movie theme park 40 mins. Madrid 1 hour drive.

Open

All year.

At a glance

Welcome & Ambience	✓✓✓✓✓	Location	✓✓✓✓✓
Quality of Pitches	✓✓✓✓✓	Range of Facilities	✓✓✓✓✓

Directions

Site is on C4000 road on the edge of the town, signed towards Puebla de Montelban; site signs also in city centre. From Madrid on N401, turn off right towards Toledo city centre but turn right again at the roundabout at the gates to the old city. Site is signed from the next right turn.

Charges guide

Per person	€ 4,40
child (3-10 yrs)	€ 3,70
caravan or tent	€ 4,24
car	€ 4,24
motorcycle	€ 3,50
motorcaravan	€ 8,49

Plus 7% VAT.

Reservations

Not made. Tel: 925 220 090.
E-mail: elgreco@retemail.es

ES9097 Camping Los Batanes

Ctra Lagunas de Ruidera, km 8, 02611 Ossa de Montiel (Albacete)

This large campsite is in a lovely setting at the side of one of the many lakes in this area. The route to get here is beautiful and it is well worth the trip, but careful driving was necessary in parts with our American motorhome. A smaller, older part of the campsite houses reception, a small shop (ask at reception they will open it in low season whenever you wish), a bar and restaurant and one toilet block. Here are medium sized pitches, shaded by pine trees with a small river running through. Over a wooden bridge is the main newer, part of the campsite with over 200 level, gravel and sand pitches of mixed size, shaded again by pine trees. There is a new toilet block (cleaner and more modern than the other) plus two barbecue areas. Another small stream runs towards the lake which can be seen from a few of the pitches. Towards one end of this new site is the swimming pool complex with two pools surrounded by hedges and grass for sunbathing, more toilets and places to eat, drink and have fun. In summer children's club activities are run from here and this is definitely the part of the campsite with a lot going on. The site is increasingly popular with Spanish campers who come to relax and enjoy watersport activities in a beautiful area. Because of its popularity it is being extended and should develop into a good large place to stay.

Facilities

One old toilet block (a slight smell) and a newer, more spacious, better one just finished. If cleaning is maintained they should cope in high season. Small shop. Simple restaurant, snacks and bar (June - Sept, and weekends). Swimming pools (19 June - Sept). Play area. Children's activities. Off site: Beautiful walks and many lakes to explore. Watersports in summer. Tourist information either at reception or 9 km. at nearest village. Bus stop in village.

Open

All year.

At a glance

Welcome & Ambience	✓✓✓	Location	✓✓✓✓
Quality of Pitches	✓✓✓✓	Range of Facilities	✓✓✓

Directions

On E5/NIV Cordoba – Madrid road (south of Madrid) take 430 road towards lbacete. Coming into Ruidera turn right (just after lake on the right) signed Lagunas de Ruideria. Drive 8 km. along this country road to site on right.

Charges 2004

Per person	€ 3,90 - € 4,80
child (1-13 yrs)	€ 3,25 - € 3,90
pitch	€ 8,50 - € 13,00
electricity (5A)	€ 2,90

Reservations

Contact site. Tel: 926 699 076.
E-mail: camping@losbatanes.com

www.alanrogers.com for latest campsite news

ES9088 Camping de Fuencaliente

km 105, N420 Cordoba-Tarragona, 13130 Fuencaliente (Ciudad Real)

This quiet site nestles in an attractive valley between the Sierra Modrona and the Sierra Morena. It is a site for getting away from it all and sampling the peaceful mountain beauty. It could also be a useful stopover if crossing Spain coast to coast or if you wish to visit the fascinating historic town of Toledo. With very few other desirable sites in this region of Castilla - La Mancha, this one is spacious with 91 generously sized pitches (over 100 sq.m.) all with electricity (6A) and water. There is both artificial shade and natural shade from pine trees and the beautiful, restful views. Areas are also allocated for tents. The large swimming pool with a separate children's area is most welcome in summer, as this part of Spain gets very hot. The site has a good restaurant overlooking the pools, with reasonable prices. The local village of Fuencaliente is 5 km. south and provides the usual village facilities including some very good Spanish restaurants and bars.

Facilities

The large, modern toilet block has excellent facilities. Laundry sinks. Swimming pool (1/6-15/9; free). Restaurant/bar. Supermarket. Playground. Barbecue area with table and benches overlooking the countryside.
Off site: Fuencaliente 5 km.

Open

2 April - 9 September.

At a glance

Welcome & Ambience	✓✓✓	Location	✓✓✓✓
Quality of Pitches	✓✓✓	Range of Facilities	✓✓

Directions

From the N420 road (Cuidad Real – Cordoba) turn by 105 km. marker (approx. 5 km. north of Fuencaliente) onto unmade road signed Camping San Isidro to site.

Charges 2004

Per person	€ 3,61
child	€ 3,31
tent	€ 3,61
caravan	€ 5,71
car	€ 2,10
motorcycle	€ 1,80

Electricity included. Plus 7% VAT.

Reservations

Contact site. Tel: 926 698 170.

ES9094 Camping La Aguzadera

Ctra N-IV, km 197.5, 13300 Valdepeñas (Ciudad Real)

This is a small, unassuming site which will be useful to travellers, especially if you wish to enjoy some excellent Spanish fare in the restaurant. There are few other campsites open all year in this area. With pleasant views of the mountains, the site is part of a huge sports complex where there is lots of activity, although the site is quite separate with lots of room to manoeuvre. The 66 pitches are of average size and are on sloping sand with a few trees providing a little shade. There is some road noise as the site is just off the N4. The sophisticated restaurant overlooks a pool with terraces and sunbathing areas but food is also available in the bar. It is primarily a transit site but useful if you are following the Valdepenas wine route.

Facilities

The central sanitary block is average, unheated, but clean. Washbasins have cold water only. Restaurant plus bar and attached eating area. Essentials from bar. Swimming pool and paddling pools (high season only). Play area. Tennis. Large sports complex alongside (charges apply). Dogs are not accepted. Torches required.

Open

1 June - 30 September.

At a glance

Welcome & Ambience	✓✓✓	Location	✓✓✓
Quality of Pitches	✓✓✓	Range of Facilities	✓✓✓✓

Directions

Site is directly off N4 Madrid - Cadiz at 197 km. marker at Valdepenas exit. Look for the 'Angel of Peace' statue – the site is directly opposite and is well signed.

Charges guide

Per person	€ 3,55
child	€ 2,57
car	€ 3,71
caravan	€ 3,95
tent	€ 3,01
motorcaravan	€ 5,88

Reservations

Contact site. Tel: 926 310 769.
E-mail: la-aguzadera@manchanet.es

The region of Madrid lies right in the middle of the Spanish mainland bordering Castilla-La Mancha and Castilla and Leon. At the centre lies the city of Madrid, which since the 16th century has been the country's capital.

The region of Madrid is a one province autonomy, also called Madrid

The mountainous region of Madrid can be divided into two areas: the sierra, in the north and west of the region, which includes part of Somosierra and Guadarrama; and the central and southern parts, where the area is flatter and forms part of the plateau of La Mancha and La Alcarria.

Founded by the Moors in the 9th Century, Madrid is now a modern, vibrant city offering innumerable attractions to the visitor. Its architectural heritage is immense. Some of the oldest parts of Madrid lie around the Puerta del Sol; a good starting place for exploring the city. Full of outdoor resturants and bars, Plaza Mayor is considered to be one of the finest in Spain, and in summer bcomes an outdoor theatre and music stage. The city also has a large number of parks and gardens, among them el Retiro, the Botanical Gardens, the Parque del Oeste and the Casa de Campo; and numerous museums and art galleries. Outside the capital, the Sierra de Madrid is ideal for winter sports and the beautiful town of Aranjuez, home to the Royal Palace and glorious gardens, is a popular retreat from the city.

Cuisine of the region

Tapas is popular with typical dishes including seafood: steamed mussels, anchovies in vinegar and pickled bonito plus croquettes and mini-casseroles. Sea bream and cod is used a lot. Local produce includes beef from the Guadarrama Mountains, olives from Campo Real, aniseed from Chinchón and asparagus from Aranjuez. Madrid is also a good place to experience every regional style of Spanish cooking

Buñuelos: a type of fritter which is filled with custard, chocolate and cream

Cocido: meat, potato and chickpea stew

Con gabardina: prawns cooked in beer

Torrijas: bread pudding

Places of interest

Alcala de Henares: university town, birthplace of Cervantes, author of Don Quixote, Cervantes House Museum, Archepiscopal Palace Cathedral

Chinchón: 15th century castle, beautiful medieval square, 19th century church with painting by Goya, home of Alchoholera de Chinchón – aniseed liqueur!

Parque Natural de la Cumbre: moutain park, highest mountains in the Madrid region.

San Lorenzo de El Escorial: town in heart of Guadarrama Mountains, Monastery of El Escorial, Royal Pantheon

Alan Rogers tip

THE VERANOS DE LA VILLA (JULY-SEPT) AND FESTIVAL DE OTONO (SEPT-NOV) IN MADRID HAS THEATRE, CINEMA, FLAMENCO AND MUSIC CONCERTS. MANY EVENTS ARE FREE.

www.alanrogers.com for latest campsite news

ES9091 Camping Municipal Soto del Castillo

Soto del Rebollo s/n, 28300 Aranjuez (Madrid)

Aranjuez, supposedly Spain's version of Versailles, is worthy of a visit with its beautiful palaces, leafy squares, avenues and gardens. It is 47 km. south of Madrid and 46 km. from Toledo, and is therefore a useful and popular site, excellent for enjoying the unusual attractions or for an en-route stop. You can visit the huge, but slightly decaying Royal Palace or the Casa del Labrador (translates as farmer's cottage) which is a small neo-classical palace in unusual and differing styles. It has superb gardens commissioned by Charles II. Two little tourist road trains run from the site to the palaces daily. This unusally well equipped municipal site is alongside to the River Tajo in a park-like situation with mature trees. The 225 touring pitches, all with electricity (10A), are set on flat grass, unmarked amid tall trees. Siting is informal but pitches are of moderate size. Canoes may be hired from behind the supermarket and there is a lockable moat gate to allow access to the river. There is good security backed up with CCTV around the river perimeter.

Facilities

The largest of three modern and good quality sanitary blocks is heated in winter and well equipped with some washbasins in cabins. Two smaller blocks of more open design have been refurbished. Washing up facilities have only cold water. Laundry facilities. Gas supplies. Small shop (15/6-15/9). Bar/restaurant (all year) with attractive riverside patio (also open to the public). Takeaway. TV room. Swimming and paddling pools (15/6-15/9). Play area. Volleyball. Bicycle hire. Boat launching and Canoe hire. Drinks machines. Torch useful. Off site: Within easy walking distance of palace, gardens and museums. Riding 5 km. Golf 20 km.

Open

All year.

At a glance

Welcome & Ambience	✓✓✓✓✓	Location	✓✓✓✓✓
Quality of Pitches	✓✓✓✓	Range of Facilities	✓✓✓✓✓

Directions

Using the A305 from Madrid to Aranjuez look for the 8 km. marker on the outskirts of town. Then follow campsite signs - these lead you back onto the A305 (going north now) and the site is signed off right at 300 m. on the first left bend. Follow signs down the narrow road for 400 m. If coming from the south ensure that you have the A305 to Madrid - there are other roads signed to Madrid. If in doubt ask as it is very confusing if the A305 road is missed.

Charges guide

Per person	€ 3,00 - € 3,91
child (3-10 yrs)	€ 2,55 - € 3,15
caravan	€ 3,45 - € 4,36
tent	€ 2,70 - € 4,21
car	€ 2,55 - € 3,30
motorcaravan	€ 3,76 - € 4,81

Plus 7% VAT. Discounts for groups or long stays.

Reservations

Write to site. Tel: 918 911 395.

ES9092 Camping Lagos Coto Cisneros

Ctra Pte Arganda - Chinchon, 28500 Arganda del Rey (Madrid)

This is a large, lively site with a very simple Spanish flavour, 20 km. from Madrid, which could be used for exploring the capital or as a stopping point if travelling to the south as it is about half-way through Spain. The 340 marked pitches are of reasonable size, all have 5A electricity and most are shaded by mature trees. There is a large representation of permanent Spanish pitches but the touring pitches are generally separate and in pleasant surroundings. There are several lakes, two near the entrance and the other is surrounding more than half the site boundary. All are safely fenced but the friendly ducks have their own accesses and may well join you for a meal. The lakes are good for fishing and watersports are available (nothing involving engines). If you arrive late out of season persevere and the security guard will let you in. We see this mostly as a transit site but you can practice your language skills here and use it as a base to visit the new Warner Brothers Movie world theme park at San Martin de la Vega just 16 km. away.

Facilities

Unsophisticated, unheated sanitary blocks but clean and neat with facilities for disabled campers. (Note one block has push button hot water with free flow cold water to the shower which is irritating). Staged area for animation in summer. Restaurant/bar (hours vary in winter and they may only open at weekends). Swimming pool and paddling pool (supervised in season). Play area. Watersports. Fishing. Football. Tennis. Bicycle hire. Petanque. Torch useful. Off site: Theme park 16 km. Madrid 20 km.

Open

All year.

At a glance

Welcome & Ambience	✓✓✓✓	Location	✓✓✓✓
Quality of Pitches	✓✓✓	Range of Facilities	✓✓✓

Directions

From Madrid - Alabcete E901/NIII take the M832 Morata de T/Chinchon road at 20.5 km. from Madrid. Chincon. The site is 3 km further on and well signed.

Charges guide

Per person	€ 3,61
child	€ 3,01
caravan or tent	€ 3,61
car	€ 3,61
motorcaravan	€ 6,62
electricity (5A)	€ 3,31

No credit cards.

Reservations

Contact site. Tel: 918 719 695.

www.alanrogers.com for latest campsite news

ES9200 Caravanning El Escorial

Apdo. Correos 8, Ctra M600, km 3500, 28280 El Escorial (Madrid)

There is a shortage of good sites in the central regions of Spain, but this is one (albeit rather expensive). It is well situated for sightseeing visits especially to the magnificent El Escorial monastery which is a short drive. Also, the enormous civil war monument of the Valle de los Caidos is very close plus Madrid and Segovia are both about 50 km. El Escorial is very large, there are 1,358 individual pitches with artificial shade (ensure you get a pitch without a low tree canopy if you have a 3 m. high motorcaravan. Of these, 750 are occupied by permanent units but are totally separate from the touring and tent areas – weekends can be lively and noisy on the site and in the bar. There are another 250 pseudo 'wild' spaces for tourists on open fields, with good shade from mature trees (long cables may be necessary for electricity). The general amenities are good and include three swimming pools (unheated), plus a paddling pool in a central area with a bar/restaurant with terrace and plenty of sitting out areas.

Facilities

Three large refurbished toilet blocks, plus two smart, small blocks for the 'wild' camping area, are all fully equipped with some washbasins in private cabins. Baby baths and facilities for disabled campers. The blocks can be heated in cool weather. Large supermarket (1/3-31/10) and souvenir shop. Restaurant/bar and snack bar (1/3-31/10). Disco-bar. Swimming pools. Three tennis courts. Two football pitches. Basketball. Fronton. Volleyball. Two well equipped playgrounds on sand. ATM. Off site: Town 3 km. Riding or golf 7 km.

Open

All year.

At a glance

Welcome & Ambience	✓✓✓✓✓	Location	✓✓✓✓
Quality of Pitches	✓✓✓✓✓	Range of Facilities	✓✓✓✓✓

Directions

From the south go through the town of El Escorial, follow the M600 - Guadarrama road - the site is between the 2 and 3 km. markers north of town on the right. If approaching from the north use the A6 autopista take exit 47 and the M600 towards El Escorial town. Site is on the left.

Charges guide

Per person	€ 4,60
child (3-10 yrs)	€ 4,45
caravan or tent	€ 4,60
car	€ 4,60
motorcaravan	€ 7,90
electricity	€ 3,30

VAT included. No credit cards.

Reservations

May be made in writing to guarantee admission.
Tel: 918 902 412.
E-mail: info@campingelescorial.com

ES9210 Camping Pico de la Miel

Ctra NI Madrid - France, km 58, 28751 La Cabrera (Madrid)

Pico de la Miel is a very large site, 70 kilometres north of Madrid. It is well signed and easy to find, two or three kilometres southwest off the main N1 road, with an amazing mountain backdrop. Mainly a long-stay site for Madrid hence there are a huge number of very well established, fairly old statics. There is a small separate area with its own toilet block for touring units. The 60 pitches are on rather poor, sandy grass, some with artificial shade. Others, not so level, are under sparse pine trees and there are yet more pitches for tents (the ground could be hard for pegs). Electricity connections are available. Tall hedges abound and trees make it resemble a giant maze, no internal signs are provided and the long walk to the pool can be a challenge. The noise level from the many Spanish customers is high and you will have a chance to practice your Spanish!

Facilities

Dated but clean tiled toilet block, with some washbasins in cabins and free hot water to laundry and washing up sinks. It can be heated and an en-suite unit with ramp is provided for disabled visitors. Motorcaravan services. Gas supplies. Shop. Restaurant/ Bar (all year). Excellent swimming pool complex, supervised (15/6-15/9). Tennis. Playground.
Off site: Bicycle hire and riding 200 m. Fishing 8 km.

Open

All year.

At a glance

Welcome & Ambience	✓✓✓✓	Location	✓✓✓✓
Quality of Pitches	✓✓✓✓	Range of Facilities	✓✓✓✓✓

Directions

Site is well signed from the N1. Going south use exit 60, going north exit 59 or 60, and follow site signs.

Charges guide

Per person	€ 4,40
child (2-9 yrs)	€ 4,00
caravan or tent	€ 4,40
car	€ 4,40
motorcaravan	€ 7,00
electricity	€ 3,00

All plus 7% VAT. Less 10-25% for longer stays.

Reservations

Contact site. Tel: 918 688 082.
E-mail: pico-miel@picodelamiel.com

Widely regarded as the 'Bible' by site owners and readers alike, there is no better guide when it comes to forming an independent view of a campsite's quality. When you need to be confident in your choice of campsite, you need the Alan Rogers Guide.

- ✓ Sites only included on merit
- ✓ Sites cannot pay to be included
- ✓ Independently inspected, rigorously assessed
- ✓ Impartial reviews
- ✓ 36 years of expertise

INSPECTED CAMPSITES & SELECTED

Castilla y León

The large region of Castilla y León is located inland, bordering Portugal to the west. It has a rich legacy dating back to the Romans, with an extraordinary wealth of castles, cathedrals and mansions, historic cities and towns.

The region is made up of the following provinces:
Avila, Burgos, Leon, Palencia, Salamanca, Valladolid, Zamora, Segovia and Soria

Steeped in history and architectural sights, the major towns and cities of the provinces all have something to offer. In the south, the town of Ávila is set on a high plain, surrounded by 11th century walls; and the graceful city of Salamanca was once home to one of the most prestigious universities in the world. Its grand Plaza Mayor is the finest in Spain. In the east, Segovia is well known for its magnificent Roman aqueduct, with 163 arches and 29 metres at its highest point; the cathedral; and the fairy-tale Alcazár, complete with turrets and narrow towers. And the attractive city of Soria still retains a Romanesque legacy in its network of medieval streets. Burgos in the north, is the birthplace of El Cid and has a Gothic cathedral of exceptional quality, making it one of the finest in Spain. The lively university city of Leon boasts a Royal Pantheon, decorated by Romanesque wall paintings, and also an impressive Gothic cathedral. There too is a Gothic cathedral in Palencia plus an archaeology museum. South of Leon, the old walled quarters of Zamora have a retained medieval appearance, with a dozen Romanesque churches. And in the centre of the region, Valladolid is famous for its extravagant and solemn processions during the Holy Week celebrations.

Cuisine of the region

The region is best known for its roast pork and lamb which has earned it the nickname *España del Asado* (Spain of the Roast). Other local products include trout from Leon and Zamora, and a variety of pulses: white, red and black beans, Castilian and *Pedrosillano* chickpeas, and various types of lentils. Soups feature a lot in winter: trout soup, typical of Órbigo de Leon; garlic soup; Zamora soup, a garlic soup with ripe tomatoes and hot chilli peppers

Bizcochos de San Lorenzo: sponge cakes

Farinatos: sausages made from breadcrumbs, pork fat and spices

Hornazos: sausage and egg tarts

Judias del barco con chorizo: haricot beans with sausage

Yemas: a sweet made with egg yolks and sugar

Places of interest

Astorga: city of Roman origin, chocolate museum, cathedral

Ciudad Rodrigo: Renaissance mansions, cathedral, 12th century walls

Coca: impressive Mudejar castle, birthplace of the famous Roman emperor Theodosius the Great

Pantano de Burgomillodo: reservoir, great for bird-watchers

Parque Natural del Cañón del Río Lobos: park created around the canyon of the River Lobos with rock formations, cave and good walking tracks

Parque Natural del Lago de Sanabria y alrededores: mountainous area with deep valleys and glacier lagoons, variety of flora and fauna including 76 types of birds and 17 large mammals

Alan Rogers tip

THE PLAZA DEL COSA IN PEÑAFIEL MAKES ONE OF THE MOST SPECTACULAR BULLRINGS IN SPAIN WHEN BULLFIGHTS ARE HELD IN AUGUST.

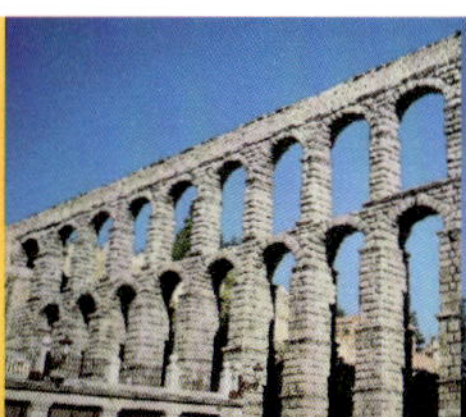

www.alanrogers.com for latest campsite news

ES9019 Camping La Pesquera

Ctra de Caceres - Arrabal, 37500 Ciudad Rodrigo (Salamanca)

This modest site has just 54 pitches and is located near the Rio Agueda looking up to the magnificent fortress ramparts of Ciudad Rodrigo. A frontier city in its heyday, it has much of historic interest including the first Parador to be located in an historic building. The cathedral belfry still has shell marks caused the Duke of Wellington's army during the 1812 war of independence. There are also wonderful treasures to be found in the golden stone buildings within the city walls. Entry to the site is through a municipal park with a large play area. Whilst the site is small it can take even the largest units, the centrally located facilities have all been refurbished to a high standard, the pitches are flat and grassy and the roads are well maintained gravel. The pitches are shaded by trees by day and there is site lighting at night although you may find torches useful due to the tree canopy. The reception and a small bar which serves snacks in summer is near the front of the site. There is a touch of old Spain directly alongside the site, an old farmhouse with its trailing grape vine and ancient well.

Facilities

Attractive new ochre/stone sanitary building with British WCs and free hot showers. Washing machine, dishwashing (H&C) and laundry (C) sinks. Facilities for disabled campers. Basics sold from bar in high season. Bar/snacks (April - Sept). Playground outside gates. Barbecue outside gate. Torches useful. Off site: Fort in town to explore. River fishing 1 km. Riding 5 km. Superb walking area.

Open

25 April - 30 September.

At a glance

Welcome & Ambience	✓✓✓✓✓	Location	✓✓✓✓✓
Quality of Pitches	✓✓✓✓✓	Range of Facilities	✓✓✓

Directions

Site is southwest of Salamancar close to Ciudad Rodrigo. From the E80 N260, any direction, take the 526 to Coria. Site is alongside river directly off the road and well signed.

Charges guide

Per person	€ 2,80
child (up to 12 yrs)	€ 2,50
tent	€ 2,50 - € 2,80
caravan	€ 2,80
car	€ 2,80
motorcaravan	€ 5,00

Reservations

Contact site. Tel: 923 481 348.

ES9026 Camping El Burro Blanco

Camino de las Norias s/n, 37660 Miranda del Castañar (Salamanca)

Set on a hill top, within the Sierra Peña de Francia is the romantic walled village of Miranda del Castañar with its charming, crumbling castle. The winding, narrow streets are similar to the Arab medinas, with quaint mediaeval style houses which seem untouched by recent centuries where donkeys are still used as means of transport. The site has been developed by a Dutch team including husband and wife Jeff and Yvonne and their friend Paul. You are welcomed at the gate and are walked around the facilities. A copy of the site regulations is provided to all campers along with your own rubbish bin. The 48 shady pitches are 60 sq.m, with two at 130 sq m and are mostly level with some terracing and all with electricity. The pitches are beautifully set in 3.5 hectares of the most attractive woodland complete with rough tables and chairs made from local stone, unusual statues, a fountain fed by a well and a small stream which traces a route though the site. The owners keep an exhaustive list of all the birds and other wildlife spotted around the campsite, and in one area (wet in winter, but dry in summer) there are beautiful luminous green tree frogs and other aquatic reptiles (you will hear their 'barking' at night in the mating season - May). This site is not suitable for bigger caravans and large motorhomes.

Facilities

One central modern sanitary facility, fully equipped includes a baby bath. Two washbasins have hot water and one hot tap serves both the dishwashing and laundry sinks. Out of season part of the unit is closed and therefore facilities are unisex. Launderette. Gas supplies. Library with book swap and small bar. Off site: Restaurants, bars, shops and ATM in village 600 m. Municipal swimming pool nearby, river swimming and fishing 1.5 km. If you wish to explore some of the unique villages in the area avoid La Alberca which has been spoiled by over exploitation. Try instead Cepeda or Casas del Conde.

Open

1 April - 1 October.

At a glance

Welcome & Ambience	✓✓✓✓	Location	✓✓✓✓
Quality of Pitches	✓✓✓✓	Range of Facilities	✓✓✓

Directions

From north - south directions take C512 (Salamanca - Coria) road southwest for about 70 km. through Vecinos, Linares de Rio Frio in direction of Coria (road numbers change but keep on this main road). This is easiest route! From east – west direction take C515 Bejar - Ciudad Rodrigo road turning south on C512 (again road numbers change). The road to Miranda del Castañar is approx. 7 km. northeast of village of Cepeda. Turn off main road signed Miranda del Castañar. After 1.2 km. going downhill towards town look for left turn on a concrete road. Follow road for 1.1 km. (a short stretch unmade) and site is on right.

Charges 2004

Per person	€ 4,00
child (0-5 yrs)	€ 3,00
pitch	€ 9,00
electricity	€ 1,20

Plus 7% VAT. Discounts after 3 days increasing to 40% after 18 days. No credit cards.

Reservations

Contact site. Tel: 923 161 100.
E-mail: elburro@internet-rural.com

www.alanrogers.com for latest campsite news

ES9025 Camping Regio

Ctra de Madrid, km 4, 37900 Santa Marta de Tormes (Salamanca)

Salamanca is one of Europe's oldest university cities, and this beautiful old sandstone city has to be visited. Find the famous frog which is hidden in the fabulous University facade and discover what unusual Spanish fortune will be granted you! Or just enjoy the wonderfully accessible Salamantine architecture and the myriad of bars around the Plaza Mayor. This is also a useful staging post en-route to the south of Spain or central Portugal. The site is seven kilometres outside the city on the old road to Madrid. It is behind the Hôtel Regio and campers can take advantage of the hotel facilities which include a quality restaurant, a cheaper cafeteria (discounts for campers), an excellent pool (small charge). There is a pool bar and a shaded patio. The site itself has a small bar and restaurant. The pitches (with a large area for tents) are clearly marked on slightly sloping ground, with some shade in parts. There are plentiful electricity points (10A) in little red-roofed towers and many water points with unusual taps.

Facilities

Very large fully equipped sanitary block has very good facilities for disabled campers. Washing machines in a dedicated room - all very clean. Gas supplies. Excellent motorcaravan services. Restaurant, cafe and swimming pool at adjoining hotel. Bar. Supermarket (1/4-30/9). Play area. Tennis. Basketball. English is spoken. Off site: Bus to town terminates at hotel car-park. Fishing 2km. Bicycle hire 4 km. Town centre and golf 7 km.

Open

All year.

At a glance

Welcome & Ambience	✓✓✓	Location	✓✓✓✓
Quality of Pitches	✓✓✓✓✓	Range of Facilities	✓✓✓✓✓

Directions

Take main N501 route from Salamanca to Avila, then to St Marta de Tormes 7 km east of the city. Hôtel Regio is on the old road into St Marta on the left at the 90 km. marker. There are yellow camping signs through the city and on the roads to the east.

Charges 2005

Per person	€ 2,70 - € 3,20
child	€ 2,40 - € 2,80
tent or caravan	€ 2,70 - € 3,20
car	€ 2,70 - € 3,20

Reservations

Write to site. Tel: 923 138 888.
E-mail: recepcion@campingregio.com

ES9022 Camping El Folgoso

49361 Vigo de Sanabria (Zamora)

A pleasant drive through the Sanabria National Park takes you to this unspoilt site alongside a beautiful lake. It is a large site with most pitches given over to tents, as the terrain is rugged and strewn with enormous rocks, whilst being sheltered by fine dense oaks. The pitches are informal and tents are placed anywhere on terraces or the lower levels. Pitches for caravans and motorcaravans are in more formal lines at the far end of the site with (5A) electricity. All buildings are primarily of wood and stone and designed to be in sympathy with the surroundings. The nearby lake shores are public areas but there are toilets and picnic facilities. There are magnificent walks all around and much to see in the area, from many spectacular canyons to Saint Martin's Monastery.

Facilities

Three sanitary blocks, two refurbished and one new unit close to the restaurant, provide pre-set showers on payment, facilities for disabled campers and a variety of washing facilities but all with cold water. Bar with snacks (all year). Self-service and full restaurants (April - Oct.). Drinks machines. Torches essential. Off site: Supermarket (April - Oct.) just outside site.

Open

All year.

At a glance

Welcome & Ambience	✓✓✓	Location	✓✓✓✓
Quality of Pitches	✓✓✓	Range of Facilities	✓✓✓

Directions

From N525 Orense/Ourense - Benavente autovia or the parallel A525, take any exit for Puebla de Sanabria and follow signs for Sanabria National Park. This will place you on the ZA 104 heading north. Pass through villages of El Puente, Cubelo and Galende to 11 km. marker and site is signed to the right.

Charges guide

Per person	€ 3,46
child (under 10 yrs)	€ 2,55
pitch	€ 5,26 - € 7,67

Reservations

Not necessary. Tel: 980 626774.

ES9021 Camping Municipal Fuentes Blancas

Ctra Cartuja - M'flore, km 3,5, 09000 Burgos (Burgos)

Fuentes Blancas is a comfortable municipal site within easy reach of the Santander ferries. There are around 350 marked pitches of 70 sq.m. on flat ground, 112 with electricity (6A) and there is good shade in parts. A small shop caters for most needs, the typically Spanish bar serves snacks and in the evening a restaurant is open. The site has a fair amount of transit trade and reservations are not possible for August, so arrive early. Burgos is an attractive city, ideally placed for overnight stop en route to the south of Spain. The old part of the city is quite beautiful and there are pleasant walks along the river banks.

Facilities

Clean, modern, fully equipped sanitary facilities in five blocks, but not all open outside July/Aug. Facilities for babies. Washing machine. Motorcaravan services. Small shop (all season). Bar/snack bar (all season). Swimming pool (15/5-15/9). Playground. Table tennis. Basketball. Football. English is spoken. Off site: Fishing 150 m. Bicycle hire 2 km.

Open

1 April - 30 September.

At a glance

Welcome & Ambience	✓✓✓✓✓	Location	✓✓✓✓✓
Quality of Pitches	✓✓✓✓✓	Range of Facilities	✓✓✓✓

Directions

From the north (Santander) follow signs for E5/N1 (E80/N620) Valladolid - Madrid on main through road. Immediately after crossing river turn left at 'Fuente Blancas Parc' signs leading to yellow camp signs and follow river east in direction of Cartuja de Miraflores for 3 km. Site is well signed on left.

Charges guide

Per person	€ 3,50
pitch incl. caravan and electricity	€ 10,75

Reservations

Not made. Tel: 947 486 016.

ES9023 Camping Camino de Santiago

Casco Urbano, 09110 Castrojeriz (Burgos)

This tranquil and uncomplicated site lies to the west of Burgos on the outskirts of Castrojeriz, an unspoilt small Spanish rural town. In a superb location, almost in the shadow of the ruined castle high on the adjacent hillside, it will appeal to those who like peace and a true touring campsite without all the modern trimmings, and at a reasonable cost. Out of main season the bar/restaurant are closed but ask to be directed to the 'Taberna' restaurant in town for a real treat of old Spanish cuisine in classical surroundings. The 50 marked pitches are level, grassy and divided by hedges, with electricity (5A), water and drainage available to all. Mature trees provide shade and there is a pretty orchard in one corner of the site. English is spoken here.

Facilities

Adequate sanitary facilities with showers (three hot per sex), British and Turkish style WCs, and washbasins with cold water only. Dishwashing sinks with hot tap. These facilities are in older style, but are well maintained and clean. Washing machine. Small shop s (1/6-31/8). Bar. Coffee shop (1/6-31/8). Games room. Tennis. Play area. Bicycle hire.

Open

1 March - 30 November.

At a glance

Welcome & Ambience	✓✓✓✓✓	Location	✓✓✓✓✓
Quality of Pitches	✓✓✓✓	Range of Facilities	✓✓✓

Directions

From N120 (Osorno-Burgos) road, turn on BU404 for Villasandino and Castrojeriz. Turn left at crossroads on southwest side of town and then left at site sign.

Charges 2005

Per person	€ 3,75
tent or caravan	€ 3,50 - € 4,00
car	€ 3,00

All plus 7% VAT.

Reservations

Write or fax site for details. Tel: 947 377 255. E-mail: campingcastro@eresmas.com

ES9250 Camping Costajan

Ctra NI/E5, km 162, 09400 Aranda de Duero (Burgos)

This site is well placed as an en-route stop for the ferries, being 80 km. south of Burgos. This is the capital of the Ribera del Duero wine region that produces many fine wines of Spain competing with the great Riojas. The welcome is warm and friendly here. With 225 unmarked pitches, all with electricity, there are around 100 for all types of tourer. Large units may find access to the variably sized pitches a bit tricky among dense olive and pine trees and on the slightly undulating sandy ground but trees provide good shade. In high season there is a good sized pool to relax in. There are many fascinating things to see in the area but we particularly recommend a visit to the suspended buildings at Gumiel de Izan.

Facilities

Good, heated, modern sanitary facilities have hot and cold water. Facilites for disabled people. Washing machine. Reception opens 08.00-14.00 and 18.00-22.00. Gas supplies. Shop with essentials (all year). Cafe with snacks and bar. Large swimming pool open to public (all 15/5-15/9). Tennis. Football. Minigolf. Riding 2 km. Fishing 3 km.

Open

All year.

At a glance

Welcome & Ambience	✓✓✓✓	Location	✓✓✓
Quality of Pitches	✓✓✓✓	Range of Facilities	✓✓✓✓

Directions

From N1/E5 take exit to North signed Aranda de Duero at 164.5 km, follow N1 towards town and the campsite is at the 162 km mark.

Charges guide

Per person	€ 3,50 - € 3,65
pitch	€ 3,50 - € 7,35

Reservations

Said to be unnecessary. Tel: 947 502 070. E-mail: costajan@circulopyme.com

ES9044 Camping Monumento al Pastor

Ctra Madrid-Irun km 308, 09219 Ameyugo (Burgos)

This is a very small simple site which makes a very good transit stop and is very special if you wish to sample traditional Spanish fare cooked to perfection whilst enjoying spectacular views. Look out for a seven metre high white sculpture of the shepherd boy towering 25 metres over the site and the road as you approach. The monument is famous. The shepherd boy was killed by a thunderbolt in 1959 whilst tending his sheep, accompanied by his dog who is also immortalised here, along with a lamb and a chapel dug into the rock. There are 15 pitches terraced on grass with one area allocated for tents. In high season there is a small hardstanding for two additional vehicles. Electricity (5A) is available to all the grass pitches. There are also some 50 permanent pitches. In high season a small hut serves as reception, otherwise go to the bar. The site itself lays at the foot of Napoleon Hill. A large bar/restaurant provides magnificent views of the Obareues mountains and surrounding hills which are designated to become a natural Park in the near future. The owner's son speaks good English.

Facilities

Sanitary facilities are quaint, clean and adequate. Essentials sold in the bar. Fabulous stylish restaurant offering campers top Spanish cuisine or a special 'menu del dia', also very popular with locals. Children's playground. Basketball. 5-a-side soccer. Off site: Local bus/train service 3 km. Bilbao 70 km. Co-located superb restaurant with smart uniformed waiters, most impressive wine list and excellent food.

Open

All year.

At a glance

Welcome & Ambience	✓✓✓✓✓	Location	✓✓✓✓✓
Quality of Pitches	✓✓✓✓	Range of Facilities	✓✓✓

Directions

Nearest large town is Miranda de Ebro. Site is very easy to find as it sits on the N1 between Gastiez Vitoria and Burgos. Madrid - Irun (A68/E80 Bilbao - Burgos) road at 308 km. marker. The monument makes it impossible to miss the site, but take care as the access is can be dangerous if crossing the main road. A safer option is off the N625 250 m. from the main road access.

Charges guide

Per person	€ 2,84
child	€ 2,35
caravan	€ 3,05
tent	€ 2,40 - € 3,36
car	€ 2,84
motorcycle	€ 1,82

Reservations

Contact site. Tel: 947 344355.

ES9253 Camping Picon del Conde

Ctra NI, km 263, 09292 Monasterio de Rodilla (Burgos)

This all year site is unusual, in that it has been amazingly decorated by the owner, Pedro Fasseler Sagredo who is extremely lively and friendly, as are his family. The experience begins as you drive under an art nouveau style entry arch and enter a pleasant site with a variety of unusual sculptures including Don Quixote and his companion Sancho Panza. The theme is continued in the friendly restaurant and bar with use of decorative local rock on most surfaces. The 60 level, grass pitches, all with electricity (5A), are of a reasonable size with separating hedges giving some privacy and trees offering shade. There is some traffic noise from the busy N1 alongside the site and the picnic site and terrace directly outside the restaurant are always busy in season, the adjacent motel being responsible for some of this. Compared to other sites in the area this is a good option for a stopover if heading for the ferry or for exploring the area. If you visit around Christmas you will see the amazing nativity scene the father constructs - again all in the local stone which is full of holes like Emmental cheese, with a profusion of working models with lights and decorations.

Facilities

The first floor, unheated sanitary block is modern, very clean and fully equipped. A central elevated Venus de Milo statue is accentuated by mirrors and natural lighting. Good facilities for disabled campers are beneath the main sanitary facilities. Motorcaravan service point. Restaurant and friendly bar. Swimming pools. Children's play area. Tennis and fronton. Off site: Burgos 15 minutes away.

Open

All year.

At a glance

Welcome & Ambience	✓✓✓✓✓	Location	✓✓✓✓
Quality of Pitches	✓✓✓✓✓	Range of Facilities	✓✓✓✓

Directions

Nearest town Monasterio de Rodilla (Burgos) From autopista A1 take exit 3 at Briviesca on the N1. Then exit 2 at Rubena heading north on N623 towards Irun. Site is on the N1 at the 263 km. marker, well signed midway between Burgos and Briviesca.

Charges guide

Per adult	€ 2,90
child	€ 2,60
caravan	€ 3,20
tent	€ 2,90 - € 3,20
car	€ 3,20
motorcycle	€ 2,70

Reservations

Contact site. Tel: 947 594 355.

ES9254 Camping Puerta de la Demanda

Ctra de Pineda, km 2, 09199 Villasur de Herreros (Burgos)

This recently built site is being improved and shows great promise. On flat ground, it is overlooked on three sides by the hills and mountains of the Sierra de la Demanda which give the site its name. There is little shade over 50 well marked large pitches all of which have electricity (5A) and drainage. The modern buildings are of local stone and wood in sympathy with the quiet surroundings, yet providing an excellent set of facilities. Just 300 m. away is a dam which may provide non-powered water sports and a river is very close for swimming and fishing. The whole site is securely fenced. It is eleven kilometres from Atapuerca a most important historical find which will be opening shortly. Set in 50 unspoilt hectares it will show the origins of prehistoric man, his culture and his move from Africa to Europe. Burgos is close by with all its attractions.

Facilities

Attractive new ochre/stone sanitary building with British WCs and free hot showers. Washing machine, dishwashing (H&C) and laundry (C) sinks. Facilities for disabled campers. Basics sold from bar in high season. Bar/snacks (April - Sept). Torches useful. Off site: River fishing 1 km. Superb walking area.

Open

Easter - September.

At a glance

Welcome & Ambience	✓✓✓✓✓	Location	✓✓✓✓
Quality of Pitches	✓✓✓✓	Range of Facilities	✓✓✓✓

Directions

From the N120 Burgos - Lograno road, exit at Ibeas de Juarros (approx 7km east of Burgos) towards Villalbura, Arlanzon, Villasur de Herreros and site on road no. 8201.

Charges guide

Per person	€ 2,81
child (up to 12 yrs)	€ 2,30
tent	€ 2,62 - € 2,91
caravan	€ 2,91
car	€ 2,91
motorcaravan	€ 4,90

Plus 7% VAT.

Reservations

Contact site. Tel: 983 796819.

ES9257 Camping Frias

09211 Ciudad de Frias (Burgos)

Located in a natural park northeast of Burgos, on the edge of the old, small Spanish town of Frias, much of this site is taken up with static units. However, an area at the end is reserved for touring caravans and motorcaravans. A beautiful river runs alongside, about 20 feet below the campsite but with access for fishing, and the level, numbered pitches have views across the really beautiful scenery surrounding the campsite. A little shade is provided from a few trees. This is very Spanish site (no English was spoken when we visited) so it may be noisy in summer with lively Spanish visitors but it was quiet when we visited in May. Facilities are basic with only cold water at washbasins and sinks. A bar houses darts, a pin ball machine and five tables for snacks, with another separate restaurant for the serious eaters. The main attraction of this site is the spectacular scenery in the surrounding area. Frias looks old and interesting with a castle reached by a trip over the bridge and fairly long walk. Beautiful scenery awaits when traveling just a few miles especially along the Rio Ebro – definitely rural Spain.

Facilities

One toilet block provides basic facilities with British style WCs, coin operated showers and 2 washing machines. Shop with good range of produce (all year). Bar and restaurant. Two swimming pools (22/6-15/9). Off site: Transport would be needed to visit any interesting places.

Open

All year.

At a glance

Welcome & Ambience	✓✓✓	Location	✓✓✓✓
Quality of Pitches	✓✓✓	Range of Facilities	✓✓✓

Directions

Site is on the north side of Frias - approach only from this side. Either from A1 exit 5 onto the A2122 towards Quintana Martin Galindez, with a few tunnels but spectacular scenery (turn right onto 625 for a short time then left to Quintana Martin Galindez.) and after about 16 km. turn left signed Frias. Campsite is 3 km. on right just before stone bridge. Or (from the west) on A1 from exit 4 on N232 then 629 to Trespaderne. Turn right towards Miranda and drive east for 10 km. then turn right to Frias. Site is on right before stone bridge (3 km).

Charges 2004

Per person	€ 2,85
child	€ 2,40
pitch	€ 7,60
electricity	€ 2,40

Less 10% in low season. Plus 7% VAT.

Reservations

Contact site. Tel: 0947 357198.
E-mail: camfrias@burgos.net

www.alanrogers.com for latest campsite news

ES9242 Camping El Acueducto

Avda. D. Juan de Borbón, 49, Ctra CL601, km 112, 40004 Segovia (Segovia)

Located right on the edge of the interesting city of Segovia with lovely views across the open plain with mountains in the background, this is a family run, typically Spanish site. The grass pitches are mostly of medium size, although a few pitches near the gate would have room for larger motorcaravans. Reception is small but the owner is very helpful and speaks good English. El Acueducto is well positioned for discovering Segovia. About three miles away, Segovia is deeply and haughtily Castilian, with plenty of squares and mansions from its days of Golden Age grandeur, when it was a royal resort. The Roman aqueduct, Cathedral and Alcazar are well worth visiting and two Bourbon palaces, La Granja and Riofrio, are a few miles from the city.

Facilities

Two traditional style toilet blocks provide basic facilities, a laundry room and dishwashing sinks, all of which are clean. Small shop for basics. Bar. Two swimming pools. Table tennis. Basketball and football pitch. Large play area. Off site: Large restaurant a few yards along the road providing good food. Bus service into city centre. Madrid is within driving distance.

Open

All year.

At a glance

Welcome & Ambience	✓✓✓	Location	✓✓✓
Quality of Pitches	✓✓✓	Range of Facilities	✓✓✓

Directions

From the north on N1 (Burgos - Madrid) take exit 99 onto N110 towards Segovia. On outskirts of city take third exit onto N603 signed Madrid. Pass one exit to Segovia and take second signed Segovia and La Granja. At roundabout turn right towards Segovia. Site is 500 yards on right at the side of the duel carriageway.

Charges 2004

Per person	€ 4,50 - € 4,95
child	€ 3,50 - € 3,85
pitch	€ 14,00 - € 15,40
electricity (5A)	€ 3,50 - € 3,85

Reservations

Contact site. Tel: 921 425 000.
E-mail: campingsg@navegalia.com

ES9240 Camping El Cantosal

Ctra de Santiuste, km 2, 40480 Coca (Segovia)

On the 'Ruta de Mudejar' (route of Mudejar castles and buildings), near the nature reserve 'Hoces del Duraton' is this tiny campsite of 50 pitches. The setting has a fairy tale air about it – the magnificent fifteenth century Castillo de Coca can be seen from most of the site. The history of the village is fascinating and the climb to the tallest tower of the castle is rewarded with views of the village, its ancient bull ring and the surrounding countryside. Designed in sympathy with the surroundings the recently built stone buildings and all the facilities are of the highest quality. The grass and sand pitches are flat and shaded by tall trees in the daytime, and lit by pretty post lights at night. The bar serves snacks and excellent coffee and has a lovely open fire for cooler evenings. There is an arrangment for campers to use the local pool at a special rate, the campsite is set alongside a river where there are lots of wooden picnic tables under the trees and stone barbeques.

Facilities

The modern sanitary building with British style WCs and free showers is central. Washing machine, dishwashing (H&C) and laundry sinks under cover. Facilities for disabled campers. Shop (high season). Bar with snacks (all season). Large playground just outside the site. Off site: Village with shops bars and restaurants. Fishing 2 km. Golf 20 km. Village of Coca with superb castle with attractive flowered gardens and bull ring 2 km.

Open

15 June - 15 September.

At a glance

Welcome & Ambience	✓✓✓✓✓	Location	✓✓✓✓✓
Quality of Pitches	✓✓✓✓✓	Range of Facilities	✓✓✓

Directions

From Valladoid south on the N601 to Olmedo then east on the vp1105 to Coca. At T-junction marked Coca 2 km, Santuiste 7 km, turn into campsite road through stone pillars situated on the left and signed Zona De Picnic El Cantasol.

Charges 2005

Per person	€ 2,80
child (up to 12 yrs)	€ 2,50
tent	€ 2,60 - € 2,80
caravan	€ 2,80
car	€ 2,80
motorcaravan	€ 5,00

Reservations

Write to site. Tel: 627 445906.
E-mail: info@asecal.net

ES9251 Camping Cañon del Rio Lobos

Ctra Burgos de Osma-S. Leonard, 42317 Ucero (Soria)

This is a smart and 'proper' site with vast amounts of flowers (a full time gardener keeps everything just so), set among attractive limestone cliffs of the Burgos canyons. The site is pricey but all facilities are immaculate and there are few others in the area. Reception is purpose built and control of the security barrier is from within - everything here is very organised. The camp logo depicts a bird of prey and you will see many of these wheeling above the site. You can practise your Spanish here as little English is spoken, but there is tourist information in English. The very attractive swimming pool is within a secure walled area, which again has many flowers and shrubs and is private from the road that runs alongside the site (some road noise). Children will need supervision in the pool as there is no barrier between the shallow and deep areas. If you wish to take advantage of the stunning scenery and explore the area the site staff will assist with routes and maps.

Facilities

Spotless fully equipped toilet blocks. Bar/restaurant (high season) or a set 'menu del dia' in the bar. Basic shopping from bar. Swimming pool (extra charge). Two excellent tennis courts (extra charge). Children's play area. Bicycle hire. Fishing. Torch useful. Off site: Local bus service 1 km. on Wed./Sat.for town. Excellent walking routes.

Open

March - November.

At a glance

Welcome & Ambience	✓✓✓✓✓	Location	✓✓✓✓✓
Quality of Pitches	✓✓✓✓✓	Range of Facilities	✓✓✓✓✓

Directions

On N234 Burgos - Soria road take right fork in village of San Leornado de Yagüe. Turn right again after village signed El Burgos de Osma. Site is on this road and well signed south of Ucero.

Charges 2004

Per person	€ 4,35
child	€ 3,55
pitch	€ 11,95
electricity	€ 4,45

All plus 7% VAT.

Reservations

Contact site. Tel: 975 363565.

ES9029 Camping El Astral

Camino de Pollos 8, 47100 Tordesillas (Valladolid)

The site is in a prime position alongside the wide River Duero (safely fenced). It is homely and run by a charming man, Eduardo Gutierrez, who has excellent English and is ably assisted by brother Gustavo and sister Lola. The site is generally flat with 154 pitches separated by hedges. They vary in size from 60 - 80 sq.m. with mature trees providing shade. We recommend a walk across the bridge to investigate the fascinating town of Tordesillas which is steeped in Spanish history. Also don't miss the Real Monasterio de Santa Clara known as the Alhambra of Castille - it is amazing. Visits to local Bodegas (wineries) can be organised. This is a friendly site ideal for exploring the area as you move through Spain. There is an electricity pylon tucked in the corner of the site but this does not detract from the pleasant ambience here and the quality stay offered.

Facilities

One attractive sanitary block including two cabins with WC, bidet and washbasin. Quality facilities provided for disabled campers, including ramps throughout site. Baby room in ladies' area. Washing machines. Motorcaravan services. Supermarket. Bar. Very good restaurant fequented by locals. Swimming and paddling pools (15/6-15/9; lifeguard at all times). Children's playground. Tennis. Minigolf. English speaking staff. Local bus service. Animation daily in high season. Torches are useful.

Open

1 April - 30 September.

At a glance

Welcome & Ambience	✓✓✓✓✓	Location	✓✓✓✓✓
Quality of Pitches	✓✓✓✓✓	Range of Facilities	✓✓✓✓✓

Directions

Tordesillas is 28 km. southwest of Valladolid. From all directions, leave the main road towards Tordesillas and follow signs to campsite or 'Parador' (a hotel near the campsite).

Charges 2005

Per person	€ 3,85 - € 5,20
child (0-12 yrs)	€ 3,00 - € 4,25
caravan or tent	€ 3,85 - € 5,20
car	€ 3,30 - € 4,40
motorcycle	€ 3,30 - € 4,40
motorcaravan	€ 6,50 - € 8,00

Plus 7% VAT. Discounts in low season and for longer stays.

Reservations

Not necessary. Tel: 983 770 953.
E-mail: info@campingelastral.com

www.alanrogers.com for latest campsite news

With a coastline of inlets and wide, rocky estuaries, sheltering traditional old fishing villages and fine beaches, Galicia is perhaps best known for Santiago de Compostela, the place where the famous pilgrim's route comes to an end.

This region is made up of four provinces: Ourense, Lugo, A Coruña and Pontevedra

The obvious highlight in the region has to be the beautiful medieval city of Santiago de Compostela, capital of Galicia and world famous centre of the old European pilgrimage. Now a World Heritage Site, the city boasts an impressive Romanesque cathedral with more churches, convents and monasteries dotted around. One of the best times to go to Santiago de Compostela is during the Festival of St James on 25 July, which has also been designated Galicia Day. Following the route into the city, are the towns of Portomarín and Samos. Near Samos, the Lóuzara valley and the Sierra do Oribio are ideal for those interested in hiking and wildlife. There are also places to go paragliding or potholing. The Galician coastline is characterized by high cliffs and estuaries collectively known as the Rías Atlas and Rías Baixas with the Costa da Morte or Coast of Death separating them; so called because of the hundreds of shipwrecks that litter the cliffs and rocks. It was also once considered by the pilgrimages to be the 'end of the world'. Along the coast are medieval towns and villages including Noia, Muros, A Coruña and Finisterre. Corcubión, Camariñas and Corme-Laxe are other rias with fishing villages and home to some of the best barnacles in the region.

Cuisine of the region

Local cuisine features heavily in fiestas and throughout the region are numerous markets. Good quality seafood is found in abundance; *percebes* (barnacles) are a favourite. *Pulpo* (octopus) is also popular and special *pulperías* will cook it in the traditional way. Vegetable dishes include the Galician broth, made with green beans, cabbage, parsnip, potatoes and haricot beans. *Aguardiente gallego*, a regional liqueur, is used to make the traditional mulled drink known as *queimada*, where fruit, sugar and coffee grains are added and then set alight.

Caldeirada: fish soup

Caldo gallego: thick stew of potato cabbage

Empanada: light-crusted pastries often filled with pork, beef, tuna or cod.

Lacon con grelos: ham boiled with turnip greens

Places of interest

A Coruña: medieval quarters, Romanesque churches, Roman lighthouse

Baiona: one of the region's best resorts

Camariñas: town on the 'end of the world', good barnacle hunting ground, lacemaking traditions

Lugo: town completely enclosed within preserved Roman walls, along which are 85 towers

Malpica: seaside harbour, jumping off point for nearby islands

Pontevedra: picturesque old town with lively atmosphere

Vigo: fishing port, beaches

Viveiro: beaches, old town surrounded by Renaissance walls

Alan Rogers tip

WITH GOOD BEACHES, WALKING TRACKS, BARS AND RESTAURANTS, THE ATLANTIC ISLANDS NATIONAL PARK HAS FOUR GROUPS OF ISLANDS INCLUDING THE CÍES AND ONS ISLANDS.

ES9024 Camping As Cancelas

Rue do 25 de Xulio 35, 15704 Santiago (A Coruña)

The beautiful city of Santiago has been the destination for European Christian pilgrims for centuries and they now follow ancient routes to this unique city, the whole of which is a national monument. There are many pilgrims' routes, including one commencing from Fowey in Cornwall. The As Cancelas campsite is excellent for sharing the experiences of these pilgrims in the city and around the magnificent cathedral. It has 156 marked pitches (30-70 sq.m), arranged in terraces and divided by trees and shrubs. On a hillside overlooking the city, the views are very pleasant, but the site has a steep approach road and access to most of the pitches can be a challenge for large units. Electrical hook-ups (5A) are available. There are many legendary festivals and processions here, the main one on 25 July, especially in holy years (when the Saint's birthday falls on a Sunday). Examine for yourself the credibility of the fascinating story of the arrival of the bones of St James at Compostela (Compostela translates as 'field of stars').

Facilities

Two very modern, luxurious toilet blocks are fully equipped, with ramped access for disabled campers. The quality and cleanliness of the fittings and tiling is outstanding. Dishwashing and laundry facilities. Small mini market (open July/Aug.). Restaurant. Bar/ TV. (open all year). Well kept, unsupervised swimming pool and children's pool. Small playground. Off site: Regular bus service runs into the city from the bottom of the hill outside site. Huge commercial centre five minutes level walk away.

Open

All year.

At a glance

Welcome & Ambience	✓✓✓✓✓	Location	✓✓✓✓✓
Quality of Pitches	✓✓✓✓	Range of Facilities	✓✓✓✓✓

Directions

From the east on N634 Lugo road site is signed at junction with N550 road (on dual-carriageway filter right following signs for right for La Coruña N550 and also site). Turn at the sports stadium and site is 800 m. on left.

Charges guide

Per person	€ 3,46 - € 4,00
child (up to 12 yrs)	€ 2,40 - € 3,07
car	€ 3,46 - € 4,18
tentor caravan	€ 3,46 - € 4,30

All plus VAT.

Reservations

Write to site. Tel: 981 580 476.
E-mail: info@campingascancelas.com

BUNGALOWS AND RURAL TOURISM ACCOMODATIONS

CAMPING

"AS CANCELAS"

Situated north of the city, access by San Cayetano and Avenida del Camino Francés.

OPEN THROUGHOUT THE YEAR

In quiet surroundings, though not far from historical pilgrims town with its famous cathedral. Good bus connection to town and its historical monuments. Site has first class installations, incl. swimming and paddling pool, as well as first class ablution blocks.

Ruo de 25 de Xulio, 35 E-15704 SANTIAGO DE COMPOSTELA (La Coruña)
Tel.: (34) 981 58 02 66 - 58 04 76 • Fax. (34) 981 57 55 53

ES8942 Camping Los Manzanos

Ctra Sta Cruz - Meiras, km 0,7, 15179 Santa Cruz (A Coruña)

This large site is to the east of the historic port of La Coruña, not far from some ria (lagoon) beaches. The site has a steep sloping access and is divided by a stream into two main sections, linked by a wooden bridge. Some huge interesting stone sculptures create focal points and conversation pieces. The lower section is on a gentle slope. Pitches for larger units are marked and numbered, all with 10A electricity and there is a fairly large, unmarked field for tents. The site impressed us as being very clean, even when full, which it tends to be in high season. Señor Sanjurjo speaks good English and visitors are assured of a friendly welcome. Some aircraft noise should be expected (but only six aircraft per day – none at night).

Facilities

Two good toilet blocks provide modern facilities including free hot showers. Swimming pool - clean, with a lifeguard, free to campers, and open all season if you are tough enough! Small shop with fresh produce daily. High quality restaurant/bar (Easter - Sept). Playground. Barbecue area. Medical post. Excellent bungalows for hire. Off site: Beach 800 m. Bicycle hire 2 km. Golf and riding 8 km.

Open

Easter - 15 September.

At a glance

Welcome & Ambience	✓✓✓✓✓	Location	✓✓✓✓
Quality of Pitches	✓✓✓✓✓	Range of Facilities	✓✓✓✓

Directions

From A9/E1 going south, take exit 7 for 'O Burgo'. The site is on the Santa Cruz – Meiras road, north of Oleiras and is well signed from there.

Charges guide

Per person	€ 4,40
child	€ 3,40
pitch	€ 4,40 - € 8,80

All plus 7% VAT.

Reservations

Write to site. Tel: 981 614 825.
E-mail: info@camping-losmanzanos.com

Asturias

Like its neighbouring province, Cantabria, Asturias also has a beautiful coastline, albeit more rugged and wild, with the Picos range separating them. In the south the Cantabrian mountains form a natural border between Asturias and Castilla-León.

This is a one province region

The capital is Oviedo

Situated between the foothills of the Picos mountains and the coast is the seaside town of Llanes, in the east. It has several good beaches, beautiful coves and given its location, is a good base for exploring the Picos del Europa. Along the coast towards Gijón are more seaside resorts including Ribadesella, with its fishing harbour and fine beach. The cities of Gijón and, in particular, Avilés are renowned for their Carnival festivities, a national event which takes place in late February. This week-long party involves dancing, live music, fireworks and locals who dress up in elaborate fancy-dress costumes. South of here towards the centre of the province is the capital, Oviedo. The city boasts a pedestrian old quarter with numerous squares and narrow streets, a cathedral, palaces, a Fine Arts Museum, Archaeological Museum plus various remarkable churches that date from the 9th century. There are also plenty of *sidrerías* (cider houses).The west coast of Asturias is more rugged. One of the most attractive towns along here is Luarca, built around a cove surrounded by sheer cliffs. With a fishing harbour and an array of good restaurants and bars, the town's traditional character is reflected in its *chigres* – old Asturian taverns – where visitors can learn the art of drinking cider.

Cuisine of the region

Local specialities include *fabada,* a type of stew made with haricot beans called *fabes*, *potes* (soups) and of course cider, which can be drunk in *sidrerías.* The customary way to serve cider is to pour it from a great height, a practice know as *escanciar*, into a wide-mouthed glass only just covering the *culín* or bottom. Rice pudding is the traditional dessert and *frixuelos* (crepe), *huesos de santo* (made from marzipan) and *tocinillo de cielo* (syrup pudding) are eaten during festivals.

Brazo de gitano: a type of Swiss roll

Carne gobernada: beef in white wine with bacon, eggs, peppers and olives

Fabada asturiana: haricot beans, chorizo, cabbage, cured pork shoulder and potatoes

Pastel carbayón: almond pastry

Places of interest

Avilés: 14th and 15th century churches and palaces

Cuillero: small, charming fishing port

Gijón: 18th century palace, beaches, museums

Villahormes: seaside town with excellent swimming coves

Villaviciosa: atmospheric old town, 13th church, cider factory

Alan Rogers tip

VISIT THE CIDER FACTORY AT VILLAVICIOSA AND SEE HOW THE *LAGARES* WORK – THE PRESSES USED TO EXTRACT THE JUICE, BEFORE SAMPLING THE LOCAL TIPPLE.

www.alanrogers.com for latest campsite news

ES8940 Camping Los Cantiles

Ctra N634, km 502,7, 33700 Luarca (Asturias)

Luarca is a picturesque little place with a pretty inner harbour and two sandy beaches, and Los Cantiles is two kilometres to the east of town on a cliff top that juts out into the sea, giving excellent views from some pitches and the sound of the waves to soothe you to sleep. The owners speak excellent English and Hubert, who is Dutch, and Cornelia, who is German, are charming and eager that you enjoy your stay here. The site is well maintained and is a pleasant place to stop along this under-developed coastline. The 230 pitches, 83 with electricity (6A) are mostly on level grass, divided by huge hedges of hydrangeas and bushes. Some pitches have gravel surfaces. There is a separate area for late arrivals in high season. You can take the car to the Laurca beaches and the small town is within walking distance downhill (the return is steep!). This is a pleasant site as a base for exploring the area or as a transit site if moving to or from Portugal.

Facilities

Two modern, fully equipped sanitary blocks (one in low season) are kept very clean, as is the whole site. Mainly British style toilets. The block used in winter is heated. Large solar heating system for hot water. Facilities for disabled people and babies. Water is recycled for flushing purposes - the owners have a 'green' attitude. Laundry. Freezer service. Gas supplies. Small shop (all year). Bar with hot snacks (15/6-1/10). Day room for backpackers with tables, chairs and cooking facilities (less gas). Lounge/reading room. Bicycle hire. Torches are required. English is spoken.
Off site: Indoor swimming pool, sauna and fitness centre 300 m. Fishing 70 m. Riding 6 km.

Open

All year.

At a glance

Welcome & Ambience	✓✓✓✓✓	Location	✓✓✓✓✓
Quality of Pitches	✓✓✓✓✓	Range of Facilities	✓✓✓✓

Directions

Turn off main N632 at 154 km. marker onto N634. At the km 502.7 point east of Laurca, site is well signed through an estate.

Charges 2004

Per person	€ 3,70
child (4-10 yrs)	€ 3,25
tent	€ 3,60 - € 3,80
caravan	€ 4,30
motorcaravan	€ 7,00
car	€ 2,80

Plus 7% VAT. No credit cards.

Reservations

Advised for mid July - end Aug and made by post with deposit (€ 15). Tel: 985 640 938.
E-mail: cantiles@conectia.net

ES8945 Camping Lagos de Somiedo

Valle de Lago, 33840 Somiedo (Asturias)

This is a most unusual gem of a small site in the mountainous Parque Natural de Somieda. Winding narrow roads with challenging rock overhangs, hairpin bends and breathtaking views (for eight kilometres) finally bring you to the lake and campsite at an elevation of 1,200 m. This is a site for 4x4s, powerful small campervans, cars, backpackers of endurance – not advised for medium or large motorhomes, and caravans are not accepted. It is not an approach for the faint hearted! The friendly Lana family make you welcome at their unique site, which is tailored for those who wish to explore the natural and cultural values of the Park without the 'normal' campsite amenities. There is no electricity, but in this extraordinary glacial valley you can leave reality behind in the exploration of the marvels of nature including bears, wolves, capercailles and a unique wild goat which frequent these mountains. A charming building, in keeping with the area, provides the amenities and contains many items of natural interest. A small bar/restaurant set tight into the vertical rock face offers traditional Asturian food, but watch out for the local's stilted wooden clogs scattered in the entrance hall. There is a cool wind here most of the time and a torch is essential at night. Cars are parked away from the pitches here.

Facilities

There are British style toilets and free hot water to clean hot showers, washbasins, laundry sinks and for dishwashing (outside, under cover). Facilities for babies and children. Washing machine. Combined reception, small restaurant, bar and reference section. Bread, milk and other essentials, plus local produce and crafts are sold in the site shop and bar. Horses for hire, trekking. Lectures on flora, fauna, history and culture. The river Valle runs through the site allowing trout fishing (licence required). Barbecue area. Small play area. Telephone. Gas supplies. Off site: The very small village is within 500 m. and it maintains the Spanish customs and traditions of this area.

Open

Easter - 15 October.

At a glance

Welcome & Ambience	✓✓✓✓	Location	✓✓✓✓
Quality of Pitches	✓✓✓	Range of Facilities	✓✓✓

Directions

From N634 via Oviedo turn left at 442 km. marker on AS-15 signed Parque Natural de Somiedo. At 9 km. marker past village of Longoria, turn left on AS-227. At 38 km. marker, turn left into Pol de Somiedo, signed Centro Urbano. Follow signs for Valle de Lago and El Valle; 8 km. of hairpin bends from Pola, passing Urria on the left, brings you to the valley. Site is signed on the right.

Charges guide

Per person	€ 3,46
child	€ 2,85
tent incl. 2 persons	€ 3,46
tent with 3 or more persons	€ 4,06
car	€ 2,85
motorcycle	€ 2,40

All plus 7% VAT.

Reservations

Not necessary. Tel: 985 763 776.

www.alanrogers.com for latest campsite news

ES8950 Camping Costa Verde

Playa de la Griega, 33320 Colunga (Asturias)

This busy site with a marked Spanish flavour some 1.5 km. from the town of Colunga, has some very nice features and the owners aim to please. The most attractive feature, just outside the gate, is a spacious, supervised beach with a low tide lagoon which is ideal for younger children. The 160 regularly laid out pitches are very busy in high season. They are flat, but with little shade, and electricity (6A) is available throughout (long leads needed in places). A new sports and play area, with a dedicated barbecue and a picnic area is at the end of the site across a bridge . Whilst the river is mainly fenced off, children could possibly find their way to the river and thus should be supervised. This area is the real Jurassic Park with the footprints of dinosaurs having been discovered and preserved locally, along with some dinosaur fossil remains. Ask at reception for details and guides.

Facilities

The single toilet block is of a high standard with a mixture of British and Turkish style toilets (all British for ladies), large showers and free hot water throughout. Laundry. Well stocked shop. Bar/restaurant is traditional and friendly. Sports field. Barbeque. Children's playground. Torches needed. Little English spoken. Off site: Nearby towns of Ribadesella, Gijón and Oviedo. Excellent beaches. Fishing in river alongside site. Golf 18 km.

Open

Easter - early October.

At a glance

Welcome & Ambience	✓✓✓✓✓	Location	✓✓✓✓✓
Quality of Pitches	✓✓✓✓	Range of Facilities	✓✓✓✓

Directions

From Santander take N634 to Ribadesella, and continue for 21 km. along the N632 coast road towards Gijón. Take right turn towards Lastres from the centre of Colunga.

Charges guide

Per adult	€ 3,70
child (over 5 yrs)	€ 3,15
tent	€ 3,25 - € 3,40
caravan	€ 4,20
car	€ 3,15
motorcycle	€ 2,85

VAT included.

Reservations

Essential for peak weeks and made for exact dates with deposit. Send for booking form.
Tel: 985 856 373.

ES8955 Camping Caravaning Arenal de Moris

Ctra 632, 33344 Caravia Alta (Asturias)

This peaceful, rural site is close to three fine sandy beaches and is surrounded by mountains in the natural reservation area known as the Sueve. A hunting reserve, this is important for a breed of short Asturian horses, the 'Asturcone'. The famous mountains, 'Picos de Europa', are only 35 km away, Covadonga and its lakes are near and Ribadesella is 12 km. It is an ideal area for sea and mountain sports, horse riding, walking, birdwatching and cycling. Camping Arenal's 350 grass pitches are of 40-70 sq.m. and electricity connections are available. With little shade, some pitches are terraced with others on an open, slightly sloping field with views of the sea. The restaurant with a terrace serves local dishes and overlooks the pool to hills and woods. In the middle distance a new autoroute viaduct supported by large concrete piers sculpts its way across the valley. There was little noise when we visited but this must be considered a possibility. The excellent beach is a short walk.

Facilities

Three sanitary blocks provide comfortable, controllable showers (no dividers) and vanity style washbasins, laundry facilities and external dishwashing (cold water). Supermarket. Restaurant. Swimming pool. Tennis. Play area in lemon orchard. English is spoken. Off site: Fishing 200 m. Golf 10 km. Riding 15 km. Shops, bar and restaurants in local village.

Open

1 June - 31 August.

At a glance

Welcome & Ambience	✓✓✓✓	Location	✓✓✓
Quality of Pitches	✓✓✓✓	Range of Facilities	✓✓✓

Directions

Site is signed from the N632 Ribadesella - Gijón road at km. 14 point.

Charges guide

Per person	€ 3,95
child	€ 3,70
caravan	€ 5,15
tent	€ 3,70 - € 3,95
car	€ 3,95
motorcycle	€ 2,90

Reservations

Contact site. Tel: 985 853 097.
E-mail: camoris@teleline.es

ES8960 Camping La Paz

Ctra N-634 Irun - Coruña, km 2, 33597 Vidiago-Llanes (Asturias)

On arrival here you may well be reminded of the fortress towns of old Spain. The reception building is opposite a solid rock face and many hundred feet below the site and the climb to the site is quite daunting but staff will place your caravan for you, although motorcaravan drivers will have an exciting drive to the top. Once there it is all worth it as the views are absolutely outstanding. The site is arranged on numerous terraces with lower areas in a valley floor. The way down to the beach is very steep but the views, both to the Picos de Europa and to seaward are most impressive. There are 434 pitches with electricity of between 30-70 sq.m, but many are only suitable for tents with no electricity. Because of the steep access, units may be positioned on upper terraces by site staff using Range Rovers. An area back from the beach is more suitable for very large units. There is a cliff-top restaurant and bar with commanding views over the ocean and beach. It is best to book in high season since the site is deservedly popular and one of the best managed along this coast. With the extreme slopes, we think it would appeal most to visitors who are not infirm. Children will require supervision on the steep slopes.

Facilities

Four first class sanitary blocks, with some interesting and unusual design features (such as being cut into solid rock), are modern, well equipped and spotlessly clean. They include hot showers with electronic controls and a baby bath. Full laundry and dishwashing facilities. Spring water is available from a number of taps throughout the site. Motorcaravan services. Mini-market. restaurant and bar. Lounge. Watersports. Table tennis. Games room. Fishing. Superb Beaches. Torches essential. English spoken. Off site: Well placed for excursions to the eastern end of the Picos de Europa.

Open

1 June - 20 September.

At a glance

Welcome & Ambience	✓✓✓✓✓	Location	✓✓✓✓✓
Quality of Pitches	✓✓✓✓✓	Range of Facilities	✓✓✓✓✓

Directions

From Santander take N634 towards Llanes. Site is signed from the main road at km.292, before you arrive in Vidiago.

Charges guide

Per adult	€ 3,58
child	€ 3,34
tent	€ 3,40
caravan	€ 4,78
car	€ 3,58
motorcycle	€ 2,98

All plus 7% VAT.

Reservations

Advised for peak weeks. Tel: 985 411 012.
E-mail: delfin@campinglapaz.com

ES8965 Camping Picos de Europa

33556 Avin-Onis (Asturias)

It is said that, due to their proximity to the sea, the Picos (peaks) are called Europa as early navigators, on sighting them, knew they were again near the continent of Europe. Indeed, it is probably best to follow the coast to reach Cangas de Onis, the gate to the Picos, when first locating the site. Once settled you can explore these dramatic limestone mountains on foot, by bicycle, by horse, etc. The site itself is newly developed and the dynamic owner, Jose is very pleasant and nothing is too much trouble. There is direct access off the AS114 in a valley situation beside a pleasant, fast flowing river. Local stone has been used for the L-shaped building at the main entrance which houses receptionand a very good restaurant. The bar has an unusual circular window and small terrace overlooking the river. The 140 marked, smallish pitches have been developed in three corridor type avenues, on level grass backing on to hedging and with electricity to most. The tent area is over the bridge past the fairly small, round swimming and paddling pool. The site specialises in caving activities and is youthful.

Facilities

The main sanitary facilities are in the reception building. Additional toilet facilities, showers, baby bath, etc are in the tent area. Laundry and dishwashing facilities. Washing machine. Shop (Jul - Sep). Bar, restaurant serves a menu of the day at lunchtimes (all local fare, filling and very unusual - try it). All year Swimming pool. Canoeing, riding and exceptional caving. Torches necessary. Excursions can be arranged in the mountains (on horseback if wished) and canoes can be hired. Off site: Site runs a most professional Speleology school with a hostel 3 km. away with 100 beds. Riding 12 km. Covadonga with its lakes and national park 13 km. Coast at Llanes 25 km. Golf 35 km.

At a glance

Welcome & Ambience	✓✓✓✓✓	Location	✓✓✓✓✓
Quality of Pitches	✓✓✓✓	Range of Facilities	✓✓✓✓✓

Directions

Site is 15 km. east of Cangas on AS114 road.

Charges guide

Per person	€ 3,30
child (under 14 yrs)	€ 3,00
small tent	€ 3,30
large tent or caravan	€ 3,90
car	€ 3,00
motorcycle	€ 2,40

All plus 7% VAT.

Reservations

Not needed outside July/Aug. Tel: 985 844 070.
E-mail: info@picos-europa.com

Open

All year.

The region of Cantabria in the north of Spain offers the best of both worlds. On the one hand there is the glorious coastline with beautiful beaches and pretty fishing villages; while inland there are a number of national parks including the mountainous, Picos de Europa.

Cantabria is a one province region

The capital is Santander

The capital, Santander, is an elegant city which extends over a wide bay with views of the Cantabrian Sea. Its historic quarter is situated against a backdrop of sea and mountains, although the town is best known for its beaches; the Playa de la Magdalena, which has a summer windsurfing school, and the popular El Sardinero beach. There is also a Maritime Museum and Museum of Prehistory and Archaeology plus a small zoo housed in the gardens of the old royal palace. A short distance from the city is the pretty medieval village of Santillana del Mar and the prehistoric Caves of Altamira. Despite being closed indefinitely for restoration work, the adjacent Altamira Museum houses a replica of these caves and their impressive prehistoric drawings. Also on the outskirts of the capital is the Cabárceno Nature Park with more protected areas scattered around the region, including those at Oyambre, Peña Cabarga and Saja-Besaya. The largest is the mountain range of Picos de Europa, a national park which shares it territory with Asturias and Castilla-León. With river gorges, valleys, woodlands and an abundance of wildlife, it is popular with walkers, trekkers and climbers.

Cuisine of the region

Seafood is used a lot, including fresh shellfish, sardines, *rabas* (fried squid), *bocartes rebozados* (breaded whitebait). Cheese is produced throughout the region; *queso de nata* (cream cheese), *picón* from Treviso Bejes, and smoked cheeses from Áliva or Pido. A typical dish of the region is the Cantabrian stew, which contains haricot beans, cabbage, rice and sausage. Desserts include the traditional cheesecakes of the Pas Valley and pastries. The local tipple is *orujo*, a strong liquor.

Maganos encebollados: squid with onion

Quesada: cheesecake

Sobaos pasiegos: sponge cakes

Sorropotún: type of fish stew

Places of interest

Castro Urdiales: beaches, Gothic church, Roman bridge, old quarter

Comillas: rural town, beaches, Gaudí-designed villa

Laredo: lively seaside resort, 13th church, 5 km. long sandy beach

Lierganes: 17th and 18th architecture, spa

Potes: on east side of Picos de Europa, mountain bike hire, paragliding available

San Vicente de la Barquera: picturesque fishing port

Alan Rogers **tip**

THERE ARE MORE PREHISTORIC CAVES AT PUENTE VIESCO, ONE OF WHICH, CASTILLO, IS OPEN TO TOURS; IT'S BEST TO BOOK IN ADVANCE. IT ALSO HAS REMARKABLE PAINTINGS.

ES8961 Camping El Helguero

Ctra Santillana-Comillas, 39527 Ruiloba (Cantabria)

This site, surrounded by tall trees and impressive towering rock formations, caters for around 240 units on slightly sloping ground. There are many marked pitches on different levels, all with access to electricity (6A), but with only a little shade in parts. There are also attractive tent and small camper sections set close in to the rocks. The reasonably sized swimming pool and children's pool has an access lift for disabled campers. This is a good site for disabled visitors, in a peaceful location, and is excellent value out of main season. One can generally find space here even in high season, but arrive early. The site is used by tour operators and there are some site owned chalets. There is a large Spanish presence at weekends, especially in high season and if you do not wish to share the boisterous culture, choose one of the many pitches away from the restaurant area.

Facilities

Three well placed toilet blocks, although old, are clean and cared for, and include facilities for disabled visitors and children. Dishwashing, laundry sinks and washing machines. Motorcaravan services. Well-stocked supermarket (July/Aug. 9 am - 1 pm). bar snacks, separate more formal restaurant. Swimming pool with (limited opening with lifeguard on duty, caps compulsory - sold on site). Playground. Animation in high season. Games machines. Activities for children and entertainment for adults. Bicycle hire. ATM. Torches required. Off site: Restaurants in village. Fishing or riding 3 km. Santillana del Mar 12 km. Beaches near.

At a glance

Welcome & Ambience	✓✓✓✓	Location	✓✓✓✓
Quality of Pitches	✓✓✓✓✓	Range of Facilities	✓✓✓✓✓

Directions

From the C6316 road from Santillana del Mar to Comillas, turn left at Sierra. Site is signed as Camping Ruiloba (we don't know why) and is 200 m. on the left.

Charges 2005

Per person	€ 3,30 - € 3,90
child (4-10 yrs)	€ 2,80 - € 3,40
caravan or tent plus car	€ 6,60 - € 7,80
motorcaravan	€ 6,60 - € 7,80
electricity	€ 3,00

Reservations

Write to site. Tel: 942 722 124.
E-mail: elhelguero@ctv.es

Open

1 April - 30 September.

ES8962 Camping La Isla Picos de Europa

Picos de Europa, 39570 Potes-Turieno (Cantabria)

La Isla is beside the road from Potes to Fuente Dé, with excellent mountain views and good shade, which makes it a popular site for families with young children. Established for over 25 years, a warm welcome awaits you from the owners (who speak good English) and a most relaxed and peaceful atmosphere exists in the site. The 160 unmarked pitches are arranged around an oval gravel track (one-way system), under a variety of fruit and ornamental trees. Electricity (3A) is available to all pitches, though some may require long leads. A small bar and restaurant is cleverly placed at a lower level, by the small river which runs through the site. Everything here is in a very pleasing traditional style . There are opportunities for riding and 4x4 safaris (site provides details) in the region, together with all the other mountain sports and active outdoor pursuits.

Facilities

Single, clean and smart sanitary block retains the style of the site. It includes washbasins, laundry and dishwashing sinks all with cold water. Washing machine. Gas supplies. Freezer service. Small shop. Restaurant/bar with local dishes. Takeaway. Small swimming pool, bathing caps compulsory (15/5-15/10). Children's playground. Barbecue and picnic area. Fishing. Bicycle hire. Riding. Drinks machine.
Off site: Interesting town of Potes, with Monday morning market 4 km. Monastery at Toribio nearby.

Open

1 April - 30 October.

At a glance

Welcome & Ambience	✓✓✓✓✓	Location	✓✓✓✓✓
Quality of Pitches	✓✓✓✓✓	Range of Facilities	✓✓✓✓✓

Directions

Site is on right hand side, 4 km. outside Potes, on N621 Potes to Espinama/Fuente Dé road.

Charges 2004

Per person	€ 3,30 - € 3,60
child (0-10 yrs)	€ 2,80 - € 3,00
tent	€ 3,30
caravan	€ 4,00
car	€ 3,30
motorcycle	€ 2,10

All plus VAT. Low season reductions.

Reservations

Write to site. Tel: 942 730 896.
E-mail: campicoseuropa@terra.es

ES8963 Camping La Viorna

Ctra Santa Toribio, 39570 Potes (Cantabria)

The wonderful views down the valley from the open terraces of this site make it an attractive base from which to tour this region or to relax by the excellent swimming pool. It is popular with both familes and couples. There are beds of flowers and the trees are maturing, providing shade on many pitches. Access is good for all sizes of unit to the 110 pitches of around 70 sq.m, all of which have electricity (3 or 6A). In high season, however, tents may be placed on less accessible, steeply sloping areas. The restaurant (fixed menu) has a terrace overlooking the pools. A pleasant feature is that all roofs are of the same design that is in sympathy with the town. This extends to a large picnic area behind the main block and even to small covered sitting out areas around the pool. All the buildings are in local stone with chunky wood fittings which look extremely attractive.

Facilities

Single, neat sanitary block of high standard, clean and modern. Washbasins with cold water. Facilities for disabled visitors double as unit for babies (key from reception). Laundry room has plenty of sinks, washing machine and ironing board. Dishwashing room with many sinks all cold water. Shop. Restaurant/bar with terrace. Heated swimming pool (23 x 13 m) and children's pool (bathing caps compulsory). Children's playground. Games room. Covered area with electronic games. Tourist information. Some English spoken. Many sporting activities can be arranged such as parascending, mountain biking, trekking, rafting and canoeing. Off site: Potes 2 km. (Monday market). Toribio Monastery close. Fuente Dé short spectacular drive.

At a glance

Welcome & Ambience	✓✓✓✓✓	Location	✓✓✓✓✓
Quality of Pitches	✓✓✓✓✓	Range of Facilities	✓✓✓✓✓

Directions

Take road N621 from Unquera to Potes. After town take left fork signed Toribio de Liebana and site is on right after 800 m.

Charges guide

Per person	€ 2,85
child	€ 2,40
caravan/tent	€ 2,85 - € 3,91
car	€ 2,85
motorcycle	€ 2,40
electricity	€ 2,10

All plus VAT.

Reservations

Write to site. Tel: 942 732 021.

Open

Easter/1 April - 30 October.

ES8964 Camping El Molino de Cabuérniga

Sopeña de Cabuérniga, Ctra C625, km 42, 39510 Cabuérniga (Cantabria)

Located in a peaceful valley with magnificent views of the mountains, beside the river Saja and only a short walk from the old and attractive village, this gem of a site is on an open, level, grassy meadow with trees. Wonderful stone buildings and artefacts are a feature of this unique site. There are 114 marked pitches, all with electricity (3/5A), although long leads may be needed and the site is lit at night. This comfortable site is very good value and ideal for a few nights (or you may wish to stay longer) whilst you explore the Cabuérniga Valley which forms part of the Reserva Nacional del Saja. The area is great for just resting or indulging in active pursuits with opportunities for mountain biking, climbing, walking, swimming or fishing in the river, horse riding, hunting, paragliding and 4x4 safaris. You will receive a warm welcome here with friendly advice on how best to enjoy your stay (for example, mountain weather forecasts). Sopeña Fiesta is in mid-July each year.

Facilities

A single, modern sanitary block provides toilets, showers and washbasins with cold water only. Dishwashing (H&C) and laundry sinks outside. Washing machines and ironing. Facilities for disabled campers planned. Small shop for basics. Restaurant/bar (June - Sept). Wonderful playground in rustic setting – supervision recommended. Fishing. Bicycle hire. Stone cottages and apartments for rent. Barbecue. No English is spoken. Off site: Fishing 200 m. Riding 4 km. Restaurants within 10 minutes drive in several directions.

Open

All year.

At a glance

Welcome & Ambience	✓✓✓✓✓	Location	✓✓✓✓✓
Quality of Pitches	✓✓✓✓✓	Range of Facilities	✓✓✓✓✓

Directions

From N634 at Cabezon de la Sal turn on C625, continue for approx. 10 km. to km. 42 where site is signed before Valle de Cabuérniga. Turn into village (watch out for low eaves/gutters on buildings), bearing right, watching carefully for small site signs through village (the locals always point for you!). automatic barrier at entrance arch.

Charges guide

Per person	€ 3,31
child	€ 3,01
pitch	€ 6,61
electricity	€ 2,10

All plus VAT.

Reservations

Contact site. Tel: 942 706 259.
E-mail: cmcabuerniga@campingcabuerniga.com

ES8970 Camping Las Arenas–Pechon

Ctra Pechon - Unquera, km 2, 39594 Pechon (Cantabria)

This campsite is in a very quiet, but rather spectacular location bordering the sea and the Tina Mayor estuary, with views to the mountains and access to an excellent beach. Otherwise, enjoy the pleasant kidney shaped pool that also shares the views. Unusually there is yet another beach on the far side of the site, this for the more adventurous as the access path is a little steep. Las Arenas is a very green, ten hectare site with lots of shade from acacias, oak and poplar trees, and is good value. Taking 337 units, half of the site is divided into marked, grassy pitches (60 sq.m) in various bays or on terraces with stunning sea and mountain views, with electricity available (5A) and connected by asphalted roads. There are some quite steep slopes to tackle - the restaurant along with reception is at the top. Children need to be supervised in some areas and infirm campers may find the slopes difficult.

Facilities

Clean, well tiled sanitary facilities are in the older style. Various blocks include showers (no divider), plus dishwashing, laundry sinks and washing machines. Well stocked supermarket Restaurant (open to public). Snack bar. (open when site open). Playground. Fishing. Opportunities for fishing, swimming, diving, windsurfing or cycling from site. Windsurfer and bicycle hire. Torches necessary. English is spoken. Off site: For older teenagers a disco/bar 1 km. Golf 28 km.

Open

1 June - 30 September.

At a glance

Welcome & Ambience	✓✓✓✓	Location	✓✓✓✓✓
Quality of Pitches	✓✓✓✓✓	Range of Facilities	✓✓✓✓

Directions

Nearest large city is Santander. Turn off the N634, Santander - Coruna road, just east of Unquera onto the road to Pechon. Site is 4.5 km.

Charges guide

Per person	€ 3,60
child	€ 3,99
caravan	€ 4,80
tent	€ 3,00 - € 3,60
car	€ 3,60
motorcycle	€ 2,60

All plus 7% VAT.

Reservations

Contact site. Tel: 942 717 188.
E-mail: lasarenas@ctv.es

ES8971 Camping Caravaning Playa de Oyambre

San Vicente de la Barquera, Finca Peña Guerra, 39547 San Vicente de la Barquera (Cantabria)

This exceptionally well managed site is ideally positioned to use as a base to visit the spectacular Picos de Europa or one of the many sandy beaches along this northern coast. The site is in lovely countryside (good walking and cycling country), with some views of the fabulous Picos mountains, and near the Cacarbeno National Park. The owner's son Pablo and his wife Maria are assisted by Francis in providing a personal service and both men speak excellent English. The 200 marked pitches are mostly of a good size (average 80 sq.m. with the largest ones often taken by tightly packed seasonal units). They are arranged on wide terraces with little shade and with electricity (10A) in most places. All pitches are flat and most have water and drainage. The site is well lit and a guard patrols at night (high season). The site gets busy with a fairly large Spanish community in season and there can be the usual happy noise of them enjoying themselves at weekends.

Facilities

Good sanitary facilities are in one, well kept block, with cleaners on duty all day and evening. Showers are spacious but have a frustrating mixture of push-button hot and ordinary cold controls. Facilities for babies and disabled visitors. Dishwashing (H&C) and laundry sinks (cold only). Washing machines (tokens from reception). Motorcaravan services. Well stocked supermarket open until 10 pm. with deliveries of fresh fish three days a week (15/6-15/9). Restaurant features fresh local dishes. Bar/TV lounge. Games area with machines. Swimming pools with lifeguard (1/6-15/9). Playground. Basketball. Football. Off site: Fishing and superb beaches 1 km. Riding 5 km. San Vicente de la Barquera 5 km.

Open

Easter/1 April - 30 September.

At a glance

Welcome & Ambience	✓✓✓✓✓	Location	✓✓✓✓
Quality of Pitches	✓✓✓✓✓	Range of Facilities	✓✓✓✓✓

Directions

Site is signed at the junction to Comillas, at km. 265 on the E70, 5 km. east of San Vicente de la Barquera. The entrance is quite steep (take care with caravans). Exercise caution as there is another 'Camping Playa de Oyambre' within 500 m. (on the beach) which is not recommended.

Charges guide

Per person	€ 3,45
child	€ 2,95
pitch	€ 6,95
electricity	€ 2,50

All plus VAT.

Reservations

Advised, particularly if you have a large unit. Write to site. Tel: 942 711 461.
E-mail: camping@oyambre.com

www.alanrogers.com for latest campsite news

ES8973 Camping Santillana

Ctra de Comilias s/n, 39330 Santillana del Mar (Cantabria)

This is an attractive site on sloping ground eight kilometres from the beaches of the north coast with full facilities. It has a fine swimming pool complex, a restaurant and self service café which operate all year. Pitches mostly for tents are informally arranged on a slope, with other pitches for caravans and motor-caravans on the lower part of the site. With numbered but unmarked pitches, some overcrowding may occur. Electricity is available (only 6A). Pitches alongside the road will experience some road noise as this is a busy arterial route. Many permanent types of accommodation on site and a large separate complex across a small street has many mobile homes. The site is directly off the main road and a fairly steep entry brings you to a reception where English is spoken. The site can be used en-route for the trip home or outbound or for exploring the northern areas of Spain. The centre of the charming medieval village of Santillana is near, and the Altamira caves are close.

Facilities

Toilet blocks are well placed (onlt one open in low season), fully equipped and with facilities for disabled campers. Washing machines and irons. Supermarket and souvenir shop (both high seasons). Bar/restaurant (popular with locals at weekends) and self service cafe (all year). Swimming pool complex with separate paddling pool. Play area for toddlers and an inventive play complex for older children. Minigolf. Tennis. Bicycle hire. Satellite TV. Drinks machines. Electronic games. Film processing service. Entertainment in high season.

Open

All year.

At a glance

Welcome & Ambience	✓✓✓✓	Location	✓✓✓✓
Quality of Pitches	✓✓✓✓✓	Range of Facilities	✓✓✓✓✓

Directions

Nearest large city is Santander. Site is directly off Santanilla - Comillas road (C6316) between the 5 km. and 6 km. markers. Exit the N634 west of Torrelavega. Alternatively, exit A67 at km. 16 and follow signs to Santillana.

Charges guide

Per person	€ 4,95
child (6-10 yrs)	€ 3,85
caravan or tent	€ 4,95
car	€ 4,80
motorcaravan	€ 6,00
electricity	€ 3,00

No credit cards.

Reservations

Advisable in July and August. Tel: 942 818 250.
E-mail: campingsantillan@ceoecant.es

ES8995 Camping Los Molinos

C/ La Ria S/N, 39180 Noja (Cantabria)

Camping Los Molinos is ideally located for touring the local area and as an overnight stop en route when travelling by ferry via Bilbao or Santander. It is close to the village of Noja, a busy Spanish tourist resort in high season, on the coast of Cantabria and is near the Playa del Ris beach which has fine sand and clear water. The site is divided into two main areas, both with a large number of permanent units. There are 500 average sized touring pitches, on level ground, but with little shade; all have electricity. There is a large separate area for tents. Each half of the site has its own main building with catering facilities. The right side has the main restaurant/bar, disco, supermarket, while the left has the reception, café/bar, supermarket and the swimming pools. Unusually the site has its own karting complex.

Facilities

The fully equipped modern sanitary building is central and kept very clean. Washing machines, dishwashing (H&C) and laundry sinks under cover. Facilities for disabled campers have access ramps. Supermarket, butcher and fishmonger (1/6-30/9).Main restaurant/bar good decoration and tablecloths with cafe bar providing tapas, pizzas or takeaway food. (1/6-30/9). Swimming pool and children's pool with life guard (15/6-10/9). Children's playground. Basketball. Tennis. Team games. Medical room. Security at gate. ATM. Torch useful. Off site: Indoor pool 100 m. Beach and fishing 300 m. Riding and bicycle hire 500 m. Golf 1 km. Boat launching 7 km. Free bus hourly to the beach and town in high season.

Open

1 June - 30 September.

At a glance

Welcome & Ambience	✓✓✓✓✓	Location	✓✓✓✓
Quality of Pitches	✓✓✓✓	Range of Facilities	✓✓✓✓✓

Directions

From E70/A8 Bilbao -Santander, take exit 185, CA 147 to Noja take first right S403. It is 10 km. to Noja. In town look for multiple campsite signs going off to left. Follow signs to Playa del Ris. At beach roundabout turn left (the sign had gone when we visited) and look for a left turn at further large signs. Reception is in the building to the left.

Charges 2005

Per pitch	€ 7,00 - € 10,50
adult	€ 3,50 - € 5,00
child	€ 2,80 - € 4,00
tent	€ 4,70 - € 6,00
car	€ 2,00 - € 3,00
electricity	€ 2,50

No credit cards.

Reservations

Write to site. Tel: 942 630 426.
E-mail: losmolinos@ceoecant.es

ES8985 Camping Valderredible

Ctra Polientes - Ruerrero, S/n, Valderredible, 39220 Polientes (Cantabria)

This is a pleasant site owned by the Gutierrez brothers who designed and constructed this site using their past campsite experience. Jose and Jesus are very keen to welcome you to their establishment. If you approach the site from the east you will enjoy the vista of limestone valleys and pass a large ornate waterfall which is worth exploring. All facilities on site are modern and kept spotlessly clean. There are 100 flat pitches with 80 for tourers and 20 for tents. Most have electricity and trees have been planted, although there is little shade at the moment. The pools enjoy river and mountain views, as does the patio to the bar/restaurant. The bustling bar, with TV, is pleasantly decorated with local artefacts and offers a range of tapas in season. There are some lovely walks in this unspoilt area (ask for guidance). The site is about 80 km. south of Santander and is good as a stopover or for longer stays if you wish for a peaceful break. On the first Sat and Sun of August there is a Fiesta here with all night celebrations so the site is full and extremely noisy.

Facilities

The good central sanitary block is fully equipped and comfortable. Washing-up sinks outside but covered. Two washing machines (free) and a dryer. No facilities for disabled campers. Small well stocked shop. Bar selling tapas and more formal restaurant, good service and reasonably priced. Swimming pool and children's pool (caps required; June - Sept). Play area (supervision required). Volleyball. Bar billiards. Table football. Torch useful. Off site: Canoeing and fishing in river Ebro 200 m. (March - June). Riding and bicycle hire 15 km. Buses run to local village which has a few bars and some restaurants.

Open

1 April - 4 November.

At a glance

Welcome & Ambience	✓✓✓✓	Location	✓✓✓✓✓
Quality of Pitches	✓✓✓✓	Range of Facilities	✓✓✓✓

Directions

Exit from A623 Burgos - Santander road around the village of Quintanilla Escalada onto minor road to Polientes. The site is clearly signed along the 21 km. of road and is just past the village of Ruijas. It is a spectacular drive in from the main road.

Charges 2005

Per person	€ 3,30 - € 3,50
child (3-10 yrs)	€ 3,00 - € 3,10
tent	€ 3,40 - € 3,60
caravan	€ 3,40 - € 3,60
car	€ 3,40 - € 3,60
motorcaravan	€ 5,50 - € 5,80

Plus 7% VAT.

Reservations

Necessary in August. Tel: 942 776 138.
E-mail: valderrecamp@mundivia.es

ES9000 Camping Playa Joyel

Playa de Ris, 39180 Noja (Cantabria)

This very attractive holiday and touring site is some 40 kilometres from Santander and 70 kilometres from Bilbao. It is a high quality, comprehensively equipped busy site, by a superb beach; providing 1,000 well shaded, marked and numbered pitches, including 80 large pitches of 100 sq.m. Electricity is available (3A with blue Euro-sockets). The swimming pool complex with lifeguard is free to campers and the superb beaches are cleaned daily 15/6-20/9. One of the beach exits leads to the main beach, or if you turn left out of the other you will find a safe, placid estuary with water at rising tide. An unusual feature is the natural park within the site boundary which has a great selection of animals to see. It overlooks a protected area of marsh where European birds spend the winter. There are security patrols at night. This good value, well managed site has a lot to offer for family holidays with much going on in high season when it gets very busy. Used by tour operators (150 pitches).

Facilities

Six excellent, spacious and fully equipped toilet blocks (voted amongst the cleanest in Europe) include baby baths and dishwashing facilities. Large laundry. Motorcaravan services. Gas supplies. Freezer service. Supermarket (all season). General shop. Kiosk. Restaurant (14/4–29/9). Bar, café takeaway and snacks (14/4–28/9). Swimming pools, bathing caps compulsory (15/5-15/9). Entertainment organised with a soundproof pub/disco (July-Aug). Games hall. Gym park. Recreation area and sports field. Tennis. Children's playground. Riding.Fishing. Natural animal park. Barbecue area. Hairdresser (July/Aug). Pharmacy. ATM and money exchange. Torches necessary in some areas. Medical centre. Dogs are not accepted. Off site: Bicycle hire 500 m. Within 1 km – large complex with multiple facilities including golf and indoor pool (fee). Golf 20 km.

At a glance

Welcome & Ambience	✓✓✓✓✓	Location	✓✓✓✓✓
Quality of Pitches	✓✓✓✓✓	Range of Facilities	✓✓✓✓✓

Directions

From A8 (E70) toll-free motorway at Beranga (km.185) take the N634 then, almost immediately, take the S403 for Noja. Follow signs to site.

Charges 2005

Per person	€ 3,70 - € 5,50
child (under 10 yrs)	€ 2,50 - € 4,10
pitch	€ 10,70 - € 16,40
electricity	€ 2,50 - € 2,70

All plus 7% VAT. No credit cards.

Reservations

Made for 1 week or more. Early arrival or reservation is essential in high season. Tel: 942 630 081. E-mail: playajoyel@telefonica.net

Open

Easter - 30 September.

TRAVEL SERVICE SITE

TO BOOK CALL 0870 405 4055 OR www.alanrogersdirect.com

Located in northern Spain, this is a region steeped in Basque traditions, which is reflected in the architecture, native language, local sports and cuisine.

There are three provinces:
Alava, Gipuzkoa and Bizkaia

The regional capital is Vitoria

The province of Gipuzkoa adjoins France in the east. Its capital, San Sebastian, is a bustling, picturesque seaside town with a strong Basque identity. Overlooking La Concha Bay and enclosed by rolling low hills, this popular resort boasts four good beaches, including the celebrated La Concha Beach. As cider production is one of oldest traditions in Basque country there are also plenty of sidrerías (cider houses) to visit. Heading along the rocky fringe of Costa Vasca towards Bilbao in Bizkaia are more excellent beaches and pretty fishing villages including Orio, Zarautz and Getaria. The biggest attraction in Bilbao is the famous Guggenheim Museum. Opened in 1997 this spectacular building is completely covered with titanium sheets and houses a collection of modern and contemporary art from around the world. The city also boasts a beautiful old quarter with a Gothic cathedral, the Plaza Nueva and a museum. Further inland in Alava is Vitoria, the region's capital. Its medieval streets intermingle with Renaissance Palaces and fine churches and are lined with lively bars and tavernas. In the summer the city plays host to a jazz festival. Elsewhere in the province are various nature reserves.

Cuisine of the region

Basque cuisine is considered to be the finest in Spain. Tapas or *pintxos* is readily available in bars, served with the local white wine *txakolí*. Fish is popular, especially *bacalao* (cod) and seafood is often used to make casseroles and sauces. Lots of milk based desserts. Founded in the 19th century, the tradition of dining clubs or *txokos* are unique to the Basque country

Alubias pochas: white haricot bean stew

Chipirones en su tinta: squid cooked in its ink

Goxua: sponge cake with whipped cream and caramel

Intxaursalsa: milk pudding with cinnamon and walnuts

Marmitaco: fish and potato stew

Pantxineta: custard slice

Places of interest

Encartanciones: one of the world's largest cave chambers Torca del Carlista, wildlife sanctuary

Hondarribia: fishing port, beaches, charming walled old town

Laguardia: old walled town with cobbled streets, historic buildings, in wine-growing district of Rioja Alavesa

Oñati: Baroque architecture, old university

Tolosa: impressive old town square, carnival in February

Zarautz: seaside town, famous for production of *txakoli*

Zumaia: beaches, good coastal walks, July fiesta with Basque sports, dancing and bull racing

Alan Rogers tip

BASQUE SPORTS FEATURE IN MANY LOCAL FIESTAS. WATCH OUT FOR *AIZKOLARITZA* (LOG-CHOPPING), *HARRI-JASOTZEA* (STONE-LIFTING) AND *SEGALARITZA* (GRASS-CUTTING)!

ES9045 Camping Angosto

Ctra Villanane-Angosto no. 2, 01425 Villanañe (Araba)

This is a smart eco-friendly site with excellent facilities surrounded by wooded hills near the Valderejo National Park. Opened in 2002, the facilities are improving every year remaining smart and clean. A keen young team run things here, and there is an emphasis on adventure sports. The site is occasionally busy with parties of local youngsters enjoying the various activities organised by the management (it can be noisy when this happens). With ample manoeuvring space, the 71 pitches are flat and of average size, 25 having electricity. There is a large area for tents. Young trees have been planted around the site and are beginning to provide shade. An attractive pool has been built with a sliding roof for inclement weather. Attractive walks start just outside the site perimeter and we spotted deer several times, and the area has one of the largest colonies of vultures in Northern Spain. As the site is one hour from Bilbao we see it as a most pleasant stopover or a chance to sample the rustic simplicity of the area and enjoy the facilities and a tranquil setting.

Facilities

Central, fully equipped sanitary block of attractive design with facilities for disabled campers. Dishwashing sinks outside, under cover. Washing machine. Good shop also used by the local villagers. Stylish bar. Attractive and terraced restaurant. Small fenced children's play area close to entrance and grass toddler play area. Mountain bike hire. Fishing. Adventure sports incl. parascending organised. Table football. Table tennis. TV. Fishing. Ice machine. Drinks machine. Torches necessary in some areas. Off site: Bus service from pretty local village 1 km. Heated municipal pool 1.4 km.

Open

April - September (plus weekends September - March

At a glance

Welcome & Ambience	✓✓✓✓✓	Location	✓✓✓✓✓
Quality of Pitches	✓✓✓✓✓	Range of Facilities	✓✓✓✓✓

Directions

Nearest town is Miranda de Ebro. From Bilbao and the Longrono autoroute, exit at village of Pobes and take road to Salinas and Espejo (N625). Site is clearly signed. If towing a caravan continue to Miranda de Ebro proceed towards Burgos for one exit (no 4) and take the N1 to the N625 then north to Villanane.

Charges guide

Per person	€ 3,16
child	€ 2,70
tent	€ 2,85
caravan	€ 3,16
car	€ 2,85
motorcaravan	€ 4,81

All plus 7% VAT.

Reservations

Contact site. Tel: 945 353 271.
E-mail: info@camping-angosto.com

ES9035 Camping Portuondo

Ctra Gernika-Bermeo, 48360 Mundaka (Bizkaia)

From some of the 119 pitches on site there are stunning views over the ocean and estuary. Among the lovely gardens, the pitches are mainly for medium size vans and tents, but there are six large pitches at the lower levels for caravans and motorhomes. In high season (July/August) it is best to ring to book your space. Before entering the site walk 20 metres up the hill and enjoy views that are difficult to beat on this coast (it is also a good idea to have a look at the approach before driving in). This well cared for, impressive little site could either be a very pleasant site to stay or a good base from which to explore the local area and the old Spanish town (9 September is a great celebration day here) and the friendly owner Inmanol is keen to help you. The site is mostly terraced, with pitches split, one section for your unit the other for your car and there is shade in parts. Most pitches are very slightly sloping and all have electricity (6A, some may need long leads). Above the larger sanitary block the building becomes a lofty picnic area with long benches, open on all sides, but perfect for occupants of tents in periods of rain. There is a stylish, safe swimming pool in the lower area of the site but no facilities for disabled campers. We stress that this site is on a steep incline.

Facilities

Two very good quality, fully equipped, sanitary units can be heated and include mostly British WCs and a smart baby bathroom. Dishwashing and laundry sinks outside under cover. Automated shop (all season). Bar and two restaurants, one open to public offering full range of meals and snacks, plus barbecue food (16/1-15/12). Takeaway (15/6-15/9). Swimming pools (15/6-15/9). Table tennis. Sky TV. Barbecue area. Bicycle hire. Washing machines and dryers. Caravan storage. Torches necessary. English spoken. Off site: Fishing 100 m. Beaches 500 m bracing walk. Surfing on Mundaka beach (500 m) is so good they hold international championships there. Boat launching 1 km. Bicycle hire, bars and restaurants 2 km. Sailing 5 km.

At a glance

Welcome & Ambience	✓✓✓✓✓	Location	✓✓✓✓✓
Quality of Pitches	✓✓✓✓✓	Range of Facilities	✓✓✓✓✓

Directions

From N634 or autopista (S. Sebastian-Bilbao), turn at Amorebieta onto the C6315 road to Gernika - Bermeo. Approach site from Bermeo direction due to oblique, steep (18%) access.

Charges 2005

Per person	€ 5,00
child (under 10 yrs)	€ 4,40
pitch	€ 10,10

All plus 7% VAT. Less 5-10% for longer stays.

Reservations

Write to site. Tel: 946 877 701.
E-mail: recepcion@campingportuondo.com

Open

All year.

www.alanrogers.com for latest campsite news

ES9038 Camping Orio

20810 Orio (Gipuzkoa)

This site has 260 pitches, with many long stay units and privately owned static units, but there should always be adequate space in the 190 pitches allocated for tourers. It is only 100 m. from the beach and there is little shade. The pitches are in rows divided by tarmac roads and hedges, all with electricity (5A). Like most of the north coast sites, it is fairly expensive in high season, with the cheaper pitches furthest from the beach, but the bonus is that they are closer to the sanitary facilities. The beach is in a pretty bay contained by towering hills which overlook the site. The beach is of soft sand (real sand-castle stuff) and shelves gently. Fishing is popular off the extremely long jetty or in the local river. This is a decent site for transit stops, west of San Sebastian or a little longer if you wish to enjoy the beach.

Facilities

The modernised main sanitary block is fully equipped and includes baby baths. Two additional smaller, older sanitary blocks are opened in the main season. Large kitchen with additional dishwashing and laundry sinks (cold water) outside under cover. Good facilities for disabled campers. Mini-market and good restaurant/bar attached to the site (open July/Aug). Swimming pools. Playground. Squash and tennis courts. Fishing. Barbecue area. Dogs are not accepted. Torches are necessary. Some English is spoken. Off site: Fishing 100 m. Golf 6 km. Sailing. Indoor pool. Aviary 100 m.

At a glance

Welcome & Ambience	✓✓✓✓✓	Location	✓✓✓✓✓
Quality of Pitches	✓✓✓✓	Range of Facilities	✓✓✓✓

Directions

Turn off N634 road at the Orio junction and follow signs to site. The approach is straightforward.

Charges guide

Per unit incl. 2 persons	€ 12,70 - € 22,55
extra adult	€ 2,30 - € 3,65
child (2-10 yrs)	€ 1,80 - € 3,10

VAT included.

Reservations

Write to site. Tel: 943 834 801.
E-mail: kaupina@terra.es

Open

1 March - 1 November.

ES9039 Gran Camping Zarautz

Monte Talai-Mendi, Ctra N634 San Sebastian - Bilboa, 20800 Zarauz (Gipuzkoa)

This friendly site sits alongside vines high in the hills to the east of the Basque town of Zarautz and has commanding views of the excellent beaches and the island of Isarria. Twenty percent of the 500 pitches are permanent which brings Spanish life and colour to the site at weekends. The pitches are of average size, shaded by mature trees, are reasonably level and have 5A electricity. We recommend a call to reserve one of the perimeter pitches which enjoy magnificent views over the bay. Between the site and the sea is a protected public area where flora and fauna flourish. You can enjoy birds and wildlife whilst exploring the ruins of a once busy iron ore works on the shore and the adjacent small island of Mollarri (children should be supervised in this area). On approaching the site you will pass a Bodega producing the local white wine, Txakoli (pronounced Char-coal-lee). The locals drink it young with shellfish. The town of Zarautz offers a cultural programme in summer and the pedestrian promenade with modern sculptures is a good vantage point to enjoy the beach and surfers.

Facilities

Two sanitary blocks - the more modern is circular and open plan with facilities for disabled campers. Two washing machines. Restaurant/bar with TV. Well stocked shop. Play area. Drinks machines. Recycling bins. English spoken. Off site: Bus/train service 1 km. Two good restaurants very close by. Below site at beach level is a 9 hole golf course. For a special treat visit the ancient sider'as (cider houses). These open in January and offer tastings with superb traditional food until the cider runs out. Ask for assistance at reception.

Open

All year.

At a glance

Welcome & Ambience	✓✓✓✓✓	Location	✓✓✓✓✓
Quality of Pitches	✓✓✓✓	Range of Facilities	✓✓✓

Directions

From N634 Donostia - San Sebastian road at 17 km. marker take sign to Zarautz and site is well marked on the roundabout at the eastern side of town.

Charges guide

Per person	€ 3,80
child (0-10 yrs)	€ 3,25
caravan or tent	€ 4,50
car	€ 3,80
motorcaravan	€ 8,30
electricity	€ 3,10

VAT included.

Reservations

Contact site. Tel: 943 831 238.

www.alanrogers.com for latest campsite news

The region of Navarra lies in the north of Spain, on the border with France separated by the Pyreenes. With mountain retreats, beautiful valleys and an array of attractive towns and historic buildings littered throughout the region, it is also popular for those wishing to follow the Pilgrim's Route to Santiago de Compostela.

There is only one province also known as Navarra

The capital is Pamplona

Founded by the Roman general Pompey in 75 BC, the region's capital Pamplona is perhaps best known for the Fiestas de San Fernmín (July), when the *encierro* takes place – a tradition which involves people running through the streets in front of bulls. The city is also boasts its fair share of sights including the old town, with its ancient churches and elegant building. Outside the city is the Sierra de Aralar, a great hiking spot with well-marked paths of all grades. A wander through here will take you past waterfalls and caves and in Excelsis you'll come across Navarra's oldest church, the Sanctuario de San Miguel, a popular pilgrimage destination. In the south, the historic medieval town of Olite is home to an outstanding 15th century castle, with turrets galore, and a Romanesque and Gothic church. To the west is the Urbasa and Andía Nature Reserve. Further north and in the east, the villages and valleys of the Pyrenees provide some of the most beautiful landscapes in the province and offer the perfect place to relax. Of particular note are the Valle de Baztán and the Valle de Salazar. For the more active, the Valle de Roncal is a good place to explore the mountains as is the Pirenaico National Park.

Cuisine of the region

Typical products found in abundance in this area include asparagus grown on the river banks, small red peppers and artichokes from Tudela, pork from Estella, cherries from Ciriza, cheese made in the Roncal Valley and *chorizo* from Pamplona

Ajoarriero: cod cooked with garlic, potato, 'choricero' peppers and tomatoes

Canutillos de Sumbilla: sweet pastry made with aniseed, filled with lemon flavouring

Chorizo: shaped like a candle, stuffed in thick tripe with pork and beef, seasoned with salt, paprika, garlic and sugars. It is eaten raw.

Cordero al chilindrón: lamb stew

Cuajada: made from sheep's milk and natural curd, sweetened by honey or sugar

Pacharán: traditional aniseed liquor

Places of interest

Andía Nature Reserve: forests, ponds, wildlife including the golden eagle, wild boar and wildcat

Camino de Santiago: ancient Pilgrim's route. There are variants but the most popular point of entry into Spain was the pass of Roncesvalles, in the Pyrenees. It then continues south through Navarra via Sangüesa, Puente La Reina and Estella, then west through the provinces of La Rioja and Castilla-León till it reaches Santiago in the Galicia province

Orreaga-Roncesvalles: a town established as a sanctuary and hospital in 1132 and first staging post for pilgrims, museum with exhibition on Pilgrim's Route.

Sangüesa: small town, 14th century churches, medieval hospital

Ujué: medieval defensive village, Romanesqe church

Alan Rogers tip

VISIT THE CAVES AT ZUGARRAMURDI. IN THE MIDDLES AGES THE CAVERN WAS A MAJOR CENTRE FOR WITCHCRAFT AS 'CELEBRATED' IN THE LOCAL WITCHES' FESTIVAL (JULY).

ES9043 Camping Caravanning Errota el Molino

31150 Mendigorria (Navarra)

This is an extremely large, sprawling site set by an attractive weir near the town of Mendigorria, alongside the river Arga. Regardless of the mini-windmill (molino) at the entrance, it really takes its name from an old disused water-mill close by (try to find it when you have a moment spare). Reception is housed in the lower part of a large prefabricated building along with the bar/restaurant which has a cool shaded terrace, there is a large separate more formal dining room and a supermarket and other support facilities. The chirpy owner Anna Beriain will give you a warm welcome. The upper floor is dormitory accommodation for backpackers. The site is split into separate permanent and touring sections. The touring area is a new development which is divided into sections. There are good-sized flat pitches with electricity and water for tourers, however there is no electricity in the tent area. Many trees have been planted around the site but there is little shade as yet. There is a small tour operator presence and backpackers and campers abound during the festival of San Fermin (bull running) in July, made famous in Pamplona (28 km.) by Ernest Hemingway. Tours of the local bodegas (groups of ten) to sample the fantastic Navarra wines can be organised by reception.

Facilities

The single, fully equipped, toilet block is very clean and well maintained, with cold water to washbasins. Services could become busy during San Fermin but then access is allowed to the sanitary facilities on the permanent side. Dishwashing (cold only) and laundry sinks (H&C). Facilities for disabled campers. Washing machine. Large restaurant, pleasant bar. Supermarket (Easter - Sept). Superb new swimming pools for adults and children. Football. Table tennis. Volleyball. Golf. Bicycle hire. Riding. Weekly animation programme (July/Aug) and many sporting activities. Pleasant river walk. Sophisticated dock and boat launching facility, pedaloes and canoes for hire and an ambitious water sport competition programme in season with a safety boat present at all times. Torches useful. Off site: Bus for town 1 km. Tours to Pamplona.

At a glance

Welcome & Ambience	✓✓✓✓✓	Location	✓✓✓✓✓
Quality of Pitches	✓✓✓✓✓	Range of Facilities	✓✓✓✓✓

Directions

From N111 Pamplona - Logroño road take exit to Puente la Reina. Take N6030 towards Mendigorria and after approx 6 km. take Larraga turn by the wide river Arga, where site is signed.

Charges guide

Per person	€ 3,60
child	€ 2,95
pitch incl. car and electricity	€ 10,50

Plus 7% VAT. Discounts outside high season.

Reservations

Made with 25% deposit. Advisable during San Fermin. Tel: 948 340 604.
E-mail: info@campingelmolino.com

Open

All year.

WIN A Caravan...

A holiday...and lots more

Alan Rogers

Prize Draw Bonanza

Alan Rogers Guides, in association with Towsure, providers of everything for the outdoors, are running a unique new prize draw for 2005. This is your chance to win a fantastic set of prizes, never before offered in the UK.

YOU COULD WIN ALL THESE!

WIN A brand new Avondale caravan

WIN A Camping Cheque holiday, including return ferry

WIN £500 of Towsure products

WIN A complete set of Alan Rogers 2005 guides

To enter, simply visit www.towsure.com

Towsure

ES9042 Camping Etxarri

Paraje Dambolintxulo s/n, 31820 Etxarri-Aranatz (Navarra)

Situated in the Valle de la Burunda the site is a peaceful oasis with superb views of the 1,300 m. high San-Donato Mountains. The approach to the constantly improving site is via a road lined by huge 300 year old beech trees, surrounding the tiny site, which nestles behind an enormous pool. Reception is a purpose built chalet with a touring reference library (mostly in Spanish). There are 100 average sized pitches on flat ground, 50 for tourers, with 6A electricity to all and water to 25. The site is well placed for fascinating walks in unspoilt countryside and is close to three recognised nature walks catering for all tastes and abilities. Animation is organised in August for children and there are many other activities available (see below). There is hostel accommodation for young Navarra students as part of their curriculum, and this is also used as standard accommodation especially at the time of the Fiestas de San Ferm'n (bull-running) in Pamplona. It is essential to make a reservation if you wish to stay for the thrilling week of 6-14 July. There is riotous non-stop celebration in Pamplona during this Fiesta, made world famous by Ernest Hemingway.

Facilities

Single, very modern sanitary block includes sinks and baby bath. Laundry. Gas supplies. Essential supplies available in high season. Bar. Restaurant with traditional fare at reasonable prices (1/6-30/9). Very large swimming pool plus children's pool (ex municipal and open to the public). Archery (small fee). Bicycle hire. Minigolf. Skateboarding. Table tennis. Small football pitch. Volleyball. Play area. Games room. Off site: Good bus services. Local village at 2 km has bars, restaurants and shops. Pamplona is recommended - parking is difficult - try to the west of the bullring, then wander down to Plaza de Toros (renamed Plaza Hemingway), to savour the atmosphere. A useful tip: it is common to use dual-naming of places and roads - one in the Spanish language the other in Basque and it can be confusing - ask for advice if in doubt.

At a glance

Welcome & Ambience	✓✓✓✓✓	Location	✓✓✓✓✓
Quality of Pitches	✓✓✓✓✓	Range of Facilities	✓✓✓✓

Directions

From A8 San Sebastian - Bilbao motorway take exit to Pamplona A15 at the junction at Irurzun (approx. 17.5 km. northwest of Pamplona) take N240 to Vitoria. At 40 km. marker take road to Etxarri-Aranatz where site is signed.

Charges 2005

Per person	€ 2,90 - € 3,80
child	€ 2,70 - € 3,40
caravan	€ 3,70 - € 4,70
tent	€ 3,50 - € 4,30
car	€ 2,90 - € 3,80
electricity	€ 3,60

Reservations

Contact site. Tel: 948 460 537.
E-mail: info@campingetxarri.com

Open

1 April - 1 October.

camping etxarri kanpina etxarri'ko

Situated amidst a leafy oakwood in the centre of the Sakana Valley.

Its magnificent setting makes it a perfect base for visiting two outstandingly beautiful areas: the mountains of Urbasa and Aralar.

These are lands of shepherds inhabitated since the paleolithic times, and they still boast many prehistoric remains.

Due to varying altitudes, they are accessible to all ages.

Camping ETXARRI . E-31820 ETXARRI ARANATZ (Navarra) . Tel./fax: (34) 948 46 05 37
info@campingetxarri.com . www.campingetxarri.com

In the north eastern part of Spain, Aragón borders France with the Pyreenes lying between them. It is a region rich in folklore, with rural mountainside villages renowned for their Romanesque architecture, beautiful valleys and awe-inspiring peaks.

Aragón is made up of three provinces: Huesca, Zaragoza and Teruel

The capital of the region is Zaragoza

The region can be separated into three different areas: the central area consisting of the Ebro basin, a vast flat lowland; the northern area where the Pyrenees lie; and the area made up of the Iberian mountain range in the northwest and south-east of the region. The northern-most province of Huesca is located in the foothills of the Pyrenees Mountains, a beautiful area with plenty of picturesque towns and villages to visit. It is also good walking country with numerous trails offering anything from short day-walks in the valleys to long-distance treks in the mountains. Skiing is popular too. Bordering Huesca, the province of Zaragoza is home to the region's capital, also of the same name. Zaragoza is a lively town with plenty of bars and restaurants, plus numerous museums and architectural treasures. Outside the capital you'll find more villages, countryside, and vineyards where the best of the region's wine is produced; the mapped out Ruta del Vino will take you through the area. The third province of Teruel is largely comprised of the Iberian mountain range, with attractive towns, medieval sights and more dramatic scenery to admire.

Cuisine of the region

Specialities include lamb, locally-produced ham and sausages; fruit is also used a lot in desserts.

Chilindrones: sauces of tomato and pepper

Frutas de Aragón: sugar-candied fruits covered in chocolate

Pollo al chilindrón: chicken (or lamb) stew with onions, tomatoes and red peppers

Salmorrejos: cold soups

Suspiros de amante: dessert with cheese and egg

Ternasco: roast lamb

Tortas de alma: made with pumpkin, honey and sugar

Trenza de Almudévar: with nuts and raisins soaked in liqueur

Places of interest

Aljafería Palace: spectacular Moorish monument

Basílica de Nuestra Señora del Pilar: Baroque temple from the 17th and 18th centuries

Benasque: attractive alpine town, gateway to Pyrenees

Casa-Museo de Goya: art museum, including engravings by Goya

Jaca: home of the country's oldest Romanesque cathedral

Monasterio de San Juan de la Peña: 17th century Baroque monastery and 10th century Old monastery in Romanesque style

Parque Nacional de Ordesa y Monte Perdido: alpine national park

Alan Rogers tip

FOR FOLK MUSIC LOVERS, THE PYRENEES FOLK FESTIVAL IS HELD IN JACA, LATE JULY AND THE CITY OF ZARAGOZA INTERNATIONAL FOLKLORE EVENT TAKES PLACE IN SEPTEMBER.

www.alanrogers.com for latest campsite news

ES9058 Camping Baliera

Ctra N260, km 355.5, 22486 Bonansa (Huesca)

With its wonderful location in a quiet river valley with views of the surrounding, mountains all around, Camping Baliera is an excellent site for enjoying this beautiful area. With two National Parks within 10 km. it is ideally positioned for activities such as walking, cycling, fishing and winter skiing. Combining camping with timber chalets and apartments, the site has 250 well kept grass touring pitches (80-120 sq.m), 200 with electricity (5/10A). The pitches are mostly located close to the attractive, stone built reception building which also houses a comfortable bar and restaurant, shop and fitness. An outdoor swimming pool is open in high season. At this time an entertainment team organises excursions in the local area and activities such as cinema, handicrafts and sports. The approach to this site is by narrow and winding mountain roads and it is 5 km. from the nearest village. However, for all but the largest units, the trip is well worth making.

Facilities

Two toilet blocks, one part of the apartment block near the entrance, the other in the reception building (this closed in low season). The heated are good with well equipped showers, vanity style washbasins and a baby room. Laundry room and drying room. Chemical disposal and motorcaravan services. Shop, bar and restaurant (all year). Swimming pool (1/7-31/8). Fitness equipment. Play area and small sports field. Entertainment in high season. Off site: National parks and outdoor activities. Nearest village 5 km.

Open

All year.

At a glance

Welcome & Ambience	✓✓✓✓	Location	✓✓✓✓✓
Quality of Pitches	✓✓✓✓	Range of Facilities	✓✓✓✓

Directions

On N230, 34 km. south of Vielha, turn onto N260 for 2-3 km, then onto A1605 signed Bonsana for 100 m. to site on left. Reception is 200 m. through the site. Approach roads are narrow and winding, but navigable.

Charges 2004

Per person	€ 3,60 - € 4,50
child (2-10 yrs)	€ 3,36 - € 4,20
pitch	€ 7,20 - € 10,50
electricity	€ 4,00
dog	€ 1,68 - € 2,10

VAT included.

Reservations

Contact site. Tel: 974 554 016.
E-mail: info@baliera.com

ES9060 Camping Peña Montañesa

Ctra Ainsa-Francia, km 2, 22360 Labuerda (Huesca)

A large, riverside site situated quite high up in the Pyrenees, near the Ordesa National Park, Pena Montanesa is easily accessible from Ainsa or from France via the Bielsa Tunnel (steep sections on the French side), and is ideally situated for exploring the beautiful Pyrenées. The site is essentially divided into three sections opening progressively throughout the season and all have shade. The 288 pitches on fairly level grass are of approximately 75 sq.m. and 10A electricity is available on virtually all. This is quite a large site which has grown very quickly and as such, it may at times be a little hard pressed, though it is very well run. Grouped near the entrance are the facilities that make the site so attractive. Apart from a fair sized outdoor pool and children's pool (lifeguard 1/3-1/10), there is a glass covered indoor pool (heated in winter) with jacuzzi and sauna (open all year) and an attractive bar/restaurant (with open fire) and terrace with the supermarket and takeaway opposite. The complete town of Ainsa is listed as a national monument of Spain and should be explored while you are here, along with the national park. There is an entertainment programme for children (21/6-15/9 and Easter weekend) and twice weekly for adults (July/Aug).

Facilities

A newer toilet block, heated when necessary, has free hot showers but cold water to open plan washbasins, facilities for disabled visitors and a small baby bathroom. An older block in the original area has similar provision. Washing machine and dryer. Bar. Restaurant. Takeaway. Supermarket. Outdoor swimming pool and children's pool (March - Oct). Pool complex (all year). Children's playground. Boules. Table tennis. Bicycle hire. Riding. Rafting. Only gas barbecues are permitted. Torches required in some areas. Off site: Fishing 100m. Skiing in season. Canoeing near.

At a glance

Welcome & Ambience	✓✓✓✓✓	Location	✓✓✓✓✓
Quality of Pitches	✓✓✓✓	Range of Facilities	✓✓✓✓✓

Directions

Site is 2 km. from Ainsa, on the road from Ainsa to France.

Charges guide

Per person	€ 4,40 - € 5,50
child (1-9 yrs)	€ 3,44 - € 4,30
pitch	€ 12,00 - € 15,00
dog	€ 2,64 - € 3,30
electricity	€ 4,30

All plus 7% VAT.

Reservations

Are made for camping with € 100 deposit by visa or giro. Tel: 974 500 032.
E-mail: info@penamontanesa.com

Open

All year.

www.alanrogers.com for latest campsite news

ES9062 Camping Boltaña

Ctra N-260, km 442, 22340 Boltaña (Huesca)

Nestled in the Rio Ara valley, surrounded by the Pyrennees mountains and below a tiny but enchanting, historic, hill top village, is the very pretty, thoughtfully planned Camping Boltaña. Generously sized, grassy pitches have good shade from a variety of trees and a stream meanders through the campsite. The landscaping includes ten charming rocky water gardens (though these can dry up in the summer months) and a covered pergola doubles as an eating and play area. A stone building houses the site's new reception, social room and supermarket. Opposite is a terrace for enjoying tapas, listening to music, casual eating, animation and games and above this is the charming stone and wood restaurant. Special meals and paellas can be ordered the day before for you to eat in the restaurant or take away. Angel Moreno, the owner of the site, is a charming host and has tried to think of everything to make his guests comfortable.

Facilities

Two modern sanitary blocks include facilities for disabled visitors and laundry facilities. A casual restaurant and bar and a more formal restaurant (April-Oct). Supermarket. Swimming pools and children's pool (15/5-30/9). Children's playground. Barbecues. Full size soccer pitch. Animation for children, music at weekends in high season. Pentanque. Guided tours organized, plus hiking, canyoning, rafting, climbing, mountain biking and caving. Torches may be necessary in some parts. Local bus service.

Open

All year.

At a glance

Welcome & Ambience	✓✓✓✓✓	Location	✓✓✓✓
Quality of Pitches	✓✓✓✓	Range of Facilities	✓✓✓✓

Directions

South of the Park Nacional de Ordesa, site is about 50 km. from Jaca near Ainsa. From Ainsa travel northwest on N260 toward Boltana (near 443 km marker). 1 km. from Boltana turn south toward Margudged. Camping Boltana is well signed and is approx. 1 km. along this road.

Charges guide

Per person	€ 4,60
child (1-10 yrs)	€ 3,70
caravan or tent	€ 5,10
car	€ 5,10
motorcycle	€ 4,10
motorcaravan	€ 9,20

Reservations

Contact site for details. Tel: 974 502 347.
E-mail: info@campingboltana.com

ES9064 Camping Gavín

Ctra N260, km 503, 22639 Gavín (Huesca)

Camping Gavín is set on a terraced, wooded hillside. At about 900 m. it is surrounded by towering peaks at the portal of the Tena Valley. One can enjoy the natural beauty of the Pyrenees and venture near or far along the great Pyrenean footpaths. The National Park of Ordesa, the valleys of Hecho, Broto and Tena and their associated ravines, lakes and rivers all offer a great variety of opportunities for physical activities. Visit the high mountain villages of Formigal, Panticosa and Balneario and watch the eagles soar overhead. The site offers 150 pitches of 80 sq m. in size and with electricity available to all (6/10A). The main site buildings are built of natural stone. There are also 11 superb, balconied apartments for 4 to 6 persons. You will find a friendly welcome with English spoken.

Facilities

Excellent shower and toilet facilities in three main buildings with subtle, tasteful décor include facilities for babies and disabled people. Dishwashing and laundry facilities. Bar and snacks. Well stocked supermarket. Swimming pool and children's pool. Tennis. Table tennis. Playground. Barbecues are not permitted at some times of the year. Off site: Windsurfing, rafting, riding, fishing, walking and climbing in the vicinity. Bicycle hire 2 km. Day excursions to the Monastery of San Juan de la Pena or over the border into France possible.

At a glance

Welcome & Ambience	✓✓✓✓	Location	✓✓✓✓
Quality of Pitches	✓✓✓✓	Range of Facilities	✓✓✓✓✓

Directions

Site is off the N260, 2 km. from Biescas at km 503.

Charges 2005

Per person	€ 3,60 - € 5,00
caravan or tent	€ 3,60 - € 5,00
car	€ 3,60 - € 5,00
motorcaravan	€ 6,05 - € 8,60

Reservations

Advisable for Holy week and July/Aug.
Tel: 974 485090. E-mail: info@campinggavin.com

Open

All year.

ES9070 Centro de Vacaciones Pirineos

Ctra N240, km 300, 22791 Santa Cilia de Jaca (Huesca)

This pretty site which is open most of the year, is directly on the pilgrimage route to Santiago. As well as the campsite, with chalets to hire, there is a small hotel. It has a mild climate, being near the River Aragon, not too high and convenient for touring the Pyrenees. The trees provide good shade. There is an attractive irregular shaped swimming pool and children's pool. The restaurant with a varied menu and a good value menu of the day has a large comfortable terrace and a patio for drinks and snacks. There is an open fronted room for barbecuing and all equipment is provided. A major feature here is the huge recreational area with all manner of sports and amusements. It is a friendly site which is useful for transit stops and off-season camping on the large, mostly level wooded area which can accommodate 250 units (no marked pitches), with electric points throughout. There is some road noise along the south side of the site.

Facilities

One heated sanitary block is open all year, providing a quite satisfactory supply, including dishwashing and laundry sinks with hot water. A second, more modern block is open April - September only. Launderette. Restaurant. Bar. Supermarket (15/6-15/9, otherwise essentials kept in bar). Swimming pools (15/6-15/9). Two tennis courts. Table tennis. Playground. Playroom with electronic games. Petanque. Bicycle hire. Gas supplies. 5-side-soccer. Torches required in some areas. Off site: Fishing and bathing in river 200 m.

Open

All year excl. 3 November - 3 December.

At a glance

Welcome & Ambience	✓✓✓	Location	✓✓✓✓
Quality of Pitches	✓✓✓	Range of Facilities	✓✓✓✓

Directions

Site is 15 km. west of Jaca on N240 at km 300 (65 km. northwest of Huesca).

Charges guide

Per person	€ 4,80
child (2-9 yrs)	€ 4,45
caravan or tent	€ 4,80
car	€ 4,50
motorcaravan	€ 8,50
electricity (6A)	€ 3,90

All plus 7% VAT.

Reservations

Made with deposit (€ 60). Tel: 974 377 351. E-mail: pirineos@pirinet.com

ES9125 Camping Lago Barasona

Ctra N - 123a, km 25, 22435 La Puebla de Castro (Huesca)

This site, alongside its associated 10 room hotel, is beautifully positioned in terraces by the shores of the Lago de Barasona (a large reservoir), with views of hills and the distant Pyrenees. There are two excellent restaurants here one being in the hotel the other with a pretty terrace with wonderful views. The menu and cooking is outstanding, specialising in the regional cuisine. The very friendly, English speaking owner is keen to please and has applied very high standards throughout the site. The grassy, fairly level pitches are generally around 100 sq.m. with 35 high quality pitches of 110 sq m for larger units. All have electricity (6/10A), many are well shaded and some have great views of the lake and/or hills. Waterskiing and other watersports are available in July and August. You may swim and fish in the lake which has a shallow area extending for around 20 m. If you prefer, the site has a round outdoor pool plus the pleasant standard pool in the hotel (these open from as early as April when the weather is often quite warm). The disco is well away from the site by the lakeside. The local administration has put together some excellent tourist and walking route information (in English) and the owner has matched this with his own quality brochure. The recently discovered Roman town of Labitolosa currently under excavation is just 1.5 kilometres away. This is a most pleasant and peaceful site in a lovely area and will suit families who wish for quality and choice in their camping. The views really are beautiful.

Facilities

Two toilet blocks in modern buildings have high standards and hot water throughout including cabins (3 for ladies, 1 for men). Bar/snack bar and two excellent restaurants (all season). Shop (15/5-15/9). Swimming pools (15/5-15/9). Tennis. Table tennis. Mountain bike hire. Canoe, windsurfing motor boat and pedalo hire. Mini-club. Lake swimming, fishing, canoeing, etc. Facilities for volleyball, football and a new children's play area were under construction. Walking (maps provided). Money exchange. Mini-disco. Off site: Riding 4 km.

Open

1 April - 30 September.

At a glance

Welcome & Ambience	✓✓✓✓	Location	✓✓✓✓✓
Quality of Pitches	✓✓✓✓	Range of Facilities	✓✓✓

Directions

Site is on the west bank of the lake, close to km. 25 on the N123A, 4.5 km. south of Graus (approx. 80 km. north of Lleida/Lerida).

Charges 2005

Per person	€ 3,70 - € 4,85
child (2-10 yrs)	€ 2,70 - € 3,70
car	€ 3,70 - € 5,20
caravan or tent	€ 3,70 - € 5,20
motorcaravan	€ 5,80 - € 8,30
electricity	€ 3,70

Plus 7% VAT .

Reservations

Made with 25-50% deposit, but probably not needed outside mid-July - mid-August. Contact site for details. Tel: 974 545 148. E-mail: info@lagobarasona.com

ES9095 Camping Ciudad de Albarracin

Junto al Polideportibo, 44100 Albarracin (Teruel)

Albarracin, in southern Aragon is set in the 'Reserva Nacional de los Montes Universales' and is a much frequented, fascinating town with a Moorish castle. The old city walls towering above date from its days when it attempted to become a separate country within Spain. This neat and clean family site is set on three levels on a hillside behind the town, with a walk of 1 km. to the centre. It is very modern and has high quality facilities including a superb building for barbecuing (all materials provided). There are 140 pitches (70 for touring units), all with electricity and separated by trees. Some require cars to be parked separately. The homely bar/restaurant, with a terrace and TV, is open all season and has a limited but very pleasant menu. The site is good value, is well run and is a good bet for exploring the area or just enjoying the peace and quiet in this area of natural beauty.

Facilities

The two spotless, modern sanitary buildings provide British style WCs, quite large showers and hot water throughout. Baby bath in the ladies' and a smart area for dishwashing and laundry with washing machines. Bar/restaurant (all season). Essentials from bar. Special room for barbecues with fire and wood provided. Play area. Fronton. 5-a-side soccer. Torches required in some areas. Off site: Municipal swimming pool 100 m. (high season). Town shops, bars and restaurants 500 m.

At a glance

Welcome & Ambience	✓✓✓	Location	✓✓✓✓✓
Quality of Pitches	✓✓✓	Range of Facilities	✓✓✓

Directions

From Teruel north on the N330 for about 8 km. then west onto A1512 for 30 km. Well signed in town.

Charges 2004

Per person	€ 2,70
child (under 14)	€ 2,00
pitch incl. car	€ 5,00 - € 5,45
electricity	€ 2,00

Plus 7% VAT.

Reservations

Contact site. Tel: 978 710 197.

Open

1 April - 31 October.

ES9105 Camping Lago Park

Ctra Alhama de Aragon-Nuevalos, 50210 Nuevalos (Zaragoza)

Lago Park is situated in an attractive area which receives many visitors for the Monasterio de Piedra just 3 km. distant and it enjoys pleasant views of the surrounding mountains. The site has a rather steep access and slopes so is considered unsuitable for disabled campers. It is just outside the attractive ancient village, between lake and mountains, and suitable as a base for exploring this really attractive area. Set on a steep hillside, the 300 pitches (250 for tourers) are on terraces. Only the lower rows of terraces are suitable for large caravans (access in some areas may be difficult). These pitches are numbered and marked by trees, most having electrical connections (10A). Facilities on site include a large pool (unheated and chilly with its mountain water), a restaurant/bar and small shop. The restaurant is disappointing with restricted hours, mediocre cooking and is pricey, but there are many good restaurants in town. The site is suitable for transit stops or if you wish to visit the monasterio as it is the only one hereabouts and appears to make the most of that fact. It is not recommended for extended stays.

Facilities

The single sanitary block has Turkish and British style WCs. washbasins with hot water and controllable hot showers (no dividers). Restaurant/bar (June-Sept). Shop (all season). Swimming pool (late June-Sept). Play area. Gas supplies. Torches needed in some areas. Off site: Fishing 300 m. Riding 2 km.

Open

1 April - 30 September.

At a glance

Welcome & Ambience	✓✓✓	Location	✓✓✓✓
Quality of Pitches	✓✓✓	Range of Facilities	✓✓✓

Directions

From Zaragoza (120 km.) take fast A2/N11/E90 road and turn onto C202 road beyond Calatayud to Nuévalos (25 km). From Madrid exit A2 at Alhama de Aragón (13 km). Follow signs for Monasterio de Piedra from all directions.

Charges 2004

Per person	€ 4,60
child (3-10 yrs)	€ 4,45
pitch incl. car	€ 8,90 - € 9,50
electricity	€ 3,90

Reservations

Contact site. Tel: 976 849 038.

Menorca, steeped in history and blanketed by mystery, is an enchanting island of roughly 270 square miles in area.

The C721 highway provides the back-bone to the island, connecting modest market towns to Mahon (the main town) in the east and Ciutadella in the west. Mahon's classic Georgian style buildings, complete with sash windows, will endear them to the British traveller. Its impressive harbour was captured by the British in 1708 during the Spanish War of Succession. In complete contrast, Ciutadella has a more Gothic feel to it. A labyrinth of tiny streets entwine the 'little city', most of which can only be accessed on foot. Monte Toro stands proudly at the centre of the island surveying all. To the south a greener lush terrain exists with long, luxurious beaches, while to the north a giant rockery erupts riddled with caves and prehistoric finds. The building of leisure facilities is now heavily taxed by the regional government and the proceeds used to buy land for National Parks and Nature Reserves, thereby protecting the island for future generations.

ES8000 Camping Son Bou

Mobile homes page 173

Ctra de San Jaime km 3.5, Apdo. de Correus 85, Alayor, 07730 Menorca

The beautiful island of Menorca cries out to be explored. It is peaceful and tranquil, with its characteristic dry stone walls, its low white buildings with terracotta tiled roof, its beautiful coastline, ancient monuments and pretty villages with their cycle of fiestas of religious origin with the noble horse as the central element. Camping Son Bou was only opened in July 1996 and has been purpose built in local style providing a large irregular shaped pool with marvellous view across to Monte Toro and overlooked by a pine shaded, terraced bar and restaurant. The 216 large pitches are arranged in circles radiating out from the main facilities and clearly edged with stones. Natural pine tree shade covers most but the outer ring. Drinking water and refuse points are well placed. Electricity (6A) is available on nearly all pitches. The ground is hard and devoid of grass except where sprinklers operate. The site gets very busy with Spanish people from the mainland in high season. Earlier in the year it is quieter and greener. If you do not fancy the ferry crossings the site has some neat wooden chalets and ready erected tents. The site is more than happy to arrange the overnight ferry crossing from Barcelona or Valencia (discounts available).

Facilities

Well designed toilet block of good quality, open plan in places. Some washbasins in cabins. Separate room with baby baths. En-suite facilities for disabled visitors and ramped access to other facilities on site. Washing up and laundry sinks all have cold water as do the washbasins. No washing machines but serviced wash available. Shop (from 1/5). Bar. Restaurant (open when site open). Outdoor pool (from 1/5). Tennis. Petanque. Football. Basketball. Volleyball. Children's play area. Bicycle hire. English spoken. Open air cinema most evenings. Occasional barbecue with guitarist. Comprehensive activity programme covering birdwatching, walking, mountain biking, canoeing, diving, windsurfing, water skiing and various excursions. Off site: Riding 3 km. The village of Son Bou itself is 0.75 km. away and very much a small tourist centre. The sandy beach is the longest in the island, well organised with lifeguards, snack bars, sun beds and umbrellas to hire with a naturist section at the far end.

At a glance

Welcome & Ambience	✓✓✓✓✓	Location	✓✓✓✓✓
Quality of Pitches	✓✓✓✓	Range of Facilities	✓✓✓✓

Directions

From Mahon (Mao) follow the main road to Ciutadella. Go past the town of Alaior (bypassed), for a further km. approx. Watch for restaurant on left and road sign for San Jaime/Son Bou. Turn left on this road (the surface is not as good as the main road). Continue for 3.5 km.and site on right.

Charges 2005

Per person	€ 5,25 - € 6,40
child (3-13 yrs)	€ 3,85 - € 4,70
tent for 1 person	€ 2,95 - € 3,60
tent for 2 persons	€ 5,80 - € 7,05
car	€ 3,55 - € 4,30
motorcycle	€ 2,70 - € 3,30

All plus 7% VAT.

Reservations

Contact site. The site can also arrange the ferries from Spain. Tel: 971 372 605.
E-mail: info@campingsonbou.com

Open

22 March - 31 October.

Portugal is a relatively small country occupying the southwest corner of the Iberian peninsula, bordered by Spain in the north and east, with the Atlantic coast in the south and west. In spite of its size, the country offers a tremendous variety in both its way of life and traditions.

Most visitors looking for a beach type holiday head for the busy Algarve, with its long stretches of sheltered sandy beaches, and warm, clear Atlantic waters, great for bathing and watersports. With its monuments and fertile rolling hills, central Portugal adjoins the beautiful Tagus river that winds its way through the capital city of Lisbon, on its way to the Altantic Ocean. Lisbon city itself has deep rooted cultural traditions, coming alive at night with buzzing cafes, restaurants and discos. Moving south east of Lisbon the land becomes rather impoverished, consisting of stretches of vast undulating plains, dominated by cork plantations. Most people head for the walled town of Evora, an area steeped in two thousand years of history. The Portuguese consider the Minho area in the north to be the most beautiful part of their country, with its wooded mountain and wild coastline, a rural and conservative region with picturesque towns.

Population: 10 million

Capital: Lisbon

Climate: The country enjoys a maritime climate with hot summers and mild winters with comparatively low rainfall in the south, heavy rain in the north

Language: Portuguese, but English is widely spoken in cities, towns and larger resorts. French can be useful

Currency: The Euro (€)

Telephone: The country code is 00 351

Banks: Mon-Fri 08.30-11.45 and 13.00-14.45. Some large city banks operate a currency exchange 18.30-23.00

Shops: Mon-Fri 0900-1300 and 1500-1900. Sat 0900-1300.

Public Holidays: New Year; Carnival (Shrove Tues); Good Fri; Liberty Day 25 Apr; Labour Day; Corpus Christi; National Day 10 June; Saints Days; Assumption 15 Aug; Republic Day 5 Oct; All Saints 1 Nov; Immaculate Conception 8 Dec; Christmas 24-26 Dec

Tourist Office:

ICEP Portuguese Trade & Tourism Office,
Second Floor, 22/25a Sackville Street, London W1S 3LY

Tel: 09063 640 610 E-mail: iceplondt@aol.com
Fax: 020 7494 1868 Internet: www.portugalinsite.com

Algarve

The Algarve, Portugal's southernmost province, is a true sunseekers paradise, offering all year round sunshine and over 150 miles of beautiful sandy beaches.

The Algarve has one district: Faro

The coast of the Algarve offers mile after mile of golden beaches and small sandy coves with interesting rock formations, interspersed with busy fishing ports. The capital, Faro, boasts excellent beaches, while the thriving fishing port and market centre of Lagos is one of the most popular destinations in the Algarve. Although the earthquake of 1755 caused great damage to Lagos, the streets and squares of the town have retained much of their charm. Within walking distance are some superb beaches, including Praia de Dona Ana, which is considered to be the most picturesque of all, and the smaller coves of Praia do Pinhão and Praia Camilo. Further inland and to the north, the hills mark the edge of a greener and more fertile region, brilliantly coloured by fig-trees, orange-groves and almond-trees that come into blossom in the winter. Here you will also find a series of typical villages that have successfully preserved their ancestral traditions. The walled town of Silves has a Moorish fortress, 13th century cathedral and archaeology musuem. It also has a lively summer beer festival. Nearby, the narrow streets of the old spa town of Monchique wind up a steep hillside, revealing magnificent views of the surrounding countryside.

Cuisine of the region

Fresh fish and seafood are popular; the local speciality is *Ameijoas na Cataplana* (clams steamed in a copper pan). One of the most traditional dishes is *caldeiradas* (stew made with all kinds of different fish) and *sardinha assada* (grilled sardines). Given the abundance of trees in the region, figs and almonds are used a lot in desserts including *bolinhos de amêndoa* (small cakes made from marzipan and almond paste), which are moulded into the shape of fruits and vegetables in all kinds of different sizes.

Places of interest

Albufeira: popular resort, daily market, good nightlife

Cape São Vicente: south westernmost point of Europe

Faro: monuments, churches, museums, Gothic cathedral, good shopping centre

Sagres: 17th century fortress

Tavira: picturesque town, 17th and 18th century architecture

Vilamoura: good sporting facilies including golf courses

Alan Rogers tip

THE ALGARVE HAS A WHOLE HOST OF GOLF COURSES, SOME OVERLOOKING THE SEA, WHERE YOU CAN PLAY ALL YEAR ROUND.

PO8230 Camping Olhao

Pinheiros de Marim, 8700 Olhao (Faro)

This site, taking around 1,000 units and open all year, has mature trees to provide reasonable shade. The pitches are marked, numbered and in rows divided by shrubs with electricity and water to all parts. Permanent and long stay units take 20% of the pitches and the tourist pitches fill up quickly in high season, so arrive early. Amenities include very pleasant pools and tennis courts, a reasonable bar and restaurant, all very popular with the local Portuguese, and a café/bar with TV and games room. There is some noise nuisance from an adjacent railway. The large, sandy beaches in this area are on islands reached by ferry and are, as a result, relatively quiet (some reserved for naturists). This site can get busy in peak periods. A large, low season British contingent was enjoying the low prices when we visited.

Facilities

Eleven sanitary blocks are adequate, clean when seen, and are specifically sited to be a maximum of 50 m. from any pitch. One block has facilities for disabled visitors. Laundry. Supermarket. Kiosk. Restaurant/bar (all year). Café and general room with TV. Playgrounds. Swimming pools (April - Sept) and tennis courts (fees for both). Volleyball. Bicycle hire. Internet. Off site: Bus service 50 m to the nearest ferry at Olhao. Riding 1 km. Fishing 2 km. Golf 20 km.

Open

All year, as are all facilities.

At a glance

Welcome & Ambience	✓✓✓✓	Location	✓✓✓✓✓
Quality of Pitches	✓✓✓	Range of Facilities	✓✓✓✓

Directions

Just over 1 km. east of Olhao, on EN125, take turn to Pinheiros de Marim. Site is 300 m. on left. Look for white triangular entry arch as the site name is different on the outside wall - a foible of the owner.

Charges 2004

Per person	€ 1,95 - € 3,60
child (5-12 yrs)	€ 1,10 - € 2,00
car	€ 1,50 - € 3,00
tent	€ 1,50 - € 4,00
caravan	€ 2,45 - € 7,00
motorcaravan	€ 2,50 - € 7,20

Less for longer winter stays.

Reservations

Contact site. Tel: 289 70 03 00.
E-mail: parque.campismo@sbsi.pt

PO8220 Orbitur Camping Quarteira

Estrada da Fonte Santa, 8125 Quarteira (Faro)

This is a large, busy attractive site on undulating ground with some terracing, taking 795 units. On the outskirts of the popular Algarve resort of Quarteira, it is 600 m. from a sandy beach which stretches for a kilometre to the town centre. Many of the unmarked pitches have shade from tall trees and there are a few small individual pitches of 50 sq.m. with electricity and water for reservation. There are 680 electrical connections. Like other sites along this coast, long winter stays are encouraged. The pools are excellent, featuring pools for adults (with a large flume) and children (with fountains), open in high season (extra charge). The large restaurant and supermarket have separate entrances for local trade.

Facilities

Five sanitary blocks provide British and Turkish style toilets, individual washbasins with cold water, hot showers plus facilities for disabled visitors. Washing machines. Motorcaravan services. Gas supplies. Supermarket, self-service restaurant (Feb - Nov). Takeaway (from late May). Swimming pools (June - Sept). General room with bar and TV. Tennis. Kiosk. Open air disco. Medical room. Off site: Fishing 1 km. Bicycle hire (summer) 1 km. Golf 4 km.

Open

All year.

At a glance

Welcome & Ambience	✓✓✓✓✓	Location	✓✓✓✓✓
Quality of Pitches	✓✓✓✓	Range of Facilities	✓✓✓✓

Directions

Turn off N125 south towards Quarteira in Almancil (8 km. west of Faro). Site is 5 km. from the junction

Charges 2004

Per person	€ 2,60 - € 5,00
child (5-10 yrs)	€ 1,30 - € 2,50
tent	€ 2,20 - € 6,70
caravan	€ 3,10 - € 7,70
car	€ 2,20 - € 4,50
motorcaravan	€ 3,80 - € 8,40

Off season discounts (up to 70%).

Reservations

Contact Orbitur - Central de Reservas, Rua Diogo do Couto, 1149–042 Lisboa. Tel: 21/811 70 00 or 811 70 70. Email: info@orbitur.pt

PO8200 Orbitur Camping Valverde

Estrada da Praia da Luz, Valverde, 8600 Lagos (Faro)

A little over one kilometre from the village of Praia da Luz and its beach and about 7 km. from Lagos, this large, well run site is certainly worth considering for your stay in the Algarve. It has 600 numbered pitches, of varying size, which are enclosed by hedges. All are on flat ground or broad terraces with good shade in most parts from established trees and shrubs. The site has a swimming pool with a long curling slide and a paddling pool (under 10s free, adults charged). This is an excellent site with well maintained facilities and good security. It attracts a good number of long-term winter visitors. The site, which is one of the better Orbitur sites, is extremely well managed by Sra. Pinto, who is helpful and friendly.

Facilities

Six large, clean, toilet blocks have some washbasins and sinks with cold water only, and hot showers. Units for disabled people. Laundry. Motorcaravan services. Supermarket, shops, restaurant and bar complex with both self-service and waiter service in season (all April - Oct). Takeaway. Coffee shop. Swimming pool with slide and paddling pool (June - Sept). Playground. Tennis court. Disco. Pub. General room with TV. Excursions. Medical post. Off site: Fishing and bicycle hire 3 km. Golf 10 km. The road to the beach is quite narrow with fast traffic.

Open

All year.

At a glance

Welcome & Ambience	✓✓✓✓✓	Location	✓✓✓✓
Quality of Pitches	✓✓✓✓	Range of Facilities	✓✓✓✓

Directions

Fork left on N125 road 3 km. west of Lagos to Praia da Luz and site is under 1 km.

Charges 2004

Per person	€ 2,60 - € 5,00
child (5-10 yrs)	€ 1,30 - € 2,50
tent	€ 2,20 - € 6,70
caravan	€ 3,10 - € 7,70
car	€ 2,20 - € 4,50
motorcaravan	€ 3,80 - € 8,40

Off season discounts (up to 70%).

Reservations

Contact Orbitur - Central de Reservas, Rua Diogo do Couto, 1149–042 Lisboa. Tel: 21/811 70 00 or 811 70 70. Email: info@orbitur.pt

PO8210 Parque de Campismo Albufeira

EN 125 Ferreiras-Albufeira, 8200-555 Albufeira (Faro)

The spacious entrance to this site will accommodate the largest of units (watch for severe speed bumps at the barrier). One of the better sites on the Algarve, it has pitches are on fairly flat ground with some terracing, trees and shrubs giving reasonable shade in most parts. There are some marked and numbered pitches of 50-80 sq.m. Winter stays are encouraged with many facilities remaining open including a heated pool. An attractively designed complex of traditional Portuguese style buildings on the hill forms the central area of the site, has pleasant views and is surrounded by a variety of flowers, shrubs and well watered lawns, complete with a fountain. The waiter and self-service restaurants, a pizzeria, bars and a sound proofed disco, have views across the three pools.

Facilities

The toilet blocks include hot showers. Washing machines. Waiter and self-service restaurants, and pizzeria. Bars. Sound proof disco. Swimming pools. Playground. ATM. Car hire. Off site: Site bus service to Albufeira (2 km).

Open

All year.

At a glance

Welcome & Ambience	✓✓✓✓✓	Location	✓✓✓✓
Quality of Pitches	✓✓✓✓	Range of Facilities	✓✓✓✓✓

Directions

From N125 coast road or N264 (from Lisbon) at new junctions follow signs to Albufeira. Site is approx. 1 km. from junctions, on left.

Charges 2004

Per person	€ 4,85
child (410 yrs)	€ 2,60
car	€ 4,60
tent or caravan acc. to size	€ 4,60 - € 6,30
motorcaravan	€ 7,70 - € 11,40

Reservations

Made without de posit or fee; contact site. Tel: 289 587629. Email: campingalbufeira@mail.telepac.pt

PO8202 Parque de Campismo Turiscampo

Estrada Nacional, 125, Espiche, 8600 Lagos (Faro)

This site has been taken over by the previous owners of Camping L'Amfora in Spain and has been recommended by our Spanish agent. With their experience and expertise, the new owners are fully refurbishing the site and are adding new toilet blocks, a large swimming pool, new bungalows and much more. It will be open all year round and should prove to be one of the best campsites in Portugal. There are 300 pitches, all with electricity and water and trees provide some shade. The sea is 2 km. and the city of Lagos 4 km. with all the attractions of the Algarve within easy reach.

Facilities

Two toilet blocks are supplemented by a further block in high season. Washing machines. Shop. Restaurant/bar. Swimming pool. Bicycle hire. Internet point. Entertainment in high season on the bar terrace. Bungalows to rent. Off site: Praia da Luz village 1 km.

Open

1 January - 31 December.

Directions

From Lagos on road N125 towards Sagres, site is 3 km.

Charges 2005

Per person	€ 2,75 - € 4,80
child	€ 1,50 - € 2,50
pitch	€ 2,25 - € 6,00
car	€ 2,25 - € 3,50
electricity	€ 2,50 - € 3,00
dog	€ 1,00 - € 1,50

Reservations

Contact site. Tel: 351 282 789 265.
E-mail: info@turiscampo.com

PO8410 Parque de Campismo de Armacao de Pera

8365 Armacao de Pera (Faro)

A modern site with a wide attractive entrance and a large external parking area, the 1,200 pitches are in zones on level grassy sand. They are marked by trees that provide some shade, and are easily accessed from tarmac and gravel roads. Electricity is available for most of the pitches. The facilities are good. The restaurant, self service café and bar, and well stocked supermarket should cater for most needs, and you can relax around the swimming pools. The disco near to the entrance and café complex is soundproofed which should ensure a peaceful night for non-revellers. The site is within easy reach of Albufeira, Portimao and is 40 km. from Faro and makes an excellent base for stays in this region and for winter sun-seekers.

Facilities

Three modern sanitary blocks provide British and Turkish style WCs, some with bidets, washbasins, showers with hot water on payment, and facilities for disabled campers. A reader reports that maintenance can be variable. Laundry. Supermarket. Restaurant (1/5-30/9). Self service café. Three bars (1/5-30/9). Kiosk. Games and TV rooms. Tennis. Well maintained play area with safe, sandy base. Swimming and paddling pools (May - Sept). ATM. Off site: Fishing, bicycle hire and watersports nearby.

Open

All year.

At a glance

Welcome & Ambience	✓✓✓✓✓	Location	✓✓✓✓
Quality of Pitches	✓✓✓✓	Range of Facilities	✓✓✓✓✓

Directions

Site is west of Albufeira. Turn off N125/ IC4 road in Alcantarilha, taking the EN269-1 towards the coast. Site is on left side before Armacao de Pêra. There are other sites with similar names in the area, so be sure to find the right one.

Charges 2004

Per person	€ 2,50 - € 5,50
child (4-10 yrs)	€ 1,60 - € 3,20
tent	€ 2,00 - € 6,00
caravan	€ 2,50 - € 6,00
car	€ 1,50 - € 3,50
motorcaravan	€ 2,50 - € 6,00

Min. stay 3 nights 1 June - 31 Aug.

Reservations

Write to site. Tel: 282 31 22 96.

PO8430 Orbitur Camping Sagres

Cerro das Moitas, 8650 Sagres (Faro)

Camping de Sagres is a pleasant site at the western tip of the Algarve, not very far from the lighthouse in the relatively unspoilt southwest corner of Portugal. With 960 pitches for tents and 120 for tourers, the pitches are sandy and located amongst pine trees giving good shade. There are some hardstandings for motorhomes and electrical connections throughout. The fairly bland restaurant, bar and café/grill provide a range of reasonably priced meals. This is a reasonable site for those seeking winter sun, or as a base for exploring this 'Land's End' region of Portugal, as it is away from the hustle and bustle of the more crowded resorts. The beaches and the town of Sagres (the departure point of the Portuguese navigators) with its fort, are a short drive.

Facilities

Three spacious toilet blocks are showing some signs of wear but provide hot and cold showers, washbasins with cold water and footbaths. Dishwashing and laundry sinks (cold water) are under cover outside. Washing machines and ironing boards. Motorcaravan services. Supermarket (1/4-1/11). Restaurant/bar and café/grill (all 1/4-30/9). TV room. Bicycle hire. Barbecue area. Playground. Fishing. Medical post. Car wash. Off site: Beach and fishing 2 km. Boat launching 8 km. Golf 12 km.

Open

All year.

At a glance

Welcome & Ambience	✓✓✓✓	Location	✓✓✓✓
Quality of Pitches	✓✓✓✓✓	Range of Facilities	✓✓✓✓

Directions

Turn off road N268 east to EN268, after about 2 km. after turn to Sagres, site (as a camping site only – no name) is signed off to right.

Charges 2004

Per person	€ 2,40 - € 4,30
child (5-10 yrs)	€ 1,20 - € 2,15
tent	€ 2,10 - € 5,90
caravan	€ 2,70 - € 6,20
motorcaravan	€ 3,40 - € 6,70
car	€ 2,10 - € 3,70

Off season discounts (up to 70%).

Reservations

Contact Orbitur - Central de Reservas, Rua Diogo do Couto, 1149–042 Lisboa. Tel: 21/811 70 00 or 811 70 70. Email: info@orbitur.pt

PO8440 Parque de Campismo Quintos dos Carriços

Praia da Salema, Vila do Bispo, 8650-196 Budens (Faro)

This is an attractive and peaceful, valley site with a dedicated naturist area. A traditional tiled Portugese style entrance leads you down a steep incline into this excellent and well maintained site which has a village atmosphere. With continuing improvements, the site has been developed over the years by the Dutch owner. It is spread over two valleys (which are real sun-traps), with the 300 partially terraced pitches marked and divided by trees and shrubs (oleanders and roses). A small stream (dry when seen) meanders through the site. The most remote part, 250 m. from the main site, is dedicated to naturists. Although the site is lit, torches may be required in more remote areas. A very popular site for summer and winter sun-worshippers, within easy driving distance of resorts. The many fine beaches in the region provide ample opportunities for diving, swimming and fishing.

Facilities

Four modern, spacious sanitary blocks, well tiled with quality fittings, are spotlessly clean and include washbasins with cold water and hot showers on payment (€ 0.60). Dishwashing, laundry sinks and washing machine. Excellent facility for disabled people. Gas supplies. Well stocked mini-market (all year). Restaurant (daily 1/3-15/10). Bar (daily in season, once a week only 15/10-1/3). TV room. Internet. Library. Games room. Bicycle, scooter, moped and m/cycle hire. Off site: Nearby tennis, squash and excellent walks. Fishing, golf and beach 1 km. Riding 8 km. Bus service operates from the site.

At a glance

Welcome & Ambience	✓✓✓✓✓	Location	✓✓✓✓
Quality of Pitches	✓✓✓✓	Range of Facilities	✓✓✓✓

Directions

Turn off RN125 (Lagos-Sagres) road at junction to Salema (17 km. from Lagos); site is signed.

Charges 2005

Per person	€ 4,20
child	€ 2,10
tent	€ 4,20 - € 5,40
caravan	€ 5,90
car	€ 4,20
motorcycle	€ 3,00

Discounts for long winter stays.

Reservations

Contact site. Tel: 282 69 52 01. E-mail: quintacarrico@oninet.pt

Open

All year.

With huge, sparsely populated plains dominated by vast cork plantations, which provide nearly half of the world's cork, Alentejo's main attractions include the historic city of Évora and the coastal resorts with their fine, sandy beaches.

Alentejo is made up of four districts: Beja, Évora, Setúbal and Portalegre

One of the most impressive cities in Portugal, Évora lies on a gently sloping hill rising out of the huge Alentejo plain. A city steeped in history, it was occupied by the Romans and Moors for centuries. With its narrow streets, of Moorish origin, and white-washed houses, it also boasts one of the best-preserved Roman temples in the country plus various palaces and monuments, the majority dating from the 14th-16th centuries. One of the more extraordinary sights can be found in the Capela dos Ossos in the church of São Francisco – adorning the walls and pillars of this chamber are the bones of more than 5000 monks.

On the Alentejo coast is the small peaceful town of Santiago do Cacém, which has two of the best beaches in Portugal. The nearby archaelogical site at Miróbriga includes ruins of a hippodrome, several houses (some of which have mural paintings) and a clearly defined acropolis. Further south along the coast is Porto Côvo and the larger, popular resort of Vila Nova de Milfontes, which has a little castle and ancient port.

Cuisine of the region

Alentejo was traditionally an important wheat-growing region (it is frequently referred to as the 'granary of Portugal'). Local specialities include *sopa de cação* (skate soup), made from fish and bread, and *ensopado de borrego* (lamb-stew). Cheeses of the region include *queijo de Serpa* and *queijos de Niza*, made from goats milk. The *queijos de Évora*, made from ewe's milk, is smaller in size with a strong, spicy flavour. *Arroz Doce* (rice pudding topped with cinnamon) is the traditional dessert for festivals and parties and is to be found all over the country.

Places of interest

Arraiolos: ancient town, 17th century castle, famous for its carpets

Beja: provincial town founded by Julius Caesar, 13th century castle

Borba: pretty town, noted for its marble and wine

Elvas: ancient fortress town, 15th century aqueduct

Estremoz: market town, medieval castle

Odemira: quiet, characterful country town

Reguengos de Monsaraz: charming, unspoiled village with whitewashed houses

Vila Viçosa: attractive hillside town, 16th century convent

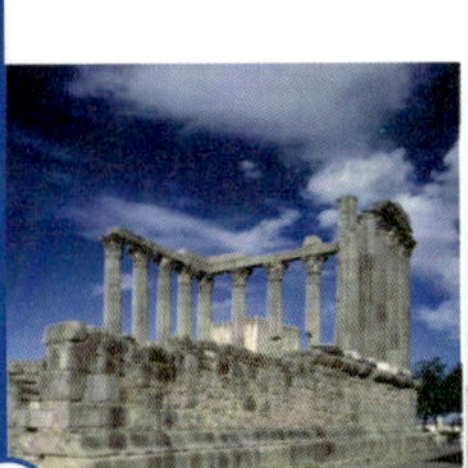

Alan Rogers tip

THE SERRA DE SÃO MAMEDE NATURAL PARK OFFERS GOOD WALKS, WITH EXCELLENT VIEWS AND ALSO HAS AN INFORMATION CENTRE HOLDING TEMPORARY EXHIBITIONS.

www.alanrogers.com for latest campsite news

PO8170 Parque de Campismo Sao Miguel

Sao Miguel, Odeceixe, 7630-592 Odemira (Beja)

Nestled in green hills near two pretty white villages, four kilometres from the beautiful Praia Odeceixe (beach) is the attractive camping park Sao Miguel. The main building (with its traditional Portuguese architecture) is built around two sides of a large grassy square. It houses reception, restaurant, bars and supermarket. There are 'Lisbon Arcade' style verandas to sit under and enjoy a drink, coffee or meal while enjoying the view across the square to the pool, tennis courts and camping which is hidden under a canopy of trees. Unusually the site works on a maximum number of 700 campers, you find your own place (there are no defined pitches) under the tall trees, there are ample electrical points, the land slopes away gently. The wooden chalet style accomodation is in a separate area, but some mobile homes share the two traditional older style but clean sanitary blocks. An outdoor cinema operates in summer showing films for children and adults. The self serve restaurant and bars are excellent, there is a pizzeria by the pool with its own terrace (summer only) and for those who want to self cater the supermarket has a bakery, as well as wide range of goods including fresh fruit and vegetables.

Facilities

Two older style sanitary buildings with British style WCs and free hot showers. Washing machines, dishwashing and laundry sinks are at the end of the block under cover. Toilets and basins for disabled campers but no shower. Shop (Jun -Sep). Restaurant/bar (March - Oct) Bar, snacks and pizzeria (June - Sept). Children's playground. Tennis courts (extra charge). Swimming pool (extra charge). No animals are accepted. Torches useful. Off site: Village has a range of shops bars and restaurants. Historic village of Odemira 2 km. Fishing/sailing 4 km. Riding 20 km. Camping is situated inside the Nature Park of Alentejo.

Open

Easter - September.

At a glance

Welcome & Ambience	✓✓✓✓✓	Location	✓✓✓✓
Quality of Pitches	✓✓✓✓	Range of Facilities	✓✓✓✓✓

Directions

Between Odemira and Lagos on the N120 just before the village of Odeceixe on the main road well signed.

Charges guide

Per person	€ 2,60 - € 4,00
child (5-10 yrs)	€ 1,40 - € 2,25
tent	€ 2,60 - € 6,00
caravan	€ 4,00 - € 5,50
car	€ 2,60 - € 3,50
motorcaravan	€ 5,00 - € 8,00

Plus 7% VAT.

Reservations

Write to site. Tel: 282 947145.
E-mail: camping.sao.miguel@mail.telepac.pt

Open

Easter - September.

PO8350 Camping Markádia

Barragem de Odivelas, Apartado 17, 7920-999 Alvito (Beja)

A tranquil, lakeside site in an unspoilt setting, this will appeal most to those nature lovers who want to 'get away from it all' and to those who enjoy country pursuits such as walking, fishing or riding. The lake is in fact a 1,000 hectare reservoir, and more than 120 species of birds can be found in the area. The open countryside and lake provide excellent views and a very pleasant environment, albeit somewhat remote. The stellar views in the very low ambient lighting are wonderful at night. The site is lit but a torch is required. There are 130 casual unmarked pitches on undulating grass and sand with ample electricity connections (16A). The friendly Dutch owner has carefully planned the site so each pitch has its own oak tree to provide shade. The bar/restaurant with a terrace is open daily in season but weekends only during the winter. One can swim in the reservoir and rowing boats, pedaloes and windsurfers are available for hire. You may bring your own boat, although power boats are not allowed on environmental grounds.

Facilities

Four modern, clean and well equipped toilet blocks are built in traditional Portuguese style with hot water throughout. Dishwashing and laundry sinks are open air. Washing machines and ironing boards. Motorcaravan services. Bar and restaurant (1/4-30/9). Shop (all year, bread to order). Lounge. Playground. Fishing. Boat hire. Tennis. Riding. Medical post. Car wash. Dogs are not accepted in July/August. Facilities and amenities may be reduced outside the main season.

Open

All year.

At a glance

Welcome & Ambience	✓✓✓✓✓	Location	✓✓✓✓✓
Quality of Pitches	✓✓✓✓✓	Range of Facilities	✓✓✓✓✓

Directions

From A2 between Setabul and the Algarve take exit 10 on IP8 signed Ferreira and Beja. Take road to Torrao and 13 km. later at 1 km. north of Odivelas, turn right towards Barragem and site is 3 km. after crossing head of reservoir following small signs (one small section of poor road).

Charges 2005

Per person	€ 4,40
child (5-10 yrs)	€ 2,00
tent or caravan	€ 4,40
car or motorcycle	€ 4,40
motorcaravan	€ 8,80
electricity	€ 2,20

Discounts of 10-20% outside June - Aug, and for longer stays. No credit cards.

Reservations

Contact site for details. Tel: 284 76 31 41.

www.alanrogers.com for latest campsite news

PO8160 Parque de Campismo Porto Covo

7520-436 Porto Covo (Setubal)

This is a site in a popular, small seaside resort where a fairly large proportion of the pitches are occupied by Portuguese units. However, it has a reasonable sense of space as you pass the security barrier to reception which is part of an uncluttered and attractively designed 'village square' area with some well established apartments for hire. The pitches are somewhat small but are hedged, reasonably level, all have electricity (5/10A), and are shaded A mini market stocks the essentials and some souvenirs. If you do not want to venture out to the beach then the swimming pools are behind the restaurant and have areas for sunbathing, the children's pool separated from the adults'. Dedicated barbecue areas are close to the pools. A jolly bar and restaurant with terrace cleverly operates across the boundary of the site and it offers a varied Portuguese menu (popular with the locals) at very reasonable prices. A second smaller restaurant operates in the site in low season. The beaches are a short walk and feature steep cliffs and pleasant sandy shores.

Facilities

The toilet blocks are clean with the usual amenities including hot showers, plus cold outside showers, foot baths and ironing facilities. Motorcaravan services. Restaurant/bar. Mini-market in season. Recreation room with games and a TV. Children's play area. Swimming pools. Tennis. Barbecue areas. Boat trips and fishing trips organised. Off site: The village is a short walk from a range of shops, bars and restaurants in pretty new roads. Bus service to Lisbon from site. Fishing 500 m. Riding 20 km. Golf 25 km.

Open

All year.

At a glance

Welcome & Ambience	✓✓✓✓✓	Location	✓✓✓✓
Quality of Pitches	✓✓✓✓	Range of Facilities	✓✓✓✓✓

Directions

From E120-1 Cercal - Sines road (note: the road changes from the E120 at Tanganheira). Take left turn (southwest) to Porto Covo. The signs are misleading hereon so look for a large white water tower with site logo for confirmation of the signs.

Charges 2004

Per person	€ 2,90
child	€ 1,45
tent	€ 3,65 - € 4,35
caravan or motorcaravan	€ 4,20 - € 4,80
car	€ 3,00
m/cycle	€ 1,90

All plus 7% VAT. Reductions in low season.

Reservations

Write to site. Tel: 269 90 51 36.

have you visited
www.alanrogers.com
yet?

INSPECTED CAMPSITES & SELECTED

Thousands have already, researching their holiday and catching up with the latest news and special offers.

Launched in January 2004 it has fast become the first-stop for countless caravanners, motorhome owners and campers all wanting reliable, impartial and detailed information for their next trip.

Alan Rogers

It features a fully searchable database of the best campsites in the UK & Ireland, and the rest of Europe: over 2,000 campsites in 26 countries. All are Alan Rogers inspected and selected, allowing you to find the site that's perfect for you, with the reassurance of knowing we've been there first.

And now it has been re-launched for the 2005 season, with more than ever before.

Visit today and find out for yourself!

With its deep-rooted cultural traditions, range of leisure activities, year-round sunshine, sandy beaches, historic towns and villages, Lisbon and Vale do Tejo has something for everyone. It is also the centre of Fado, the traditional haunting folk song of Portugal.

This region divided into four districts: Leiria, Lisbon, Santarém and Setúbal

(Part of Setúbal also features in the Alentejo region)

Standing on the banks of the river Tagus, Lisbon has been the capital of Portugal since 1255. Places of interest in the city include the medieval quarters of Alfama and Mouraria, with their cobbled streets and alleys, colourful buildings, markets and castles, and Belém, with its tower and the 16th century Jerónimos monastery. Lisbon also boasts an assortment of museums. Not far from the capital lies the romantic town of Sintra, which has an array of cottages, manor houses and palaces. Its mountains also form part of the Sintra-Cascais Natural Park.

Along the Atlantic coast, high sweeping cliffs lead down to white sandy beaches, backed by lagoons. Europe's westernmost point, Cabo da Roca, is found here as are plenty of coastal towns and villages including Peniche, Nazaré and Óbidos, a small medieval walled town with cobbled streets, tiny whitewashed houses and balconies brimming with flowers. Further inland, at Alcobaça, Tomar and Batalha, are ancient monasteries and convents, with castles in Leiria, Tomar and Santarém. Recreational pursuits include water sports, fishing and golf; courses are found throughout the region. In summer there are also open air music festivals.

Cuisine of the region

Fish soups, stews and seafood are popular, including *sardinha assada* (grilled sardines) and *Bifes de Espardarte* (swordfish steaks). Sintra is famed for its cheesecakes, which according to ancient documents were already being made in the 12th century, and were part of the rent payments. Wine-producing regions include Azeitão, Bucelas, Carcavelos and Colares.

Caldeiradas: fish stews

Queijadas: cheese tarts

Pastéis de Belém: custard tarts

Travesseiros: puff pastries stuffed with a sweet eggy mixture

Places of interest

Estoril: casino, golf course and racing track

Fátima: one of the most important centres of pilgrimage in the Catholic world

Leiria: medieval royal castle, 16th century cathedral, Romanesque church

Mafra: 18th century Palace-Convent, the largest Portuguese religious monument

Santarém: castle, archaeology museum, Gothic convent and churches

Sesimbra: picturesque small fishing town, medieval castle, the Lagoa de Albufeira is a favourite spot for windsurfers

Setúbal: natural reserve, beaches, golf courses,

Tomar: 12th century Templars' Castle, Gothic and Renaissance churches, 15th century synagogue

Alan Rogers tip

INTERESTED IN LOCAL CRAFTS AND CUISINE? VISIT THE ESTORIL HANDICRAFTS FAIR (JULY-AUG) OR THE NATIONAL GASTRONOMY AND HANDICRAFTS FESTIVAL IN SANTARÉM (OCT-NOV).

PO8130 Orbitur Camping Guincho

E.N. 247, Lugar da Areia - Guincho, 2750-053 Cascais (Lisbon)

Although this is a popular site for permanent Portuguese occupants with 1,295 pitches, it is nevertheless quite attractively laid out among low pine trees and with the A5 autostrada connection to Lisbon (30 km), it provides a useful alternative to sites nearer the city. Located behind sand dunes and a wide, sandy but somewhat windswept beach, the site offers a wide range of facilities. These include a fairly plain bar/restaurant, supermarket (all year), general lounge with pool tables, electronic games, TV room and a good laundry. There is a choice of pitches (small - mainly about 50 sq.m.) mostly with electricity, although siting amongst the trees may be tricky, particularly when the site is full. This is viewed as an alternative for visiting Lisbon, not a holiday site.

Facilities

Three sanitary blocks, one refurbished, are in the older style but are clean and tidy. Washbasins with cold water but hot showers. Dishwashing sinks have cold water. Three washing machines, two dryers. Facilities for disabled visitors. Motorcaravan services. Gas supplies. Supermarket. Restaurant, bar and terrace (all year). General room with TV. Tennis. Playground. Entertainment in summer. Medical post. Car wash. Off site: Excursions. Riding 500 m. Beach 800 m. Fishing 1 km. Golf 3 km.

Open

All year.

At a glance

Welcome & Ambience	✓✓✓✓	Location	✓✓✓✓
Quality of Pitches	✓✓✓✓	Range of Facilities	✓✓✓✓

Directions

Approach from either direction on N247. Turn inland 6.5 km. west of Cascais at camp sign. Travelling direct from Lisbon, the site is well signed as you leave the A5 autopista.

Charges guide

Per unit icl. 2 persons, electricity, water	€ 15,20 - € 28,30
extra adult	€ 2,40 - € 4,40
child (5-10 yrs)	€ 1,20 - € 2,20

Off season discounts (up to 70%).

Reservations

Contact Orbitur - Central de Reservas, Rua Diogo do Couto, 1149–042 Lisboa. Tel: 21/811 70 00 or 811 70 70. Email: info@orbitur.pt

PO8140 Lisboa Camping – Parque Municipal de Monsanto

Estrada da Circunvalacao, 1400-061 Lisboa (Lisbon)

Lisbon council completely rebuilt this site for Expo 98. It is very large (38 hectares) and is professionally operated by many uniformed staff, providing a quality service at a good price. The wide entrance with its ponds, fountains and the trees, lawns and flowering shrubs leading up to the swimming pool, is a most attractive feature. On sloping ground, the site's many terraces are well shaded by trees and shrubs. The 400 extremely good pitches include 170 on concrete hardstandings, each with its own services electricity (6/16A) There is a huge separate area for tents, and 70 chalet style bungalows are for hire. You are 8 km. from central Lisbon with two bus routes giving a regular service from the gate, and 10 km. from a decent beach. Although a city site it is big enough to generate a park atmosphere and when we visited we spotted many red squirrels and an abundance of birds. This is a most pleasant site for visiting Lisbon or just relaxing using the impressive facilities.

Facilities

Eight solar-powered toilet blocks contain quality facilities, including those for disabled people. Launderette. Motorcaravan service point and car wash. Shops, bar and restaurants (all year). Two superb swimming pools (with lifeguard; May - Sept). Tennis. Minigolf. Sports field. Playgrounds. Roman theatre. Entertainment in high season. General and TV rooms. English papers. Organised excursions. Travel agent on site. Off site: Lisbon city. Beaches 10 km. Golf 5 km. Riding 16 km. Bicycle hire 2 km.

Open

All year.

At a glance

Welcome & Ambience	✓✓✓✓✓	Location	✓✓✓✓✓
Quality of Pitches	✓✓✓✓✓	Range of Facilities	✓✓✓✓✓

Directions

From Lisbon take A5 motorway towards Estoril and the site is signed from junction 4 onto the 1C17. The site has huge signs off this road at the first exit to Buraca. The site is immediately on the right. Enter to the right of the fountain on the tiled road. Do not be put off by the scruffy areas between the autoroute and the site – inside all is well.

Charges guide

Per person	€ 3,50 - € 4,70
child (6-12 yrs)	€ 1,75 - € 2,30
pitch incl. electricity	€ 15,00 - € 20,00

Electricity included.

Reservations

Not made. Tel: 217 623 100.

PO8150 Orbitur Camping Costa da Caparica

Ava. Alfonso de Albuquerque, Quinta de Ste Antonio, 2825 Costa da Caparica (Setubal)

This is very much a site for 600 permanent caravans but it has relatively easy access to Lisbon (just under 20 kilometres) via the motorway, by bus or even by bus and ferry if you wish. It is situated near a small resort, favoured by the Portuguese themselves, which has all the usual amenities plus a good sandy beach (200 m. from the site) and promenade walks. There is a small area for touring units which includes some larger pitches for motorcaravans. We see this very much as a site to visit Lisbon rather than for prolonged stays. Activities and shows are organised in season in an outdoor disco/entertainment area.

Facilities

The three toilet blocks have mostly British style toilets, washbasins with cold water and some hot showers - they come under pressure when the site is full. Facilities for disabled visitors. Washing machine. Motorcaravan services. Supermarket. Large bar/restaurant (Feb-Nov). Playground. Doctor calls daily in season. Gas supplies. Off site: Fishing 1 km. Riding 4 km. Golf 5 km.

Open

All year.

At a glance

Welcome & Ambience	✓✓✓✓	Location	✓✓✓✓
Quality of Pitches	✓✓✓	Range of Facilities	✓✓✓✓

Directions

Cross the Tagus bridge (toll) on A2 motorway going south from Lisbon, immediately take the turning for Caparica and Trafaria. At 7 km. marker on IC20 turn right (no sign) - the site is at the second roundabout.

Charges 2004

Per person	€ 2,40 - € 4,50
child (5-10 yrs)	€ 1, 20 - € 2,45
tent	€ 2,20 - € 6,50
caravan	€ 3,10 - € 6,50
car	€ 2,20 - € 4,40
motorcaravan	€ 3,80 - € 7,80

Off season discounts (up to 70%).

Reservations

Contact Orbitur - Central de Reservas,
Rua Diogo do Couto, 1149–042 Lisboa.
Tel: 21/811 70 00 or 811 70 70.
Email: info@orbitur.pt

PO8450 Parque de Campismo Colina do Sol

2465 Sao Martinho do Porto (Leiria)

Colina do Sol is a well appointed site with its own swimming pool and near to the beach. Only one kilometre from the small town of S. Martinho do Porto, it has around 350 pitches marked by fruit and ornamental trees on grassy terraces. Electricity (6 or 10A) is available to all, although some may need long leads. The attractive entrance with its beds of bright flowers, is wide enough for even the largest of outfits, and the surfaced roads are very pleasant for manoeuvring. There is a warm welcome and good English is spoken. A well stocked supermarket and a restaurant, cafeteria, and a bar with a delightful paved terrace beside the large clean swimming pools, one for children. The beach is at the rear of the site, with access via a gate which is locked at night (22.00-08.00). This is a convenient base for exploring the Costa de Prata and for excursions to old town of Leiria, with its crenellated walls towering high above the rock faces, and to the famous shrine of Fátima. Market in Sao Martinho do Porto is on Sunday.

Facilities

Two large, clean and modern toilet blocks provide British style WCs (some with bidets), washbasins - some with hot water. Dishwashing and laundry sinks are outside but covered. Ironing facilities. Motorcaravan services. Supermarket, restaurant/café with ba Off site: Shop, restaurant and bar within 200 m.

Open

All year except 15 December - 15 January.

At a glance

Welcome & Ambience	✓✓✓✓	Location	✓✓✓✓
Quality of Pitches	✓✓✓✓	Range of Facilities	✓✓✓✓

Directions

Turn from EN 242 (Caldas-Nazaré) road northeast of San Martinho do Porto. Site is clearly signed.

Charges guide

Per person	€ 2,87
child (4-10 yrs)	€ 1,37
small tent	€ 2,47
large tent	€ 2,92
caravan	€ 3,29 - € 3,57
car	€ 2,37

Less 25-50% in low seasons.

Reservations

Contact site. Tel: 262 98 97 64.
E-mail: geral@colinadosol.com

PO8480 Orbitur Camping Foz do Arelho

EN360 - km 3, Foz do Arelho, 2500 Caldas da Rainha (Leiria)

This is a large and roomy ex-municipal site, new to the Orbitur chain and improvements are still taking place. It is two kilometres from the beach and has a new central complex with a most impressive swimming pool and separated children's pool with lifeguard. The large two storey, brick-faced building contains all the site's leisure facilities but has no ramped access and there are no sanitary facilities anywhere on site for disabled campers. The building is somewhat sterile and the furniture is bland but there are pleasant views over the pool from the restaurant and terrace. Pitches are generally sandy with some hardstandings,vary in size and are unmarked on two main levels with wide tarmac roads. There is a little shade and some permanent Portuguese units occupied in high season and weekends at other times. All touring pitches have electricity (5/15A). This is a site with work in progress and it will improve to the usual Orbitur standards but if you have special needs we recommend a telephone call first.

Facilities

Four identical modern sanitary buildings (solar heating) with seatless British and Turkish style WCs and free showers. Washing machine in one, dishwashing and laundry sinks have cold water only. No facilities for disabled campers. No chemical disposal point. Supermarket. Children's club. Games room. Table tennis. Small new amphitheatre. Electronic games. Bar/snacks and restaurant. (April - Sept). Children's playground – supervision needed . Bus service. Doctor's room. Torches useful. Off site: Bus 500 m. Seaside town has a range of shops, bars and restaurants 2 km. Fishing 2 km. Watersports 3 km. Riding 15 km. Golf 35 km.

At a glance

Welcome & Ambience	✓✓✓✓	Location	✓✓✓✓
Quality of Pitches	✓✓✓	Range of Facilities	✓✓✓✓

Directions

Site is north of Lisbon west of Caldos. From A8 Take N360 to Foz de Arelho. Site is well signed.

Charges 2004

Per person	€ 2,10 - € 4,00
child	€ 1,05 - € 2,00
tent	€ 1,70 - € 5,60
caravan	€ 2,25 - € 6,00
car	€ 1,80 - € 3,70
motorcaravan	€ 2,50 - € 6,50

Reservations

Contact Orbitur - Central de Reservas, Rua Diogo do Couto, 1149–042 Lisboa.
Tel: 21/811 70 00 or 811 70 70.
Email: info@orbitur.pt

Open

All year.

PO8460 Camping Caravaning Vale Paraiso

Mobile homes page 174

E.N. 242, 2450-138 Nazaré (Leiria)

A pleasant, well managed site, Vale Paraiso is by the main N242 road in eight hectares of undulating pine woods. It provides over 600 shady pitches, many on sandy ground only suitable for tents. For other units there are around 250 individual pitches of varying size on harder ground with electricity. A range of sporting and leisure activities includes a good outdoor pool with sunbathing areas, a new pool and a play area for children, plus a small adventure playground. There is a bar, takeaway and a slightly bland restaurant/bar. Several long beaches of white sand are within 2-15 kilometres allowing windsurfing, sailing, surfing or body-boarding. Animation for children and evening entertainment is organised in season. Nazaré is an old fishing village with narrow streets, a harbour and marina, with a lift to Sitio. There is much of historical interest in the area although the mild Atlantic climate is also conducive to just relaxing. The owners are keen to welcome British visitors and English is spoken.

Facilities

Toilet facilities are good, with hot water for washbasins, showers, laundry and dishwashing sinks. Facilities for disabled people. Baby baths to borrow. Washing machine and dryers. Motorcaravan services. Shop. Restaurant (March - Sept). Café/bar with TV (all year). Takeaway. Tabac. Supermarket (March - Sept). Swimming pool and paddling pool (March - Sept; free for children under 11 yrs). Petanque. Volleyball. Basketball. Football. Badminton. Leisure games. Amusement hall. Bicycle hire. Safety deposit. Gas supplies. E-mail and fax facilities (read free, send for a fee). Bus service from gate. Apartments to rent. Off site: Fishing 1.5 km. Boat launching 2.5 km. Riding 5 km.

At a glance

Welcome & Ambience	✓✓✓✓	Location	✓✓✓✓
Quality of Pitches	✓✓✓✓✓	Range of Facilities	✓✓✓✓✓

Directions

Site is 2 km. north of Nazaré on the EN242 Marinha Grande road.

Charges 2005

Per person	€ 3,00 - € 4,00
child (3-10 yrs)	€ 1,50 - € 2,00
caravan	€ 3,60 - € 4,40
motorcaravan	€ 4,50 - € 5,50
tent	€ 2,60 - € 5,00
car	€ 2,80 - € 3,40

Reservations

Contact site. Tel: 262 56 18 00.
E-mail: info@valeparaiso.com

Open

1 January - 18 December & 27-31 December.

PO8110 Orbitur Camping Valado

E.N. 8-5 Alcobaca - Valado, 2450 Nazaré (Leiria)

This popular site is close to the traditional fishing port of Nazaré which has now become something of a holiday resort. The large sandy beach in the town (about 2 km. steeply downhill from the site) is sheltered by headlands and provides good swimming. The campsite is on undulating ground under tall pine trees, has 503 pitches and, although some smallish individual pitches with electricity and water can be reserved, the bulk of the site is not marked out and units could be close together especially during July/August. The functional restaurant, bar and supermarket are contained in one white-walled block.

Facilities

The three toilet blocks have British and Turkish style WCs, washbasins (some cold water) and 17 hot showers, all very clean when inspected. Laundry. Motorcaravan services. Gas. Supermarket. Bar, snack bar and restaurant with terrace (Feb - Nov). TV/general room. Playground. Tennis. Medical post. Car wash. Off site: Bus service 20 m. Fishing and bicycle hire 2 km.

Open

1 February - 30 November.

At a glance

Welcome & Ambience	✓✓✓✓	Location	✓✓✓✓
Quality of Pitches	✓✓✓✓	Range of Facilities	✓✓✓✓

Directions

Site is on the Nazaré - Alcobaca N8-5 road, 2 km. east of Nazaré.

Charges guide

Per unit incl. 2 persons, electricity, water	€ 12,30 - € 22,20
child (5-10 yrs)	€ 0,95 - € 1,70

Off season discounts (up to 70%).

Reservations

Contact Orbitur - Central de Reservas, Rua Diogo do Couto, 1149–042 Lisboa.
Tel: 21/811 70 00 or 811 70 70.
Email: info@orbitur.pt

PO8100 Orbitur Camping Sao Pedro de Moel

Rua Volta do Sete, 2430 Sao Pedro de Moel (Leiria)

This quiet and very attractive site is situated under tall pines, on the edge of the rather select small resort of Sao Pedro de Moel. The attractive, sandy beach is about 500 m. walk downhill from the site (you can take the car, although parking may be difficult in the town) and is sheltered from the wind by low cliffs. The shady site can be crowded in July/Aug, and the 525 pitches are in blocks and unmarked (cars may be parked separately) with 404 electrical connections. A few pitches are used for permanent units. Although there are areas of soft sand, there should be no problem in finding a firm place. The large restaurant and bar are modern as is the superb swimming pool, paddling pool and flume (there is a lifeguard).

Facilities

Four clean toilet blocks have mainly British style toilets (some with bidets), some washbasins with hot water. Hot showers are mostly in one block. Laundry. Motorcaravan services. Gas supplies. Supermarket. Large restaurant and bar with terrace (April-Sept). Swimming pools (June-Sept). TV and games room. Playground. Table tennis. Tennis. Medical post. Car wash. Off site: Bus service 100 m. Beach 500 m. Fishing 1 km.

Open

All year.

At a glance

Welcome & Ambience ✓✓✓✓✓ Location ✓✓✓✓✓
Quality of Pitches ✓✓✓✓✓ Range of Facilities ✓✓✓✓✓

Directions

Site is 9 km. west of Marinha Grande, on the right as you enter Sao Pedro de Moel.

Charges guide

Per unit ncl. 2 persons, electricity, water	€ 13,70 - € 24,90
extra adult	€ 2,10 - € 4,00
child (5-10 yrs)	€ 1,05 - € 2,00

Off season discounts (up to 70%).

Reservations

Contact Orbitur - Central de Reservas, Rua Diogo do Couto, 1149–042 Lisboa. Tel: 21/811 70 00 or 811 70 70. Email: info@orbitur.pt

PO8400 Campismo O Tamanco

Casas Brancas II, 3100-231 Louriçal (Leiria)

O Tamanco is a peaceful countryside site, with a homely almost farm-stead atmosphere, you will have chickens and ducks wandering around and there is a Burro here. The young Dutch owners, Irene and Hans, are sure to give you a warm welcome at this delightful little site. The swimming pool is very pleasant as is the small bar and a restaurant (with vegetarian menu options). Courses in printing and sculpture are arranged at certain times of the year. There may also be entertainment for the children during the day. The site is very popular with the Dutch, mature couples and winter campers. The 100 good sized pitches are separated by cordons of all manner of fruit trees, ornamental trees and flowering shrubs, on level grassy ground. There is electricity (6/16A) to 72 pitches and 5 pitches are suitable for large motorhomes. The site is lit and there is nearly always space available. One can fish or swim in a nearby lake and the resort beaches are a short drive. There may be some road noise on pitches at the front of the site.

Facilities

The single toilet block provides very clean and generously sized facilities including washbasins in cabins, with easy access for disabled visitors. As facilities are limited they may be busy in peak periods. Dishwashing and laundry sinks outside, under cover. Hot water throughout. Washing machine. Bar/restaurant. New roofed patio with fireplace. TV room/lounge. Swimming pool. Off site: Lake 2 km. Beach 11 km. Market in nearby Lourical every Sunday.

Open

1 February - 31 October.

At a glance

Welcome & Ambience ✓✓✓✓✓ Location ✓✓✓✓✓
Quality of Pitches ✓✓✓✓✓ Range of Facilities ✓✓✓✓

Directions

From N109/IC1 (Leira-Figuera de Foz) road, 25 km. south of Figuera in Matos de Carriço, turn on to N342 road (signed Louri≤al 6 km). Site is directly off the behind high hedges 1.5 km. on left.

Charges 2004

Per person	€ 3,15
child (up to 5 yrs)	€ 1,70
tent	€ 2,35 - € 3,05
caravan	€ 3,40
car	€ 2,35
motorcaravan	€ 5,65

Winter discounts up to 40%. No credit cards.

Reservations

Contact site. Tel: 236 95 25 51.
E-mail: campismo.o.tamanco@mail.telepac.pt

Beiras & Centre

Beiras is the traditional name for a strip of land flanked by Portugal's two main rivers – the Douro and the Tagus. This region is made up of two contrasting areas: white sandy beaches, fishing villages and pine forests lie along the coast, while inland the mountains dominate the landscape.

Beiras has five districts:
Aveiro, Coimbra, Castelo Branco, Guarda and Viseu

One of Europe's oldest university towns, Coimbra was Portugal's capital from 1143 to 1255. The university, founded in 1290, has kept its academic traditions, as seen in the black-capped students, in the soulful tones of the *fado de Coimbra* (traditional song sung to the sound of guitars by the students) and in the Queima das Fitas (Burning of the Ribbons), a boisterous celebration of graduating students. Coimbra also boasts a Romanesque cathedral and south of the town lies Conímbriga, with the most important Roman remains in Portugal. Surrounded by the original walls, the archaeological site features an early Christian burial ground, a set of hot springs and a museum. Further north lies Aveiro. Famous for its lagoon, the town is crisscrossed by canals where colourfully painted moliceiro boats sail. To the east lies the Serra de Estrela, the highest mountain range in the country. It is home to the textile town of Covilha, various attractive villages including Gouveia, Manteigas and Seia, plus the mountain resort of Guarda. Skiing is popular. Along the coast, the pretty seadside resorts of São Martinho do Porto, Nazaré and Figueira da Foz offer fine sandy beaches, good seafood restaurants and water sports facilities.

Cuisine of the region

Roast pork, lamb stew, seafood and fresh fish are popular, including *truta* (trout) from the mountains of Serra da Estrela. The famous ewe's milk cheese Queijo da Serra, is also a produced in the mountains, and can be bought at Cheese Fairs held in villages and towns throughout the region during February and March. Regional desserts include hard and sweet biscuits, pancakes and sponge cake (*ovos-moles*, *pão-de-ló*).

Chanfana: lamb stewed in red wine

Leitão assado da Bairrada: roast pork

Places of interest

Belmonte: hilltop town, castle, Romanesque-Gothic church

Bussaco: national park founded by monks in the 6th century

Castelo Branco: 13th century castle, medieval quarter, 16th-18th century churches

Curia and *Luso*: spa towns

Monsanto: historic village, 12th-century castle, 18th-century manor-houses

Viseu: remains of Gothic walls, cathedral

Alan Rogers tip

BUY THE LOCALLY PRODUCED HANDICRAFTS: EMBROIDERED SILK BEDSPREADS FROM CASTELO BRANCO, CERAMICS FROM COIMBRA, AND GLASS AND CRYSTAL FROM ALCOBAÇA.

PO8070 Orbitur Camping Mira

Estrada Florestal no. 1 - km 2, 3070 Mira (Coimbra)

A small seaside site set in pinewoods, Orbitur Camping Mira is situated to the south of Aveiro and Vagos, in a quieter and less crowded area. It fronts onto a lake at the head of the Ria de Mira, which eventually runs into the Aveiro Ria. A back gate leads directly to the sea and a wide quiet beach 300 m. away, a road runs alongside the site where the restaurant complex is situated resulting in some road noise. The site has around 225 pitches on sand, which are not marked but with trees creating natural divisions. Electricity and water points are plentiful. The site provides an inexpensive restaurant, snack bar, lounge bar and TV lounge. A medium sized supermarket is well stocked, with plenty of fresh produce. The Mira Ria is fascinating, with the brightly painted, decorative 'Moliceiros' (traditional fishing boats).

Facilities

The modern toilet blocks are clean, with 14 free hot showers and washing machines. Motorcaravan services. Gas supplies. Shop, restaurant and bar (March - Nov). Snack bar. TV room. Smart playground. Off site: Bus service 150 m. Bicycle hire 200 m. Fishing 500 m. Golf 1 km. Indoor pool, lake swimming and riding at Mira 7 km.

Open

1 March - 30 November.

At a glance

Welcome & Ambience	✓✓✓✓✓	Location	✓✓✓✓✓
Quality of Pitches	✓✓✓✓	Range of Facilities	✓✓✓✓

Directions

Turn off N109 at Mira, about 27 km. south of Aveiro towards Praia de Mira. After about 5 km. (watch for speed bumps close to site!) a small sign shows a left turn which leads direct to the site. If you miss it, the site is signed from the beach resort. Make sure you ask for the Orbitur site if stuck - there are others here which are not as pleasant!

Charges 2004

Per person	€ 2,10 - € 3,80
child (5-10 yrs)	€ 1,05 - € 1,90
caravan	€ 2,25 - € 5,80
tent	€ 1,70 - € 5,30
car	€ 1,80 - € 3,50
motorcaravan	€ 2,50 - € 6,20

Off season discounts (up to 70%).

Reservations

Contact Orbitur - Central de Reservas, Rua Diogo do Couto, 1149–042 Lisboa. Tel: 21/811 70 00 or 811 70 70. Email: info@orbitur.pt

PO8090 Orbitur Camping Figueira da Foz

E.N. 109 - km 4 - Gala, 3080 Figueira da Foz (Coimbra)

This site of around 450 pitches is on sandy terrain under a canopy of pine trees and well cared for. Some pitches near the road may be rather noisy. One can drive or walk the 300 m. from the back of the site to a private beach; you should swim with caution when it is windy - the warden will advise. The site fills in July/August and units may be very close together, but there should be plenty of room at other times. Besides the beach, Coimbra and the nearby Roman remains are worth visiting.

Facilities

The three toilet blocks have British and Turkish style toilets, individual basins (some with hot water) and free hot showers. Laundry. Motorcaravan services. Gas supplies. Supermarket and restaurant/bar with terrace (all May - Sept). Lounge. Playground. Tennis. TV. Doctor visits in season. Car wash area. Off site: Beach 300 m. Fishing 1 km. Bicycle hire and riding 3 km.

Open

All year.

At a glance

Welcome & Ambience	✓✓✓✓✓	Location	✓✓✓✓✓
Quality of Pitches	✓✓✓✓	Range of Facilities	✓✓✓✓✓

Directions

Site is 4 km. south of Figueira da Foz beyond the two rivers; turn off N109 1 km. from bridge on southern edge of Gala, look for Orbitur sign on roundabout it is then 600 m. to site.

Charges 2004

Per person	€ 2,20 - € 4,30
child (5-10 yrs)	€ 1,10 - € 2,15
caravan	€ 2,40 - € 6,20
tent	€ 1,90 - € 5,90
car	€ 1,90 - € 3,80
motorcaravan	€ 2,80 - € 6,70

Off season discounts (up to 70%).

Reservations

Contact Orbitur - Central de Reservas, Rua Diogo do Couto, 1149–042 Lisboa. Tel: 21/811 70 00 or 811 70 70. Email: info@orbitur.pt

PO8050 Orbitur Camping São Jacinto

E.N. 327, km 20, São Jacinto, 3800 Aveiro (Aveiro)

This small site is in the São Jacinto nature reserve, on a peninsula between the Atlantic and the Barrinha, with views to the mountains beyond. The area is a weekend resort for locals and can be crowded in high season - it may therefore be difficult to find space in July/Aug, particularly for larger units. Swimming and fishing are both possible in the adjacent Ria, or the sea, 20 minutes walk from a guarded back gate. There is a private jetty for boats and the manager will organise hire of the decorative 'Moliceiros' boats used in days gone by to harvest seaweed for the land. This is not a large site, taking 169 units on unmarked pitches, but in most places trees provide natural limits and shade. A deep bore-hole supplies the site with drinking water.

Facilities

Two toilet blocks, very clean when inspected, contain the usual facilities. Dishwashing and laundry sinks. Washing machine and ironing board in a separate part of the toilet block. Motorcaravan services. Shop. Restaurant/bar (all May - Sept). Playground. Table tennis. Tourist information.
Off site: Bus service 20 m. Fishing 200 m. Bicycle hire 10 km.

Open

February - November.

At a glance

Welcome & Ambience	✓✓✓✓✓	Location	✓✓✓✓✓
Quality of Pitches	✓✓✓✓	Range of Facilities	✓✓✓✓

Directions

Turn off N109 at Estarreja to N109-5 to cross bridge over Ria da Gosta Nova and on to Torreira and São Jacinto. Or from Porto go south N1/09 turn for Ovar on the N327 which leads to São Jacinto.

Charges 2004

Per person	€ 2,00 - € 3,50
child (5-10 yrs)	€ 1,00 - € 1,75
caravan	€ 2,20 - € 5,70
tent	€ 1,65 - € 4,90
car	€ 1,80 - € 3,40
motorcaravan	€ 2,40 - € 6,10

Off season discounts (up to 70%).

Reservations

Contact Orbitur - Central de Reservas, Rua Diogo do Couto, 1149–042 Lisboa. Tel: 21/811 70 00 or 811 70 70.
Email: info@orbitur.pt

PO8330 Camping Municipal Arganil

E.N. 17 - km 5, Sarzedo, 3300 Arganil (Coimbra)

This quiet, inland site is attractively located in the hamlet of Sarzedo, some two kilometres from the town of Arganil. A spacious and well planned site, it is high quality for a municipal and prices are very reasonable! Delightfully situated among pine trees above the River Alva where one can swim, fish, canoe and windsurf. The 150 pitches, most with electricity (15A), are of a reasonable size, mainly on flat sandy grass terraces shaded by tall trees. The site is kept beautifully clean and neat and access roads are tarmac. A small but excellent restaurant serves local food and has an unusual attached bar with terrace.

Facilities

Sanitary facilities are clean and well maintained, with Turkish and British style WCs, controllable hot showers, washbasins in semi-private partitioned cabins and a hairdressing area with electric sockets. Ramped entrances make it suitable for disabled visitors. Washing machines. Bar, restaurant and snacks (all year). Shop (July - Sept). TV room. Tennis. Car wash. Off site: Bus service 50 m. River beach and fishing 100 m. Watersports 200 m. Swimming pool in nearby Arganil. Golf 25 km.

Open

All year.

At a glance

Welcome & Ambience	✓✓✓✓✓	Location	✓✓✓✓
Quality of Pitches	✓✓✓✓✓	Range of Facilities	✓✓✓✓

Directions

From EN17/N2 Coimbra - Sarzedo at 324.4 km marker exit to Sarzedo site is signed. Ignore first campsite sign to Avelar as there is a much better access some 500 m. further up the road on the right also signed.

Charges 2004

Per person	€ 1,50 - € 1,70
child (5-10 yrs)	€ 1,00 - € 1,20
caravan	€ 2,00 - € 5,00
tent	€ 1,40 - € 2,80
car	€ 1,50 - € 2,00
motorcaravan	€ 2,20 - € 5,00

Plus 7% VAT.

Reservations

Contact site. Tel: 235 20 57 06.
E-mail: campingcma@hotmail.com

Porto & North

Originally inhabited by Celtics, Romans and Moors, the North is a region steeped in history. Renowned for its beautiful countryside, the River Douro winds its way past mountains, valleys, vineyards and cliffs until it reaches the sandy beaches of the Atlantic coast near the city of Porto.

The region is comprised of five districts: Braga, Bragança, Porto, Viana do Castelo and Vila Real

Situated in the north western corner of Portugal, the Costa Verde boasts lush green pine forests and unspoilt sandy beaches, dotted with picturesque seaside villages, including Caminha and Vila Nova de Cerveira. It is also renowned for its wine, being the home of Port and Vinho Verdo. Located on the banks for the River Douro, the attractive city of Porto is the centre of the Port wine trade – free tastings are offered at the wine cellars in Vila Nova de Gaia – and terraced vineyards can be found across the Douro Valley.

The region is also a perfect place for walking, mountain trekking, canoeing or simply relaxing in the spa towns of Carvalhelhos, Chaves and Pedras Salgadas. Vidago has a magnificent park with swimming pools and a golf course, while the mountains of Peneda, Soajo and Gerês form the Peneda Geres National Park, an area covering 170,000 acres, with an abundance of wildlife. Vila Nova de Foz is the centre for visits to the Côa Archaeological Park, which houses one of the world's largest collections of outdoor Palaeolithic rock art, dating back 22,000 years.

Cuisine of the region

Typical dishes include *bacalhau* (dried and salted cod), *rabanadas*, *papos-de-anjo* and *barrigas-de-freiras* (sweetmeats). Porto has its own tripe dish *Tripas à moda do Porto*.

The Minho region is renowned for its *Vinhos Verdes*, whose vines are grown on trellises (being suspended high in the air on special frames). In the Douro region, the vines are grown on terraces, giving the impression of huge natural staircases leading down to the banks of the river. Both red and white wines are produced here including the famous *Vinho do Porto* (Port Wine).

Caldo verde: thick soup made with green cabbage, potatoes and spicy sausage

Feijoada à transmontana: bean stew

Places of interest

Barcelos: medieval walled town with dungeon, ceramics museum, archaeology museum

Bragança: medieval castle and walls, 16th century cathedral, railway museum with 19th century locomotives and carriages.

Chaves: Roman bridge, 14th century castle with Archaeology and Epigraphy Museum.

Guimarães: medieval castle and walls, palace

Lamego: medieval castle, 12th century fortress

Ponte de Lima: beautiful small town, Roman bridge, medieval towers, manor houses

Viana do Castelo: town famous for its handicrafts and colourful regional costumes

Vila do Conde: ancient medieval shipyard, famous for its manufactured lace

Alan Rogers tip

TAKE A BOAT TRIP ALONG THE RIVER DOURO AND ADMIRE THE BEAUTIFUL TERRACED VINEYARDS WHERE THE GRAPES ARE GROWN FROM WHICH PORT WINE IS MADE.

PO8020 Orbitur Camping Viana do Castelo

Rua Diogo Alvares, Cabadelo, 4900-161 Darque (Viana do Costelo)

This site in northern Portugal is worth considering as it has the advantage of direct access, through a gate in the fence (locked at night) to a large and excellent soft sand beach (400 metres) which is popular for windsurfing. There are 225 pitches on undulating sand, most with good shade and with electricity in all areas. Some flat good sized pitches are reserved for caravans. As usual with Orbitur sites, most pitches are not marked and it could be crowded in July/August. A pleasant restaurant terrace overlooks the swimming pool and the site. A ferry crosses the river to the town centre. The site is also convenient for visiting the medieval town of Ponte de Lima (24 km), with its white-washed houses, towers and Roman bridge, and Viana do Castelo is famous for its beautiful embroideries and festival processions.

Facilities

Clean, well kept toilet facilities are in two blocks. Both blocks have washbasins with cold water and hot showers. Good facilities for disabled campers. Laundry. Motorcaravan services. Gas supplies. Supermarket. Small restaurant with terrace and bar (all May-Sept). Reading room with TV, video and fireplace. Playground. Tennis. Medical post.
Off site: Fishing 1 km. Riding 2 km.

Open

16 January - 30 November.

At a glance

Welcome & Ambience	✓✓✓✓✓	Location	✓✓✓✓✓
Quality of Pitches	✓✓✓✓	Range of Facilities	✓✓✓✓

Directions

On N13 coast road driving north to south drive through Viana do Castelo and over estuary bridge. Turn immediately right off N13 towards Cabedelo and the sea. Site is the third camp signed, the other two are not recommended.

Charges 2004

Per person	€ 2,20 - € 4,30
child (5-10 yrs)	€ 1,10 - € 2,15
pitch and car	€ 3,80 - € 9,60

Off season discounts (up to 70%).

Reservations

Contact Orbitur - Central de Reservas, Rua Diogo do Couto, 1149–042 Lisboa. Tel: 21/811 70 00 or 811 70 70. Email: info@orbitur.pt

PO8030 Orbitur Camping Rio Alto

E.N. 13 - km 13 - Rio Alto-Est, 4490 Póvoa de Varzim (Porto)

This site makes an excellent base for visiting Porto (by car) which is some 35 kilometres south of Estela. It has around 700 pitches on sandy terrain and is next to what is virtually a private beach (access via a novel double tunnel under the dunes). The beach shelves steeply at some tidal stages. The 18 hole golf course is adjacent and huge nets along one side of the site protect campers from any stray balls. There are some hardstandings for caravans and motorcaravans and electrical connections to most pitches. The area for tents is furthest from the beach and windswept, stunted pines give some shade. There are special arrangements for car parking away from camping areas in peak season. There is a quality restaurant, snack bar and a large swimming pool plus a paddling pool across the road from reception. The beach tunnel is open 09.00-19.00 and the beach has a lifeguard 15/6–15/9.

Facilities

Four well equipped toilet blocks have hot water. Dishwashing and laundry sinks under cover. Washing machines and ironing facilities. Facilities for disabled campers. Gas supplies. Restaurant, bar and snack bar (1 Jan - 30 Nov), mini-market (15 May - 15 Sept). Swimming pool (1 June - 30 Sept). Tennis. Playground. Games room. Surfing. TV. Medical post. Car wash. Evening entertainment twice weekly in season. Off site: Fishing 800 m. Golf 1 km. Bicycle hire 13 km. Riding 19 km.

Open

All year.

At a glance

Welcome & Ambience	✓✓✓✓✓	Location	✓✓✓✓✓
Quality of Pitches	✓✓✓✓	Range of Facilities	✓✓✓✓✓

Directions

Site is reached via a cobbled road leading directly off the EN13 coast road towards the sea (just north of Estela), 12 km. north of Póvoa de Varzim. Travel 2.6 km. along the narrow cobbled road and look to the right for an Orbitur sign (well back from the road). Take this for 0.8 km. to site (beware speed bumps). You travel through intensive greenhouse farming for the last 2 km. but keep going it is worth it!

Charges 2004

Per person	€ 2,40 - € 4,50
child (5-10 yrs)	€ 1,20 - € 2,25
tent	€ 2,20 - € 6,50
caravan	€ 3,10 - € 7,40
motorcaravan	€ 3,80 - € 7,80
car	€ 2,20 - € 4,40

Off season discounts (up to 70%).

Reservations

Contact Orbitur - Central de Reservas, Rua Diogo do Couto, 1149–042 Lisboa. Tel: 21/811 70 00 or 811 70 70. Email: info@orbitur.pt

PO8010 Orbitur Camping Caminha

E.N. 13 - km 90 - Mata do Camarido, 4910 Caminha (Viana do Costelo)

A pleasant site in northern Portugal close to the Spanish border, this site is just 200 metres from the beach. It has an attractive and peaceful setting in woods alongside the river estuary that marks the border with Spain. With a pleasant, open feel about it, fishing is possible in the estuary and swimming, either there or from the rather open, sandy beach. The site is shaded by tall pines with other small trees planted to mark the large sandy pitches. The main site road is surfaced but elsewhere take care not to get trapped in soft sand accessing some pitches. Pitching and parking can be haphazard.

Facilities

The clean, well maintained toilet block has British style toilets, washbasins (cold water) and hot showers, plus beach showers, extra dishwashing and laundry sinks (cold water). Laundry with ironing boards. Motorcaravan services. Small restaurant, snacks and supermarket (all April - Sept). Off site: Beach 100m. Bus service 800 m. Fishing 1 km. Riding 5 km. Golf 40 km.

Open

16 January - 30 November.

At a glance

Welcome & Ambience	✓✓✓✓✓	Location	✓✓✓✓
Quality of Pitches	✓✓✓✓✓	Range of Facilities	✓✓✓✓

Directions

Turn off main coast road (N13-E50) just after camping sign at end of embankment, about 1.5 km. south of ferry.

Charges 2004

Per person	€ 2,10 - € 3,80
child (5-10 yrs)	€ 1,05 - € 1,90
pitch and car	€ 3,50 - € 9,30

Off season discounts (up to 70%).

Reservations

Contact Orbitur - Central de Reservas, Rua Diogo do Couto, 1149–042 Lisboa. Tel: 21/811 70 00 or 811 70 70. Email: info@orbitur.pt

PO8380 Parque Natural de Vilar de Mouros

4910 Vilar de Mouros (Viana do Costelo)

Located some 15 minutes walk above the village of Vilar de Mouros and very close to the Spanish border, this small site is ideal for those looking for an uncomplicated campsite giving really good prices. Along with several permanent units, the 45 marked pitches for touring units, all with electricity, are on slightly sloping, grassy terraces, with a separate area for tents, all set amongst trees and vines on a hillside. Not many are suitable for larger units. This friendly site has a good range of other amenities which include one large and one unusual small stone swimming pools. There is a small but good café/bar, takeaway, a simple self-service restaurant with shady terrace, and a mini-market.

Facilities

The two toilet blocks, very much in the quainter, older Portuguese style, provide British style WCs (some with bidets), washbasins (cold water), and hot showers. Washing machine and dryer in a separate building. Mini-market (high season). Café/bar. Self-service restaurant. Swimming pool. Tennis court. TV room. Washing machine. Children's pool and playground. Medical post. Bicycle hire. Little English spoken. Dogs are not accepted. Off site: Fishing 4 km. River Minho 4 km. Riding 5 km. Golf 20 km.

At a glance

Welcome & Ambience	✓✓✓✓✓	Location	✓✓✓✓
Quality of Pitches	✓✓✓✓	Range of Facilities	✓✓✓✓

Directions

Site is signed from the N13, just north of Seixas, turn towards Vilar de Mouros. Site is on right just before village.

Charges guide

Per person	€ 2,10 - € 3,50
child	€ 1,02 - € 1,70
pitch	€ 2,04 - € 4,40

Reservations

Contact site. Tel: 258 72 74 72.

Open

All year.

PO8370 Parque de Campismo de Cerdeira

4840 Campo do Gerês (Braga)

Placed in the National Park of Peneda Gerês, amidst spectacular mountain scenery, this excellent site offers modern facilities in a truly natural area. The well fenced, professional and peaceful site has some 600 good sized unmarked, mostly level, grassy pitches in a shady woodland setting. Electricity (5/10A) is available for most pitches, though some long leads may be required. A very large timber complex, tastefully designed with the use of materials, granite and wood provides a superb restaurant with a comprehensive menu. There are unlimited opportunities in the area for fishing, riding, canoeing, mountain biking and climbing, so take advantage of this quality mountain hospitality.

Facilities

Three very clean sanitary blocks provide mixed style WCs, controllable showers and hot water. Laundry. Gas. Mini-market. Restaurant/bar (15/4- 30/9). Playground. Bicycle hire. TV room. Medical post. Good tennis courts. Mini Golf. Car wash. Barbecue area. Torches useful. Dogs not accepted in July/August. Off site: Fishing and riding 800 m.

Open

All year.

At a glance

Welcome & Ambience	✓✓✓✓✓	Location	✓✓✓✓✓
Quality of Pitches	✓✓✓✓✓	Range of Facilities	✓✓✓✓✓

Directions

From north, N103 (Braga-Chaves road), turn left at N205 (7.5 km north of Braga). Follow N205 to Caldelas Terras de Bouro and Covide where site is clearly marked to 'Campo do Geres'.

Charges 2004

Per person	€ 3,15 - € 4,20
child (5-11 yrs)	€ 1,90 - € 2,65
pitch	€ 4,20 - € 8,95

Reservations

Contact site. Tel: 253 35 1005.
E-mail: parque.cerdeira@portugalmail.pt

home from home

Over recent years many of the campsites featured in this guide have added large numbers of high quality mobile homes and chalets. Many site owners believe that some former caravanners and motorcaravanners have been enticed by the extra comfort they can now provide, and that maybe this is the ideal solution to combine the freedom of camping with all the comforts of home.

Quality is consistently high and, although the exact size and inventory may vary from site to site, if you choose any of the sites detailed here, you can be sure that you're staying in some of the best quality and best value mobile homes available.

Home comforts are provided and typically these include a fridge with freezer compartment, gas hob, proper shower - often a microwave and radio/cassette hi-fi too but do check for details. All mobile homes and chalets come fully equipped with a good range of kitchen utensils, pots and pans, crockery, cutlery and outdoor furniture. Some even have an attractive wooden sundeck or paved terrace - a perfect spot for outdoors eating or relaxing with a book and watching the world go by.

Regardless of model, colourful soft furnishings are the norm and a generally breezy décor helps to provide a real holiday feel.

For your convenience and as a result of feedback from many of our readers, we have now included a distinct section on mobile homes and chalets.

Although some sites may have a large number of different accommodation types, we have restricted our choice to one or two of the most popular accommodation units (either mobile homes or chalets) for each of the sites listed.

The mobile homes here will be of modern design, and recent innovations, for example, often include pitched roofs which substantially improve their appearance.

Design will invariably include clever use of space and fittings/furniture to provide for comfortable holidays - usually light and airy, with big windows and patio-style doors, fully equipped kitchen areas, a shower room with shower, washbasin and WC, cleverly designed bedrooms and a comfortable lounge/dining area (often incorporating a sofa bed).

In general, modern campsite chalets incorporate all the best features of mobile homes in a more traditional structure, sometimes with the advantage of an upper mezzanine floor for an additional bedroom.

Our selected campsites offer a massive range of different types of mobile home and chalet, and it would be impractical to inspect every single accommodation unit. Our selection criteria, therefore, primarily takes account of the quality standards of the campsite itself. However, there are a couple of important ground rules

- ☑ Featured mobile homes must be no more than 5 years old, and chalets no more than 10 years old.
- ☑ All listed accommodation must, of course, fully conform with all applicable local, national and European safety legislation.

For each campsite we given details of the type, or types, of accommodation available to rent, but these details are necessarily quite brief. Sometimes internal layouts can differ quite substantially, particularly with regard to sleeping arrangements, where these include the flexible provision for ‘extra persons’ on sofa beds located in the living area. These arrangements may vary from accommodation to accommodation, and if you're planning a holiday which includes more people than are catered for by the main bedrooms you should check exactly how the extra sleeping arrangements are to be provided!

INSPECTED CAMPSITES & SELECTED

Charges

An indication of the tariff for each type of accommodation featured is also included, indicating the variance between the low and high season tariffs. However, given that many campsites have a large and often complex range of pricing options, incorporating special deals and various discounts, the charges we mention should be taken to be just an indication. We strongly recommend therefore that you confirm the actual cost when making a booking.

We also strongly recommend that you check with the campsite, when booking, what (if anything) will be provided by way of bed linen, blankets, pillows etc. Again, in our experience, this can vary widely from site to site.

On every campsite a fully refundable deposit (usually between 150 and 300 euros) is payable on arrival. There may also be an optional cleaning service for which a further charge is made. Other options may include sheet hire (typically 30 euros per unit) or baby pack hire (cot and high chair).

ES8102 Camping Mas Patoxas

Ctra Palafrugell-Pals, km 339, 17256 Pals (Girona)

For our full description of this campsite see page 33

All featured accommodation are situated in a tranquil area within this attractive site.

AR1 – Luxe – Mobile Home

Sleeping:
2 bedrooms, sleeps 6: 1 double, 1 twin with 2 single beds, sofa bed; pillows & blankets provided

Living area:
living / kitchen area, TV, shower & WC

Eating:
fitted kitchen with cooking hobs, microwave & fridge

Outside:
table & chairs, parasol

Pets:
not accepted

AR2 – Gitotel – Chalet

Sleeping:
2 bedrooms, sleeps 6: 2 double, 1 twin with 2 single beds; pillows & blankets provided

Living area:
living / kitchen area, shower & WC

Eating:
fitted kitchen with cooking hobs & fridge

Outside:
table & chairs, parasol

Pets:
not accepted

Weekly Charges

	AR1	AR2
Low season *(from)*	€ 457	€ 367
High season *(from)*	€ 779	€ 711

ES8050 Camping Aquarius

Playa s/n, 17470 Sant Pere Pescador (Girona)

For our full description of this campsite see page 27

AR1 – Roller – Mobile Home

Sleeping:
2 bedrooms, sleeps 5: 1 double, 1 twin with 2 single beds and bunk bed, 2 single beds; pillows & blankets provided

Living area:
living / kitchen area, satellite TV, heating, shower & WC

Eating:
fitted kitchen with cooking hobs, microwave, toaster, coffee machine & fridge

Outside:
table & chairs, covered terrace

Pets:
not accepted

Weekly Charges

	AR1
Low season *(from)*	€350
High season *(from)*	€840

ES8390 Camping Vilanova Park

Ctra de l'Arboc, km 2.5, 08800 Vilanova i la Geltru (Barcelona)

For our full description of this campsite ▶ see page 47

The chalets are situated in several different areas throughout the site.

AR1 – Series 500 – Chalet

Sleeping:
2 bedrooms, sleeps 4-6: 1 double, 1 twin with 2 single beds, 1 double sofa bed; pillows & blankets provided

Living area:
living / kitchen area, stereo, shower & WC

Eating:
fitted kitchen with cooking hobs, microwave & fridge

Outside:
table & chairs

Pets:
not accepted

AR2 – Series 800 – Chalet

Sleeping:
2 bedrooms, sleeps 6: 1 double, 1 twin with 2 single beds, 1 double sofa bed; pillows & blankets provided

Living area:
living / kitchen area, stereo, shower & WC

Eating:
fitted kitchen with cooking hobs, microwave & fridge

Outside:
table & chairs

Pets:
not accepted

Weekly Charges

	AR1	AR2
Low season *(from)*	€ 515	€ 603
High season *(from)*	€ 774	€ 1012

ES8502 Camping Caravaning Montblanc Park

Ctra Prenafeta, km 1,8, 43400 Montblanc (Tarragona)

For our full description of this campsite ▶ see page 49

The featured accommodation has fine locations within this idyllic site - often benefiting from stunning mountain views.

AR1 – Miramar – Bungalow

Sleeping:
2 bedrooms, sleeps 6: 1 double, 1 twin with 2 single beds, 1 sofa bed

Living area:
living / kitchen area, TV, heating, shower & WC

Eating:
fitted kitchen with cooking hobs & fridge

Outside:
table & chairs

Pets:
not accepted

AR2 – Rojals – Mobile Home

Sleeping:
2 bedrooms, sleeps 5: 1 double, 1 twin with 2 single beds, sofa bed

Living area:
living / kitchen area, TV, shower & WC

Eating:
fitted kitchen with cooking hobs & fridge

Outside:
table & chairs

Pets:
not accepted

Weekly Charges

	AR1	AR2
Low season *(from)*	€ 430	€ 360
High season *(from)*	€ 702	€ 564

ES8481 Camping Cambrils Park

Apartado de Correos 123, 43850 Salou (Tarragona)

For our full description of this campsite see page 56

AR1 – Aloha – Bungalow

Sleeping:
2 bedrooms, sleeps 6: 1 double, 1 twin with 2 single beds, sofa bed; pillows, sheets & blankets provided

Living area:
living / kitchen area, TV, heating, air conditioning, bath & WC

Eating:
fitted kitchen with cooking hobs, oven, microwave & fridge

Outside:
table & chairs, terrace

Pets:
not accepted

Weekly Charges

	AR1
Low season *(from)*	€ 320
High season *(from)*	€ 1015

ES8480 Camping & Bungalows Sanguli

Prolongacion Calle, Apdo de Correos 123, 43840 Salou (Tarragona)

For our full description of this campsite see page 54

The mobile homes and bungalows are located in a very pleasant part of the site, between the swimming pool and shopping centre.

AR1 – Tahiti Suite – Bungalow

Sleeping:
2 bedrooms, sleeps 6: 1 double, 1 twin with 2 single beds, sofa bed; pillows, sheets & blankets provided

Living area:
living / kitchen area, satellite TV, bath & WC

Eating:
fitted kitchen with cooking hobs, oven & fridge

Outside:
table & chairs, terrace

Pets:
not accepted

AR2 – Louisiane – Mobile Home

Sleeping:
2 bedrooms, sleeps 6: 1 double, 1 twin with 2 single beds, 1 double sofa bed. Pillows, sheets & blankets provided

Living area:
living / kitchen area, satellite TV, air conditioning, heating, shower & WC

Eating:
fitted kitchen with cooking hobs, microwave & fridge

Outside:
table & chairs, parasol

Pets:
not accepted

Weekly Charges

	AR1	AR2
Low season *(from)*	€ 310	€ 270
High season *(from)*	€ 1015	€ 868

ES8482 Camping La Pineda de Salou

Ctra Costa Tarragona - Salou km 5, 43481 La Pineda (Tarragona)

For our full description of this campsite see page 58

AR1 – B1 – Mobile Home

Sleeping:
1 bedroom, sleeps 2-4: 1 double, 1 double sofa bed; blankets, sheets, pillows and towels supplied

Living area:
living / kitchen area, TV, heating, shower & WC

Eating:
fitted kitchen with cooking hobs, microwave & fridge

Outside:
table & chairs, parasol

Pets:
not accepted

Weekly Charges

	AR1
Low season *(from)*	€ 401
High season *(from)*	€ 658

ES8479 Camping Playa Cambrils - Don Camilo

Ctra Cambrils - Salou km 1.5, 43850 Cambrils (Tarragona)

For our full description of this campsite see page 59

AR1 – O'Hara Luxe – Mobile Home

Sleeping:
2 bedrooms, sleeps 5: 1 double, 1 twin with 2 single beds, sofa bed

Living area:
living / kitchen area, shower & WC

Eating:
fitted kitchen with cooking hobs & fridge

Outside:
table & chairs

Pets:
not accepted

AR2 – Gitotel Premium – Chalet

Sleeping:
2 bedrooms, sleeps 5: 1 double, 2 twin with 2 single beds, sofa bed

Living area:
living / kitchen area, shower & WC

Eating:
fitted kitchen with cooking hobs & fridge

Outside:
table & chairs

Pets:
not accepted

Weekly Charges

	AR1	AR2
Low season *(from)*	€ 208	€ 197
High season *(from)*	€ 793	€ 719

ES8470 Camping La Siesta

Calle Ctra Norte 37, 43840 Salou (Tarragona)

For our full description of this campsite see page 60

The bungalows featured are situated in a quiet and shady part of the campsite, not far from the entrance and main facilities.

AR1 – B4 – Bungalow

Sleeping:
1 bedroom, sleeps 4: 1 double, 1 double sofa bed; pillows & blankets provided

Living area:
living / kitchen area, shower & WC

Eating:
fitted kitchen with cooking hobs & fridge

Outside:
table & chairs, parasol

Pets:
not accepted

AR2 – B6 – Bungalow

Sleeping:
2 bedrooms, sleeps 4: 1 double, 1 twin with 2 single beds; pillows & blankets provided

Living area:
living / kitchen area, shower & WC

Eating:
fitted kitchen with cooking hobs & fridge

Outside:
table & chairs, parasol

Pets:
not accepted

Weekly Charges

	AR1	AR2
Low season *(from)*	€ 273	€ 399
High season *(from)*	€ 420	€ 644

ES8540 Yelloh! Village La Torre del Sol

Ctra N340, km 1136, 43300 Montroig (Tarragona)

For our full description of this campsite see page 63

AR1 – Gitotel – Chalet

Sleeping:
2 bedrooms, sleeps 6: 1 double, 1 twin with 2 single beds, 1 sofa bed

Living area:
living / kitchen area, shower & WC

Eating:
fitted kitchen with cooking hobs & fridge

Outside:
table & chairs

Pets:
not accepted

AR2 – Mobile Home

Sleeping:
2 bedrooms, sleeps 6: 1 double, 1 twin with 2 single beds, 1 double sofa bed

Living area:
living / kitchen area, shower & WC

Eating:
fitted kitchen with cooking hobs & fridge

Outside:
table & chairs

Pets:
not accepted

Weekly Charges

	AR1	AR2
Low season *(from)*	€ 329	€ 301
High season *(from)*	€ 889	€ 805

ES8000 Camping Son Bou

Ctra de San Jaime km 3.5, Apdo. de Correus 85, Alayor, 07730 Menorca

For our full description of this campsite see page 143

AR1 – Casitas de Madeira – Mobile Home

Sleeping:
2 bedrooms, sleeps 6: 1 double, 1 twin with 2 single beds, 1 double sofa bed; sheets, pillows & blankets provided

Living area:
living / kitchen area, shower & WC

Eating:
fitted kitchen with cooking hobs & fridge/freezer

Outside:
table & chairs

Pets:
accepted

Weekly Charges

	AR1
Low season *(from)*	€ 448
High season *(from)*	€ 693

ES8620 Camping L'Alqueria

46730 Gandia (Valencia)

For our full description of this campsite see page 70

AR1 – Mediterraneo – Mobile Home

Sleeping:
2 bedrooms, sleeps 5: 1 double, 1 twin with 2 single beds, sofa bed

Living area:
living / kitchen area, TV, wash basin & WC

Eating:
fitted kitchen with cooking hobs & fridge

Outside:
table & chairs

Pets:
small dogs only

AR2 – Gitotel – Chalet

Sleeping:
2 bedrooms, sleeps 5: 1 double, 1 twin with 2 single beds, sofa bed

Living area:
living / kitchen area, TV, shower & WC

Eating:
fitted kitchen with cooking hobs & fridge

Outside:
table & chairs

Pets:
small dogs only

Weekly Charges

	AR1	AR2
Low season *(from)*	€ 255	€ 255
High season *(from)*	€ 652	€ 652

PO8460 Camping Caravaning Vale Paraiso

E.N. 242, 2450-138 Nazaré (Leiria)

For our full description of this campsite see page 157

AR1 – Block B – Appartment

Sleeping:
2 bedrooms, sleeps 5-6: 1 double, 1 twin with 2 single beds, 1 sofa bed

Living area:
living / kitchen area, TV, heating, shower & WC

Eating:
fitted kitchen with cooking hobs & fridge

Outside:
table & chairs, parasol

Pets:
not accepted

Weekly Charges

	AR1
Low season *(from)*	€ 360
High season *(from)*	€ 750

WIN A Caravan...

A holiday...and lots more

Prize Draw Bonanza

Alan Rogers Guides, in association with Towsure, providers of everything for the outdoors, are running a unique new prize draw for 2005. This is your chance to win a fantastic set of prizes, never before offered in the UK.

YOU COULD WIN ALL THESE!

- **WIN** A brand new Avondale caravan
- **WIN** A Camping Cheque holiday, including return ferry
- **WIN** £500 of Towsure products
- **WIN** A complete set of Alan Rogers 2005 guides

To enter, simply visit **www.towsure.com**

the travel service

Mobile Home Holidays

INSPECTED & SELECTED CAMPSITES

QUALITY ACCOMMODATION AT HUGE SAVINGS

Superb campsites, ideal for families and couples, offering state-of-the-art fully equipped mobile homes. Huge savings - just turn up and move in!

- ✓ Around 75 top sites in France, Italy, Holland
- ✓ All Alan Rogers selected and inspected
- ✓ Spacious mobile homes
- ✓ Free children's clubs on many sites
- ✓ Superb facilities on all sites
- ✓ Great destinations including Brittany, Mediterranean, Dordogne, Venice, Lake Garda

Don't leave it to chance,
leave it to us

Alan Rogers

For your FREE colour brochure

0870 405 4055

alanrogers**direct**.com

book on-line and save

OPEN ALL YEAR

The following campsites are understood to accept caravanners and campers all year round, although the list also includes some sites that are open for at least ten months. These are marked with a star (*) – please refer to the site's individual entry for details. It is always wise to phone them to check as the facilities available, for example, may be reduced.

SPAIN

Cataluña-Catalunya

ES8072 Les Medes*
ES8102 Mas Patoxas*
ES8130 Calonge
ES8063 El Llac*
ES9123 El Solsones
ES9121 Vall d'Ager
ES8240 Bona Vista Kim
ES9140 Pedraforca
ES8390 Vilanova Park
ES8392 El Garrofer*
ES8502 Montblanc Park
ES8235 Bon Repos
ES8506 Serra de Prades
ES8508 Poboleda
ES8395 Arc de Bara
ES8483 Tamarit
ES8535 Cala d`Oques
ES8536 Ametlla

Comunidad Valenciana

ES8560 Playa Tropicana
ES8558 Vinaros
ES8570 Torre La Sal 2
ES8580 Bonterra
ES8590 Monmar
ES8615 Kiko
ES8625 Kiko Rural
ES8612 Euro Camping (Oliva)
ES8675 Vall de Laguar
ES8680 Armanello
ES8682 Villamar
ES8681 Villasol
ES8685 El Raco
ES8683 Benisol
ES8754 Javea
ES8755 Moraira
ES8686 Excalibur Medieval
ES8687 Cap Blanch
ES8742 La Marina
ES8689 Playa del Torres
ES8743 Marjal
ES8741 Florantilles

Murcia

ES8752 El Portus
ES8748 Los Madriles
ES8745 La Fuente
ES8753 La Manga

Andalucia

ES8749 Sopalmo
ES8751 Cuevas Mar
ES9270 Suspiro-Moro
ES8765 La Garrofa
ES9296 Castillo de Banos
ES9285 Las Lomas
ES9275 Los Avellanos
ES8782 Laguna Playa
ES9295 Don Cactus
ES9290 El Balcon
ES8783 Almanat
ES8803 La Buganvilla
ES8790 La Laguna
ES8800 Marbella Playa
ES8809 El Sur
ES8802 Cabopino
ES8850 Paloma
ES8855 Tarifa
ES8865 Playa Las Dunas
ES8873 La Aldea
ES8889 Los Alcornocales
ES8871 Giralda
ES9081 Villsom
ES9078 Los Villares
ES9082 Sevilla
ES9080 El Brillante
ES9085 Carlos III
ES9089 Despenaperros
ES9084 La Campiña*

Extremadura

ES9087 Merida
ES9027 Monfrague
ES9028 Villueracas

Castilla La-Mancha

ES9090 El Greco
ES9097 Los Batanes

Madrid

ES9091 Soto-Castillo
ES9092 Coto Cisneros
ES9200 El Escorial
ES9210 Pico-Miel

Castilla y Leon

ES9022 El Folgoso
ES9025 Regio
ES9250 Costajan
ES9253 Picon del Conde
ES9044 Monumento
ES9257 Frias
ES9242 El Acueducto

Galicia

ES9024 As Cancelas

Asturias

ES8940 Los Cantiles
ES8965 Picos-Europa

Cantabria

ES8964 Molino
ES8973 Santillana

Pais Vasco-Euskadi

ES9035 Portuondo
ES9039 Gran Zarautz

Navarra

ES9043 Errota el Molino

Aragón

ES9058 Baliera
ES9060 Peña Montañesa
ES9062 Boltana
ES9064 Gavín
ES9070 Pirineos*

PORTUGAL

Algarve

PO8220 Quarteira
PO8230 Olhao
PO8210 Albufeira
PO8200 Valverde
PO8202 Espiche
PO8410 Armacao-Pera
PO8430 Sagres
PO8440 Quintos

Alentejo

PO8350 Markádia
PO8160 Porto Covo

Lisbon & Vale do Tejo

PO8140 Monsanto
PO8130 Guincho
PO8150 Caparica
PO8480 Foz do Arelho
PO8450 Colina-Sol*
PO8110 Valado*
PO8460 Vale Paraiso*
PO8100 S Pedro-Moel

Beiras & Centre

PO8090 Figueira da Foz
PO8040 Vagueira
PO8050 Sao Jacinto*
PO8330 Arganil

Porto & North

PO8030 Rio Alto
PO8020 Viana-Castelo*
PO8370 Cerdeira
PO8010 Caminha*
PO8380 Vilar de Mouros

DOGS

For the benefit of those who want to take their dogs with them or for people who do not like dogs at the sites they visit, we list here the sites that have indicated to us that they do not accept dogs. If you are, however, planning to take your dog we do advise you to contact them first to check – there may be limits on numbers, breeds, etc. or times of the year when they are excluded.

Never – these sites do not accept dogs at any time:

SPAIN

Cataluña-Catalunya

ES8005	
ES8090	Cypsela
ES8101	Playa Brava
ES8103	El Maset
ES9143	Pirineus
ES9123	El Solsones
ES8420	Stel (Roda)
ES8481	Cambrils
ES8530	Playa Montroig
ES8540	Torre del Sol
ES8537	Templo del Sol

Comunidad Valenciana

ES8560	Playa Tropicana
ES8620	L`AlqueriaL
ES8681	Villasol
ES8682	Villamar
ES8741	Florantilles

Murcia

ES8748	Los Madriles

Andalucia

ES8751	Cuevas Mar

Castilla y Leon

ES9251	Rio Lobos

Cantabria

ES9000	Playa Joyel

Pais Vasco-Euskadi

ES9038	Orio

PORTUGAL

Alentejo

PO8170	São Miguel

Porto & North

PO8380	Vilar de Mouros

Maybe – accepted at any time but with certain restrictions:

SPAIN

Cataluña-Catalunya

ES8060	Ballena Alegre 2	Special Area
ES8072	Les Medes	not July-Aug
ES8075	Estartit	not 20/6 - 20/8
ES8080	Delfin Verde	not 12/7-15/8
ES8160	Cala Gogo	not 1/7 - 26/8

Comunidad Valenciana

ES8580	Bonterra	not in July/Aug

Andalucia

ES9295	Don Cactus	not in July/Aug
ES8803	La Buganvilla	not in July/Aug

PORTUGAL

Alentejo

PO8350	Markádia	not July/Aug

Porto & North

PO8370	Cerdeira	not July/Aug

FISHING

We are pleased to include details of sites which provide facilities for fishing on site. However, it is always best to contact sites directly to check that they provide for your individual requirements.

SPAIN

Cataluña-Catalunya

ES8010	Castell Mar
ES8015	La Laguna
ES8030	Nautic Almata
ES8035	Amfora
ES8040	Las Dunas
ES8050	Aquarius
ES8060	Ballena Alegre 2
ES8063	El Llac
ES8074	Paradis
ES8080	Delfin Verde
ES8101	Playa Brava
ES8135	Eurocamping
ES8140	Treumal
ES8160	Cala Gogo
ES8200	Cala Llevadó
ES8230	El Pinar
ES8232	Bella Terra
ES8235	Bon Repos
ES8238	Caballo de Mar
ES8312	Tres Estrellas
ES8410	Playa Bara
ES8420	Stel (Roda)
ES8483	Tamarit
ES8486	Torre de la Mora
ES8520	Marius
ES8530	Playa Montroig
ES8535	Cala d`Oques
ES8536	Ametlla
ES8537	Templo del Sol
ES8540	Torre del Sol
ES9142	Solana del Segre
ES9143	Pirineus

Comunidad Valenciana

ES8560	Playa Tropicana
ES8570	Torre La Sal 2
ES8612	Euro Camping (Oliva)
ES8615	Kiko
ES8687	Cap Blanch
ES8689	Playa del Torres
ES8743	Marjal

Murcia

ES8752	El Portus
ES8753	La Manga

Andalucia

ES8765	La Garrofa
ES8782	Laguna Playa
ES8783	Almanat
ES8855	Tarifa

Castilla La-Mancha

ES9090	El Greco

Madrid

ES9091	Soto-Castillo
ES9092	Coto Cisneros

Castilla y Leon

ES9257	Frias

Asturias

ES8945	Lagos-Somiedo
ES8950	Costa Verde
ES8960	La Paz
ES8965	Picos-Europa

Cantabria

ES8962	La Isla
ES8970	Arenas-Pechon
ES9000	Playa Joyel

Pais Vasco-Euskadi

ES9035	Portuondo
ES9045	Angosto

Navarra

ES9043	Errota el Molino

Aragón

ES9060	Peña Montañesa
ES9125	Lago Barasona

PORTUGAL

Alentejo

PO8350	Markádia

Porto & North

PO8030	Rio Alto

BICYCLE HIRE

We understand that the following sites have bicycles to hire on site or can arrange for bicycles to be delivered. However, we would recommend that you contact them directly to check as the situation can change.

SPAIN

Cataluña-Catalunya

ES8030 Nautic Almata
ES8033 Las Palmeras
ES8035 Amfora
ES8040 Las Dunas
ES8050 Aquarius
ES8060 Ballena Alegre 2
ES8072 Les Medes
ES8074 Paradis
ES8080 Delfin Verde
ES8135 Eurocamping
ES8160 Cala Gogo
ES8180 Sant Pol
ES8210 Tucan
ES8225 La Masia
ES8392 El Garrofer
ES8482 Pineda de Salou
ES8502 Montblanc Park
ES8506 Serra de Prades
ES8530 Playa Montroig
ES8536 Ametlla
ES8537 Templo del Sol
ES8540 Torre del Sol
ES9123 El Solsones
ES9140 Pedraforca
ES9144 Stel

Comunidad Valenciana

ES8560 Playa Tropicana
ES8570 Torre La Sal 2
ES8580 Bonterra
ES8612 Euro Camping (Oliva)
ES8615 Kiko
ES8625 Kiko Rural
ES8686 Excalibur Medieval
ES8743 Marjal

Murcia

ES8745 La Fuente
ES8748 Los Madriles
ES8752 El Portus

Andalucia

ES8803 La Buganvilla
ES9290 El Balcon

Extremadura

ES9027 Monfrague
ES9087 Merida

Madrid

ES9091 Soto-Castillo

Castilla y Leon

ES9023 Santiago

Galicia

ES9024 As Cancelas

Asturias

ES8940 Los Cantiles

Cantabria

ES8961 El Helguero
ES8962 La Isla
ES8964 Molino
ES8970 Arenas-Pechon

Pais Vasco-Euskadi

ES9045 Angosto

Navarra

ES9042 Etxarri
ES9043 Errota el Molino

Aragón

ES9060 Peña Montañesa
ES9062 Boltana
ES9064 Gavín
ES9125 Lago Barasona

Balears

ES8000 Son Bou

PORTUGAL

Algarve

PO8202 Espiche
PO8210 Albufeira
PO8230 Olhao
PO8430 Sagres
PO8440 Quintos

Alentejo

PO8160 Porto Covo

Lisbon & Vale do Tejo

PO8460 Vale Paraiso

Beiras & Centre

PO8040 Vagueira

Porto & North

PO8370 Cerdeira

HORSE RIDING

We understand that the following sites have horse riding stables on site. However, we do recommend that you contact the campsite to check that they meet your requirements.

SPAIN

Cataluña-Catalunya

ES8015 La Laguna
ES8030 Nautic Almata
ES8506 Serra de Prades

Comunidad Valenciana

ES8625 Kiko Rural

Andalucia

ES8751 Cuevas Mar
ES9290 El Balcon

Extremadura

ES9027 Monfrague

Asturias

ES8945 Lagos-Somiedo

Cantabria

ES8962 La Isla
ES9000 Playa Joyel

Navarra

ES9043 Errota el Molino

Aragón

ES9060 Peña Montañesa

PORTUGAL

Alentejo

PO8350 Markádia

BOAT LAUNCHING

We understand that the following sites have boat slipways on site. Where facilities are within easy reach and we have been given details, we have included this information in the individual reports. However, we recommend that you contact them directly to check that they meet your requirements.

SPAIN

Cataluña-Catalunya

ES8030 Nautic Almata
ES8101 Playa Brava
ES8135 Eurocamping
ES8530 Playa Montroig
ES8540 Torre del Sol

Comunidad Valenciana

ES8570 Torre La Sal 2
ES8612 Euro Camping (Oliva)
ES8615 Kiko
ES8689 Playa del Torres

Murica

ES8752 El Portus

Andalucia

ES8765 La Garrofa
ES8782 Laguna Playa
ES8855 Tarifa
ES8871 Giralda

Madrid

ES9091 Soto-Castillo

Cantabria

ES8970 Arenas-Pechon

Navarra

ES9043 Errota el Molino

Aragón

ES9125 Lago Barasona

PORTUGAL

Alentejo

PO8350 Markádia

REPORTS BY READERS

We always welcome reports from readers concerning sites which they have visited. Generally reports provide us with invaluable feedback on sites already included in the Guide or, in the case of those not featured in our Guide, they provide information which we can follow up with a view to adding them in future editions. However, if you have a complaint about a site, this should be addressed to the campsite owner, preferably in person before you leave.

Please make your comments either on this form or on plain paper. It would be appreciated if you would indicate the approximate dates when you visited the site and, in the case of potential new sites, provide the correct name and address and, if possible, include a campsite brochure. Send your reports to:

Alan Rogers Guides, Spelmonden Old Oast, Goudhurst, Kent TN17 1HE

Name of Site and Ref. No. (or address for new recommendations)

____

____

Dates of visit: ______________________________

Comments:

Reader's Name and Address: ________________________

____

____

____

Sail overnight to Spain

Direct with your car

Cruise overnight in luxury from Plymouth to Santander in almost half the time of any other direct ferry service. While on board you'll enjoy award-winning service and top-class facilities. Now there's a real alternative to flying or driving through France, and all for less than you'd expect.

Call **0870 908 1261**

or book online and save

www.brittanyferries.com

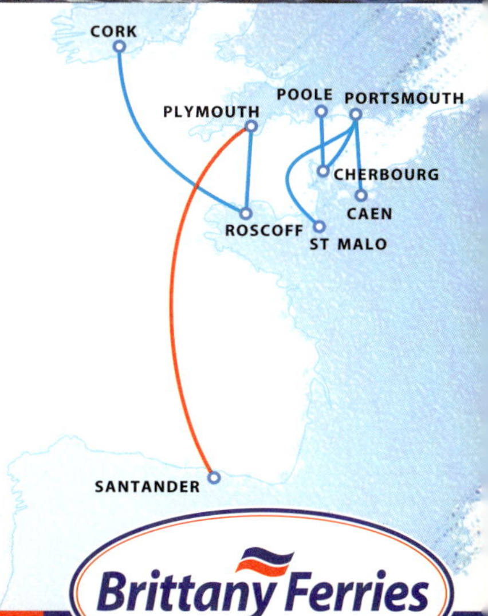

Brittany Ferries

If you are planning to take your caravan, tent, trailer tent or motorcaravan to the continent you will need to be familiar with the rules, regulations and customs that pertain to driving abroad.

A recent survey looked at why many Britons would not entertain a holiday abroad and why many foreigners would not contemplate coming here. According to the findings, the biggest single put-off was driving on the 'wrong' side of the road. However, statistics clearly show that you are less at risk of being involved in accidents – and that includes minor shunts – when driving in another country. The theory is that motorists of that country recognise that the nationality plate on your vehicle means that you might be slightly hesitant and give you that extra few inches which makes the difference between a minor ding and a trouble free journey. Of course it could also be that when driving in another country we take things a bit easier, so we are less at risk of being involved in an accident.

With European harmonisation eliminating most of the differences between driving in your home country and another, there has never been a better time to consider driving abroad. Where there are differences, they are in the detail.

For example all European countries require you to carry your driving documents whenever you are behind the wheel; there's no three day's grace to get to your local police station. Amongst the documents you are required to carry is your vehicle registration document, the V5 (what used to be called the log book). If yours is a hire or company vehicle you may have difficulties getting your hands on the V5. However the police will accept a photocopy of the V5 provided it is accompanied by a brief letter – signed by the vehicle owner – saying you have their permission to take the vehicle abroad.

European harmonisation also means that most common road signs are the same in all countries. Where mainland Europe differs from the UK is in the use of direction signs. If you are following signs through a town and arrive at a junction without signage – don't panic. The logic is that if all major routes are straight on, you don't need another sign to tell you the obvious.

As to language difficulties, you will find that most continental road signs are similar in style to those in the UK, although what is written on them will be in the language of the country concerned (for example Barcelona is spelt Barcelone in French), so it's worthwhile mugging up some of the more important and/or more usual ones. See articles on individual countries – the main signs have been translated for you.

When it comes to traffic regulations around school entrances, the Europeans are also ahead of us. In mainland Europe the law, or common practice, is that you should not pass a parked school bus unless it is absolutely safe to do so. If you can pass, you must keep your speed to a walking pace. It is the same when you drive past a school when the children are outside. The law, or best practice, says you should reduce your speed to a crawl.

We would never dream of suggesting that you would ever break the speed limit, but if you are tempted it is worth remembering that European police seem to have as many speed cameras as British police. The difference between speeding in the UK and mainland Europe is in the way fines can be levied. If you are caught in a manned speed trap you may be expected to pay an on-the-spot fine, so it's no good arguing that you haven't got enough money to pay the fine. Most manned speed traps will take cash, traveller's cheques, debit and credit cards.

Checklist

Before you set off for a holiday abroad it's worth making yourself a checklist of things to do, and what to pack – we've been travelling abroad several times a year for more than thirty years and we still don't rely on our memory for this, so it's best to consult a checklist; here's the one we use:

- ☐ Passports
- ☐ Tickets
- ☐ Motor Insurance Certificate, including Green Card or Continental Cover clause
- ☐ V5 Registration Document and/or (if not your own vehicle) the owners authority
- ☐ Breakdown Insurance Certificate
- ☐ Driving Licence (The new PHOTO style licence is now MANDATORY in most European countries)
- ☐ Form E1-11 (to extend NHS Insurance to European destinations)
- ☐ Foreign Currency (EUROS, and Swiss Francs if appropriate) and/or Travellers Cheques
- ☐ Credit Card(s)
- ☐ Campsite Guide(s) and Tourist Guide(s)
- ☐ Maps/Road Atlas
- ☐ GB Stickers on car and caravan/trailer
- ☐ Beam deflectors to ensure that your headlights dip towards the right hand side
- ☐ Red Warning Triangle
- ☐ Spare vehicle/caravan driving light bulbs
- ☐ Torch
- ☐ First-Aid Kit, including mosquito repellent
- ☐ Fire extinguisher
- ☐ Basic tool kit (e.g screwdriver, pliers, etc)
- ☐ Continental mains connector/adaptor, and a long cable – for continental sites
- ☐ Polarity tester
- ☐ Spare fuses for car and caravan
- ☐ Spare fan/alternator belt

Finally bear in mind it's well worth having your car and caravan serviced before you go, and do check that your outfit is properly 'trimmed' before you set off.

Be sensible at all times and do not leave valuables in your vehicle or leave anything visible which could tempt a petty thief. Take care if waved down by anyone; in the past tactics like this have been used to get you to leave your car so an accomplice can have a field day rummaging through your belongings.

Spain

Driving in Spain presents few problems, but there is one piece of advice in particular which we would highlight, namely the need to have a Bail Bond (obtainable via your motor insurers) to avoid the risk of your car being impounded following an accident. It is also necessary to carry two warning triangles in Spain, as well as a spare set of bulbs.

Seat belts for all passengers are compulsory, and children under 12 years of age are not allowed to sit in the front unless using a proper child seat/harness; motorcyclists must wear crash hats. The maximum speed limits are roughly similar to those in the UK: 120 kph, or 75 mph on motorways, known as Autopistas, and 90 kph on main roads – there is a lower limit of 80 kph when towing.

The following are some of the more important road signs:

Ceda el Paso	Give Way
Despacio	Slow Down
Peligro	Danger!
Prioridad	Right of way
Peaje	Toll Booth
Prohibicion	Prohibited
Salida	Exit (from Autopista)

Portugal

Unfortunately Portugal has a very poor road safety record, particularly around the Algarve coastal area. Quite why this should be so is not entirely clear, but it may well have something to do with the fact that road surfaces vary from excellent to dreadful, sometimes with little or no warning! It is not uncommon to be driving along a well surfaced smooth tarmac road one moment only to be confronted with a stretch of cobbled road the next – somewhat unnerving to say the least, so concentration and care are the order of the day. Be prepared to give way to traffic on your right, even if it looks as if you have the right of way.

Speed limits are 120 kph (75 mph) on motorways (Auto-Estradas) and 90 kph on other main roads, but there are lower limits for towing (100 kph and 70 kph respectively).

Essential equipment consists of a warning triangle and spare set of light bulbs. Seat belts all round are mandatory, and children under 12 years of age are not allowed in the front seats unless wearing a child restraint; motorcyclists are required to wear crash hats and keep their headlights on at all times.

In theory European law means that a vehicle insured for use in the UK is still insured in any other European country. But some insurers know that doesn't really mean what you think it means. Somewhere in the fine print on page 37 of your policy you could find that if you take your vehicle abroad your insurance coverage is reduced to third party only. So two weeks before you venture abroad contact your vehicle insurer and find out if you need additional coverage.

Most vehicle breakdown insurance schemes claim to offer pan-European cover. But again it is worth asking just how good that cover is. If you car expires beside the road in a cloud of steam you don't want to have to try explaining the problem to a telephone receptionist who is fluent in every language – except yours.

The travel insurers Alan Rogers work with (see advert on page 187) operate language-specific call centres. If anything goes wrong you'll speak to somebody totally fluent in your language. What all insurers will insist on is that your vehicle must be in good condition before you set off on holiday. A full service a few weeks before your departure date will take care of that.

There is probably no subject which causes campers, caravanners and motor-caravanners venturing abroad more worries than insurance, so notwithstanding the notes above, if you're in any doubt about insurance it may be worthwhile you giving the subject some further thought, and the following will hopefully help to clarify things:

The problem with insurance is that there is often an 'overlap', so that sometimes one aspect is apparently covered on two insurance policies. To avoid confusion let's cut through the hype and take a clear look at the different types of insurance.

If you are planning on camping, caravanning or motorcaravanning abroad, this is what you will need.

Road traffic insurance

As previously stated, your ordinary car or motorcaravan road insurance will cover you anywhere in the EU. *However* many policies only provide minimum cover. So if you have an accident your insurance may only cover the cost of damage to the other person's property.

To maintain the same level of cover abroad as you enjoy at home you need to tell your vehicle insurer. Some will automatically cover you abroad with no extra cost and no extra paperwork. Some will say you need a Green Card (which is neither green or on card) but won't charge for it. Some will charge extra for the green card. Ideally you should contact your vehicle insurer 3-4 weeks before you set off, and confirm your conversation with them in writing.

A good insurance company will provide a European recognised accident report form. On this you mark details of damage to yours and the other party's property and draw a little diagram showing where the vehicles were in relation to each other. You give a copy of your form to the other motorist; he gives you a copy of his. It prevents all the shouting which often accompanies accidents in this country.

Holiday insurance

This is a multi-part insurance. One part covers your vehicles. If they breakdown or are involved in an accident they can be repaired or returned to this country. The best will even arrange to bring your vehicle home if the driver is unable to proceed.

Many new vehicles come with a free breakdown and recovery insurance which extends into Europe. Some professional motoring journalists have reported that the actual service this provides can be patchy and may not cover the recovery of a caravan or trailer. Our advice is to buy the motoring section of your holiday insurance.

The second section of holiday insurance covers people. It will include the cost of doctor, ambulance and hospital treatment if needed. If needed the better companies will even pay for English language speaking doctors and nurses and will bring a sick or injured holidaymaker home by air ambulance.

The third part of a good holiday insurance policy covers things. If someone breaks in to your motorhome and steals your passports and money, one phone call to the insurance company will have everything sorted out. If you manage to drive over your camera, it's covered.

An important part of the insurance that is often ignored is the cancellation section. Few things are as heartbreaking as having to cancel a holiday because a member of the family falls ill. Cancellation insurance can't take away the disappointment, but it makes sure you don't suffer financially as well.

There are a number of good insurance policies available including those provided for their members by the two major clubs and those offered by the leading camping holiday agents already mentioned in this guide.

Which ever insurance you choose we would advise not picking any of the policies sold by the High Street travel trade. Whilst they may be good, they don't cover the specific needs of campers, caravanners and motorcaravanners. And ideally you should arrange your holiday insurance at least four weeks before you set off.

Form E111

By arrangement between the British Government and rest of the European Community Governments, British holiday-makers can enjoy similar health care as that Government offers its own citizens. The form which shows you are entitled to take advantage of this arrangement is called E111.

E111 doesn't replace holiday insurance, but is in addition to. The form is available from all main UK Post Offices. Fill out one for every adult member of your family (children under 16 should be marked as dependents on your form). Get it stamped by the counter staff and take it on holiday with you.

Form E111 is valid indefinitely (unless you change your address).

And that is all you need to know about insurance. You know what they say about insurance, don't you? You'll only need it if you haven't got it.

www.insure4europe.com

PRICES HELD FROM 2004

Taking your own tent, caravan or motorhome abroad?
Looking for the best cover at the best rates?

Our prices considerably undercut most high street prices and the 'in-house insurance' of many tour operators whilst offering equivalent (or higher) levels of cover.

Our annual multi-trip policies offer superb value, covering you not only for your european camping holiday but also subsequent trips abroad for the next 12 months.

Total Peace of Mind

To give you total peace of mind during your holiday our insurance policies have been specifically tailored to cover most potential eventualities on a self-drive camping holiday. Each is organised through Voyager Insurance Services Ltd who specialize in travel insurance for Europe and for camping in particular. All policies are underwritten by UK Underwriting Ltd, on behalf of a consortium of insurance companies that are members of the Association of British Insurers and the Financial Ombudsman services.

24 Hour Assistance

Our personal insurance provides access to the services of Inter Group Assistant Services (IGAS), one of the UK's largest assistance companies. European vehicle assistance cover is provided by Green Flag who provide assistance to over 3 million people each year. With a Europe-wide network of over 7,500 garages and agents you know you're in very safe hands.

Both IGAS and Green Flag are very used to looking after the needs of campsite-based holidaymakers and are very familiar with the location of most European campsites, with contacts at garages, doctors and hospitals nearby.

SAVE with an Annual policy

If you are likely to make more than one trip to Europe over the next 12 months then our annual multi-trip policies could save you a fortune. Personal cover for a couple starts at just £95 and the whole family can be covered for just £115. Cover for up to 17 days wintersports participation is included.

Low Cost Annual multi-trip insurance

Premier Annual Europe self-drive	Premier Annual Europe self-drive
including 17 days wintersports	including 17 days wintersports
£95.00 per couple	**£115.00** per family

Low Cost Combined Personal & Vehicle Assistance Insurance

Premier Couples Package	Premier Family Package
10 days cover for vehicle and 2 adults	10 days cover for vehicle, 2 adults plus dependent children under 16
£61.00*	**£75.00***

* Motorhomes, cars towing trailers and caravans, all vehicles over 4 years old and holidays longer than 10 days attract supplements – ask us for details. See leaflet for full terms and conditions.

One call and you're covered – ask us for a leaflet or no-obligation quote.

0870 405 4059

DELTA EUROCARD MasterCard SWITCH VISA

Policies despatched within 24 hours insure4europe.com is a trading name of Mark Hammerton Travel Ltd.

3 FREE ISSUES!

THE UK'S FAVOURITE MOTORHOME MAGAZINES...

The UK's best selling motorhome magazine for 38 years, MMM is considered to be the only place to look for the latest news from the motorcaravanning world.

The UK's leading magazine for motorhome buyers, Which Motorcaravan has more hot news of new models and in-depth vehicle tests than any rival publication.

Reply now and you will get the next **3 issues of MMM for just £1 each** or the next **3 issues of Which Motorcaravan FREE!**

Then, if you like what you see - do nothing! Your subscription will continue at the LOW RATE of just £8 every 3 months for MMM, or £5 every 3 months for Which Motorcaravan, giving you a saving of up to 44% off the shop price!

100% RISK FREE OFFER
If you feel that the magazine is not for you simply write to us within 10 days of receiving your third issue and you won't pay a penny more! Additionally, you may cancel your subscription at any time and we will refund in full the cost of all unmailed copies.

Call our Hotline today on **01778 391180**
(Please have your bank details ready & quote ref: ALANROGERS05)

Offer is open to UK residents and is a Direct Debit offer only. Your subscription will start with the next available issue. Please note, only one trial offer per magazine will be processed per household during a 12 month period.

Paying too much

for your mobile home holiday?

Travel off peak

and Pay Just £27.50 per night

with Holiday Cheque

Holiday Cheque gives you exclusive off peak access to quality mobile homes and chalets on over 100 of Europe's finest campsites. You'll find superb family facilities, including sensational pools, great value restaurants, friendly bars and real hospitality. And the kids can have the time of their lives! All for just £27.50 per night.

- Over 100 top campsites
- All just £27.50 per night
- High quality mobile homes
- Luxury high specification chalets
- Fully equipped - down to the corkscrew!
- Plus unbeatable ferry prices

Huge savings - but hurry

HOLIDAY CHEQUES COST JUST £27.50 PER NIGHT. THAT'S A SPECIAL PROMOTIONAL RATE, SAVING UP TO 50% OFF CAMPSITE'S STANDARD PRICES. BUT IT'S FIRST COME, FIRST SERVED, SO THERE'S NO TIME TO LOSE IF YOU WANT TO BOOK THE CAMPSITE OF YOUR CHOICE.

HOLIDAY CHEQUE

Call today for your FREE brochure

0870 405 4058

it will save you £££'s on your holiday

www.holidaycheque.co.uk

Alan Rogers

3 ISSUES FOR £1

Practical Caravan is the UK's biggest and best selling caravan magazine. Written by enthusiasts for enthusiasts, each issue is packed full with holiday tips, technical advice, reader reviews, superb photography, reader offers… and much more!

Try the next 3 issues for just

£1

Then, if you like what you see - just sit back and relax! Your subscription will continue at the discounted rate of £7.80 every 3 issues for Practical Caravan or £7.15 for Practical Motorhome. That's **20% off** the shop price.

We and thousands of subscribers guarantee you will love it!

This offer is also valid on

Practical Motorhome

NOW EVEN BIGGER AND BETTER!

CALL 08456 777 812 NOW

or visit **www.haymarketsubs.com** and quote ALG04

Offer closes 31 December 2004

Save up to 55% on your holiday

Camping Cheque ©

Last year over 150,000 people used well over 1 million Camping Cheques and enjoyed half-price holidays around Europe. Make sure you don't miss out this year.

Huge off peak savings

511 quality campsites, in 18 European countries, including the UK, all at just £9.95 per night for pitch + 2 adults, including electricity. Go as you please and save up to 55% off normal site tariffs.

ferry savings

Ask about our famous special offers

- ☑ Caravans/trailers Go **FREE**
- ☑ Motorhomes Priced As Cars

Conditions apply – ask for details

CALL NOW for full details of how to save up to 55% on your holiday

Alan Rogers

0870 405 4057

For full information visit

www.campingcheque.co.uk

Buy Cheques, check ferry availability, book everything on-line AND SAVE!

the travel service

Save Time, Save Money

THE LOW COST PITCH AND FERRY RESERVATION SERVIC
FOR READERS OF THE ALAN ROGERS GUIDES

INSPECTED CAMPSITE & SELECTED

We'll book your preferred campsite(s)
Choose from 150 of the finest inspected and selectec sites across Europe (look for the highlighted site descriptions in all Guides). We can even book site-owned mobile homes and chalets (visit www.alanrogersdirect.com or ask for details).

Ask about our incredible Ferry Deals:

- ✓ Caravans GO FREE
- ✓ Motorhomes Priced as Cars

We'll organise your low cost Channel crossing - call us for a quote or visit **www.alanrogersdirect.co**

We'll provide comprehensive information
Leave it to the experts and enjoy peace of mind.

Don't leave it to chance, **leave it to us**

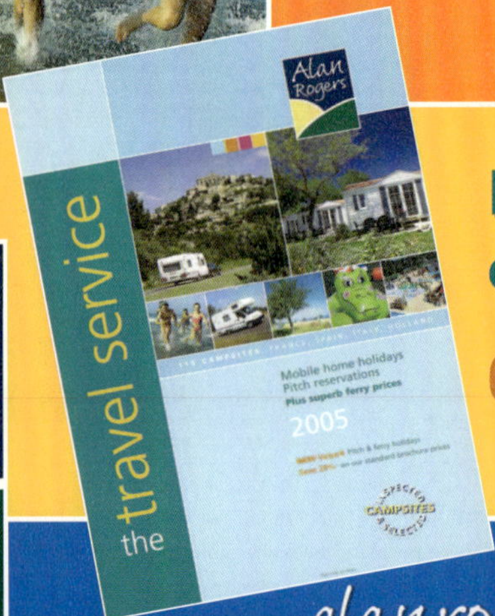

For your FREE colour brochure

0870 405 405

Alan Rogers

alanrogers**direct**.com
book on-line and save

POWR-PRODUCTS

POWRTOUCH

The Remote Control Caravan Mover

POWRTOUCH is the remote control caravan mover which attaches direct to your chassis and caravan tyres, giving you fingertip control over the positioning of your caravan. Innovative and powerful, whichever model you choose, parking your caravan will never be a struggle again.

All major debit/credit cards accepted

With a POWRTOUCH there's no risk of injury, no risk of damage and no embarrassing scenes! Just simple, precise, easy movement when pitching, hitching and parking.

- *Single or Twin Axle Models*
- *ISO 9001:2000 & TUV Approved*
- *Price Match any comparable unit*

FREE 5 YEAR NO QUIBBLE GUARANTEE

UKAS QUALITY MANAGEMENT

TÜV Approved

A QUALITY OF LIFE PRODUCT

POWRTOUCH HOTLINE:

0870 7521762

www.powrwheel.com

Information & Customer Service: 01425 623123

Powrwheel Ltd, 8 Queensway, New Milton, Hampshire BH25 5NN

WIN A Caravan...

A holiday...and lots more

Alan Rogers

Prize Draw Bonanza

Alan Rogers Guides, in association with Towsure, providers of everything for the outdoors, are running a unique new prize draw for 2005. This is your chance to win a fantastic set of prizes, never before offered in the UK.

YOU COULD WIN ALL THESE!

- WIN A brand new Avondale caravan
- WIN A Camping Cheque holiday, including return ferry
- WIN £500 of Towsure products
- WIN A complete set of Alan Rogers 2005 guides

To enter, simply visit **www.towsure.com**

Towsure

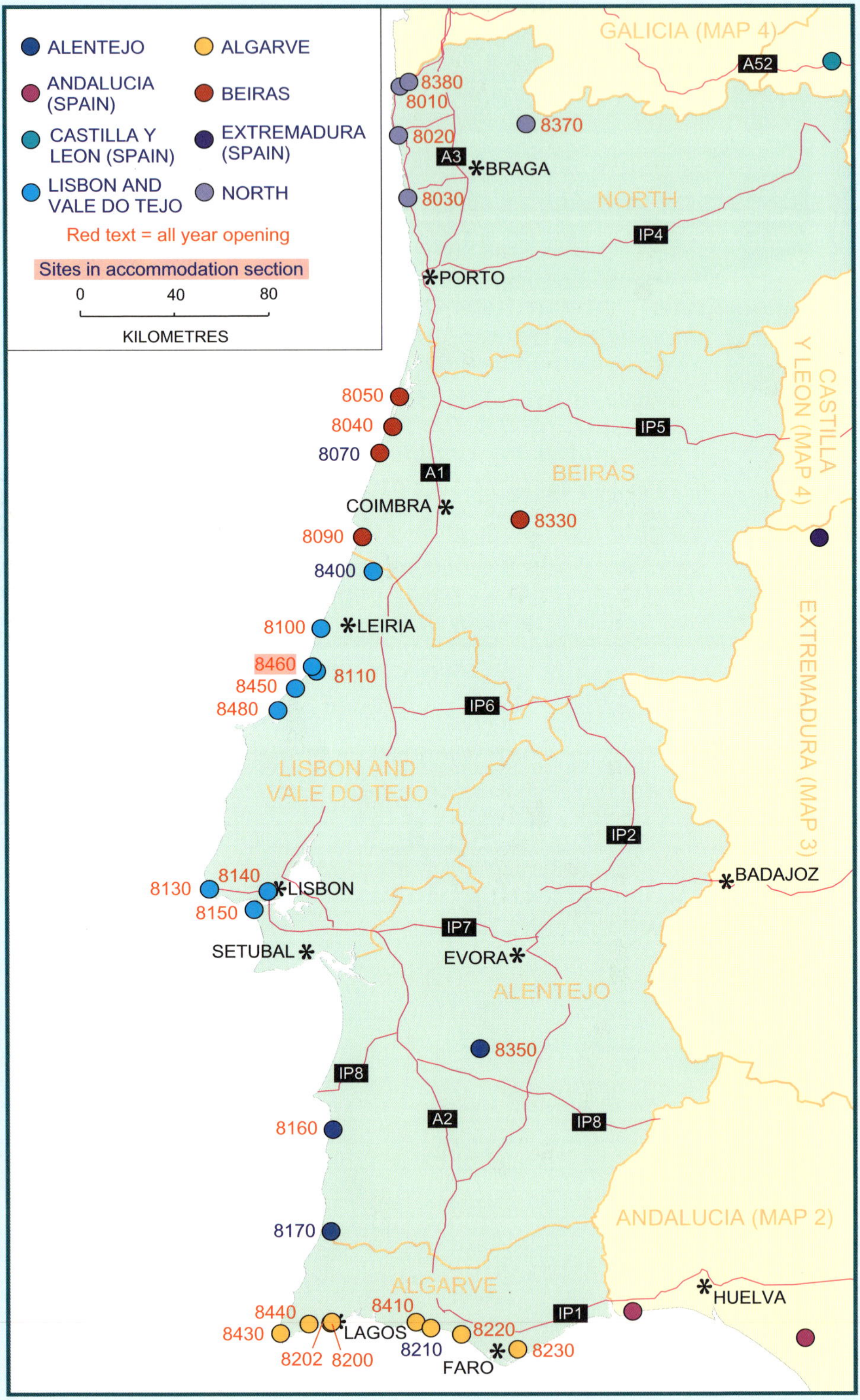

Please refer to the numerical index for campsite page reference

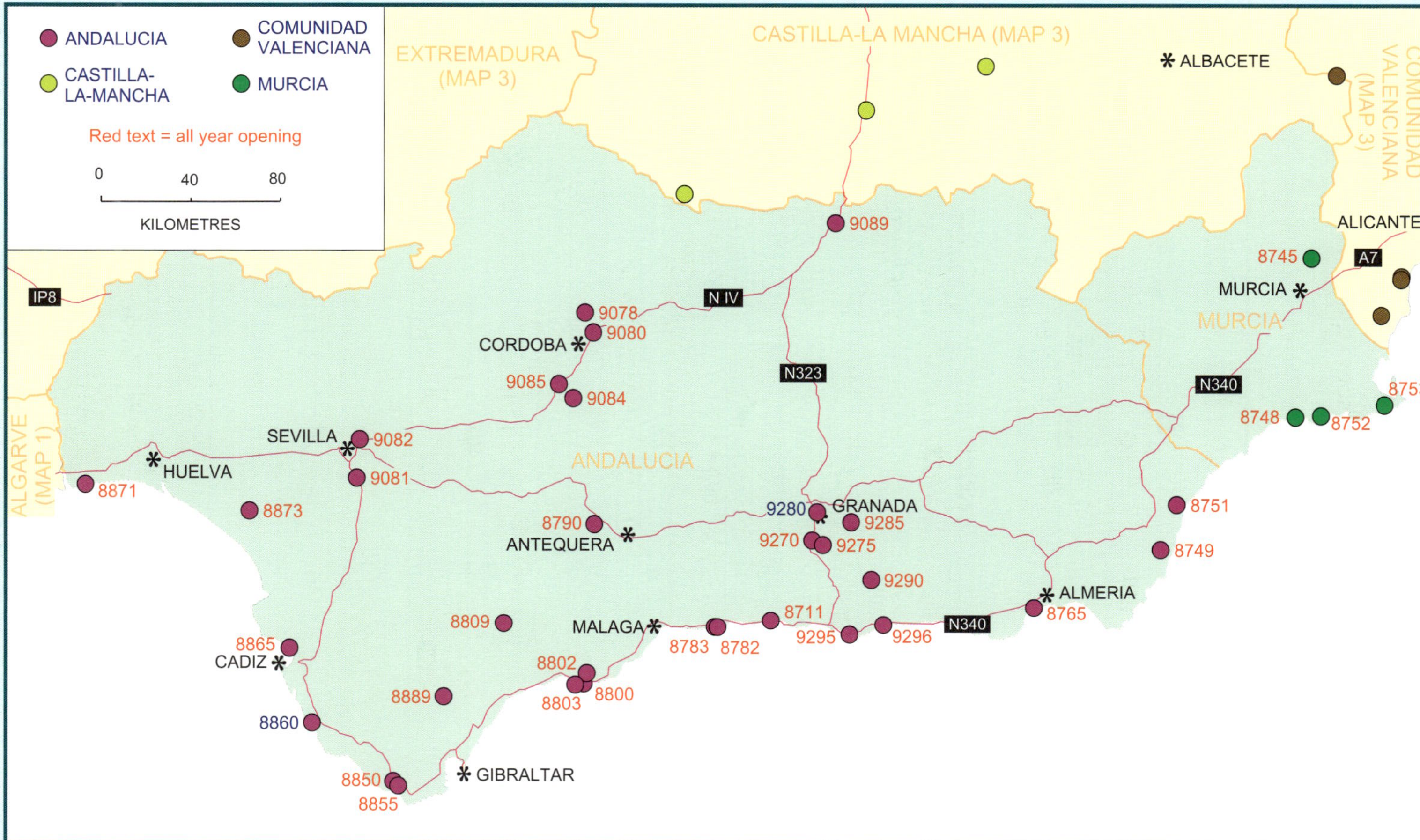

Please refer to the numerical index for campsite page reference

Please refer to the numerical index for campsite page reference

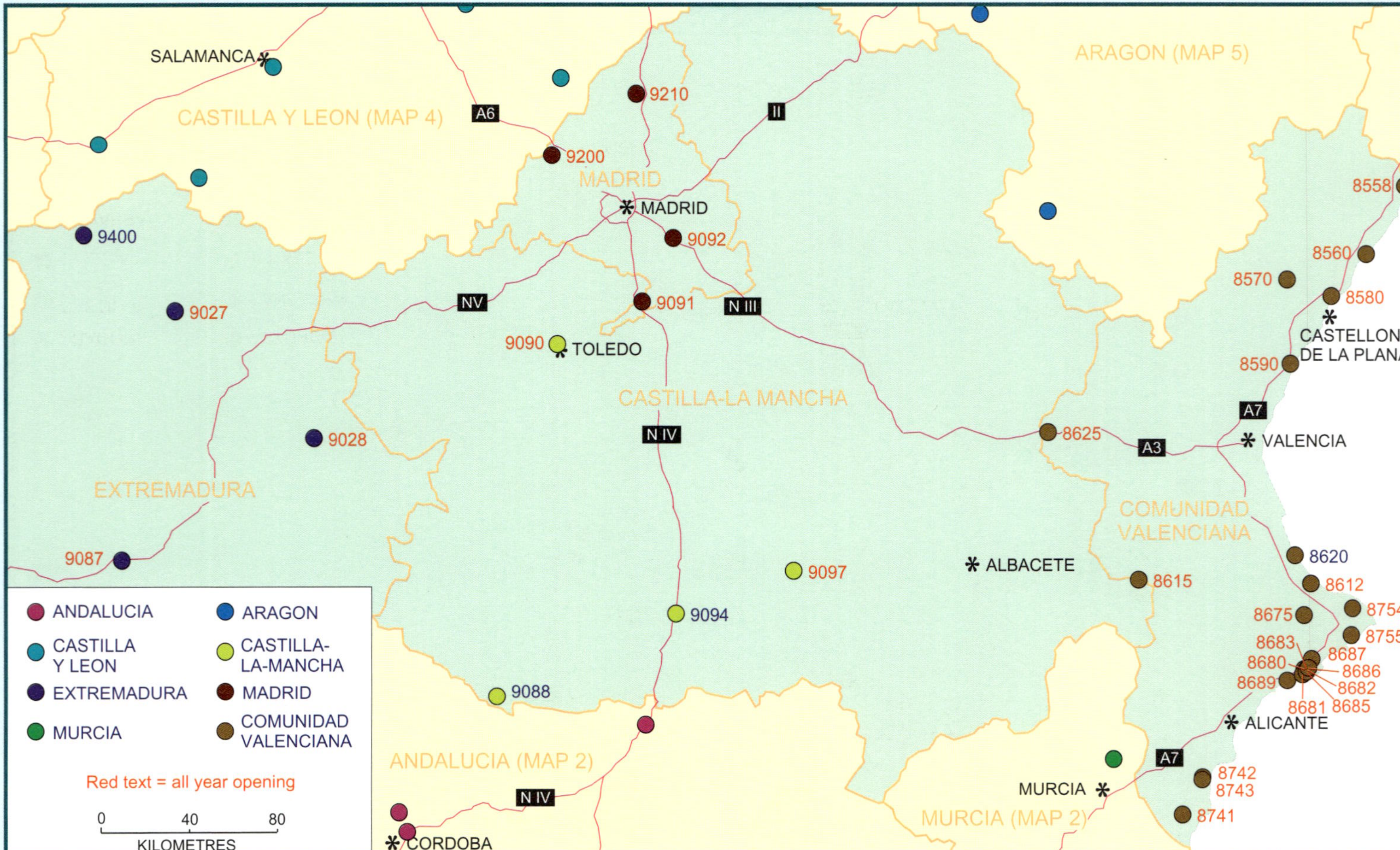

Extremadura, Castilla La-Mancha, Madrid & Comunidad Valenciana – Map 3

Galicia, Asturias, Cantabria, Pais Vasco-Euskadi, Castilla y León & La Rioja – Map 4

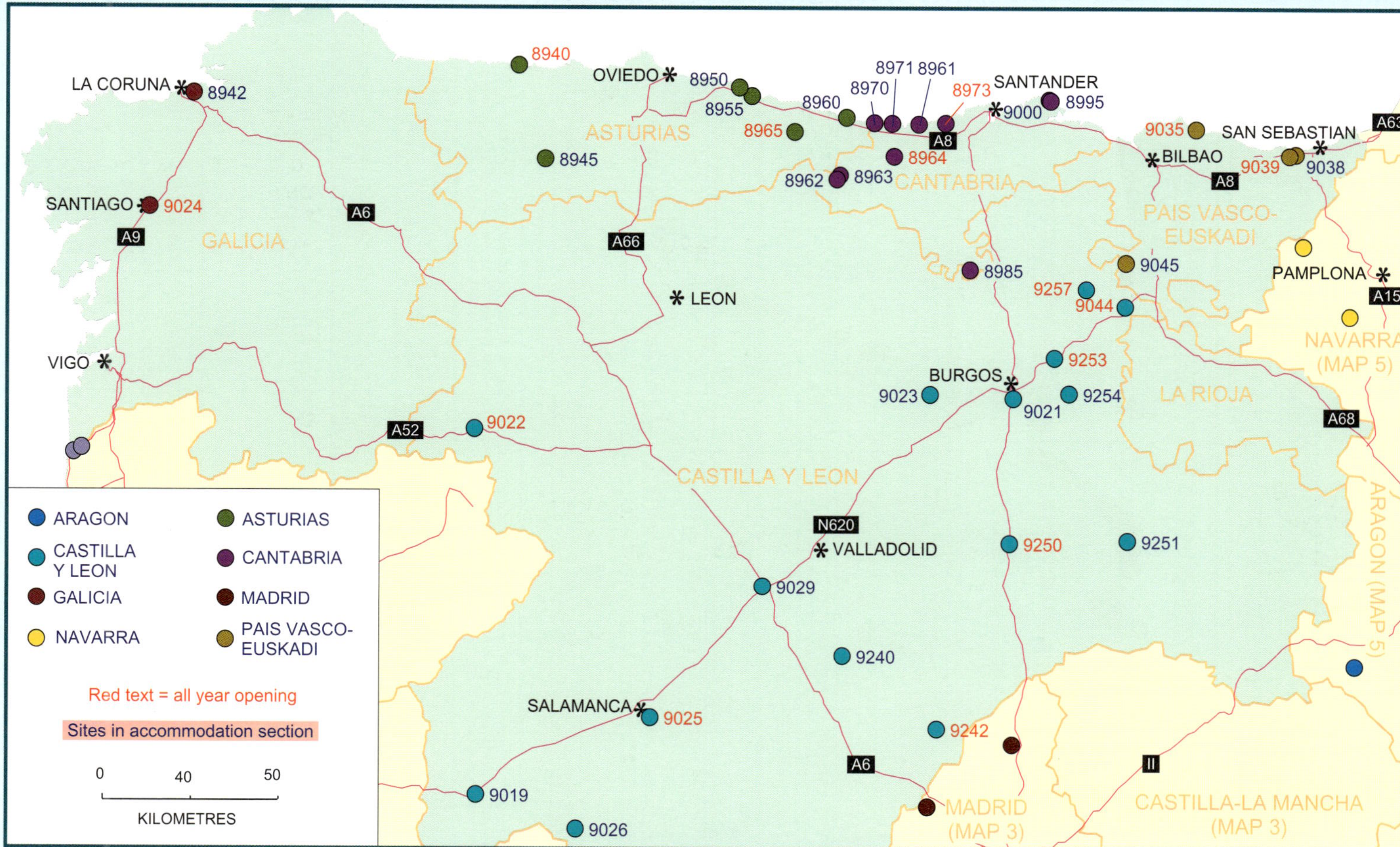

Please refer to the numerical index for campsite page reference

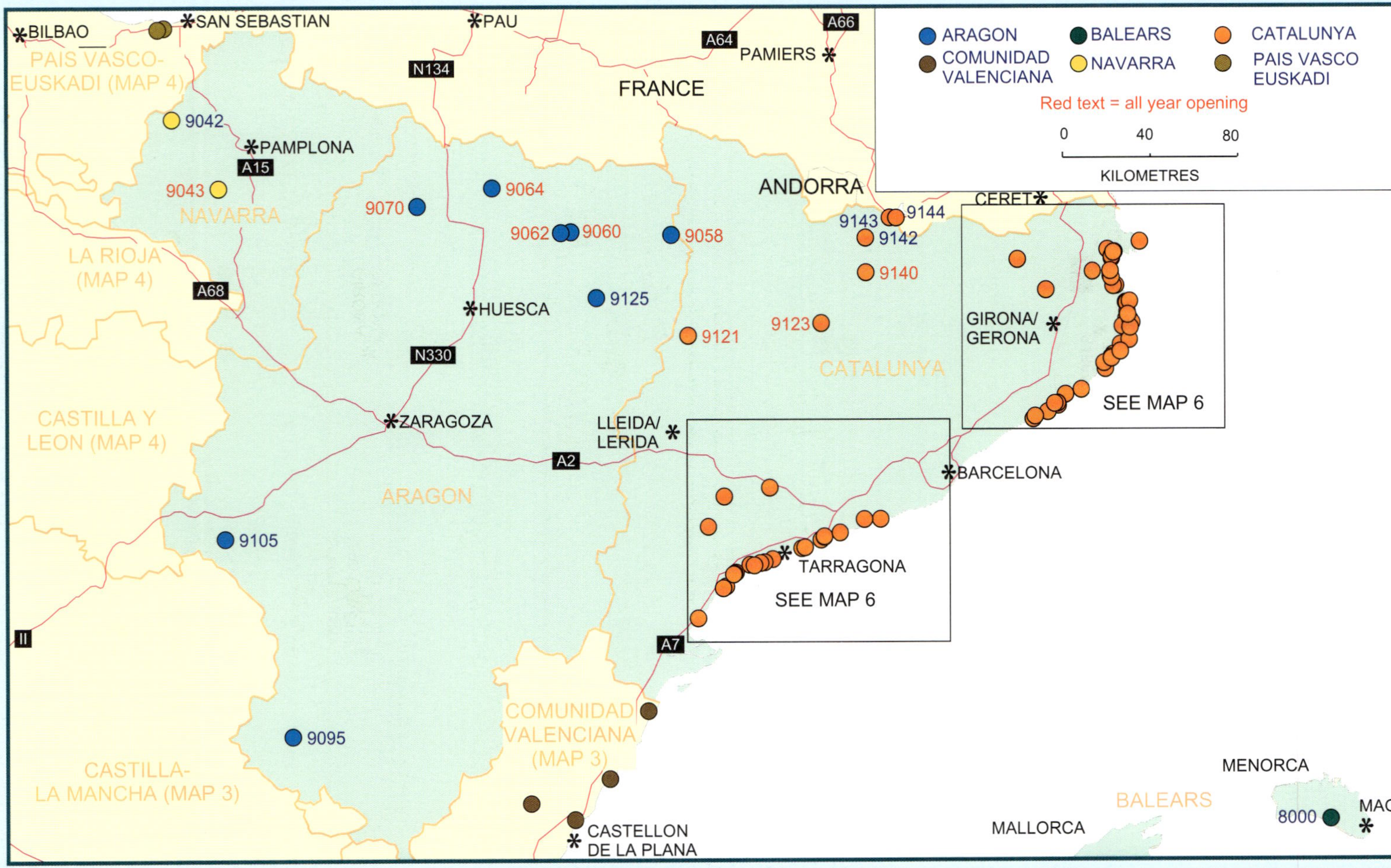

Please refer to the numerical index for campsite page reference

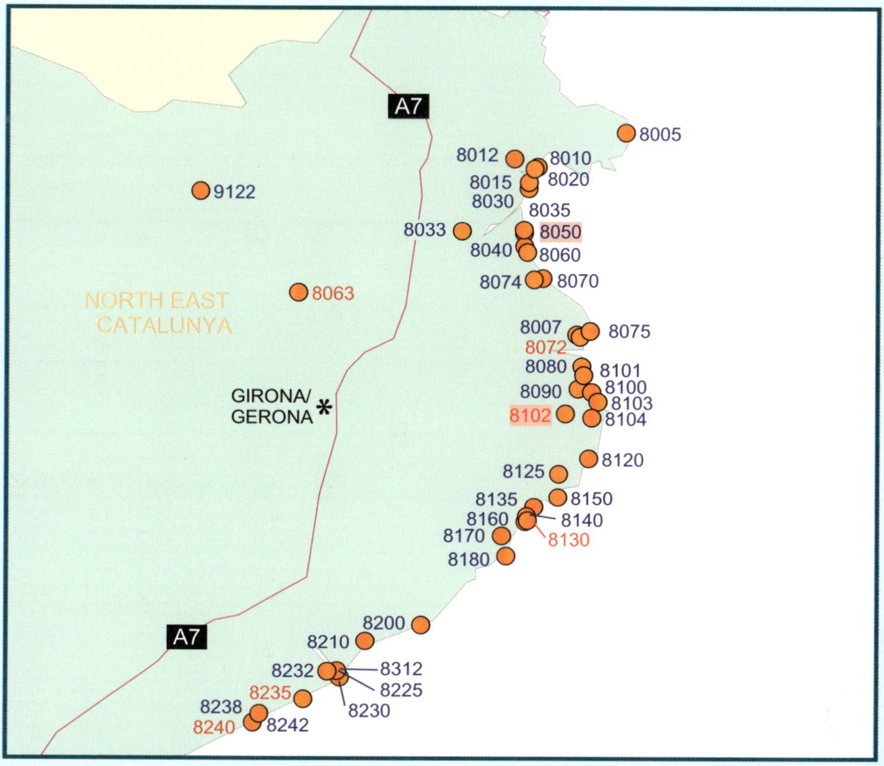

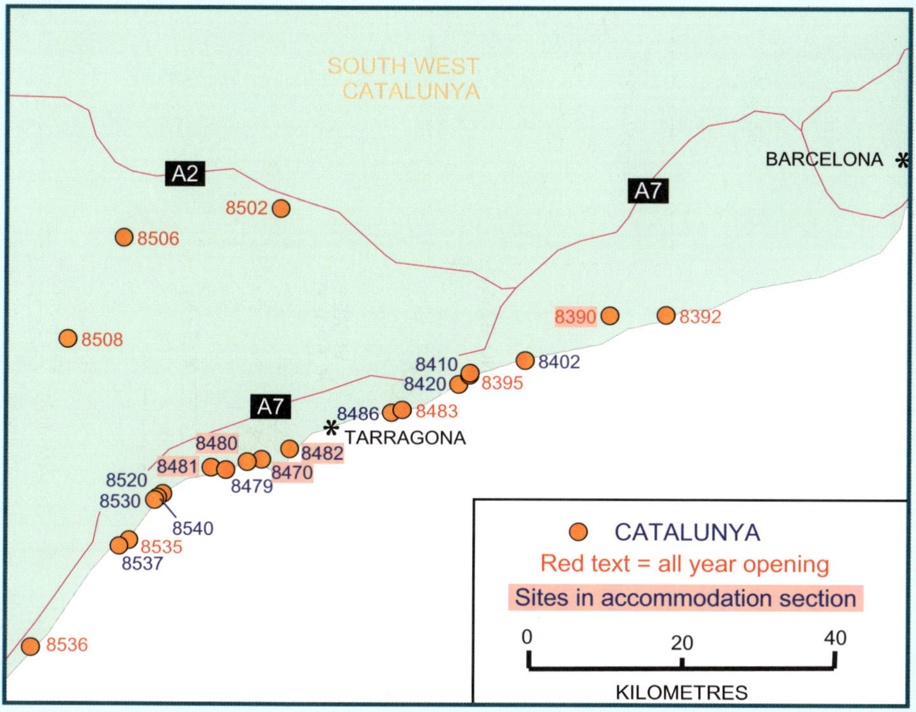

Please refer to the numerical index for campsite page reference

have you visited
www.alanrogers.com
yet?

INSPECTED CAMPSITES & SELECTED

Thousands have already, researching their holiday and catching up with the latest news and special offers.

Launched in January 2004 it has fast become the first-stop for countless caravanners, motorhome owners and campers all wanting reliable, impartial and detailed information for their next trip.

Alan Rogers

It features a fully searchable database of the best campsites in the UK & Ireland, and the rest of Europe: over 2,000 campsites in 26 countries. All are Alan Rogers inspected and selected, allowing you to find the site that's perfect for you, with the reassurance of knowing we've been there first.

And now it has been re-launched for the 2005 season, with more than ever before.

Visit today and find out for yourself!

SPAIN

INSPECTED & SELECTED CAMPSITES

SPAIN

Cataluña-Catalunya

Comunidad Valenciana

Murcia

Andalucia

PORTUGAL

Algarve

Alentejo

Lisbon & Vale do Tejo

Beiras & Centre

Porto & North

Widely regarded as the 'Bible' by site owners and readers alike, there is no better guide when it comes to forming an independent view of a campsite's quality. When you need to be confident in your choice of campsite, you need the Alan Rogers Guide.

- Sites only included on merit
- Sites cannot pay to be included
- Independently inspected, rigorously assessed
- Impartial reviews
- 36 years of expertise

INSPECTED & SELECTED CAMPSITES

Tell Us About the Alan Rogers Guides!

We're keen to constantly improve our service to you and the key to this is information. If we don't know what makes our readers 'tick' then it's difficult to offer you more of what you want.

WIN A COMPLETE SET OF ALAN ROGERS GUIDES

Return this completed questionnaire and you could win a complete set of 2006 Alan Rogers Guides. Why not complete an on-line version of this? Go to www.alanrogers.com/feedback

About the Alan Rogers Guides

1 **For how many years have you used the Alan Rogers Guides?**

Never 1-2 yrs 3-6 yrs 7-10 yrs Over 10 yrs

2 **How frequently do you refer to it?**

Never Each year Every 2 yrs Every 3 yrs

3 **How frequently do you buy a new copy?**

Never Each year Every 2 yrs Every 3 yrs

4 **If you lend it to friends, how many others might refer to it?**

1 2 3 4 Over 4

5 **Please rate the Alan Rogers Guides on a scale of 1–10 where 10 is excellent and 1 is extremely poor**

1 2 3 4 5 6 7 8 9 10

6 **Do you have any comments about the Alan Rogers Guides?**

....

....

7 **What do you consider to be the best thing about the guides?**

Independent reviews Honest descriptions Accurate information Range of sites Depth of information

Other ....

8 **What do you consider to be the worst thing about the guides?**

....

9 **How many sites featured in the guides have you visited in the past?** *(best estimate)* ....

10 **Can you comment on any other campsite guides?**

Title .... Your opinion ....

About Your Holidays

11 **a) Do you own any of the following?**

Caravan Motorhome Trailer Tent Tent

Other *(please specify)* ....

b) How many times a year do you use it?

1 2-3 4-6 7-10 More than 10

12 **When on holiday, do you participate in any of the following?**

Fishing Golf Cycling Sailing/Boating Walking Bird Watching

Other *(please specify)* ....

13 **How many years have you been camping / caravanning?**

3 yrs or less 4 – 7 yrs 8 – 12 yrs 13 – 15 yrs 16 – 20 yrs Over 20 yrs

WIN A COMPLETE SET OF ALAN ROGERS GUIDES

WIN A COMPLETE SET OF ALAN ROGERS GUIDES

About You

Mr/Mrs/Ms, etc. .... Initial .... Surname ....

Address ....

.... Post code ....

e-mail address .... @ .... Telephone ....

14 **Your age** 30 and under 31-50 51-65 Over 65

15 **Do you have children – if so, how old is the youngest?**
6 and under 7-12 Over 12

16 **Do you work (full or part time)?** Yes No

17 **Are you retired?** Yes No

About Your Leisure Time

18 **Are you a member of any caravan/motorhome clubs?**
The Caravan Club The Camping & Caravanning Club The Motor Caravanners Club

Other *(please specify)* ....

19 **Are you a member of the following?**
National Trust English Heritage RSPB CSMA Ramblers

20 **Which (if any) camping/caravanning magazines do you read regularly?**
MMM Practical Motorhome Practical Caravan Caravan Life Which Motorcaravan Motor-caravan Caravan

21 **Which other magazines do you read regularly?** ....

22 **Which newspapers do you read regularly?**
Express Mail Telegraph Times Guardian Observer Sun

Other (please specify) ....

23 **Do you enjoy any particular hobbies?** *(please specify)* ....

24 **Do you have regular access to the internet?** Yes No

If yes, which camping/caravanning websites do you visit regularly? ....

And Finally

25 **Do you have any useful camping/caravanning tips?**

....

26 **If you could change one thing about camping/caravanning holidays what would it be?**

....

We may wish to publish your comments, please tick this box if you would prefer us not to.

Might you be interested in becoming an Alan Rogers site inspector?
If so, please tick the box and we will send you further information

Camping Cheque and Alan Rogers may use this data to send you information and Special Offers.
Please tick here if you do not wish to receive such information

Thank you very much for your time and trouble in completing this questionnaire
Please return to: Alan Rogers Travel Service, FREEPOST NAT17734, Cranbrook, TN17 1BR